D1095350

Robert Ryan

Robert Ryan

A Biography and Critical Filmography

by

Franklin Jarlett

FOREWORD BY
JOHN HOUSEMAN

McFarland & Company, Inc., Publishers
Jefferson, North Carolina, and London

Frontispiece: Ryan in a late '40s publicity still.

British Library Cataloguing-in-Publication data are available

Library of Congress Cataloguing-in-Publication Data

Jarlett, Franklin, 1947–
    Robert Ryan : a biography and critical filmography / by Franklin
Jarlett.
       p.   cm.
    [Includes index.]
    Includes bibliographical references.
    ISBN 0-89950-430-2 (lib. bdg. : 50# alk. paper) ∞
    1. Ryan, Robert, 1913–1973.   2. Actors—United States—Biography.
I. Title.
PN2287.R88J37   1990
791.43'028'092—dc20
[B]   89-42725
                                                             CIP

Manufactured in the United States of America

McFarland & Company, Inc., Publishers
  Box 611, Jefferson, North Carolina 28640

To Linda, who gained strength from me,
To me, who gained strength from her,
To Nafisa, who had the strength
to put up with all of it,
To our collective spirits
For going against the grain

Man wishes to be confirmed in his being by man, and wishes to have a presence in the being of the other. Secretly and bashfully he watches for a yes which allows him to be, and which can come only from one human person to another.

Martin Buber

Acknowledgments

My efforts in writing this work were encouraged and aided by the following, each of whom provided a small or large piece to completing the puzzle of Ryan: David Chierichetti, John Hall, and Ruth Zitter, RKO Pictures; Marion Hanscom, Max Reinhardt Archives at the State University of New York at Binghamton; Jack London, Esquire; Janice Muirhead, Longwharf Theatre; John Tirpak, U.C.L.A. Theatre Archives; Jeffrey Mintz, National Film Information Service; Elaine Ebo, Geraldine Duclow, and William Harding, Free Library of Philadelphia; Charles Silver and Terry Geesken, New York Museum of Modern Art; Jean Soderlund and Mary Ellen Clark, Swarthmore College Peace Collection; the Motion Picture Sound and Recording Division, Library of Congress; the New York Public Library at Lincoln Center for the Performing Arts; Bernard Dinken, Amalgamated Clothing and Textile Workers of America; Jack Sutters, American Friends' Service Committee; National Committee for a Sane Nuclear Policy; American Civil Liberties Union; World Federalist Association.

Also, MGM/UA, Paramount, Films Incorporated, Swank Films, Don Bosco Films, Budget Films, the Hollywood Book Store, the Alan Henwood Cinema, Jerry Ohlinger's Movie Material Store, the Movie Poster Place.

I feel a special indebtedness to the late author William Torbert Leonard for his immeasurable assistance.

Table of Contents

Acknowledgments	vi
Foreword (John Houseman)	ix
Introduction	xi

Part I. Biography

Early Years	3
RKO and the War	15
Caught in the Crossfire	25
On Dangerous Ground	42
Film Noir	56
Family Versus Career	65
A Return to the Stage	78
Between Character Actor and Leading Man	84
Television and Other Diversions	91
Entering the Sixties	110
A Move to New York	122
Cameo Appearances	135
Stage Satisfactions	149
Long Day's Journey	159
The Loss of Jessica	163
Final Days	171

Part II. Creative Output

Chronological Filmography with Selected Criticism	179
Stage Performances	271
Television Performances, 1955–1973	273
Narrations, Appearances and Recordings	277
Ryan Films on Videocassette	278

Appendix A: Film Noir in the United States   279
Appendix B: The Oakwood School Today   282
Chapter Notes   283
Bibliography   287
Index   289

Foreword

Robert Ryan was an extraordinary man and an extremely talented actor. This biography succeeds in capturing the conflicts and contradictions that made him one of the most powerful, compelling actors of his time. Throughout his long and distinguished career as a film and stage star, he was deeply and passionately concerned with social and political problems. As an actor and a citizen, he did not hesitate to support his convictions—sometimes at considerable personal risk.

John Houseman

Introduction

Although I never knew Robert Ryan, I was drawn to something about him, something intangible, since my childhood in the early fifties when I first saw his movies on television. I used to sit in front of the set with a fixed attentiveness, watching certain movements, gestures, attitudes.

In high school, I saw his definitive Master-at-Arms Claggart in *Billy Budd* as a chapter to an elusive text of which I did not know the title. I searched the television and cinema schedules, stayed up late at night, studying what I thought was a message. It was in his face, his voice, his posture, his walk. Later, his Deke Thornton in *The Wild Bunch* had the same pained awareness.

In graduate school, my chronic passion became an acute obsession. I had to find out more about him to understand what he was saying, and used a psychology term paper to justify my emotional indulgence. When I saw his Larry Slade in *The Iceman Cometh*, I finally comprehended.

He depicted life, random pain, short-lived joys, loneliness, death. Better than any other American actor, he communicated man's existential dilemma. In his life and in his films he chronicled that struggle.

I wrote a letter to Patricia Bosworth, who had known and liked Ryan in a special way, and made a wild request of her.

"Would you consider writing a biography on Ryan?" I inquired. She told me that she was working on another piece, and then she said, "Why don't you tackle it?"

Robert Ryan was a man of undercurrents. In many of his movies he remained on the outer fringe of things, whether as a hero or a villain, watching and seeming to anticipate things. His screen image was the exact opposite of his real self, yet there were echoes of ambivalence, relics of his experience of the world. In his bad-guy roles, he often inspired pity as well as dread, but when he played a good-guy, one still felt a little sad for him, because he frequently ended up with the short end of the stick.

In the public eye he was an elusive spirit, religiously avoiding widespread fame and recognition, and despite his obvious talents, he appeared in relatively few big budget films, often accepting billing beneath actors of decidedly less talent. He saw acting as an art form, as a vehicle for self-expression, and his work delivered a profound message, albeit a dark one. He strove to create and to grow as an actor, rather than to appear in some spectacle just to make a buck. Part of him wanted to be a star in the traditional sense, and he flirted with it, even as resistance to it tugged at him always.

He felt that having been raised essentially as an only child had caused him to be too self-absorbed, and as an actor he became very aware of the narcissism that often is part of the stardom package. Perhaps Ryan didn't think he had what it took to get to the top in the first place, but if he had truly wanted more glamor, he could have gotten it. Why he did not is difficult to say.

Above all, Ryan gave unstintingly of himself, in public and in private. That his acting ability was of the first order, that many of his films are artistic masterpieces, and that he chose his roles always with the object in mind of saying something important, are reasons enough to take a serious look at his life.

Just as important, however, were his political and social accomplishments. He probably would have preferred to be remembered for them, as he truly wanted to make a contribution to the world. This he did, but he reached more people than he ever would have imagined. In life, he always had a modesty about his work, almost as if to compensate for any weaknesses. One wonders, then, about the irony of being a movie star, since it is a career that thrives on attention and popularity.

This work intends to examine some contradictions, to try to put together the puzzle of Ryan, but his privateness precludes gaining access to all of the pieces. His best friend and wife, Jessica, died in May 1972, a year before his death on July 11, 1973. A few people who truly knew him remain.

The experience of talking to Ryan's children, Timothy, Cheyney, and Lisa, revealed the to be just what I had hoped, warm, sincere, and intelligent. Other immensely helpful people with whom I had conversations and or exchanged correspondence included Robert Wallsten, Millard Lampell, John Houseman (whom I thank for his Foreword to the present work), Philip Dunne, Robert Wise, John and Evans Frankenheimer, Lamont Johnson, Samuel Fuller, Philip Yordan, Sidney Harmon, Harold and Lynne Mayer, Arvin Brown, Fred Zinnemann, Katharine Hepburn, Janet Leigh, Maureen Stapleton, Elizabeth Schappert, Virginie van Bark, Albert Hackett, John Springer, Harold J. Kennedy, Norman Cousins, George Slaff, Walter Hoffmann, Ted R. Leutzinger, and William Conrad.

All unattributed quotes throughout this book are a result of the author's communications with the above-named.

When I left their company and retreated to the recesses of my study to try to assemble a coherent piece about this remarkable man, his essence at times eluded me. Emerging after three years with alternating feelings of success and failure, I hope my work has done justice to the spirit of Robert Ryan, and that it will illuminate the message he strove to communicate in his life and in his films, that of man's essential dignity.

Part I
Biography

1. Early Years

When Timothy and Mabel Ryan bore their first son, Robert Bushnell Ryan, on November 11, 1909, in Chicago, Illinois, they were determined he would be educated, polite, and would take over the family business. Three years later, when a second son, John, was born, they began to plan his future as well. Security was important to the Ryans.

Tim Ryan was an industrious man who had inherited enough money from his father's ship-building business to begin his own, the Ryan Contracting Company, in Chicago. His parents had emigrated from Tipperary, Ireland, to Lockport, Illinois, in the late 1850s, with no money but a lot of Black Irish perseverance. The barrenness of the potato famine gradually became a memory as the Ryans struggled upward from the menial jobs usually relegated to Irish immigrants at the time to a life of comfortable security. The Ryans always retained the soul of their past, though, even in the ethnic melting pot of Chicago in the early 1900s.

By the time young Robert was of school age, Tim and Mabel Ryan had progressed to a country-club existence of private schools, two cars, and summers at the lake. The price of this luxury was back-breaking construction jobs, as Chicago madly built itself above and below ground. Tim Ryan landed a number of large city contracts which were responsible for the city's rapid growth in the teens and twenties.

Although Tim Ryan was Roman Catholic and Mabel was Episcopalian, they enrolled Robert at Jesuit-taught Loyola Academy, giving Catholicism the upper hand. The Ryans chose Loyola for its academics rather than its religious atmosphere, and in their raising of Robert, they avoided most of the Church's ritualism. He was confirmed in neither parent's religion.

Later in life when Ryan was asked about the depth of his religious beliefs, he hedged, stating with typical Ryan equanimity, "emotionally and intellectually, I am a Catholic, but since I've never been a practicing one, I assume the Church wouldn't agree."[1] The influence of Roman Catholicism on his emotional development ran much deeper than his glib downplaying of it, and in fact, many of his roles reflected the imprint of Catholic dogma, at whose core was a nexus of sin, guilt, and expiation.

When Ryan was eight years old, his brother died from influenza. There was only a faint moan of grief within the family, though, since Irish tradition dictated that death be accepted silently and stoically. Children were to be seen rather than heard, thus whatever feelings Ryan had about the loss of John faded into his unconscious where they remained for most of his life. When he faced his own mortality at age 60, he admitted having been haunted by John's death his whole life.

Tim and Mabel Ryan's grief about John's death was symbolized by anxiety over Robert. He was a shy boy, and when he complained of loneliness, Mabel viewed his vulnerability as a lack of self-confidence. She enrolled him in violin classes. On the other hand, Tim thought that violin lessons would sissify his son, and decided that Robert should take boxing lessons. The violin eventually fell by the wayside when the young Ryan's natural athletic ability in the ring easily won out over the graceful confinement of chamber music.

Mabel began sending Ryan to the movies, which quickly turned into a retreat for him. Every weekend he could be found at the matinées, where he became enthralled with the spectacle of the cinema. In his youth, his first idol was swashbuckler Douglas Fairbanks, Sr., but in early adulthood, he graduated to the realism of stars such as James Cagney and Spencer Tracy.

After studying for 12 years at Loyola, Ryan emerged, "perfectly well educated," as his friend, John Houseman, later observed. An essential aspect of the Jesuit philosophy was its emphasis on educating the intellect as a means of becoming more consciously human. Within that sphere, the classics of literature played an important role.

In his junior year at Loyola, Ryan was drawn to the works of William Shakespeare when a teacher concentrated on *Hamlet* for a semester. From then on, literature became Ryan's main focus of attention, and he read all of Shakespeare, as well as the works of Bernard Shaw and Anton Chekhov.

Ryan was exposed to the attraction of show business early in life, having grown up in the neighborhood in which the Essanay film studios were located. For a time, Charlie Chaplin, Gloria Swanson, and Wallace Beery lived on the same street as did the Ryan family, and in his youth, Ryan often slipped into the spectators' crowd when Essanay was shooting.

On Saturdays, he used to show up at Essanay, eager to be picked as one of the extras in one of the two reelers being churned out. He was on hand to watch the filming of several pictures featuring the first child star, Mary Macalastry, and he appeared as a walk-on in two silent pictures, *The College Widow* (1927), directed by Archie Mayo, and *Strong Boy* (1929), from John Ford.

In 1927, Ryan went East to New Hampshire and Dartmouth College. After living in Chicago, he never got used to the pastoral New England setting, and to fight his boredom he went to work for the college newspaper. While writing

A young Ryan with father Tim Ryan on fishing outing.

for the campus magazine, his interest in the penning of words grew. Perhaps he was drawn to the permanence of print and to its seeming immortality.

Ryan lost some of his shyness at Dartmouth, and was involved in antiprohibition activities on campus. He excelled in sports, winning letters in track and football, and became Dartmouth's first freshman to win the heavyweight boxing title. For the next four years, he remained undefeated.

By that time in his life, Ryan was a perfect specimen of Black Irish youth. Standing six-feet four-inches and weighing 190 pounds, he had tight, sinewy muscles, and not an ounce of fat. With his dark, curly hair, and sparkling brown eyes that lit up when he smiled, he could have been the glowing, all–American boy-next-door, or the somber Irish pug, emptying tankards of stout in a gin-mill.

At Dartmouth, Ryan's passion for literature stirred up questions and thoughts with which to wrestle regarding the meaning of life. He concluded that to understand the matter of his existence, it was necessary to ponder the concept of death. His Jesuit training had taught him how to examine rationally issues of conscience.

Ryan expressed his inner search on paper in his junior year when he wrote a one act play, *The Visitor*. The title was a metaphor for death, and when Ryan later recalled the play, he described it as, "exactly the kind of thing that a young writer thinks about."[2]

Ryan graduated from Dartmouth in 1931, with a Bachelor of Arts degree in literature, ambitiously hoping to land a job as a newspaper reporter. He had no interest in joining his father in the family business, and instead headed for New York City with a few like-mindedly innocent friends. His optimism met one disappointment after another, and he was unable to find even a menial job at the newspapers.

As the United States was in the throes of the Depression, the stark reality of gaunt faces wearily queued up at the soup lines brought Ryan face to face with poverty such as he had never seen. To make matters worse, in a bid for independence from his family, Ryan had declined any financial help. In any case, his father was in no position to support him after the crash had nearly ruined his business.

Later in life, when Ryan looked back on his abrupt awakening from a life of convenience, he said wryly, "I was a child of the '20s, when life was a ball. But it was a dream world that is gone forever."[3]

Ryan got desperate one day and decided to take any job he could find. His footsteps led him to the Brooklyn waterfront, where he grabbed a job on one of the freighters being loaded. The ship was bound for Africa via the Cape of Good Hope, Ryan would be the engine room janitor, and he would be gone for two years.

Ryan spent a long two years in the freighter's hot bowels, but learned a lot about life there. In his rite of passage, he stoked coal, cleaned bilges, sweated bullets, got filthy dirty and soaking wet, and ate lousy food. While enduring that, he also gained a wisdom that belied his years and background. He learned what it was like to suffer physical hardship as one of the "black crew" in the engine room. Life got especially tough around the hot East African coast and in the turbulent weather around the Cape.

Ryan developed a rough camaraderie with the crew, some of whom he never forgot. One was Joe Curran, a feisty Irishman who later became the head of the National Maritime Union. Ryan recalled that Curran was a "decent, noisy guy who kept the ship in an uproar," and told a story of how Curran initially broke the ice of social distance. When Curran learned that Ryan had been a fighter at Dartmouth, he informed him in the best barroom tradition, "I won't take you on because you're a boxer, unless I can get you on the floor." Ryan laughed and said, "Joe was always handy with a chair."[4]

When the voyage ended, Ryan's return to New York was hardly glorious. His funds were low, and so were his spirits. Worse yet, shortly after berthing at the port, he received word from his mother that his father had been run down by an automobile, and that he was critically injured. Ryan rushed home to help, and had to supervise a big sand-hogging job for the Chicago subway. Having had no previous experience in such matters, he worked elbow to elbow with the workers by day, while managing the mechanics of the business at night. As his father recuperated, Ryan's firsthand glimpse of the headaches of private enterprise convinced him that he could never be happy taking over the family business. When Tim Ryan returned to work, Ryan took to the road again.

His quest continued when he set out for northern Montana with a childhood friend in search of a gold mine they thought would be "a sure thing." People were still chasing after the dream of instant wealth, and Ryan's friend had heard that El Dorado might yet be found one hazy night when he had one beer too many. In the face of the Depression, such fantasies seemed attainable.

After a frustrating period of false starts and no gold, Ryan retreated to a one-horse town named Missoula, where he found a job punching cattle for $8 a week, plus room and board. He took to the task easily, having been taught how to ride a horse by his father years earlier.

While languishing in Missoula, waiting for something to happen, Ryan got an emergency call from Chicago: Tim Ryan had just died of complications from his recent car accident. Ryan took a train home immediately, particularly numb and grief-stricken since his father had died so suddenly and he had not been there at the end. At 26 years of age then, he went through a trying period, caring for his mother while jumping from one job to another.

He first landed a temporary job as a clothes model in one of the department stores downtown. Although he felt ill at ease with the spectacle of that kind of work, something good came from his discomfort. One of the women with whom he worked was a part-time actress, who asked him to take a small role in a play her amateur theater group was doing at a local women's club. Ryan enjoyed the experience, and began to have vague thoughts of acting for a living, but he realized that most stage actors barely existed on what they earned.

Mabel Ryan failed to share her son's enthusiasm about acting as a career, and encouraged him to find a job that would provide a steady income. It was 1936 and the Depression had lifted, enabling Ryan to work at a number of off-beat and generally unsuccessful jobs, each less rewarding than the last. He was a bodyguard for a union boss, a cemetery plot salesman, a salesman for a steel company, a WPA worker, and a bill collector for a loan company on Chicago's West Side.

Venturing into the slums on the West Side and demanding money from the poor depressed Ryan so much that he only lasted two weeks there. On his final day, while returning to the office with his collections, he felt such guilt that he gave a payment back to one of his customers, and went home.

Ryan finally got a job that he could at least call respectable, working for the city of Chicago, after Mabel Ryan got in touch with a childhood friend, Mayor Kelly. Mabel and Kelly shared the same dyed-in-the-wool Democratic politics, as well as their Irish background. Kelly promised Mabel that he would find her son something with a future, but unfortunately, the job involved handing out supplies for Chicago's Board of Education. Since Ryan's office was in the basement, there was no place to go but upward, and the job quickly became the most boring of all the positions he had held during the past several years.

For much of the day he sat behind a desk doing nothing, alternating with the handing out of supplies just at the moment when he might be dozing off. Ryan became depressed about his situation of being 27 years old with a college degree, apparently going nowhere.

To pass the time and to exercise his mind, he began writing notes for Dartmouth's alumni magazine, which brought him back to reassessing his past strengths and interests. He thought about having won a prize for *The Visitor* when he had been a student at Loyola, and he still had a fantasy of being a playwright.

While Ryan was reading the newspaper one day, he noticed that a local private girls' school, the Stickney School, was searching for someone to direct its annual play. Having developed a certain nerve for approaching people in uncertain situations, he presented himself to the school's principal as if he had experience as a stage director. He gave a convincing interview and got the call.

The play was *Dear Brutus*, it was a success, and a light bulb flashed in Ryan's mind. He later recalled "getting bitten by the acting bug, watching those kids,"[5] and came to a decision about his next step in life. He enrolled in a drama class taught by Edward Boyle, who was a veteran stock-company actor turned instructor.

For the past several years, Boyle had been teaching stagestruck Chicagoans, for $5 a week, all he had learned in a lifetime of acting. Ryan admired Boyle's honesty, and kept one of his axioms always in mind. Boyle told him, "Whatever you do on stage, be *very* positive — whether it's good or bad — be *positive*."

Ryan's impetuous side soon collided with the nuances of good acting, and Boyle calmed his anxious enthusiasm in his straightforward way, saying, "Boy, you have all the faults of a young actor. You don't know anything, but you always act as if you did."[6] Ryan accepted the comment as matter-of-fact Ed Boyle, told with kindness.

While working with Boyle, Ryan made plans to continue his acting studies at the Pasadena Playhouse, and then to make his move on a Hollywood career. After investing $300 in savings on an oil drilling venture in northern Michigan, he hit pay dirt and netted $2,000. By mid–1939, he was ready to leave home for the last time, and in the summer he left for California.

Ryan arrived in California too late for an acting class which had just begun at the Pasadena Playhouse, and he was briefly left hanging with anticipation. Luckily, a young actor at the Playhouse suggested another acting school in Los Angeles, Max Reinhardt's Actors' Workshop. Following the actor's advice, Ryan enrolled in Reinhardt's school, and began classes.

Reinhardt had founded his acting school in New York City in the late 1930s, after fleeing from Nazi Germany. He moved the school to Hollywood in 1939, and quickly built a reputation by the time Ryan arrived at the school that year. One of Ryan's first teachers was Vladimir Sokoloff, who had recently come to Hollywood from the Moscow Art Theatre. The understated acting style which Ryan later perfected owed much to Sokoloff, who was a noted exponent of the Stanislavsky method of dramatic interpretation. Both Sokoloff and Reinhardt liked Ryan's honest, boy-next-door enthusiasm, and Reinhardt told him one day, "You do things with gusto — you are *never* shy!"[7]

When Ryan began classes, one of the first people in the class whom he noticed was a tall, pretty, dark-haired woman named Jessica Cadwalader. She had been an actress for several years, first with the Wayfarers, a San Francisco theater group, and then she came to Reinhardt's Workshop when it was in New York. The initial attraction which brought Ryan and Jessica together may have been her well-bred Quaker upbringing, although with her delicate aquiline features and lively wit, she could have come from Irish extraction. Jessica was also a quiet person, but she had the right amount of assertiveness to complement Ryan's basic shyness. They fell in love with each other on the spot. Ryan and Jessica didn't wait to graduate, and on March 11, 1939, they were married at St. Thomas' Episcopal Church in Los Angeles.

After a brief honeymoon, the reality of their financial situation prevailed. Neither had a steady job, and they quickly learned one of the anxieties in the love-hate relationship of the acting business, that earning a decent living at it is one of life's trials. But while they were on the stage performing, or listening to Reinhardt lecture on the art of acting, it was easy to forget their uncertain futures.

The plays in which Reinhardt gave his students practical experience were classics of the theater, and Ryan had strong roles in several of them. He was Bottom in *A Midsummer Night's Dream*; the father in Pirandello's *Six Characters in Search of an Author*; Prince Beladore in Maeterlinck's *Sister Beatrice*; and Silvio to Jessica's Beatrice in Goldoni's *At Your Service*.

Group portrait of Ryan's graduating class of 1939 from Max Reinhardt's Acting School. Jessica and Robert (second and third from left), Reinhardt (at center). Also pictured, Walter Brooke, standing at far right, Herbert Anderson, fourth from right, Nanette Fabray, seated at right. Courtesy Max Reinhardt Archives.

Among Ryan's classmates were a few with whom he later worked, including Nanette Fabray *(Mr. President)*, Herbert Anderson *(The Set-up)*, and Walter Brooke *(Lawman, Executive Action)*. When Ryan's class graduated, there was a joyous celebration at Reinhardt's home in Hollywood, and he never forgot the powerful learning experience of studying under Reinhardt, whom some observers have called Germany's most talented stage producer and director of the early twentieth century.

At the time of his graduation, Ryan was barely aware of what he had learned from Reinhardt, because it was intangible. Thirty-two years later, when Ryan wrote a poignant eulogy on the magic of Reinhardt's genius, he referred to his "obsession with the inner life of man, and with the mysterious spirit that flickers and flames in all of us," and said, "Max Reinhardt was the most tremendous and important person to have ever influenced my career and my work."[8]

After graduation, Ryan kept his eye on the school's bulletin board, on which were posted a few auditions for local theater groups. He spotted a part he liked in Somerset Maugham's *Too Many Husbands*. Although the prospective part was minor and the play was a musical, Ryan needed the money and

"Golden Gloves" (Paramount), 1940. Paramount's plan to give Ryan the starring role as a strapping young boxer in his film debut was changed, and Richard Denning ended up with the part.

the experience. He auditioned for the part and was accepted. Then, something very good happened in his life.

A talent scout for Paramount Studios, who had been in the audience of the Belasco Theatre in Los Angeles when *Too Many Husbands* opened, approached Ryan after the show. His question was simple. Would Ryan be interested in signing a contract with Paramount for $75 a week? He was taken aback because he had taken a screen test for Paramount in 1938, and had been rejected as "not the right type." He accepted the offer immediately.

Ryan was ecstatic about his contract with Paramount, and about the opportunity of coming into contact with stars he respected and admired, such as Gary Cooper, Ray Milland, Fred MacMurray, Claudette Colbert, and others. In his first film, however, a "B" directed by Edward Dmytryk called *Golden Gloves*, reality intervened.

In his book *It's a Hell of a Life, but Not a Bad Living*, Dmytryk described how Ryan was chosen to star in *Golden Gloves*, and how he ended up with a bit part. A Paramount casting director had recommended Ryan for the lead role as boxer Bill Crane, and Dmytryk gave him a screen test. Afterward, said Dmytryk, Paramount decided that "Bob wasn't quite ready for us." In later years, Dmytryk confessed sheepishly, "Perhaps *we* weren't ready for *him*."

Appearing as one of the "ringers" brought into the boxing match to take a fall at the right moment, Ryan seemed to be a natural in front of the camera. Dmytryk was also impressed by his athletic ability, and said, "Bob hit like a mule." The film's star, Richard Denning, verified the force of Ryan's punches, when he went for X-rays three times because he thought he had a cracked rib.

Ryan's dialogue in *Golden Gloves* was limited to one ironic line. After taking a dive in a bout, Ryan slowly regains his senses and says to his crooked manager, played by J. Carrol Naish, "I thought you could get me more."

Ryan's other three efforts for Paramount were no better. In *Queen of the Mob*, he was cast as an office worker, appearing briefly in two scenes; in Cecil B. DeMille's *Northwest Mounted Police*, he had no dialogue; in *Texas Rangers Ride Again*, he was an extra. After one dismal year, Paramount declined renewal of his contract, and he was released with another actress deemed "unsuitable" for movies, Susan Hayward.

While Ryan had been working for Paramount, Jessica had been doing some modeling, but she had nearly decided to give up acting. Though she had the talent for acting, she disliked the stress of show business, and didn't have the burning desire to help her through the inevitable lean periods. But she had a writer's self-discipline, and could sit down for hours at a time at the typewriter, practicing and developing her craft.

After no other studio picked up Ryan's contract, he went back to his old standby, the stage. It was Spring, 1940, and summer stock was about to begin on the eastern "Straw-hat circuit." Ryan and Jessica first traveled to Dennis, on Cape Cod, where *A Kiss for Cinderella*, starring Luise Rainer, was to be done at the Cape Playhouse.

Casting had been nearly completed when Ryan approached the theater's producer for a job, but with only one professional performance to his credit, he was an unlikely prospect. Moreover, as Luise Rainer was starring in the play and the other members of the cast were experienced, perhaps he should have been intimidated, but he persisted.

The manager finally gave him a part, but stipulated that his pay would be room and board only. As soon as he was hired, Ryan planted himself in the auditorium to watch the rehearsals. Shortly after, he put himself in the position to give advice to one of the younger actors, Robert Wallsten.

It was slightly impertinent of him to advise someone with much more experience about the fine points of acting than himself, but he was polite enough about it, and Wallsten was modest enough to preclude any misinterpretations.

During a break in rehearsals, Ryan introduced himself and asked if he could make a comment on how Wallsten was holding a pistol during a particular scene. When Wallsten replied, "Please do," Ryan asked him if he knew how to hold a gun.

Wallsten said, "No, but by all means, show me." In a very official manner, Ryan demonstrated. (Eight years later, Ryan got a little egg on his face when Howard Hughes criticized him for not holding a pistol properly during the filming of *The Woman on Pier 13*.)

Their casual meeting developed into a close friendship that endured for the rest of Ryan's life. When Wallsten tried to describe why he and Ryan liked each other from the start, he ventured to say that they viewed the world through similar eyes. Wallsten had graduated from Harvard in 1932 with a degree in fine arts, and had been a stage actor for several years prior to meeting Ryan. Later, he wrote short stories and articles for magazines, numerous television scripts, and coedited the letters of John Steinbeck. A native of New York City, he had grown up sophisticated and literate, but more importantly, he was compassionate and sensitive. His personality complemented Ryan's.

When Wallsten looked back on his first impression of Ryan playing a bright-eyed cockney soldier in *A Kiss for Cinderella*, he saw a chemistry with the potential for stardom. He remembered seeing Ryan's "stellar charm," and envisioned his "magic grin that could turn on and entrance people with its warmth."

Ryan also made an impression on Luise Rainer, and when the acting company moved the play to Maplewood, New Jersey, she introduced him to her husband, playwright Clifford Odets. Odets was casting his new play, *Clash by Night*, which was to open in New York on Broadway, starring Tallulah Bankhead, Joseph Schildkraut, and Lee J. Cobb, with Lee Strasberg directing. Odets liked Ryan, and hired him to play the clean-cut, clearheaded Joe Doyle.

In the New York stage scene, any new play from Odets was an important theatrical event, and a great deal of anticipation surrounded the arrival of *Clash by Night*. After a one-week tryout in Philadelphia at the Schubert Theatre, though, the play received less than enthusiastic reviews, and difficulties began to crop up. First, Bankhead caught the flu, then Schildkraut, Ryan, and a few other cast members became ill. Next, backstage tempers flared, and by the time *Clash by Night* struggled to the Belasco Theatre in New York in December 1941, everyone's energy had waned. After 39 performances, the play closed.

The only cast member to emerge from *Clash by Night* unscathed was Ryan. In the *New York Times*, Brooks Atkinson called his portrayal "manly and clearheaded." Filmmaker Pare Lorentz, who was working for RKO Radio at the time, also noticed Ryan when he saw the play, and offered him a $600 a week contract at RKO.

A few years earlier, Lorentz had directed documentaries for Franklin Roosevelt's Resettlement Administration, and was about to direct his first non-documentary, *Name, Age, and Occupation*, starring Frances Dee and Erford Gage. Lorentz had been searching for someone to play the part of a young man working his way out of the Depression, and thought Ryan looked typically American. Ryan signed up with RKO, and headed back to Hollywood with Jessica.

2. RKO and the War

Although RKO Radio Pictures was the smallest of the major Hollywood studios and had an erratic history, it also made a name for itself by attracting a number of creative artists who dealt with unorthodox subject matters. Thus, many of the cinema's great successes were born at 780 Gower Street, such as *Citizen Kane, Gunga Din, The Magnificent Ambersons, The Best Years of Our Lives,* and others. It seems fitting that Ryan should have begun his career there, but he never appeared before Lorentz's cameras.

Since *Name, Age, and Occupation* was Lorentz's first dramatic feature, he was uncertain in his method and ran into problems during production. After having gone way over budget with 90 days of shooting and nothing to show for the effort, RKO decided to shelve the unfinished film. Studio executives were prompted to interrupt the already losing financial project by America's entrance into World War II, which made the film's story suddenly anachronistic and totally unsalable.

The image for which RKO first groomed Ryan depicted him as the epitome of the American male, strong, eager, and patriotic. His emergence as a star happened at a perfect time, since World War II had caused a change in not only the type but the tone of Hollywood films. The romanticized, worldly, and often glossy state of reality seen in motion pictures of the thirties gave way to more down-to-earth themes involving average Americans doing everyday tasks.

During the next two years, Ryan appeared in seven films, while RKO continued to mold him into a bankable actor. He quickly moved up the ladder toward stardom, from sixth billing in *Bombardier* to second billing in *Marine Raiders,* while in each film he demonstrated varied aspects of his acting ability. Even at this stage of his career, the roles which came his way were tinged with tragedy, while the sincerity of his portrayals caught the attention of critics and some influential people at RKO. Actor Pat O'Brien was one of them.

O'Brien had established his kindly, paternal image at Warner Bros. in the thirties, and he was now one of RKO's biggest stars. When Ryan was assigned the part of a youthful, gung-ho airman in *Bombardier,* O'Brien took an immediate liking to him, partly because of his professional manner while shooting,

"Bombardier" (RKO), 1943. Airman Joe Connors (Ryan, at right on platform), being instructed in the use of the Norden bombsight. (Photo courtesy the Museum of Modern Art/Film Stills Archives.)

and partly because of his infectiously honest way of relating to people. But the friendship between Ryan and O'Brien ran deeper, to the loyalty of their shared Irish heritage. Ryan soon saw the depth of O'Brien's loyalty when O'Brien specifically lobbied for him in two films later on.

After 1943's *Bombardier*, RKO continued to explore Ryan's good-guy image, and cast him as one of Fred Astaire's jovial Air Force buddies in *The Sky's the Limit*. But in his next film, *Behind the Rising Sun*, directed by Edward Dmytryk, his character suggested more complexities and a darker side.

In the picture, Ryan played a rough American baseball player with a ruthless streak but a patriotic spirit, who shoots a cat when it disturbs his poker game, later defeats a huge Japanese wrestler in a boxing match, and is ultimately tortured to death for suspected spying. Thirty-five years later, when Dmytryk recalled *Behind the Rising Sun*'s rousing fight scene between Ryan and Mike Mazurki, its impression had not faded. Dmytryk called the scene " a beautifully choreographed battle between two superior athletes."[1]

Ryan's next four pictures had a shared similarity in theme, all concerning

World War II. Each explored a different aspect of his ability, yet all depicted him as having a quiet inner strength. In John H. Auer's *Gangway for Tomorrow*, he played a race car driver seriously injured in the big race just before military enlistment, who struggles onward to fulfill his patriotic duty in a defense plant. The film was considered a "little" picture, but it had a European flavor that kept it from falling into typical war exploitation fare.

Wanting to capitalize on the success of Pat O'Brien's recent film, *Knute Rockne – All-American*, RKO set the wheels in motion for another biography. This time it was in *The Iron Major*, as Frank Cavanaugh, Dartmouth's legendary football coach, who became a hero in World War I but who later died of war injuries. O'Brien had plenty of influence at RKO and recommended Ryan for the part of Father Tim Donovan, the Jesuit priest from Notre Dame who was Cavanaugh's close friend. The suggestion worked well, as Ryan played Donovan with a sincerity O'Brien had patented in similar roles. In his autobiography, O'Brien wrote that Ryan was "magnificent," but there was a hint of envy in his comment that Ryan "stole some of my usual ecclesiastic glory."

When RKO producer David Hempstead began his search for a male lead for Ginger Rogers in *Tender Comrade*, he spotted favorable preview cards of Ryan's performances in *Bombardier*, *The Sky's the Limit*, and *Behind the Rising Sun*. He suggested him to Rogers, who was at first unimpressed after screening parts of three of his pictures. She thought he was too big, and that he looked mean.

Hempstead went back to his desk, and bounced around in his mind several actors who might be appropriate for the role of the young man who was to have the enviable position of doing 17 love scenes with Ginger Rogers. A week later, when Rogers visited Hempstead at his office, he was busily going through preview cards of *The Sky's the Limit*, and he showed her some of them. What Rogers looked at were reviews of Ryan's performance, and they were all favorable. Time was running out for the search for a leading man for Rogers, so she decided to have another look at him. Ryan was conveniently waiting in a nearby office for just such a possibility.

Hempstead picked up his phone and spoke briefly to his secretary. Less than a minute later, Ryan appeared at Hempstead's door. For a few moments the three talked, then Rogers unobtrusively slipped Hempstead a small piece of paper. On it she had written, "I think this is the guy."[2] Today, that same piece of paper hangs on the wall in plain sight above Cheyney Ryan's desk, in his study.

Tender Comrade had moderately high production costs, thus it naturally attracted more attention than Ryan's previous pictures, and became the big career leap he needed. Opposite one of RKO's most glamorous and popular stars, Ryan firmly established his romantic screen presence, while delivering a performance of certainty. In the *New York Morning Telegram*, Leo Mishkin

Self-portrait which Ryan painted when he was a Marine Corps drill instructor at Camp Pendleton during World War II.

wrote prophetically, "Robert Ryan, a heretofore secondary player, is elevated to the male lead for Miss Rogers in the role of her husband, turning in a quiet, sure job in a work that will have him long remembered."

The picture did well financially, earning $843,000 in profits for RKO, mainly because its tone of patriotic righteous indignation registered in the public's mind at a peak emotional time. As serious political commentary, though, *Tender Comrade* offered hype instead of substance, and it quickly disappeared from attention. A few years later, the picture would surface again, this time under congressional scrutiny, when the Screenwriters' Guild was accused of harboring Communist propagandists.

After *Tender Comrade*, Ryan landed another solid role, combining the rugged with the romantic in RKO's *Marine Raiders*, opposite Pat O'Brien and Ruth Hussey. When the studio conferred with O'Brien regarding casting the film's second lead, he lobbied for Ryan to play the part of a battle-fatigued paramarine, who falls in love with a comely nurse (Hussey) while on furlough. Again, he gave an impressive portrayal, prompting one critic to compare his style to that of a young Gary Cooper, and which insured his status at RKO.

Opposite, top: "Behind the Rising Sun" (RKO), 1943. American athlete Lefty (Ryan) lands left hook on jaw of Japanese fighter (Mike Mazurki). Bottom: "The Iron Major" (RKO), 1943. Father Tim Donovan (Ryan) comforts football coach Frank Cavanaugh (Pat O'Brien) in his hour of need.

"Marine Raiders" (RKO), 1944. Paramarine Captain Dan Craig (Ryan) directs machine-gun fire during land assault in the South Pacific.

At the time when Ryan seemed on the verge of reaching a definable category as an actor, the war intervened to interrupt his progress.

While Ryan was working on his career, the United States had been headlong into World War II, and patriotic duty surged. Hollywood was churning out war pictures with a zeal rivaling that of a defense plant. The fervor in tinsel town was not due to nationalistic passion, but it was an intense game between studios competing for the big buck.

From an actor's viewpoint, it became a prudent gesture to take part in the war effort, and a number of actors joined the military to build their images with the public. In January 1944, Ryan enlisted in the Marine Corps, and became a drill instructor at the Camp Pendleton barracks, in San Diego, California. His motivations for selecting a training specialty and branch of service which were incongruous to his personality remain unclear, but Robert Wallsten speculated that his reasons were mainly professional. Also, having appeared in several war-related films recently may have set him into a Marine Corps frame of mind. As an added incentive, RKO guaranteed Ryan's contract through the war, and he became the first Hollywood actor to enjoy the privilege.

During the war years, Ryan underwent internal changes and began to see the world differently. Although he never experienced the direct trauma of combat, at Camp Pendleton he witnessed an endless procession of returning

"Trail Street" (RKO), 1947. Ryan's first picture after returning from World War II cast him opposite George "Gabby" Hayes (left) and Randolph Scott (not pictured).

G.I.s, physically and emotionally maimed. Of the few close friends Ryan saw during his service period, Robert Wallsten, then in the Navy and shipping out for Australia, remembered talking to a preoccupied Ryan en route through Camp Pendleton, and sensing an uneasiness he had not noticed before.

Ryan talked to Wallsten in general terms about being frustrated, and the allusion that came to Wallsten's mind suggested a gathering dark side in Ryan's soul. While waiting out his stint, he had begun to dabble in art, and focused his energy on an abstract painting which startled Wallsten when he first saw it. Ryan had not finished the painting, but Wallsten described it as a "great, agonized face," and wondered whether Ryan was depicting the face of war or a self-portrait. When he finished the painting, it was indeed himself represented on canvas, revealing his anguish during that period. He later framed the picture, and hung it in a prominent place as a silent reminder.

Before World War II, Ryan was scarcely aware that his military enlistment gave tacit approval to becoming part of a very efficient killing machine. Afterward, his heroic prewar roles may have turned into hollow triumphs as he

"The Woman on the Beach" (RKO), 1947. Ryan confers with costar Joan Bennett and director Renoir on the set.

beheld the war's tragic by-products, first, the lives lost in Hiroshima and Nagasaki, then, the abomination of the Holocaust.

By the time Ryan was discharged from the Marines in November 1945, any previous notions he had regarding the rightness of war had disappeared among the debris of its inhumanity. He had also been strongly influenced by Jessica's Quaker sensitivity and pacifistic views, and despite being subjected to a military philosophy for nearly two years, he emerged from the war devoted to peace.

Ryan made a curious move in 1945 while at Camp Pendleton, which resulted in a profound social statement two years later. He had read a provocative novel by Richard Brooks called *The Brick Foxhole*, whose theme dealt with the angry aftereffects war imposes on returning G.I.s. Ryan asked Brooks to be considered for the role of the story's central character, a murderous bigot, if the book ever made it to film. Brooks agreed to his request.

While her husband was in the Marines, Jessica had become a professional writer and had articles published in *Coronet*, *Mademoiselle*, and *Photoplay*. Her patience with the pen also turned out two novels, *The Man Who Asked Why* (1943), and *The Crack Within the Ring* (1944). She went on to become an accomplished mystery novelist and a writer of children's books.

Ryan had a several month hiatus from activity when he was discharged, because the labor unrest in Hollywood during the war years had not diminished.

By 1946, most studios had been forced to reduce the number of films being made. Of those that were undergoing major changes, RKO was probably the hardest hit until corporate head Charles Koerner reversed things in 1945, turning in RKO's most profitable year ever. But when he died suddenly from leukemia in February 1946, RKO went into another period of flux.

Ryan may have felt secure knowing he still had a steady income and a very comfortable existence, because on April 13, 1946, Jessica gave birth to their first son, Timothy, at the Cedars of Lebanon Hospital in Los Angeles. He had a little time off from films to practice parenting, and as he watched young Timothy grow, one of the things he was proud of was the boy's strength. Robert Wallsten recalled Ryan recounting to him in awed terms how Tim had picked up a typewriter with one hand at the tender age of three or four. It was almost as if the feat of strength symbolized a future which Ryan had himself lost, that of being a writer.

Ryan's first film after returning to Hollywood was his first starring role in a Western, *Trail Street*, directed by Ray Enright. By that time he was 36 years old, thus his rugged "cowboy" look and his skill on horseback gave RKO a ready-made image to sell. *Trail Street* was the second of 19 Westerns in which Ryan appeared, and by the end of his career, they composed nearly a third of his repertory.

In contrast to many of his Westerns, though, in *Trail Street* he played an earnest, good-natured land agent who comes to Kansas to farm, not to fight. Taking a close look at his portrayal of a law-abiding citizen, however, gave an indication that in that type he seemed almost too good and nice to be taken seriously. Since his last role in *Marine Raiders* had shown his ease at projecting intensity, *Trail Street* provided little challenge. Although the picture was more action than substance, it was one of RKO's few profit-making releases of 1947.

Ryan's next film of 1947, *The Woman on the Beach*, was the opposite of *Trail Street*, and as directed by Jean Renoir, it was imaginative, sophisticated, and misjudged. Renoir had been having difficulty with RKO moguls for a while, thus the commercial failure of *The Woman on the Beach* spelled out his swan song in Hollywood.

The critics' comments on *The Woman on the Beach* varied from one extreme to the other. In the *New York Herald-Tribune*, one reviewer wrote:

> There's a line midway in this turgid drama of hard-breathing passion on the Maine coast, where a character demands, "What are we doing here?" That question will find a resentful echo among many a puzzled audience.

But *Variety* was impressed with the picture, while prophesying:

> Another original creation from the striking imagination of Jean Renoir. . . . Its

box-office merits may be limited by its disturbing strangeness, but it is a *tour de force* bound to provoke a hubbub of critical controversy.

In the prestigious *Hollywood Quarterly*, writer Nathan Norman Weiss lauded Ryan's performance, but presaged his future struggles in the business:

> Robert Ryan is very much an actor and not at all the usual personality male, and it is very encouraging to see him interpret so worthy a role as Hero.

Despite the relative failure of *The Woman on the Beach*, Ryan had a commanding role as a battle-fatigued Coast Guard officer, and landed second billing to Joan Bennett. Being listed in the credits ahead of costar Charles Bickford demonstrated RKO's promotional intentions for Ryan, since at the time, Bickford had played second leads in nearly 60 films, while Ryan had appeared in a mere 12.

Curiously, Ryan never liked *The Woman on the Beach* very much, and when he was asked to talk about the film in later years at a seminar in New York, he concealed his real feelings. Since the picture had not at the time been recognized as a *film noir* classic, it also had an esoteric style that made it a strange hybrid, perhaps too avant-garde for Ryan's taste.

3. Caught in the Crossfire

One of Ryan's most important career moves happened in 1947, when he took a role that gained wide critical acclaim, but which set an image that he fought from then on. It is ironic that he later viewed with mixed emotions his part as an anti–Semitic bully in RKO's controversial film *Crossfire*, since he had specifically asked to play the role two years before.

Ryan's exact reasons for wanting to play such a negative character remain unclear, since when he talked about the role in later years, he didn't elaborate. He always seemed a bit mystified and amused by the public's enthusiasm over his interpretation of the loudmouthed bigot, Montgomery, and failed to see the "bone-chilling evil I presumably projected." He viewed *Crossfire* as a "fast murder mystery rather than a social polemic."[1]

Although much internal strife, mostly motivated by political divisiveness, existed in post–World War II Hollywood, a number of show business people saw the opportunity to use the screen to make social statements. One such person, RKO producer Adrian Scott, took the initial courageous move toward the creation of *Crossfire* when he bought the screen rights to Richard Brooks' novel, *The Brick Foxhole*.

Scott conferred with screenwriter John Paxton and executive producer Dore Schary about changing the book's theme from hatred of homosexuals to anti–Semitism. Schary was initially skeptical about this idea, but RKO heads took a gamble and approved the switch.

When *Crossfire* hit the screen, its story laid bare America's hidden history of prejudice, and the picture became the "Liberal message film" of the forties. Being the first Hollywood film to deal with the problem of anti–Semitism, *Crossfire*'s novelty increased its potential for box-office success. It also holds a unique status in the cinema, since a number of observers believe that *Crossfire* helped trigger the McCarthy era.

Crossfire won unanimous critical acclaim for its insightful treatment of a taboo topic. In an article which John Houseman wrote for the *Hollywood Quarterly*, entitled "Violence, 1947: Three Specimens," he noted:

> As an element in the business of contemporary picture making, *Crossfire* turns out to be a thoroughly organic and highly significant event. Aesthetically, the energy

"Crossfire" (RKO), 1947. Monty (Ryan) is accosted by a detective (Tom Keene) at the scene of a crime. "Film noir" aspects include heavy shadow detail and oblique camera angles.

and intensity of feeling which sparked the creators of the picture into attacking the racial issue have fired the rest of their work, transmuted it from an efficient "whodunit" into the best American picture I have seen this year.

Suddenly, Ryan's name was buzzing around movie circles, since his perceptive interpretation of the cagey Montgomery transcended what others might have played as a stereotyped routine. *Photoplay* magazine commented on the "excellent acting by Robert Ryan," while the *New Republic*'s Shirley O'Hara called his performance "wonderful."

The topicality of *Crossfire* has withstood the test of time. In 1982, author Nora Sayre wrote in her book, *Running Time: Films of the Cold War*, that "*Crossfire* skillfully imparts the post-war mood of those who were still searching for an identifiable enemy, plus the habits of hatred encouraged in wartime."

Sayre lauded Ryan's performance and commented on it from a sociopolitical perspective:

> Ryan achieves a harsh yet subtle portrait of a racist who is also a traditional reactionary: as an ex-policeman, he is deferential to authority, and his genial moments underline the violence that flares up within him despite his efforts to disguise it. . . . Throughout, the word "stinking" recurs with the savagery of an old-fashioned obscenity—it conveys the fury of the racist in a way that was new to the screen.

Another author, Foster Hirsch, took note of Ryan's strength in capturing the subtle gradations of his sociopathic character in *Crossfire*. In *The Dark Side of the Screen: Film Noir*, Hirsch applauded, ". . . Robert Ryan's powerful performance resists the kind of neat, limiting social classification that the film wants to attach to his sickness. He plays with an intensity that transcends the film's own boundaries as a liberal social document."

In examining the mysterious and hard-to-define qualities which became Ryan's trademarks, Hirsch compared *Crossfire*'s bigoted Montgomery with the psychopathy of four other films' villains: "Anti–Semitism alone does not fully account for the character's insane behavior—like the Sheriff (Orson Welles) in *Touch of Evil*, the corrupt mentalist (Tyrone Power) in *Nightmare Alley*, the has-been actress (Gloria Swanson) in *Sunset Boulevard*, and the gangster (Richard Conte) in *The Big Combo*, the Ryan character's derangement is complex and finally mysterious; it eludes analysis."

In *Hollywood in the Forties*, authors Charles Higham and Joel Greenberg confirmed Ryan's accessibility to convey the virulent nature of his character. Lauding *Crossfire* as a "beautifully organized and proportioned melodrama, written, directed and acted with unostentatious excellence," Higham and Greenberg asserted that of all these qualities, "it is Robert Ryan's psychopath, Montgomery, that stays most in mind: deceptively soft-spoken, seething with suppressed tension and feelings of inferiority, it is a frightening portrait. . . ."

Ryan's electrifying performance impressed the Oscar nominating committee, which placed his name in the bid for Best Supporting Actor of 1947. It was an uncharacteristic move by the Academy of Motion Picture Arts and Sciences to nominate a negative character fore the coveted statuette. Not surprisingly, those on behalf of Ryan ultimately capitulated in favor of Edmund Gwenn's portrait of Santa Claus in the inoffensive *Miracle on 34th Street*.

"Crossfire" (RKO), 1947. From left, Floyd (Steve Brodie) attempts to steady Mitch
(George Cooper), as Monty (Ryan) intimidates Samuels (Sam Levene).

From a career standpoint, the nomination was crucial as well as being a
sudden progression of his development as an actor. His next step ought to have
been toward larger budgeted films, roles which would enlarge on a potential
as yet only suggested, and a more mainstream recognition. This partly came
true; however, throughout his career he generally chose to avoid the obsessive
drive for head billing which his contemporaries Kirk Douglas, Burt Lancaster,
and Robert Mitchum pursued.

Besides its winning accolades as an intense socially conscious film, *Crossfire*
made uncomfortable waves in the Hollywood right, and with the wrong people
in Washington. Suspicious eyes fell on Adrian Scott and Edward Dmytryk (who had directed *Crossfire*), among others, and in late 1947 Dore
Schary got a phone call from the House Committee on Un–American
Activities.

Forthwith, investigators were dispatched to Schary's office to gather information on several RKO employees, including Dmytryk, Scott, RKO producer
Paul Jarrico, and Ryan. Schary quickly dismissed questions about Ryan's

"Berlin Express" (RKO), 1948. From left, Ryan, Merle Oberon, Charles Korvin. Film noir photography emphasizes shadows.

political leanings with a terse reply about his Marine Corps background, and the matter was thereafter left to rest.

In that Ryan had worked or associated with a number of left-thinking artists, including Clifford Odets, Jean Renoir, director John Berry, Ring Lardner, Jr., Dalton Trumbo, and others, and had made no secret about his liberal sentiments, the paranoia in Hollywood and elsewhere might have flustered him. At the head of the Hollywood rightists were vocal celebrities, headed by Cecil B. DeMille, John Wayne, Hedda Hopper, Robert Montgomery, and Adolph Menjou.

"Return of the Badmen" (RKO), 1948. A sadistic Sundance Kid (Ryan) prepares to gun down somebody.

When the smoke finally cleared, Dmytryk, Scott, and Dalton Trumbo had been convicted of contempt of Congress, and were sentenced to a year in prison. Scott's career was ruined, Trumbo was blacklisted and wrote under a pseudonym for many years, but Dmytryk returned to direct a number of important films, such as *The Caine Mutiny* and *The Young Lions*.

During the late forties, most show business figures were glancing fearfully behind themselves, and Ryan saw prudence in rebelling more skillfully, through constructive social activism. A close friend of Ryan's, screenwriter Philip Yordan, recalled his even-minded political stance, which he termed,

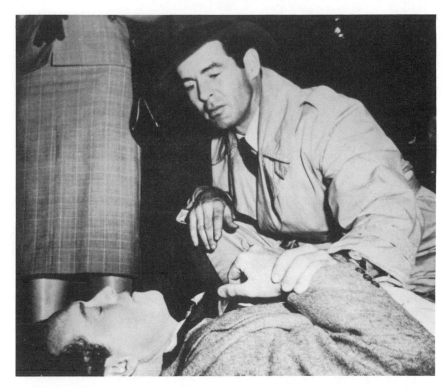

"Act of Violence" (MGM), 1948. Joe Parkson (Ryan) kneels over body of former friend Frank Enley (Van Heflin), who betrayed him during the war.

"liberal, not left-wing." When the House committee periodically reviewed its list of people to scrutinize, Ryan's name always seemed above reproach. Later, he off-handedly referred to his being "Irish-Catholic and an ex–Marine,"[2] as having saved him from the Hollywood hit list.

From then on, Ryan began to ally himself with various groups, such as the United World Federalists, and the American Friends' Service Committee. Both groups advocated a nonpartisan approach to preventing war through international cooperation between countries. After returning from World War II convinced about the insanity of war, Ryan became determined to do whatever he could to promote world peace.

His first picture of 1948, *Berlin Express*, may have contributed to his vehement antiwar stance when he traveled on location for seven weeks of shooting in Berlin and Frankfurt, Germany. Having remained stateside during the war, Ryan saw firsthand what he had been spared earlier. The vast areas of bombed-out ruins suggested an apocalypse which he would later see as imminent.

Berlin Express gave Ryan a semiromantic liaison with Merle Oberon and a wholly positive role, but he was still only courting full-fledged leading man status. Moreover, his last several pictures other than *Crossfire* had been less than spectacular in terms of changing or increasing his visibility and image.

In fact, his next film, *Return of the Badmen*, climbed in at the back gate of the horse operas. Except for Ryan's intense portrait of a psychopathic gunman and straightforward direction from Ray Enright, the film was mainly a reprise of stereotypes.

But by now the powers at RKO seemed to be channeling Ryan toward roles that required mean, often violent interpretations. Other studios were following suit, and for his third film of 1948, *Act of Violence*, he optioned out to MGM, again as an emotionally unstable person, feverishly seeking vengeance on a former Army buddy (Van Heflin). Directed by Fred Zinnemann and costarring Janet Leigh and Mary Astor, the picture bore the meticulous signature that Zinnemann brought to other modest black-and-white efforts, such as 1950's *The Men*, Marlon Brando's first film.

Ryan's reputation as an actor who couldn't give a bad performance was circulating in Hollywood at a time when three contemporaries were also making their bids for stardom. Robert Mitchum, Burt Lancaster, and Kirk Douglas had come up through the ranks at RKO as had Ryan, but from the late 1940s on, they resolutely advanced toward top billing in major productions, while he settled for second place. (Ryan was top-billed in 17 of his 70-odd films, while in the same period of time, Lancaster, Douglas, and Mitchum had logged in at least 40 each.)

The references Ryan sometimes made regarding his missing the Clark Gable or Cary Grant parts may have been idle musings, since he often talked to friends about wanting to avoid films having little meaning. Despite his strong desire to make pictures which said something profound, the fare which came his way was a succession of "program" pictures, in which he managed to create a variety of understated portrayals.

After *Act of Violence*, Ryan returned to RKO for a cameo role in director Joseph Losey's first feature film, *The Boy with Green Hair*, in which he costarred with Pat O'Brien and Barbara Hale. Having proven his bankability, if not his superstar quality, Ryan had become one of RKO's highest paid actors, thus his appearance in *The Boy with Green Hair* was a subtle gesture of support for the film's antiwar theme. But although the pacifist message of the picture was told in terms which scarcely could have been viewed as anti–American, it brought Losey under the gaze of the House committee.

In 1951, while Losey was in Europe, he was named as a former Communist and was blacklisted. He remained overseas and became a much respected craftsman, whose pictures revealed his continuous concern about issues of conscience, as in *The Damned* (1961), *King and Country* (1964), and *Mr. Klein* (1976).

"The Boy with Green Hair" (RKO), 1948. As a court psychiatrist in one of Losey's first antiwar films (at left, a shorn Dean Stockwell).

While Ryan was continuing to produce a high output of films, Jessica gave birth to their second son, Cheyney, on March 10, 1948, at the Cedars of Lebanon Hospital in Los Angeles. They were living in a modest ranch-style house in the San Fernando Valley then, and could have passed for a middle-class family, except for the presence of their black chauffeur, Solomon Smith, and his wife, Williana.

Williana did the cooking and Solomon the driving, and the kind, middle-aged couple were considered as "family." They remained as a stable force in the house for nearly 15 years, from 1948 until 1962.

In late 1948, Ryan went to MGM for the second time, after he contracted to play another neurotic character, in this case, an obsessive millionaire. By working on *Caught*, though, Ryan met the challenge of coming into contact with the gifted German director Max Ophuls, in a film which some critics have described as the best of Ophuls' work in America.

Caught is notable not only as a creative work: Ophuls is alleged to have made the film as a subtle revenge against Howard Hughes, after Hughes, for unknown reasons, humiliated Ophuls repeatedly in public. The behind-the-scenes politics of *Caught* were not openly known until many years later, thus Ryan seemed to have had no inkling that he may have been an instrument of retaliation.

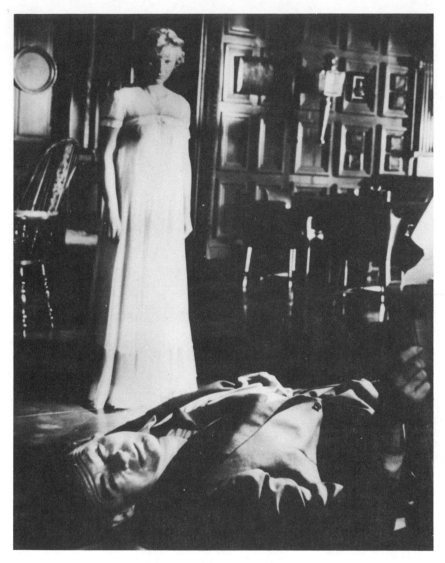

"Caught" (MGM), 1949. Smith Ohlrig lies prone after an angina attack as Leonora (Barbara Bel Geddes) observes without pity.

One observer, author and film critic Pauline Kael, believed *Caught* symbolized the intense enmity Ophuls felt toward Hughes, and that its screenplay paralleled people and events in Hughes's life. In an article, Kael reported that director Preston Sturges instigated Hughes's antagonism toward Ophuls by blaming Ophuls for running up a $1,000,000 production tab on Hughes's showcase vehicle for starlet Faith Domergue, the mediocre costume drama *Vendetta*.

From then on, Hughes publicly referred to Ophuls as "the Oaf," and shortly thereafter, Ophuls left RKO for MGM. When he collaborated with screenwriter Arthur Laurents on *Caught*, Ophuls' vengeance was sublime, because the screenplay depicted unpleasant similarities connecting Hughes with Ryan's character, which are too coincidental to be readily dismissed.

If, as Kael has asserted, Ryan's role was a parody on Hughes, it is ironic, since the two had little in common other than being tall and sharing a leanness in their features. One quality, however, that they both possessed was one of a mysterious solitude, which was integral to *Caught*'s theme of isolation.

Others have explored the Hughes/Ohlrig hypothesis. After writer Gary Carey read John Keats's unauthorized biography of Hughes, he felt confident enough to tie *Caught*'s storyline to Hughes's life. In *Film Comment*, Summer 1971, Carey noted that Ryan physically resembled Hughes, and compared two cast members, Barbara Bel Geddes and Curt Bois, to people in Hughes's narrow sphere of contact. The Bel Geddes character, Leonora Eames, meets Ohlrig in a situation closely resembling the first encounter between Hughes and Faith Domergue at a yachting party, while Ohlrig's lackey, Franzi (Bois), may have been equivalent to Hughes's barber, Eddie.

Further, Carey wrote that Hughes's habit of deserting his women for long periods of time was analogous to Ohlrig's callous neglect of Leonora. Carey also speculated that Ophuls might have been giving Hughes another slap in the face by casting Bel Geddes as Leonora, after Hughes had dismissed her from the RKO roster when he took over in 1948.

In light of the intrigue surrounding Hughes's life, Ryan's interpretation of Ohlrig's psychological workings merits consideration. In his studied depiction of one man's narcissistic loneliness, he communicated not only an emotional affliction of people in general, but he also encapsulated the essence of Hughes's troubled life.

Carey's pungent description of Ryan's portrayal of suppressed rage indicates that he dominated *Caught*. The first, with his psychiatrist:

> One is drawn into the scene, partially by the vehemence of Ryan's performance . . . [but] by the abrasive tension and vicious atmosphere which Ophuls gives it.

A second scene, at Ohlrig's mansion:

> During a moment of stress, Ohlrig slams into a pinball machine in his game room. . . . As handled by Ryan, this is a sublime meeting between actor and prop, and one is caught short by the violence of the encounter. It seems, at the time, to be one of those glorious, extraneous little touches that in movies often have more life than the story they are meant to decorate.

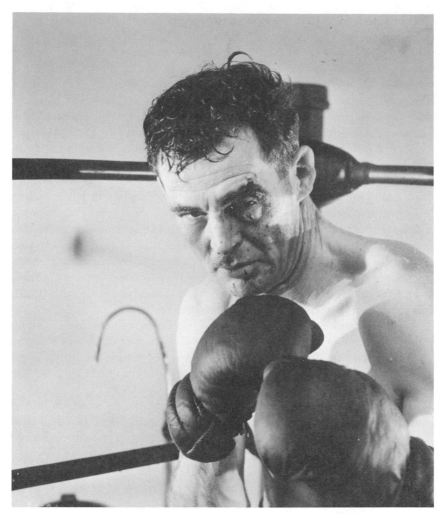

"The Set-up" (RKO), 1949. Close-up of a pummeled Stoker Thompson (Ryan). The boxing scenes were choreographed by trainer and former boxer John Indrisano.

Carey summed up Ryan's performance:

> Ryan is superb: uptight, belligerent, repulsive, he skates on stiletto blades across the icy surface of Ohlrig's personality, while managing to suggest that the façade is more than skin deep.

Although *Caught* was well received by several critics, its story of an adulterous woman who endures mental cruelty and a miscarriage for the sake of money was too disturbing to be widely appreciated. In later years, a few diligent film scholars have retrieved it for further consideration. When *Caught* was shown at the U.C.L.A. Film Archives in 1981, *Los Angeles Reader* film critic Myron Meisel wrote:

> *Caught* brilliantly mixes elements of continental sophistication, "film noir," sociological observation, class analysis, American gothic, and the myth of Howard Hughes into a coherent, precise expression of one artist's sublime sensibility.

When Dore Schary chose to make *The Set-up* in 1948, he knew he had to make lower-budget films, since RKO's resources were again fluctuating. In a bid to replenish the studio's assets, RKO board chairman Floyd Odlum sold a controlling interest to Howard Hughes, and chaos broke out immediately thereafter.

In the middle of preparation for *The Set-up*, Schary and Hughes had irreconcilable differences with each other, and Schary left RKO to return to MGM as its production head. In the director's chair on *The Set-up* sat Robert Wise, who had recently made several low-budget gems for RKO. After scrambling together whomever he could from the studio's decimated staff, in 19 days he completed a 72-minute picture which surprised everybody.

It was Schary's tenacity which resulted in Wise getting the job, since before leaving, he had insisted on Wise to Hughes. But it was an insane period at RKO, and with people coming and going due to what Wise termed, "Hughes's Don Quixote–like way of running a studio," Wise believed his days at RKO were numbered. His premonition came true: *The Set-up* was his last film for the studio.

In an interview in *L'Avant-scène* magazine, Wise said, "Even so, Hughes gave us the green light. For all of us, *The Set-up* was an act of love." The "us" included Ryan, producer Richard Goldstone, screenwriter Art Cohn, cinematographer Milton Krasner, and former boxer/trainer John Indrisano, who dealt with the film's technical end. (Indrisano apparently fell upon hard times in later years. On July 9, 1968, he hanged himself at his home in the San Fernando Valley.) For one of the few times in his career, Ryan got involved in the creation of a script, and worked closely with Wise and Indrisano to choreograph the boxing scenes.

Wise reported that Ryan's boxing background had been essential to casting him as the film's main character, over-the-hill boxer Stoker Thompson, but that it was necessary to modify his stance for the camera. Also, trainer Indrisano felt that Ryan needed to build up his muscle bulk, and being Italian, fed him spaghetti until he lost his taste for it. But the regimen of stuffing himself with carbohydrates and the daily workouts at the gym built him up while honing down any fat, leaving sinew only.

When the idea for *The Set-up* first circulated among the various screen-writers at RKO, some thought it would be difficult to cast the main character. Director Samuel Fuller had only glowing words for the poem by Joseph Moncure March, on which the story for *The Set-up* was based, and spoke of "falling for the cadence of the black fighter called Candy Jones." But when Fuller learned that Ryan was to play Jones, he had doubts about the casting of a white man in place of a black.

Seeing Ryan's performance, though, Fuller came away amazed, and lauded it with the flashy style he had learned as a newspaper crime reporter in the late 1920s and early 1930s:

> Ryan *was* that Black fighter. Under the skin, he *was* Candy Jones. Bob caught all the nuances of guts and shattered hopes, and small-time aspirations of a never-was beating the hell out of the desperation of being a club fighter.

Screenwriter Art Cohn deftly developed an intensely cynical screenplay from March's poem, and adhered to its storyline except for the ending, which he presumably changed to leave audiences with a thread of optimism. In the poem, Candy Jones, chased by gangsters after refusing to throw a fight, finds refuge in a subway station. He jumps down on the tracks just as a train approaches. Jones hunches up, one arm uplifted instinctively before the train strikes him, and his image is frozen for eternity. Fuller registered his disappointment about the changed ending, but spoke with relish about "imagining the expression Ryan would have given a second before the train struck him with a haymaker."

Ryan was drawn to *The Set-up* because its story involved a conclusion which reversed how typical boxing films ended. Wise explained, "In the majority of boxing films, good wins while evil is defeated. Here, the hero wins the battle but loses the war, since by defeating his opponent, Jones [in the movie, the character was named Stoker Thompson] causes the end of his career.

"All of the elements appealed to Bob, because *The Set-up* was not your average, run-of-the-mill B-plus picture at RKO," continued Wise. "It offered a completely different vision of boxing, not Madison Square Garden and not the universe of great champions, but a nitty-gritty look at the small-time fighter in the poor section of town."

When *The Set-up* was released, much irony surrounded its distribution as a budget feature on the lower half of a double bill. Spectacular reviews greeted its arrival, as critics and moviegoers alike excitedly discussed it and Ryan's performance. At the Cannes Film Festival of 1949, he received the Best Actor award, while in the States *The Set-up* overpowered another boxing film, United Artist's *Champion*, starring Kirk Douglas, which was released the same year. (The contention between the two films waged beyond the theaters. After United Artists attempted to release the Douglas film using *The Set-up* as its title, RKO sued United Artists and won the case.)

Many observers, including Ryan's friend John Houseman, believe that *The Set-up* is the best film ever made about the fight game. In *Hollywood in the Forties*, authors Higham and Greenberg asserted, "The scenes have a harshness, a sure feeling for cruelty and mob hysteria, that have seldom been surpassed." *The Set-up*'s stature as a cult piece has increased over the years, as Leonard Maltin commented in *T.V. Movies: 1985–86*: "a gutsy account of a washed-up fighter refusing to give up or go crooked. Ryan has never been better."

In *L'Avant-scène* magazine, writer Thierry Génin lauded Ryan's performance as an existential hero:

> Without a doubt because of his sober acting and his handsome, tired face, Ryan will always remain the giant cast by Wise in *The Set-up*. He is a deceived boxer, startled to find the dignity to resist a gang of thugs and getting beat up in an alley that represents what he had been. With his veiled stare, his weary face, and his bitter voice, Ryan trails behind him all the lassitude and solitude of the world.

From their work on *The Set-up*, Ryan and Wise developed a lasting professional and personal relationship. Both liberal thinkers, they shared many of the same friends during Ryan's Hollywood years, and Wise recalled his "even-mindedness in the best sense of the word." Jessica Ryan had the same concern for social issues, and throughout the fifties, Wise was aware of their continued activism.

It is significant that Ryan rated *The Set-up* as his most meaningful picture (at least prior to *The Iceman Cometh*), because it symbolized one man's struggle and triumph over impossible odds of venality and predation. Even so, his comments on the picture were curiously noncommittal, and he generally referred only to the film's economical structure rather than to his own winning performance. In fact, his opinions of his contributions toward any of his films were usually self-effacing, possibly as a way of compensating for any real or imagined mistakes.

Years later, when Ryan's son Timothy went into acting, he asked his father about the intricacies of the art. Ryan constantly referred to "the underplaying, the doing as much as you can with as little going on as possible." He told Tim simply, "It's all in the eyes. That's where you do most of your work."

The special quality that Ryan brought to his portrayals could only have been accurately described by someone else, though, since he tended to view his performances with a jaded eye. Samuel Fuller thought Ryan had "a charismatic gift for making you like the bastard he played, because he understood what made that bastard tick—and he made the audience understand it." Fuller believed that one of Ryan's talents was "his basic honesty in whatever role he was playing."

Philip Yordan considered Ryan's nonchalant references to his acting techniques as characteristically modest, and held that they involved much more than mere eye movements. "Bob knew exactly what he was doing," said Yordan. "Every gesture he made was carefully planned and rehearsed."

Yordan had worked with many of Hollywood's best, and classed Ryan with actors like Spencer Tracy and Edward G. Robinson. He recalled, "Bob worked very hard to perfect his craft, and no matter what the part was, he put everything into it." Yordan remembered Ryan being struck with stereotyped roles in many pictures, and that he "created something out of nothing." But, Yordan emphasized, what Ryan created was "always subtle, never flamboyant."

When *The Set-up* garnered glowing reviews, RKO arranged a private screening at the studio which sparked one of Ryan's most unforgettable experiences. Twenty-odd years later, he recalled the event to his friend Arvin Brown, who was directing him on the New York stage in *Long Day's Journey into Night.*

"As Bob left the screening room one night after a preview of *The Set-up,*" said Brown, "Cary Grant approached him on the street, stuck out his hand and announced, 'You're Robert Ryan.'

"Almost as an afterthought, Grant added, 'Uh, my name's Cary Grant.' Then he said to Bob, 'I want you to know that I just saw *The Set-up,* and I thought your performance was one of the best I've ever seen.'

"The funny part of the story was that Grant introduced himself as if Bob might not know who he was," stated Brown. Brown remembered being emotionally moved by Ryan's humility as he related the story, and heard in his voice a hero-worshipping tone which Ryan reserved for only a few actors.

When Brown saw the emotion well up in Ryan's face as he talked about the honor, he knew he had gained his trust. "Bob didn't want to be seen as a sentimental man, which he was, but it really tore him up when he told the Cary Grant incident."

As Ryan's friends translated their perceptions of his personality into understandable terms, a common theme emerged, one combining an unusual mixture of sensitivity and machismo. John Houseman believed Ryan exuded an aura of suppressed tension, and commented on an initial emotion one might feel upon seeing him for the first time. "Bob had the look of a boxer which suggested he might be a violent man, but internally, he was a *very* sensitive person," said Houseman.

Ryan's role in *The Set-up* exemplified the dichotomy Houseman perceived, of a boxer who defies the image of the pugilist. It seems appropriate that author Joan Mellen would discuss Ryan in her book *Big Bad Wolves — Masculinity in the American Film,* since virility was a part of his image.

Mellen observed, "Robert Ryan offers a unique image of the prize fighter — or of the screen male. He is gentle and soft-spoken. If he is a boxer, out of the ring he is complex and often emotionally insecure, and shuns aggression as the norm of male behavior."

Arvin Brown suggested that the paradox Ryan presented was more than make-believe, and that he possessed a degree of insecurity and a lack of aggressiveness which diminished his impact on the public. When Brown recalled meeting Ryan for the first time, his impression of him was one of shyness and possibly of retreat. Conversely, though, in describing Ryan's demeanor as "totally laid back," Brown believed that "Bob was essentially comfortable with his view of himself."

After *The Set-up*'s winning box-office notices, Ryan accepted a part in another low-budget picture for RKO, but the same degree of determination that made *The Set-up* a success failed to raise his next effort from "programmer" status.

4. On Dangerous Ground

The internal chaos which existed at RKO after Howard Hughes took over was perfectly symbolized by the title, screenplay, direction, and misleading promotional campaign for *I Married a Communist*. In late 1948 and early 1949, Hughes briefly came out of seclusion to use the picture to kick off his red-baiting period.

That Ryan landed the lead role in *I Married a Communist* is curious, since his political views contrasted strongly with everything it represented. Also, since several writers have reported that Hughes used the picture as a kind of loyalty test for actors, it remains unclear as to why he and Ryan never bumped heads.

Perhaps Ryan's liberal point of view had not filtered through to the reclusive Hughes, or his Marine Corps background may have automatically placed him above reproach. For that matter, Ryan had no way of knowing that the results of his efforts on *I Married a Communist* would be crude exploitation material, because RKO had originally signed director John Cromwell (*Of Human Bondage*) and screenwriter Herman Mankiewicz (*Citizen Kane*) to work on the picture.

After Hughes vetoed several script rewrites and various writers had departed, Cromwell backed out of the film, calling the screenplay, "without a doubt the worst I have ever read in my life." Next, Nicholas Ray agreed to direct the film, but he also dropped out at the last minute. Finally, Robert Stevenson (*Jane Eyre*) took the helm, and *I Married a Communist* went into production in April 1949. Principal shooting lasted one month, but two days of retakes were necessary after Hughes carefully examined and found fault with many aspects of the film.

In one scene, Hughes ordered Laraine Day's profile to be reshot from a different angle when he noticed a blemish on her face. He criticized the kiss sequences between Janis Carter and John Agar, and wanted them to be made sexier. He also felt "very definitely" that "Bob Ryan and Bill Talman should be helped in their pistol shooting."

As had happened in the case of *Crossfire*, initial audience research polls indicated *I Married a Communist* was an unwise venture, and in October 1949, after less than average previews in Los Angeles and San Francisco, Hughes announced a delayed national release of the picture. To mollify him, RKO personnel suggested a last minute change in the title, but Hughes snapped back in a memo, "This is ridiculous—I have always liked the title. In fact, the title is one of the most valuable parts of the picture."

Nevertheless, shortly thereafter, RKO undertook a search for an appropriate title which would "sell" the film, and nearly a hundred were suggested, each carrying a different connotation. Before Hughes finally decided on *The Woman on Pier 13*, in January 1950, he gave serious thought to lurid titles such as *San Francisco Melodrama*, *Waterfront at Midnight*, and *Where Danger Lives*. Strangely enough, Hughes's ultimate choice first surfaced scrawled on a memo pad by an unknown hand, and its author remains anonymous to this day, as if in silent nullification of the project.

The Woman on Pier 13 opened in June 1950 and had a whopping box-office deficit, partly because the public had been misled by a carefully orchestrated promotional campaign which failed to deliver what it had promised. And since the picture's dialogue reflected Hughes' fractured views via the pens of seven different writers, its ultimate message sounded like a schizophrenic propaganda piece.

The final screenplay contained fear-mongering lines such as "It's a pity that some of our members don't understand . . . they can never leave the Party . . . until the Party's ready to let them go," and, "To create an international Soviet Republic, all means will be used, including force of arms." Since America was deeply enmeshed in the Cold War, films like *The Woman on Pier 13* were almost guaranteed to fail, for they aroused only fear, despite their anti–Communist messages.[1]

As Ryan finished one low-budget film, he moved on to a succession of others that were of decidedly less quality than his talent indicated. His reputation as an actor who could elevate whatever came his way was stretched mightily in his next film, *The Secret Fury*, which was directed by actor and sometime director Mel Ferrer.

RKO banked on Ryan and Claudette Colbert to make sense of a less than believable script, but neither did so consistently under Ferrer's unsubtle direction. However, the film gave Ryan another solid romantic lead and followed his goal of seeking varied roles.

In 1950, Ryan's patience was tested by two more films after *The Secret Fury*'s failure. Although his next effort, *Born to Be Bad*, was directed by Nicholas Ray, it is virtually forgotten for unknown reasons in the repertories of both. As a high-class soap opera, much in the tradition of other "high society" films of the thirties and forties, *Born to Be Bad*'s San Francisco setting and sophisticated dialogue should have been better received.

Perhaps RKO's desire to make the film was another ill-advised maneuver, since its creation happened after that type of picture had exhausted its

"The Woman on Pier 13" (RKO), 1949. Above: Brad Collins (Ryan) meets Communist bully Vanning (Thomas Gomez) in a basement headquarters. Opposite: The seductive Christine (Janis Carter) tries to rekindle former romance with Brad (Ryan).

potential. It fell into a hazy category as a *film noir* as well, despite the established melodramatic credentials of *Born to Be Bad*'s stars. And since RKO was less known of late for its classier acts than for its quickie potboilers, the public and critics alike seem to have been unprepared for *Born to Be Bad*.

RKO's casting of Ryan opposite Joan Fontaine reflected a confidence in him as a virile male presence, while his role as a successful writer with a shrewd sense about women seemed natural. He was also able to share acting distinctions with two stars he greatly respected, Cary Grant and Laurence Olivier, Fontaine's leading men in two early forties box-office smashes, Alfred Hitchcock's *Suspicion* and *Rebecca*. For unclear reasons, the more influential film critics failed to give *Born to Be Bad* more than a cursory glance, and it disappeared from theaters after a brief run.

The early- to mid-fifties seem to have signaled Ryan's point of no return as a leading man. By then he had hovered at the periphery of the top for several years, while his contemporaries had all reached it. A few important reasons contributed to his wavering status near the pinnacle, and though other speculations may be in order, some aspects of his situation seem clear.

Ryan's physical characteristics were doubtless important, since by 1950 he was 41 years old, and had already developed deep character lines around the eyes, forehead, and mouth. His ruddy, youthful Irish look was fast being replaced by a mature ruggedness that studios decided worked best in action or outdoor pictures. Possessing an athletic prowess and a willingness to put it to use if a director asked, he performed much of his own stunt work. Also, his size was much more imposing in person than it might have appeared in his movies, made more formidable by his broad shoulders. Thus, casting directors were often disinclined to consider him for the debonair types in which he professed an interest.

Philip Yordan looked at Ryan's career pragmatically, referring to the "old Hollywood caste system" as his chief nemesis, and to studio heads who "felt Bob didn't exude the glamour nor the sex appeal of a Gable." But his black, curly hair and dark, intense eyes, offset by a full, open smile that appeared unrestrained in comparison with his quiet charisma, combined for an irresistible charm. Yordan socialized with Ryan often and had seen his magnetic effect on women. "They chased Bob," said Yordan.

Yordan also saw a side of Ryan which seemed to reflect how he viewed the Hollywood community, despite his fascination with some aspects of it. "Bob was an old-fashioned American who really belonged in a small town," explained Yordan, and added with a hint of sorrow, "he wasn't cut out for the Hollywood life."

Ryan's small circle of friends was antithetical to the show business mentality, and when he was away from the screen, most of his acquaintances had nothing to do with the entertainment industry. Yordan fondly referred to Ryan as "family," and recalled the nights when he would "just come over to

Top: "The Secret Fury" (RKO), 1950. From left, Philip Ober, Elisabeth Risdon, and Ryan tend to Claudette Colbert at a mental institution after she is accused of murder and has a nervous breakdown. Bottom: "Born to Be Bad" (RKO), 1950. Christabel Caine (Joan Fontaine) makes a clandestine telephone call as Nick Bradley (Ryan) listens in the background. (Courtesy the Museum of Modern Art/ Film Stills Archives.)

Bob's house, and we would sit around, smoke cigarettes, and drink beer." When he was asked to comment on Ryan's inner workings, Yordan said simply "Bob had no ego."

Another of Ryan's close friends, director Lamont Johnson, believed Ryan felt ambivalent about the glamour of stardom, but that, "There was a part of Bob that enjoyed being a star, and a Hollywood star, at that." Johnson remembered the period when "Bob moved out of the San Fernando Valley and into a very chic Beverly Hills house for a few years," but that paradoxically, "he never seemed comfortable there, although there was a part of him that loved it."

Johnson thought back to one of the most intriguing aspects of Ryan's personality, describing him as an "eminently balanced person." Within the Hollywood sphere, neither Ryan nor Johnson made a point of hiding his liberal viewpoints, and Johnson felt rebellious glee when he recalled how Ryan played the celebrity game. Johnson believed that Ryan fit into it when he felt inclined, but that he had the ability to maintain a distance from it, sometimes as a sardonic observer or to test his ego strength.

Though Johnson witnessed firsthand Ryan's cynical attitude toward the show business arena, he also believed Ryan flirted at the brink of glamour long enough to nearly fall victim to it. Johnson said, "Bob was a sort of lace-curtain Irishman who loved not only keeping up with the Joneses, but on the other hand, he loved to beat the shit out of them."

Ryan and Johnson first worked together on several projects in the early fifties, and a friendship grew from their having important things in common. Both had been raised Roman Catholic and came close politically, and they viewed the world through similar eyes, although Johnson had gone much further to the left in his searching twenties.

After having started a career as an actor in the late forties (his clear voice can be heard in *On Dangerous Ground*, as one of the police radio announcers), Johnson was blacklisted in Hollywood for several years because of his earlier beliefs. Out of work until 1955, he finally turned the tide in his favor when he returned as a director of television dramas such as *Peter Gunn* and *The Naked City*.

In the sixties, he began to direct motion pictures, and has had a prolific career treating a wide variety of subjects with sensitivity and wit. Johnson's most notable works include *The Last American Hero* (1973), *One on One* (1977), and *Cattle Annie and Little Britches* (1979).

Johnson has also won acclaim in the past several years for his television specials, *The Execution of Private Slovik* (1974), *Wallenberg: A Hero's Story* (1985), and *Unnatural Causes* (1986).

Johnson was not surprised that Ryan had completely avoided any adverse publicity during the hectic years of the blacklisting. He remembered his own idealistic reasons for joining the Communist Party while he was in college in the thirties, and called the experience "part of the whole learning process." Johnson came to realize that some of people's responses to the extreme leftist movements were based on "romantic and emotional notions" of making the world better.

As Johnson searched for an appropriate description for Ryan's way of dealing with social repercussions in the aftermath of World War II and during the McCarthy era, the term "curious even-handedness" seemed to fit. "Although Bob was an impetuous person," said Johnson, "on the other side of it, he was a weighing and measuring person."

Over the years, Ryan and Johnson worked and socialized with each other in entertainment and in social activism. Johnson spoke with admiration about Ryan's ability to exchange ideas freely and to sort through information, weeding out the unrealistic or the illogical. "Bob saw a lot of crap going on in the world, but he also recognized that under all the emotional, liberal persuasions, there was genuinely a Communist threat underneath the disguise," said Johnson.

Ryan's steadiness of purpose was a valuable asset for a small studio such as RKO. RKO had lately increased its output of films in a convoluted effort to lower its huge deficits, and with tight shooting schedules lasting between 15 and 21 days, the studio counted on Ryan to produce as needed. In fact, his commitment to the acting profession aided in the creation of one of his most underrated films, director Nicholas Ray's brooding, existential allegory, *On Dangerous Ground*.

From the outset of RKO's production of *On Dangerous Ground*, ominous clues indicated it was traversing territory similar to its title. Despite recent misfires in his last three pictures, Ryan agreed to play the lead role as an alienated city detective in a film which nearly wasn't made, and which appealed to an esoteric minority when it was released.

In his first book of memoirs, *Front and Center*, John Houseman described the protracted journey of *On Dangerous Ground* from the mind of Nicholas Ray to the theaters. Houseman, who was producing for RKO in 1948, decided to make the film at the request of Ray, who had worked with him a few years earlier on *They Live by Night*. Ray had just read an English novel, *Mad with Much Heart*, by Gerald Butler, and he was eager to make a movie of it, but after Houseman read the book, he did not entirely share Ray's enthusiasm. Although he saw what attracted Ray to the story, he had reservations about transferring the idea to film.

Before he approved the production for the film, Houseman needed to sort through two other opinions on the novel. An RKO story editor, William Fadiman, expressed his doubts to Houseman in a memo stating, "This is an unpleasant but powerful novel. It is likely to emerge as an 'art' production which may receive critical acclaim but no sizable box-office returns." Executive producer Sid Rogell, whom Houseman described as a "competent hack without imagination or courage," concurred with Fadiman.

Hoping to find a judgment he respected, Houseman sent a copy of *Mad with Much Heart* to his friend, novelist/screenwriter Raymond Chandler, who responded in a short letter in the negative, and said "I don't feel enthusiastic about it . . . it has no humor for me at all."

Houseman spared Nicholas Ray the foreboding news from Chandler, partly because of contractual obligations to RKO, and set about arranging a first-rate production. To calm Sid Rogell's anxiety over the picture's viability, Houseman contacted Ryan to play the lead role, opposite Ida Lupino. Having considered the successes of *Crossfire* and *The Set-up*, Houseman believed Ryan's presence in *On Dangerous Ground* could overcome some of the picture's limitations.

The screenplay for *On Dangerous Ground* had not yet been completed, but Ryan had wanted to work with Ray again, and committed himself to the film, subject to script approval. Houseman felt that Ryan was RKO's most ideally suited player for the part of loner detective Jim Wilson, which called for a taciturn physicality within an intellectual framework. Houseman then hired screenwriter A.I. Bezzerides to adapt a script from the novel based on his reputation as the author of two hard-edged novels about blue-collar life in California, and several screenplays whose themes had dealt with the chase (*They Drive by Night*, *Northern Pursuit*, and *Thieves' Highway*).

The warning signs assailing *On Dangerous Ground* in pre-production continued during the filming. Houseman and Ray had chosen an area in the Colorado Rockies near Granby for the location shooting, and sent a 40-man company there for two weeks. Heavy snowstorms caused a number of delays varying in duration from 30 minutes to three-and-a-half hours, and cinematographer George Diskant was put to the test attempting to keep continuity in the backgrounds. Even so, in the final cut, a few bare spots where snow had melted crept into the scenery.

During the time spent in Granby, the troupe stayed at the El Monte Inn, where Ryan became the center attraction of the townspeople. He accepted an invitation to demonstrate his boxing technique to students at a local high school, and handed out scores of autographs. He had less difficulty accepting the type of star adulation he saw in Granby, since it came within the context of doing a service for someone.

Whatever reservations Houseman felt about the picture's chances for commercial success, he knew that tremendous care went into the creation of *On Dangerous Ground*. He recalled that "the film *was* made with love," and that the styles of Ray and Bezzerides complemented each other. He described their chemistry as "a combination of an almost feminine sensitivity with a strong macho streak."

Ray's preparation for *On Dangerous Ground* was meticulous. He began his research by riding on patrol with police detectives in Boston's tough South End, and when he returned to Los Angeles just before filming began, he became immersed in his task. Houseman recalled how Ray and Bezzerides went out "night after night in Los Angeles Police Department squad cars to study the psychopathology of violence."

The essense of Ray's cinema expressed a preoccupation with the theme of violence, tightly intertwined with the theme of solitude. Within that context, he concerned himself with man's struggle toward a better life, yet paradoxically, he also saw the quest as a solitary one. Ray once described his experience of the world with the bleak comment, "I am a stranger here myself."[2]

Though Ray's existential concerns may have appealed to Ryan's sense of tragedy, Ryan's predilection for appearing in films dealing with the raw truths of existence sometimes prompted queries about his attraction to the melancholic. He was once asked why he never played comedy roles and he responded, "I play them as I see them."[3] In his book about Nicholas Ray, author James Kreidl discussed On Dangerous Ground and Ryan's performance, and concurred that he had an affinity for tragedy. Calling the picture "deadly serious and completely cut off from the romantic comedy," Kreidl described Ryan's interpretation as "subdued, controlled, understated—almost expressionistic."

Other writers agree that the styles of Ryan and Ray mixed together comfortably. In Film Comment, March-April 1975, author George Morris wrote, "Ryan's Wilson is the classically alienated Ray protagonist . . . isolated from every person with whom he comes in contact." Morris discussed Ryan's skill in handling Ray's frequent use of "montage" in the film, especially in his scenes opposite costar Ida Lupino. Calling attention to Ryan's exploration of his full range of expression, Morris remarked "the close-ups that follow their [Ryan and Lupino] tear-stained faces are as beautiful and eloquent as any in the cinema."

RKO's long delay in releasing On Dangerous Ground further validated the appropriateness of its title. Ray completed the studio footage in May 1950, but distribution was withheld for nearly two years.

When On Dangerous Ground finally struggled onto the screen in early 1952, the extraordinary efforts that went into its creation met with mixed reviews. One trade paper, the Hollywood Reporter, agreed with earlier premonitions, stating, "a good, sound story weakened by a switch from action to character unfoldment," but also noted, "To Ryan goes top credit for enacting a difficult role . . . in a manner that makes his performance acceptable even if the sudden change in characterization is not."

Despite being undervalued in 1952, On Dangerous Ground has resurfaced often for study by serious film scholars. George Morris concluded that On Dangerous Ground is "the one true masterwork that can hold its own with Nicholas Ray's other films . . . it reverberates with a depth of feeling that qualifies it as sublime cinematic art."

As Ryan's acting signature grew more distinct, several film critics began to

"On Dangerous Ground" (RKO), 1951. Top: From left, Detective Bailey (Charles Kemper) and Lucky (Gus Schilling) observe Wilson (Ryan) asking young woman (Nita Talbot) for identification. Bottom: Wilson's partners Pop (Charles Kemper) and Pete (Anthony Ross) guide the frustrated Wilson away from another possible assault.

reserve a category for him. He first gained notice in Europe when the prestigious French film periodical *Cahiers du Cinéma* recognized his artistic contributions and elevated him to cult stature. Unsung pictures, such as *The Woman on the Beach* and *Caught*, shared accolades with commercially suc-cessful films such as *Crossfire* and *The Set-up.*

Considering that Ryan developed his style working with artists who were trained in Europe, it is not surprising that his pictures attracted a wide follow-ing overseas. Robert Wise was amused when he went to Europe in 1953 to direct *Helen of Troy*, and discovered that *The Set-up* was being shown at theaters to sell-out audiences. "When the press showed up for interviews on the set of *Helen of Troy*. . .," said Wise, "all they wanted to talk about was *The Set-up*."

Although *The Set-up* had received substantial critical praise in America, its relegation to budget status lessened its general public recognition. Wise recalled having a conversation with director Billy Wilder concerning the irony in *The Set-up*'s reception in Europe and in the United States. "If *The Set-up* had been made in France or Italy and had come over here," Wilder told Wise, "it would have been acclaimed to the heavens by the critics."

By the early fifties, film critics posited psychoanalytic explanations for what set Ryan's acting style apart from that of other actors. When *Coronet Magazine* reviewed his distinctive portraits in a 1963 article, it asserted that they shared an affinity paralleling Nicholas Ray's solitary statement on life:

> The figures that Robert Ryan creates with such authority are all, in different ways, isolated; if their aloofness is not due to some violent obsession, it conceals something else—the secret of failure, or personal unhappiness, or extreme discontent. It is this persisting inner quality of restlessness, of disturbance, that gives him his individuality. . . .

One writer, Thierry Génin, wrote in an article in the French film periodical *L'Avant-scène* that Ryan's screen persona expressed a "lacerated humanity" that was "strong, yet tormented." Génin saw other levels of expres-sion in Ryan's portrayals that were intriguing contrasts in emotion, and perceived a tranquil fortitude suggesting that Ryan had been through a lot and had survived. Génin concluded that his message concerned the dilemma of the human condition.

Robert Wise believed that Ryan had a talent for eliciting sympathy for the characters he played, and that "part of Bob's art made one feel that he was a victim in some way, and not just an out-and-out son of a bitch." When Wise called to mind a contemporary American actor who most closely approached the intensity of temperament that Ryan molded, he suggested the name of Jon Voight.

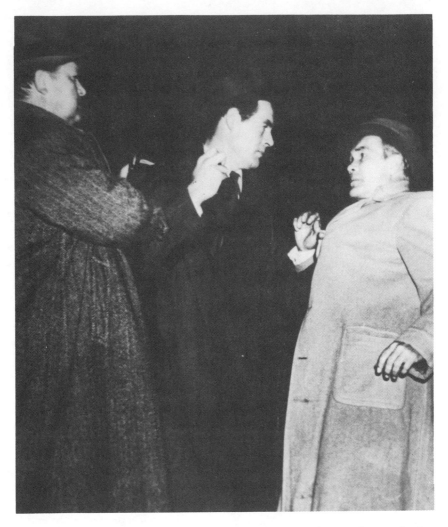

Pop Daly and Pete Santos attempt to restrain Wilson from inflicting further mayhem (from left, Charles Kemper, Ryan, William Challee).

In 1985, Voight received the Golden Globe Best Actor award for his portrayal of a manic escaped convict in *Runaway Train*. In his acceptance speech, Voight expressed gratitude for having the opportunity to play a role which made him more aware of the internal conflicts that confront mankind.

Wise was seated in the audience at the Golden Globe affair that night, and heard similarities in the tone of Voight's speech that reminded him of what Ryan might have said. Wise ventured, "I think the two shared the same inner qualities in their souls."

For his own part, Ryan seemed on the surface not to be as concerned with an exact labeling of his style as were others, and at least earlier in his career, he may not have been consciously aware of tragic undertones in his roles. It was as if by maintaining an emotional distance from his parts when he was not on a set, he could avoid the acting pitfall of becoming emotionally immersed in a type.

As Ryan's career continued and his own life progressed, he flirted ever more intimately with a tragic persona, and finally epitomized it in his last film.

5. Film Noir

While *On Dangerous Ground* languished at RKO Studios, Ryan patiently watched. He had been counting on a critical hit after his last few pictures had fizzled at the box office, but his next effort after *On Dangerous Ground* was nearly its antithesis. *Best of the Badmen* placed Ryan in the sagebrush again, in an RKO attempt to repeat the commercial success of 1948's *Return of the Badmen*.

As if to upgrade *Best of the Badmen*, which shared few plot similarities with *Return of the Badmen*, RKO elevated Ryan to top billing and gave him a love interest with costar Claire Trevor. The film turned out to be little more than a workman-like vehicle in which several Hollywood veterans, including Robert Preston, Walter Brennan, and Bruce Cabot, joined Ryan to labor over dialogue that tested their abilities to convince people.

Best of the Badmen ignited no critical note, but it appealed to the masses, while its box-office proceeds secured Ryan's knowledge that he could always lean on the Western if all else failed. *Variety* magazine stated, "Ryan's portrayal measures up to all the demands of the outdoor role."

The circumstances surrounding Ryan's next film, Nicholas Ray's indistinct *Flying Leathernecks*, warrant speculation as to whether Howard Hughes' influences on Ryan's career were coincidental or intentional, pro or con. In that Hughes' involvement with most of the studio's films was conducted in absentia, and was motivated by intentions which John Houseman called "pervasive and sinister," his perfunctory treatment of Ryan is curious.

In *The Woman on Pier 13*, Hughes criticized Ryan's pistol technique, and in most of Ryan's RKO films, he ended up relegated to a second or third lead. Also, did Hughes ever learn of the elaborate parody Max Ophuls had allegedly designed for him in *Caught*, and if so, did it have repercussions on Ryan's career?

Inasmuch as some observers have posited that Hughes' films were often "loyalty tests" for actors, *Flying Leathernecks* registered at the upper level of patriotic cant. As if to disguise its dated screenplay, which was replete with World War II clichés and stereotyped characters, Hughes ordered it shot in Technicolor.

At the head of the cast was John Wayne, one of Hollywood's most vocal right-wingers, laying the groundwork for a familiar scenario of gung-ho Marine fighter pilots, living and dying in the Pacific theater. Since Ryan had recently starred in *On Dangerous Ground* with Ward Bond, another actor of decidedly conservative views, one wonders whether Hughes may have had a deeper reason for teaming Ryan with Wayne, other than for his marquee value.

Nicholas Ray agreed to direct *Flying Leathernecks* as a favor to Howard Hughes, but he had little interest in putting much personal effort into the film, and it emerged minus his stylized genius. Ryan considered the picture to be a step backward as well, but he stood to gain from sharing top billing with John Wayne. At least, he could be certain he was in the company of professionals whose combination might be a fair box-office gamble.

Ryan's wager paid off, in part due to the Howard Hughes hype which prefaced its release, but mostly due to the well-matched acting of Ryan and Wayne, and to Nicholas Ray's direction. *Variety* noted, "the marquee pull of Ryan and Wayne promises a payoff," and lauded Ryan's "very good performance."

In this first of two films Ryan and Wayne made together, they formed a sound working relationship in which their radically opposite political views stayed in the background of their interaction. Both men had a pragmatic approach to the acting profession, and they strictly separated their personal and professional lives.

While the House Committee on Un–American Activities plowed ahead relentlessly in the early fifties, the paranoia overshadowing Hollywood polarized people's political allegiances and destroyed friendships. Ryan witnessed associates succumb to the committee's vociferous character assassinations at the same time that his career continued unaffected.

His facile explanation about escaping the fate of more vocal dissenters because of his ancestry, religion, and military background seems too simple a rationale. Lamont Johnson speculated that a more complicated reason probably concerned "Bob's inner balance."

Inasmuch as Johnson knew Ryan held strong inner convictions, he was also aware that self-preservation was equally important to him. Since Ryan's livelihood depended on his popularity with the public, his reticence may have increased as the heads rolled in front of Joe McCarthy's guillotine. Johnson remarked of that time period, "We were all anxiously tending our careers."

Dore Schary, who was no stranger to dealing with the offscreen problems of the blacklisting period and their effects on a performer's ability to work under stress, highly valued Ryan's reliability. Whereas other actors might have shown up for rehearsals script in hand, Ryan's concentration never swayed. He continued to methodically work through the subtlest details of his characters, and generally required little help with forgotten lines of dialogue.

Schary classed Ryan among actors of "talent, humor, and good disposition," such as Spencer Tracy, Cary Grant, Richard Widmark, and Melvyn Douglas, calling it a "joy working with them."[1]

"Flying Leathernecks" (RKO), 1951. Left center, John Wayne, Ryan, and William Harrigan discuss troop morale on South Pacific airfield.

Part of their stature in show business grew from people's confidence in their absolute stability on the set, and they had been around long enough to have experienced the annoying delays caused by prima donna stars with myriad personality problems and quirks. Ryan seemed almost to feel a personal sense of embarrassment from watching such people in distress, for which he may have compensated by exerting more control over his own actions.

Yet his steadfast hold on his emotions helped to enlarge his image of pent-up energy, ready to explode. Many years later in Ryan's career, his introspective trademark stubbornly stayed in the studios' minds, which they emphasized to the public in pressbooks stating ominous observations about his personality: "Ryan's slow response to questions reinforces the impression of the silent man who lives much of his life within himself, and is perhaps not at all that comfortable with strangers. . . . He certainly is not comfortable talking about himself."

The promotional ads describing Ryan as an isolated man off the screen helped to build a case against him in terms of changing his status with moviegoers. Unhappily, he discovered that many people related to him emotionally,

as if he were the embodiment of one of his negative screen roles, and that few
remembered his sympathetic portraits.

Thus, his positive roles in smaller, less publicized films of the late forties
through the fifties were often ignored. *Berlin Express, Born to Be Bad, Inferno,
About Mrs. Leslie,* and others took the back seat, while pictures such as
Crossfire, Clash by Night, Bad Day at Black Rock, House of Bamboo and *Odds
Against Tomorrow* grabbed the public's attention.

Arvin Brown attested to feeling a larger-than-life impression emanating
from Ryan when he first met him. One day in early 1971, Ryan telephoned
Brown, then a young New York stage director, and asked him to consider
directing *Long Day's Journey into Night,* and to drop by his apartment at the
Dakota to talk it over.

Brown laughed when he brought back his first thoughts about the idea of
working with Ryan, since his strongest sense of the actor's personality seemed
to originate from the dark side of his screen persona. Because the scenes that
immediately jumped out in Brown's mind concerned Ryan as a "bubbling
bigot," he responded emotionally to the dichotomy between Ryan the man
and Ryan the actor. In recalling his primary associations with Ryan's negative
screen images, Brown said, "Bob was brilliant at playing that tight-lipped, reticent type, with a sense of violence brewing underneath."

Brown talked about Ryan's aura in a way that made a fear of him almost
instinctively intimidating. "The men Bob was so adept at playing were often
men of very limited intelligence, but with just enough of it to know how to
be violent," said Brown. Before his first meeting with Ryan, Brown had time
to put his impressions of him into proper perspective, and recalled, "When I
searched out people from the theatre and films who knew Robert and his accomplishments in social activism, I was relieved to learn about a man who was
the opposite of what I had erected in my mind."

When Brown arrived at Ryan's Dakota address for their first meeting,
though, his security was again challenged upon greeting Ryan, and he encountered an initial demeanor which brought back his earlier emotional
preconceptions about Ryan. Brown observed that "Bob was an intensely shy
man," and believed that he sometimes reacted to uncomfortable situations by
withdrawing into introversion, suggestive of one of his screen types. Just at the
moment when Brown inferred that "Bob's laid-back, almost noncommittal
manner seemed to be indifference," Ryan began to talk about doing *Long Day's
Journey into Night,* and the words began to flow more easily.

"Within 15 minutes," Brown said, "I saw a man emerge who was totally the
opposite of his screen persona." As Brown became friends with Ryan, he saw
"a tremendous vulnerability and honesty" coupled with "a sense of modesty
and humility." The possession of these qualities seems to have both helped and
hindered his career.

Ryan's formidable image followed him in his next film, *The Racket.* Once more, Howard Hughes popped into the scenario to order an updated version of a property he had bought and produced in 1928, which he was convinced was worth another go-around. Ryan again ended up as the villain in a Hughes pet project, second-billed to Robert Mitchum.

As in most of the films which excited a Hughes obsession, in this case gangsterism, there was trouble on the set of *The Racket*. Nicholas Ray bowed out gracefully after trying to cope with Hughes' interference, and John Cromwell tried to patch things together. The whole affair resembled the fate of *The Woman on Pier 13*.

The Racket could have been a huge success, but after numerous script revisions and delays in shooting, the results were skewed by Hughes' exaggerated and paranoid perspective. Despite its deficits, *The Racket* did well commercially and was among RKO's top money earners of 1951.

When *The Racket* was released, it joined ranks with a type of film that was slowly gaining recognition as a legitimate art form, the *film noir*. The term, literally meaning "black film," had been coined by French film critics after World War II to designate a film structure indigenous to American cinema. At first, pictures dealing with crime and its alienating influences on the individual and society defined the genre, but critics and film scholars later broadened the category. Within its widened scope, one thematic concept predominated over others, that of human conflict.

In that genre Ryan was a central figure who usually dominated the proceedings. Foster Hirsch followed his *film noir* career closely, and considered several of his portrayals in his book, *The Dark Side of the Screen: Film Noir*. He concluded that Ryan was "unfailingly powerful, investing his tormented characters with a brooding intensity that suggests coiled depths. Cut off from the world by the strength of their feelings, his characters seem to be in the grip of torrential forces. . . . Ryan's work has none of the masked, stylized aura of much 'noir' acting—he performs with an emotional fullness that creates substantial, complex characters rather than icons."

Ryan may have been unconsciously drawn to the tragic aspects of the Nick Scanlon role in *The Racket*, since he is ultimately betrayed by his fellow criminals. In *The Racket*, Scanlon discovers there is no honor, even among thieves. As Ryan's career progressed, themes of trust and loyalty recurred frequently, as if to verify their importance in his personal life.

Despite the film's relative financial gain for RKO, neither its budget nor its critical value had the impetus to propel Ryan forward. Thus, both the picture and Howard Hughes again faded into the background of his experience at RKO. In later years, it achieved more recognition as noted by Leonard Maltin in *T.V. Movies*, who called it an "unusual 'film noir' with strong performances, especially Ryan's, and a bizarre ending."

In the two-year period of 1950 and 1951, Ryan completed six pictures of widely varying quality, among which one, *On Dangerous Ground*, still lay fallow

"The Racket" (RKO), 1951. From left, Officer Johnson (William Talman) confronts Nick Scanlon (Ryan) at police headquarters.

at RKO Studios. Since he had begun a pattern of settling for less than top billing in all but one, he was in danger of becoming entrenched in a subordinated status as a second lead. But if he felt any anxieties about the direction in which his career was headed, he kept them out of obvious view.

Away from a show business world which glorified star adulation and worldliness, Ryan's friends witnessed his consistent commitment to social activism as threatening at times to eclipse his career. His closest associates believed he was probably as concerned with the pursuit of a better world as with his livelihood as an actor.

Indeed, he apparently expended much emotional energy sorting through the paradox in which he felt he was a participant, and although he viewed acting as a valid profession, there were times when he questioned its value to society, as well as his motives for becoming an actor. Jessica Ryan was privy to his deepest thoughts in this regard, but he also spoke of his inner conflicts with other close friends.

Some of Ryan's self-doubts related to his early religious development in a Victorian household, and others were vestiges from his Irish descent and the

Protestant work ethic. In his conversations with Lamont Johnson, Ryan sometimes talked about the extent to which his Roman Catholic upbringing had affected his emotional state, and they often commiserated with each other over their various religious scars. The most nagging remnants concerned elements of guilt, while the anger resulting from a fear of retribution in the next world exacted a toll for each in similar forms.

As Johnson described the relics he thought haunted Ryan, his words summoned up a religious imagery of fire and brimstone, for sins known and unknown. "Bob talked a lot about the hangovers we shared as ex–Catholics," said Johnson, "and the deep, deep burns that leave scars on Catholics lifelong. I could sense that a hell of a lot of Bob's residual anger came from having been brought up Catholic.

"Also," said Johnson, "Bob had a good Black Irish element of anger and madness in there someplace," and wryly recalled the numerous times he and Ryan sat down with a bottle of scotch, and sifted through each other's thoughts about the works of Irish writers, such as Eugene O'Neill, Dylan Thomas, and T.S. Eliot.

Ryan was fascinated with O'Neill's tormented vision of man alone in the world, a victim of his own fears and of fate, and Johnson affirmed that "Bob literally worshipped O'Neill."

Johnson believed that Ryan felt akin to O'Neill in the matter of O'Neill's difficulties with alcoholism. Although Ryan never totally succumbed to the insidious seductions of alcohol, he once confessed to Johnson that he could easily have gone the way of the O'Neill alcoholic. "Bob was always on the edge," said Johnson. "He flirted with it, but he always stayed on top of it."

Johnson believed that if Ryan sometimes became introverted when he drank, he was probably mulling over some relic from the past. Searching for an apt description for what might have been eating at Ryan at such moments, Johnson called it, "endlessly regurgitating sour stuff that keeps coming up. You could see the anger fizzing, and the steam coming out of his ears as the booze went down."

Others in Ryan's life who were involved with him professionally as well as socially saw the subtle undercurrents of simmering, controlled emotion. Robert Wise recalled seeing Ryan at parties and marvelling at how he stayed ahead of the martinis he downed. "Bob was one of those Irishmen who could really put them away. He could drink one after the other, and it never seemed to show," said Wise with a laugh.

Ryan made no secret about his alcohol use, and seemed to regard it as a necessary evil of life, as if it were a perverse friend during solitary moments of pain. In times of stress it could soothe a soul while its pernicious influence might go on, unnoticed or ignored until it was too late.

Ryan's friends felt he possessed a combination of morality and personal pride, which may have helped him stay one step ahead of the bottle. Being resolved to keep his personal life separate from professional affairs, he exerted the same control over his struggles with alcohol. There was also the family history of stoicism to uphold, and perhaps a streak of machismo that measured a man's worth by the quantity of liquor he could consume.

Ryan believed that the image of an actor was important, and he cultivated a picture of himself and his profession which was exemplified by people he respected. He also felt that a person's true nature showed in his every action, and that the real giants in show business had stature as humans. His inclusion of himself in this echelon seems to have been one of his few brushes with the euphoria of star egotism.

Although Ryan had the potential star power to have competed with actors like John Wayne, Burt Lancaster, Kirk Douglas, and Robert Mitchum, he seemed to have consciously avoided it. He saw pitfalls in the quest for fame. One was the danger of losing touch with his family, and with the realities of the world. Perhaps his fear of estrangement became a driving force for his appearances in numerous intense films. He once sarcastically paraphrased a favorite aphorism of Louis B. Mayer about his destiny as a movie maker: "Mayer said he wanted to make pictures about beautiful people doing beautiful things in beautiful places, meaning a great, romantic illusion of life."[2]

Ahead of his career goals, Ryan's two other major concerns had to do with providing a stable home life for his children, and in making a contribution to the world. Jessica shared his commitment to that endeavor, and as they became more aware of mounting global problems, their resolution to take action solidified. Jessica had been continuing her work with the American Friends' Service Committee, and Ryan had been there to support her. Both had been emotionally affected by the rise of McCarthyism, and they were also disturbed by the domestic problems of civil rights infringements, racial prejudice, and a growing labor unrest. (Ryan was among the first volunteers from the Hollywood community to involve himself unabashedly with the American Civil Liberties' Union. In the ACLU's early endeavors in civil rights defense, Ryan raised funds with a vigorous yet thoughtful approach at a time when right-wing hysteria was in full swing.)

By the end of 1951, the Hollywood purge had claimed several people with whom Ryan had been associated. Besides Edward Dmytryk, Adrian Scott, Dalton Trumbo, and Joseph Losey, two friends, director John Berry and screenwriter Ring Lardner, Jr., fell before the domino effect. Despite Ryan's connections with these blacklisted persons and his own clearly stated liberal views, he continued to go about untouched. At the end of the blacklist period, Ryan's rationale for having been spared may have turned out to be the best answer to the question.

Ryan's last film of 1951, *Beware, My Lovely*, was one of the most classic examples of his overlooked talent. Lasting only 77 minutes, every aspect of the picture illustrated the economic artistry of a number of imaginative talents at

RKO, from its photography to its editing. It was the kind of film that attracted Ryan immediately, because it was to be directed by art director Harry Horner, who had trained under Max Reinhardt, and the camerawork was in the capable hands of George E. Diskant.

From their work together on *On Dangerous Ground*, Ryan admired Diskant's ingenuity and willingness to take risks with his camera. Diskant was one of the first cinematographers to photograph at night, and he used the technique to remarkable effect in a genre tailor-made for it, the *film noir*. Ryan was drawn to *Beware, My Lovely* because it was adapted from a Broadway play whose author, Mel Dinelli, had written its screenplay.

Beware, My Lovely suffered a fate similar to that of *On Dangerous Ground* when RKO withheld its release for over a year, until August 1952. By that time, Ryan and everybody else had gone ahead, and *Beware, My Lovely* was thrown into "programmer" status at theaters. Nevertheless, *Cue* magazine called it a "taut and terrifying film that stretches its suspenses to the breaking point."

As with many Ryan films, the picture later found more noticeable critical acclaim. In *Film Noir: An Encyclopedic Reference to the American Style*, Robert Porfirio confirmed Ryan's "excellent performance, in drawing much pathos from an essentially negative character."

Although 1951 arrived and departed leaving Ryan with a dearth of film successes, he had important options brewing elsewhere. He and Jessica had grown increasingly distressed with the educational system in North Hollywood, and had endeavored to accustom themselves to what they felt was a general decline in education. Even though Tim and Cheyney were attending a private preschool, the classes were still overcrowded, while children and parents alike were forced to put up with double sessions.

Ryan and Jessica wanted to have more control over what and how their children learned. One day they realized that their idea of education could only happen if they did something more directly than importune bureaucratic school officials. Moreover, Jessica was expecting their third child in the fall of 1951, and they wanted to start its schooling properly. They believed they had the best solution to their dilemma, and decided to put it into effect immediately.

6. Family Versus Career

The Ryans' idea to start their own school germinated from a conversation they had with their friends Ross and Wendy Cabeen, and Liz and Sidney Harmon. (Liz Harmon remarried under the name of Schappert.) Shortly afterward, the Oakwood Elementary School took root in their backyard, and by the fall of that year it went into bloom. It was a daring venture to undertake, one about which nobody knew anything other than having an intense desire to make it work.

Jessica was the prime mover in the founding of the Oakwood School, because she had the courage to persevere and push ahead despite the school's rough beginnings. For its first two years of existence, things were chaotic as everybody scrambled to get the school moving. When Sidney Harmon found an empty synagogue on Magnolia Boulevard in North Hollywood, Ryan and Ross Cabeen donated money to buy the building for $6,000. By the time Oakwood began full-fledged classes in September 1951, Ryan and many others had pitched in their sweat equity to make the building serviceable.

At the beginning, Oakwood was set up as a cooperative, thus, on weekends families came together at the school, ready to paint, patch, and repair. Among the early supporters in this endeavor were a number of concerned citizens, including Marion and D.A. Doran, Heidi Edwards, Morine and Sid Kuller, and Sylvia and David Lipton.

As word circulated about what the Ryans and others were doing, the school attracted many show business people and their families, such as Lamont and Toni Johnson, Hugh and Kathryn Beaumont, Emily and Charles Haas, John Sturges, Philip Yordan, Buddy Ebsen, John Beal, and Hy Averback. All of these volunteered to donate the initial capital, which temporarily settled the money questions, but a few other important matters remained to be resolved.

Foremost in Jessica Ryan's mind was the issue of finding qualified teachers and building the right curriculum. She wanted to create a special learning atmosphere for children, one that would promote a humanistic educational philosophy. It took a while for this to happen, as a few less than satisfying teachers and administrators came and left before the right combination was discovered.

Lamont Johnson remembered the nights spent at people's houses, when ideas and policies were vehemently discussed, and since many parents were in the entertainment business, their anxious desires to be heard often turned into shouting matches between egos. Recalling those moments with the humor of hindsight, Johnson said, "We had wonderfully stormy meetings where everyone disagreed. But it was Jessica's very good mind, and Bob's perseverance and patience that helped us through that welter of temperament. In fact, they were the soul and spine of the whole thing."

For the first few years, when the inevitable deficit was greeted with cries of frustration from some who knew better, Ryan automatically went into his pocket. Johnson remembered Ryan donating thousands of dollars to the Oakwood cause, and said, "It was Bob's steady hand at the tiller and on the checkbook that kept us going."

As Ryan worked steadily under the pressures of the Oakwood project, his film career, and his family demands, he grabbed the attention of people in show business who helped him professionally. When Ryan and Sidney Harmon first met, Harmon was a young Hollywood producer. Having been associated with Oakwood since its beginnings, Harmon got to know Ryan well. He became impressed with his readiness to push onward, even in tough times when people's feelings of failure threatened a premature demise for Oakwood.

Since Harmon handled some of the school's business matters, he also witnessed its behind-the-scenes problems, and said, "There wasn't a time when I called upon Bob to do something for the school that he didn't enthusiastically do it." In the mid-fifties, their association led to working together professionally when Harmon produced *Men in War*, and later, on three more films, *God's Little Acre*, *Day of the Outlaw*, and *The Battle of the Bulge*, when Ryan most needed the loyalty of friends.

Other friends of Ryan recalled his generosity with his time and money. Philip Yordan, who worked with Ryan and Harmon on the above films, had a succinct definition of Ryan's personality: "Bob didn't compute things in dollars and cents."

It seems apparent that Ryan's indifference to the attachments of major stardom was responsible for his placement beneath the top rung in Hollywood. While other actors used most of their energies attaining exclusive popularity as "movie stars," Ryan's conscience bothered him whenever he felt himself falling into the enmeshed self-absorption of a matinee idol.

Lamont Johnson was aware of Ryan's ambivalence concerning being an actor, and said he often seemed to be dealing with the conflict that he should be doing something more valuable to society. On the other hand, Johnson remembered Ryan as "an interesting spectacle of an actor, because Bob was never a rabid 'can't live without the movies' type."

For several years when he wasn't working on a film, Ryan kept busy making phone calls, and setting up and participating in benefits to keep the Oakwood

"Clash by Night" (RKO), 1952. Ryan's Earl Pfeiffer nurses his blues with alcohol as he observes people cavorting on the beach.

School afloat. Johnson had vivid memories of stars converging in tented-in tennis courts in the backyards of Beverly Hills celebrities. One event that had remained in Johnson's memory featured Sammy Davis, Jr., Peggy Lee, Peter Gennaro, Dean Martin, and others.

In the face of Oakwood's support from many people in the entertainment business, murmurs of displeasure were emanating from the neighborhood in which it was located. The governing powers at Oakwood were decidedly liberal, or in Ryan's words, "watered-down progressive,"[1] and when the United Nations flag was hoisted up the school's flagpole one day, a rash of hostile acts greeted its symbol of unity.

On a couple of occasions, vigilantes pelted the school with eggs, while on another, swastikas were scrawled on the building. Ironically, the vandalism served to underscore the need for schools like Oakwood, while providing a grim reminder that prejudice was alive and well in the United States.

As if to announce the Oakwood School's first year's triumph, Jessica Ryan gave birth to a girl on September 10, 1951, in Los Angeles. Ryan and Jessica both agreed on the name Lisa in honor of Vladimir Sokoloff's wife. Lisa grew up physically resembling Jessica, while Tim and Cheyney each bore similarities to their father, but in different ways; when they matured, both were tall, with dark hair and eyes. Tim was a stockier version, at six feet one inch, while Cheyney was a lean six feet four inches. All three children reached adulthood having absorbed some of both parents' artistic talent, as well as their sensitivity to world issues.

Of the many people Ryan met over the years, those that resulted in friendships had longevity. One such meeting occurred in 1951, when Ryan was between films. Harold J. Kennedy, a New York stage producer and director who was in Hollywood to do a play, telephoned Ryan one day and presented to him the starring role in a West Coast production of a play which Kennedy had recently finished directing on the New York stage. Kennedy suggested a meeting over lunch to discuss the particulars.

When Ryan entered Lucey's Restaurant across the street from RKO Studios, Kennedy felt his presence immediately, and saw heads swing in Ryan's direction. Kennedy perceived that the women in the room appeared "noticeably titillated. When Bob walked through the door," he recalled, "I was amazed at how tall he was, and what a strikingly handsome figure he cut."

Kennedy offered Ryan a choice part in *The Detective Story*, written by Sidney Kingsley, but he politely turned Kennedy down. The play didn't interest him because its story, which centered around a day in the life of a New York City police detective, was too similar to what he was being assigned in his movies. Ryan told Kennedy he was searching for the kind of stage role which would help him break out of an established mold. "If you ever find that kind of property," concluded Ryan, "give me a call and I'll do it for nothing."[2] He kept his word when, six years later, Kennedy brought him a proposal that met his stipulation.

As 1951 ended, Ryan reached another career milestone when he reprised the filmed version of his Broadway debut, ten years earlier, in *Clash by Night*. He was elevated to the role of Earl Pfeiffer, which Joseph Schildkraut had played in New York, and breathed manic life into a part that Schildkraut had portrayed as a mannered playboy.

Ryan rightly looked back on *Clash by Night* as one of his best pictures, because the directorial reins, which had been placed in Fritz Lang's brilliant hands, rarely strayed from a course of cinematic genius. RKO spent a little more money than usual on *Clash by Night*, hiring Barbara Stanwyck, Paul Douglas, and J. Carrol Naish as Ryan's costars, and gave Lang the luxury of two weeks of rehearsals prior to shooting.

Ryan liked Lang's decision to film *Clash by Night* as if it were a stage production, and was also drawn to Lang's structured European style, which adhered to a certain strict precision. Lang's "Germanic" interpretation conformed to Ryan's own method of leaving nothing to chance.

Clash by Night was one of RKO's few successful pictures of 1952, partly because of the producing team of Jerry Wald and Norman Krasna, who had come up with several hits since becoming partners. Jerry Wald was an indefatigable worker, who had written numerous high-quality scripts for Warner Bros.; *Clash by Night*'s screenplay, although penned by Alfred Hayes, may also have borne Wald's mark, since he collaborated on many scripts without asking for screen credit.

Norman Krasna had a dramatic background as a playwright, and approved of Lang's strong wish to have rehearsals, since *Clash by Night*'s story centered mainly around three people. When Lang discussed the film with Peter Bogdanovich in the latter's book, *Fritz Lang in America*, one area of discord came to light. Jerry Wald had borrowed fledgling actress Marilyn Monroe from 20th Century–Fox, and wanted to give her equal billing with Ryan, Stanwyck, and Douglas. This angered Douglas, in particular, who thought the idea was ridiculous. Stanwyck agreed, however, perhaps identifying with the fantasy of being young again and on the rise.

Ryan was noncommittal on the matter, possibly not wanting to hurt Monroe's obviously shaky feelings. He plainly saw that she was fragile and disorganized when she arrived on the set late every day with her personal acting coach in hand as a security blanket. When her tardiness vexed Lang sufficiently, in true teutonic form he belittled her with icy sarcasm, until Ryan had witnessed enough and asked him to go easy on her. Monroe ended up with equal billing in the credits.

In early 1952, at about the same time that Ryan finished work on *Clash by Night*, RKO released *On Dangerous Ground* to dim public reception. Fortunately, shortly thereafter, *Clash by Night* met with considerably greater applause, to overshadow his disappointment about *On Dangerous Ground*. *Beware, My Lovely* also came to the theaters that summer as a valid, if minor, bid to keep RKO from drowning. But 1952 was the studio's most calamitous year, as Howard Hughes became enmeshed in lawsuits and corporate headhunting. In a bid to consolidate his interests, he terminated the contracts of Ryan and a few others.

That Hughes let Ryan go is perplexing, given his interest, albeit indirect, in having Ryan star in several pet obsessions. But again, the offhandedness with which Hughes summarily dismissed Ryan prompts speculation as to what was really going on. The question as to why is more intriguing since Ryan continued to get excellent reviews for his performances, regardless of the quality of the film.

Perhaps Hughes wanted to get rid of anyone with left-wing ties. By this time, although much damage had been done in Hollywood, Ryan had grown more public in espousing his allegiances. Is it possible that Hughes's convoluted unconscious drove him, like the captain of a sinking ship, to take any supposed malcontents with him? Curiously, Hughes would later reappear in Ryan's life a few more times, but always peripherally.

"Beware, My Lovely" (RKO), 1952. Psychotic Howard Wilton (Ryan) is concerned about Mrs. Gordon's (Ida Lupino) phone call.

As soon as Ryan left RKO, he entered the free-lance market with a two-picture deal at Universal, in *Horizons West* and *City Beneath the Sea*. No longer impeded by the constraints of a studio contract, Ryan seemed to be moving toward full leading-man status. In both films he went for star billing and got it, while also getting the girl.

Directed by Budd Boetticher, each picture shared a theme having to do with loyalty and betrayal among men. In *Horizons West*, the setting was the ambivalent post–Civil War period, wherein Ryan's character succumbs to mental weaknesses brought on by the war; in *City Beneath the Sea*, he was a flamboyant deep sea diver, while Anthony Quinn got the bad guy part which might have ordinarily been offered to Ryan. Unfortunately, neither picture took off at theaters, although *Horizons West* had a fairly strong screenplay and Budd Boetticher's sturdy direction. But editing room scissors and uninspired cinematography resulted in a strangely stilted, abbreviated film.

In Ryan's next film, MGM offered him another Western, again as a villain. *The Naked Spur* was the first of three pictures he made with director Anthony Mann, each of which earned critical acclaim as well as financial gain for their producers. Metro-Goldwyn-Mayer sent Ryan on location in the Colorado

Rockies near Durango, with costars James Stewart, Janet Leigh, Ralph Meeker, and Millard Mitchell. Despite Mann's reputation for being nearly monosyllabic in his direction of actors, Ryan liked working with him.

Ryan had no difficulty dealing with Mann's unintrusive style, and would rather have been under- than over-directed. Inexperienced actors sometimes interpreted Mann's manner as impatience, but Ryan instinctively understood his personality, sensing that his introversion, although ingrained, was scarcely malicious. Ryan may also have empathized with an emotional demeanor that resembled his own tendency toward inwardness.

The Naked Spur joined the list of Ryan films whose prevalent theme concerned man against fate in a predatory world. His character, outlaw Ben Vandergroat, sees himself as an outcast from society, while the other cast members are in unfortunate circumstances, as well. When author Jim Kitses discussed the picture in his book *Horizons West*, he referred to its "dark, extreme men trapped in an impossible dilemma . . . driven by forces over which they have no control to face themselves, reliving the very experiences they flee."

In his book *T.V. Movies*, Leonard Maltin asserted that *The Naked Spur* is "one of the best Westerns ever made; a tough, hard little film . . . strikingly directed and photographed on location." In *L'Avant-scène*, Thierry Génin agreed that *The Naked Spur*'s physical setting contributed to the film's impressionistic structure in which "nature becomes a character within the story." Some observers have also called *The Naked Spur* a Western *film noir* due to its existential tone, and Ryan's finest effort in the cowboy genre.

In his next film, 20th Century–Fox's *Inferno*, Ryan switched sides of the law, and became a grim protagonist battling man and nature. Although the picture was similar to others in his repertory in its wilderness setting and torturous physical requirements, Ryan's part was different in one respect: throughout most of the movie, his character, a man marooned in the desert with a broken leg, had little spoken dialogue. The role was a particularly challenging one, and in playing it Ryan kept in mind Vladimir Sokoloff's advice from 1939 about using "action, not memory of emotion."[3] He may have been moved by a hint of nostalgic homage to Sokoloff to include *Inferno*, "a picture that nobody ever heard of,"[4] on his list of favorites.

Since leaving RKO, Ryan's free-lance status had not yet brought him the film roles he thought he could attract, but his offscreen activities were helping to divide his attention away from his career. The Oakwood School was doing well for its youthfulness, while he, Jessica, and others in charge continued the search for the ideal combination to administrate the school and teach the students. But since local fire officials still were finding fire code violations in the revamped synagogue, there was an added pressure of locating a new building before the school would be closed.

In the political arena through his association with Sidney Harmon, Ryan

"The Naked Spur" (MGM), 1953. From left, Millard Mitchell, Ryan, Janet Leigh, Ralph Meeker, James Stewart. Bounty hunter Howard Kemp (Stewart) gets the drop on fleeing murderer Ben Vandergroat (Ryan), as the others decide to become Kemp's unwilling partners.

was becoming a more visible presence. When Adlai Stevenson embarked on his bid for the presidency in 1952, the head of the Democratic Party asked Ryan to accompany Stevenson on the campaign road. Despite the implied risk of allying himself with a candidate who had been suspected by some conservatives of having radical viewpoints, Harmon remembered that Ryan had no hesitation about his decision. But though he appeared to have sustained no direct repercussions from openly airing his politics, his closer attention to affairs of his country versus those of his career exacted a different price.

When Ryan stumped around the country with Stevenson's campaign party in the fall of 1952, he savored his first taste of the peculiar kind of attention that greets politicians. In New York when he appeared with a few other celebrities at a Madison Square Garden rally for Stevenson, he found himself standing beside Humphrey Bogart. The crowd contained people who wanted autographs as much as a political huzzah, and Ryan became involved in inadvertent competition with Bogart before faint-of-breath women. After this popularity clamor Ryan came away surprised that he seemed to be the obvious preference.

Robert Wallsten, who had attended the rally with Ryan, retained the humorous memory of Bogart's chagrin upon seeing more and younger women

"Inferno" (20th Century-Fox), 1953. Ryan's David Carson searches the skies for help.

extending their eager hands for autographs from Ryan instead of from him. But Ryan's effect on people face-to-face was something about which he felt a self-effacing modesty. He tended to be impressed by the traditional ideal of the boyishly handsome screen star, referring with some envy to the aquiline features of Clark Gable, Cary Grant, or perhaps Douglas Fairbanks, Sr.

It seems that Ryan didn't clearly see his own charisma, instead focusing critically on his facial appearance. Wallsten recalled Ryan telling him one day, "You know, I consider myself lucky, because if one looks at my features one by one, they're not very good. Notice how small my eyes are." Ryan was aware on some level that he appealed to women, Wallsten believed, yet he had a diffidence about it that made it more alluring. "Whether Robert meant to attract them or not, it happened."

With the Stevenson presidential loss behind him as a dismaying reminder of America's impotence in electing a strong leader, Ryan returned to Paramount for the first time since 1941 (when Paramount had failed to renew his contract after four inconsequential films). *Alaska Seas* was a remake of the 1938 film *Spawn of the North*, and as had been the case with most updates, the new version brought forth no novelty or freshness.

There was plenty of work in Hollywood during the prosperous early fifties, and Ryan could have landed a number of film assignments which would have appealed to the masses. In 1952, Burt Lancaster had taken a risk appearing in an offbeat role for his type, in director Daniel Mann's *Come Back Little Sheba*, opposite Shirley Booth. The film landed Booth an Oscar and kudos to Lancaster for taking a part inconsistent with his established persona.

In 1954, Ryan decided to attempt a similar change in characterization, starring with Booth in another Mann vehicle, *About Mrs. Leslie*. That venture, however, met with a less enthusiastic commercial and critical response, because its story of interrupted love didn't fit in with audiences' "happy ending" syndrome. The picture made it past their myopia, though, to critics who saw a message in its painful story. Among those who appreciated the poignant tale and the interplay between Ryan and Booth, author David Shipman praised the film in his book *A Story of Cinema* as a "curious and almost splendid film," noting that Ryan played his part with "just the right amount of shyness and decency."

As Ryan attempted to break out of typecast status, he was faced with stiff resistance from the public. John Houseman tried to help him out by offering him a firm romantic lead opposite Greer Garson in MGM's *Her Twelve Men*, but again the combination failed. Garson had also been trying to keep her momentum going in Hollywood, but had passed her zenith in the forties, shortly after *Mrs. Miniver*.

In *Coronet* magazine, one writer considered the predicament that Ryan was up against, referring to him as an "unconventional personality," whom "the public would not accept as a hero." The author offered one line of reasoning for what was happening to Ryan's bid for a more visible romantic image, comparing his "combination of introspective sensibility and physical force" with that of Marlon Brando: "It [Ryan] needs the veil of glamour and intimacy such as Brando supplies for audiences to identify themselves unreservedly with it [him]." But, he added, "there is no such direct appeal in Ryan's personality, and for this reason the tension his performances communicate is more disconcerting. There is something vital not fully yielded up," which led the writer to state, "he seems essentially as much removed from his audience as they from him; and so his talent remains exceptional but mysterious and solitary."[5]

Ryan's last film of 1954, *Bad Day at Black Rock*, seemed to validate the assertion that his penchant for playing alienated characters made him into an intriguing, as well an inaccessible, personality.

The plot centered around racial intolerance, but it peripherally dealt with man's emotional estrangement in an anachronistic setting. In this case, the alienation arose from a theme of modern civilized behavior encroaching on

"About Mrs. Leslie" (Paramount), 1954. Mr. and Mrs. Leslie (Ryan and Shirley Booth), deep sea fishing off the coast of California during their six-week sojourn together each summer.

territoriality, with Ryan's character symbolizing man's inhumanity toward an adjudged enemy. Since the film's storyline concerned a taboo topic in America, the abysmal treatment of Japanese-Americans during and after World War II, it achieved a cinematic milestone.

When Ryan's character, Reno Smith, became the principal embodiment of man's propensity for heinous acts toward his fellows, it imprinted itself in people's consciences. Like *Crossfire*, *Bad Day at Black Rock* earned Ryan significant critical acclaim, while reinforcing his image of fear. Philip Yordan discussed Ryan's role with regard to the nuances of its execution. Comparing his technique with that of costar Lee Marvin, Yordan said, "If you look at the performances of the two, Marvin suggested badness but Ryan was downright *dangerous*."

In an article in *Films and Filming*, writer John Cutts linked Ryan's interpretation of Reno Smith to his training in the Stanislavsky method under Vladimir Sokoloff. Cutts noted that "his technique has an edge to it," and that

"Bad Day at Black Rock" (MGM), 1954. From left, Walter Brennan, Lee Marvin, Ryan, and John Ericson confer about the mysterious stranger who has disturbed their peace.

he *reveals* his characters, not only in the delivery of dialogue, but by making physical movement mean something in terms of character."[6]

Despite being cast in another psychopathic portrait, *Bad Day at Black Rock* was one of Ryan's most enjoyable assignments, because for a change it contained the right ingredients. In addition to a supporting cast including Dean Jagger, Ernest Borgnine, and Walter Brennan, working with Spencer Tracy was a fantasy Ryan had entertained for years. He became excited like an apprentice actor when he worked with stars of the magnitude of Tracy, although by that time his own name had acquired a similar reputation in film circles.

In Sidney Skolsky's book, *Don't Get Me Wrong, I Love Hollywood*, Skolsky declared of Ryan's performance, "It is perhaps the finest portrayal Ryan ever gave in a picture, and Ryan gave plenty of fine performances. The scene where Ryan and Tracy meet and speak to each other is as starkly beautiful as anything ever put on celluloid."

"Bob was the type that, the older he got, the better he got," affirmed Philip Yordan. "He could have played on and on, like Eddy Robinson, and never stopped. And there was never a bit of temperament from Bob on the set. Once they signed him up, you never heard a peep."

Yordan had labored on enough pictures to know the importance of meeting tight budgets and shooting schedules. As a bevy of Adonis-like actors and winsome starlets had assaulted Hollywood with their eyes focused on themselves, many producers depended on the old guard, who arrived on time with their lines down cold. Even-tempered performers like Ryan played the show business game by the rules of professionalism, although as an icon of the sudden impulse ilk, one feared he might resort to a screen counterpart at any moment and become violent on the set. He prided himself in being able to work with those whose views he opposed, or whom he didn't like, and he carefully kept his personal opinions in check.

Yordan remembered Ryan's calm, self-assured manner during shooting, and could recall only one instance when Ryan lost his aplomb, but it was off the set. One night, Yordan, Ryan, and John Wayne went out for dinner, and as the liquor flowed, Yordan saw the conversation between Ryan and Wayne shift from a friendly exchange to a testy battle of opposite ideologies:

> Wayne had a devilish sense of humor and he baited Bob. Duke was very right-wing, and Bob was at the other end of the spectrum, and they got into an argument, which was heightened by the fact that they were both a little drunk.
>
> Bob was the kind of guy who would fight for what he believed in, even though he wasn't a troublemaker, and there was a limit to how far you could push him. The debate got to the point where Bob had had enough, and all of a sudden he said, "Okay, let's go outside and settle this!"
>
> The Duke was a big man, but Bob was bigger, and the thought hit me that Bob had been the heavyweight boxing champion in college. Duke had no intentions of going outside with Bob, and he realized he had gone too far. We both calmed Bob down, and the evening wound up pretty good.

Yordan believed that Ryan and Wayne shared many personality traits, and a "sibling loyalty," and said of the two, "To use a cliché, 'They don't make them like that anymore.' Bob and the Duke were real men."

7. A Return to the Stage

In late 1953, John Houseman approached Ryan with a proposition they had discussed previously, that of working jointly on a theatrical production. The play, Shakespeare's *Coriolanus*, was, as John Houseman stated in his book of memoirs, *Front and Center*, "one of the most impressive starring vehicles in the Shakespearean canon"; it was also "the least grateful of the great tragic roles . . . evoking none of the empathy that *Othello* or even *Macbeth* can wring from an audience."

After considering several actors for the title part, Houseman thought of Ryan. Houseman realized that Ryan possessed "many of the qualities of this stiff-necked, emotional warrior," and that he could handle the character in an "unconventional but exciting manner."

"With growing enthusiasm," Houseman recalled, "I felt that Ryan's disturbing mixture of anger and tenderness," coupled with his "magnificent physical presence," had "all the required look of nobility and dark power." However, Houseman noted one deficiency in Ryan's vocal range, and had a long talk with him about it before committing himself.

Also in his book, Houseman wrote, "Though Bob's speech was that of an educated man, it was pitched rather higher than it should have been in a man his size, and had the ineradicable nasality of his Chicago origin. Also, he had a lack of experience with blank verse on the stage."

Ryan was well aware of his vocal limitations, but he had long been anticipating an opportunity to do Shakespeare. That his debut would be graded by the always rigorous New York theatre critics may have heightened his excitement about the challenge. In addition, it was rare for a Hollywood actor to attempt such a variance. Ryan told Houseman that he was willing to take the chance.

But Ryan was hedging a bit when he agreed to do *Coriolanus*. He knew the play was not well known (it had not played in New York since 1885), and had no history of great actors. In an article in *Cue* magazine, Ryan later said, "I frankly expected devastating reviews, but I was determined to do Shakespeare somewhere. And I thought, there is no way in the world for me to get my feet wet unless I do it—and do it under fire!"[1]

Coriolanus opened Off Broadway at the Phoenix Theater on January 17, 1954, to reviews which Houseman described as "respectful to excellent." Brooks Atkinson of the *New York Times* wrote:

> Mr. Houseman has illustrated the play's complex and candid examination of every kind of demagoguery with enormous clarity. . . . In exploring the eternal clash between the rulers and the ruled, Shakespeare took no sides. Mr. Houseman has been scrupulously faithful to the psychological twists and turns for their own sake, and with rueful fascination.

Noting Ryan's interpretation, Clive Barnes asserted,

> Robert Ryan plays [Coriolanus] like an attractive, well-bred son of the upper classes who despises the people more out of intellectual sluggishness than out of malice. . . . This is a refreshing interpretation of the massive personality of Coriolanus. Mr. Ryan plays it with warmth, candor, grace, and a kind of artless sincerity.

John Keating of *Cue* magazine commented, "Robert Ryan is a strong, aggressive general; it is easy to believe he crashed the gates of Corioles, unattended, and put the Volscians to rout." And Walter Kerr of the *Herald-Tribune*: "Robert Ryan, tackling his first Shakespearean role, is a virile, headstrong, commanding Coriolanus."

While Ryan was in New York, he interviewed a brilliant educator, Marie Spottswood, for the director's position at the Oakwood School. After a short consultation across the country with Jessica and Liz Schappert, Spottswood was hired. She had immediately impressed Ryan when she proposed a curriculum for Oakwood that embraced the progressive philosophy its founders envisioned.

Spottswood had done much research toward creating a social studies program that would truly educate people. Having absorbed a sound intellectual base from Quaker thought, and having read extensively the works of Sir Herbert Read, Spottswood instituted a course of study at Oakwood, promoting a multicultural awareness and a philosophy of world peace. From Read's book, *Education for Peace*, Spottswood adopted the concept of the "aesthetic education—the education of the senses, of the heart and the hand as well as the mind, with the goal toward wholeness."[2]

Without reservation, the Oakwood parents supported Spottswood's plans for a social studies program inspiring a pacifist, humanist ethic. When Ryan returned to California after *Coriolanus*, he felt renewed vigor in the direction the school was headed. It now was in the position to provide the education he had promised people. Not only would Oakwood students receive a strong foundation in the intellect, but their learning would be tempered by an understanding of the emotions. In the back of Ryan's mind he remembered his

"Escape to Burma" (RKO), 1955. Ryan as a fleeing murder suspect preparing for a getaway.

own Jesuit education, which although invaluable, had left his inner self stranded with conflicting feelings. He had come out into the workings of the world, filled with the certainty of logic, but lacking an understanding of what really directed man's actions.

The plight of the Depression, the tired, agonized faces along the way, then the chaos of World War II followed by the inexplicability of racism, had given him unexpected practical experience in the pain of existence. As their own children grew, Ryan and Jessica had resolved to prepare them to make decisions for the good of their futures as well as those of the world.

Ryan's first film after returning to Hollywood was as insignificant as *Coriolanus* was auspicious. In an attempt to reprise the passions that he and Barbara Stanwyck ignited in *Clash by Night* (Pauline Kael had called their interlude "so

"House of Bamboo" (20th Century–Fox), 1955. From left, Robert Stack, Harry Carey, Jr., Ryan, DeForrest Kelley. Just before the robbery of a diamond jeweler in downtown Tokyo, weapons are handed out.

intensely sexual that the film momentarily achieves real, if stagey, power"[3]), RKO threw them into the jungle in *Escape to Burma*. But director Allan Dwan, whose prolific career had spanned over four decades and 400 films, was nearing the end of his creative energy. However stolid his director's eye had become, it was matched by a useless screenplay and unimaginative cinematography, resulting in one of Ryan's worst pictures.

After the tremendous critical acclaim that had been heaped on *Bad Day at Black Rock*, *Escape to Burma* was analogous to a deepening rift among ever-decreasing pinnacles. When films such as *Escape to Burma* and *Alaska Seas* turned out to be such mediocre enterprises, Ryan dealt with the anxiety of failure in much the same way as did many other actors, namely, to agonize over it but to never really resolve the conflict. Perhaps it was an insoluble dilemma, to be one minute the object of intense if superficial admiration, and the next to be reduced to a ludicrous spectacle of bad acting.

Tim Ryan grew up being aware of how the side effects of the acting business affected his father. "Dad had a fear that is very common among actors, good or bad. It was a sense of, 'Well, I'm going to do this picture and then there'll never be another job again.'" Tim said, "I think that even when it was going well there was always that feeling in the back of his mind."

But Ryan's friends saw few signs that anything was ever amiss in his life.

Robert Wallsten recalled that the subject of how Ryan was doing with his career rarely came up during conversations, and that money never seemed to be a problem. At home there was also little talk of what was happening in his career. Cheyney Ryan referred to his father's stoic reactions to stress as something he had learned growing up, and said, "Dad had a certain notion of maleness, that 'You do what you have to do, and you shouldn't complain about it.'"

When the acting bug had bitten Ryan nearly 20 years earlier, he scarcely realized that it would be a perpetual love-hate relationship. As he slowly came to acknowledge the reality of the hills and valleys of acting, it began to resemble a struggling yet committed marriage. Lamont Johnson had gone through the same rites and knew how Ryan felt. "Like most intelligent people in the industry, Bob was of the opinion that 'you can't live with it, you can't live without it.'"

Thus, when the Oakwood School was developing into a stronger educational entity, Ryan decided to use it to gain a better foothold as an actor. In 1955, he and several Oakwood parents began throwing fund-raising benefits for the school, using the theater as their sales arena. For their first production, Lamont Johnson suggested doing a staged reading of George Bernard Shaw's *Major Barbara*.

"Bob thought it was a wonderful idea, so we took over a women's club in Sherman Oaks and put up a pretty respectable production. Bob played Undershaft, Marsha Hunt was Barbara, and Jim Whitmore was Bill Walker. We had a knock-out cast, and it became far more than just a staged reading. On stage the actors carried small, black-bound library paperbacks in their hands, but we had rehearsed the play sufficiently so that people scarcely needed to refer to their books." As Johnson recalled the contagious excitement everybody felt during the two or three readings of Shaw's play, he remembered that "the sparks really flew once the audiences sat down. It was bloody exciting."

Johnson reflected, "I think the production gained more momentum because we did it at a time of desperation for Oakwood's cause, and also because Bob was going through the anxiety of the career crisis himself."

When 20th Century–Fox head Darryl Zanuck called a meeting in his office with producer Buddy Adler and director Samuel Fuller, they had difficulty deciding who should play the starring role in *House of Bamboo*. Fuller had recently completed several gritty, black-and-white features, and was anxious to get the right person for his first large-scale movie. The picture was to be shot in Tokyo, and Fuller wanted to cast the star heavy with someone who would not be easily recognized by the avid Japanese moviegoers.

Zanuck and Adler suggested a few names to Fuller before he came up with Ryan as the best choice. Fuller had wanted to work with him since seeing him in *The Set-up:* "Bob was perfect as the over-the-hill fighter getting his brains scrambled for a few bucks." Although Fuller had not met Ryan prior to doing

House of Bamboo, he "knew right away that Bob was the guy to play Sandy Dawson."

"I wanted a sympathetic heavy, a psycho with charm, manners, and the balls to disturb audiences." Fuller stated with confidence, "Zanuck and Adler went for him like a bullet. Adler called him up on the phone, Bob said 'Yes,' and we did the picture right after that."

Ryan and Fuller hit it off from the start. Ryan thought that Fuller was a dynamic director, with an active eye and a strong sense of timing. He also liked Fuller's willingness to experiment and knew of his growing recognition as a director with a signature. He respected Fuller even more when the latter coached him through a few difficult scenes in *House of Bamboo*.

Fuller remembered staging an important scene in which he used Ryan's walk to make his point: "I rehearsed Bob at a billiard table as he tried to figure out which of his henchmen had betrayed him to the police. I had him slowly walk a long distance from the table, away from the men, as he tossed a billiard ball in his hand—thinking—trying to figure out who the Judas was."

"You'll cut this long, long walk out in the cutting room," he said. "It's just too long. As an actor I love it, but people will not sit for it," was Ryan's comment. "They'll sit," I told him, "because it's important that we show you *thinking* while we're on your back." The scene worked successfully in the final cut.

Of his experience working with Ryan, Fuller said, "It was unforgettable for me. His assiduous digging into the character of Sandy Dawson was intense, and the result was that he had the scene and dialogue down pat the first time we shot."

From the conversations Ryan and Fuller had when they went out to dinner a few times during the filming of *House of Bamboo*, Fuller came away knowing Ryan better than had many others. Having grown up in the newspaper business as a crime reporter, Fuller knew how to get a story. He and Ryan exchanged tales from their pasts; Fuller, about the Depression years when he wandered around the country on freight trains, Ryan, about his own tough times after a rude awakening in 1932.

Talking with Ryan over T-bone steaks in a small Tokyo restaurant, Fuller got a chance to look into his soul, and perceived a rare quality in him. "There was no phony ego in Bob," said Fuller. Fuller also became intrigued by the paradox between his bad-guy image and his real self, noting ironically that, "Bob was a liberal and a hater of racism—yet the racist characters he played from *Crossfire* to *Bad Day at Black Rock* were so intensely accurate that he swept me back to my reporter days in the South. . . . Bob reminded me of the time when I was sent to Little Rock, Arkansas, to interview some Klansmen in the back of a plumbing shop at 10 at night."

Fuller concluded, "Ryan wore their faces."

8. Between Character Actor and Leading Man

In Fox's *The Tall Men*, Ryan sank to third billing below Clark Gable's toothy smile and Jane Russell's cluttered bodice, and manfully accepted a role that reduced him to embarrassment. His portrayal as a slightly dishonorable cattle baron might have made him wince, but when he was offered the part opposite Gable, he jumped at the chance.

Moreover, director Raoul Walsh, one of the giants in the business, had a forte in the Western, and Ryan was impressed by Fox's willingness to go big-budget on *The Tall Men*. Unfortunately, the resultant fare scored several notches below satisfactory, as the picture reduced Ryan and Gable to endless squabbling over Russell's treasures, while audiences fell asleep in droves.

But the pleasure Ryan gained from working with Gable may have belonged less to an admiration for him as a great actor, than to a vicarious appreciation of Gable's complacency with his dashing, yet unvarying portrayals. Ryan said of Gable, "He belonged to that type of actor who always plays the same role, but the difference is that he was *happy* to do it." Ryan naively thought that Gable was "a man without any frustrations."[1]

For all the arduous location conditions besetting those who made *The Tall Men*, Ryan ended up being the only star to become ill during filming in Durango, Mexico. Whether it was the food or drink, or lowered resistance, he came down with hepatitis, which put him out of action for several weeks. Reminiscing about the experience years later in an interview, Ryan blamed it on demon rum, and talked about his "vague recollections" of Durango. "In those days I went through the location in a haze," he said, recalling "sitting around with Gable and Jane and getting swacked."

The hepatitis bout came at an opportune time since he was going through a period of drinking a lot. He commented wryly, "I couldn't take a drink for a year, not even a glass of beer. I damn near died when I heard that."[2] For several years after, he brought under control what Lamont Johnson had termed "dangerous symptoms on the line." In the sixties, his nemesis returned off and on, corresponding to crises not necessarily having to do with his career.

(Tim Ryan reported that his father switched from hard liquor to Lowenbräu beer in an illusory effort to stem the tide of alcoholism always looming in front of him.)

As Ryan approached middle age, the old Hollywood studio system was on its way out, and many film actors and directors were branching out, by choice or necessity, into television. By the mid-fifties the general fare of game shows and popcorn serials was slowly being supplanted by programs of a more mature nature. Ryan was one of the first to star in the innovative Screen Directors' Playhouse series, appearing as Abraham Lincoln in an episode directed by H.C. Potter, entitled "Lincoln's Doctor's Bag." However, the weekly dramatic presentations, which were created as a testing ground for motion picture directors, were sketchily written, and the series ended after nine installments.

The Lincoln role briefly brought out the lighter side of Ryan. Cheyney Ryan remembered seeing his father, dressed in his Abe Lincoln costume, driving down the street in his convertible with people gaping at him as he clowned it up. It was one of the few times Ryan brought the job home.

The advent of television as a viable medium had created competition with the movie industry, and what inadvertently proceeded was a change in the subject matter with which studios felt capable of dealing. Independent film companies sprang up, bringing fresh perspectives into a medium that had begun to stagnate. As movie producers tried to better the technical level of motion pictures to prove their superiority over television, advancements in visual techniques became permanent additions or short-lived novelties.

Bad Day at Black Rock had demonstrated the former in its use of Cinemascope (Ryan called it "the first good use of 'Scope"[3]), while the 3-D photography in Roy Baker's *Inferno* had been greeted with scarcely a ripple of excitement. (Yet in *Hollywood in the Fifties*, Gordon Gow lauded *Inferno*'s 3-D as "the first and only example of the dramatic value of depth.")

Having been one of the first to explore the newer forms of cinema expression, Ryan could have come to truly identify with the underdog. When he starred in Fox's Cinemascope production of *The Proud Ones*, his was a curious role. Fox cast him opposite one of its young stars, Jeffrey Hunter, hoping to attract the old and the young, but ironically, much of the film's attention fell on Hunter's callow youth coming of age. Moreover, Ryan's romantic involvement with costar Virginia Mayo approached a distressingly platonic state. It was as if every new and different way of casting a leading man was falling in Ryan's lap, while he labored to keep his name alive against a stacked deck.

But his durability galvanized in the face of the temporariness of much of the new talent. When his career had a resurgence in the seventies, he reflected on the transitory fame of the scores of handsome but vacuous stars who had threatened his security for years. Ryan believed that "young actors often play for themselves and overlook the mechanical skills an actor must have like speech, or how to ride a horse, or at least *look* right on one." He thought they

"The Tall Men" (20th Century–Fox), 1955. Jane Russell falls into Ryan's arms for a few moments, but she ultimately belongs to Clark Gable.

"wait for the magic moment as if their mere presence is God's gift to humanity, and find out over the years that this isn't the case." As the demise of the star system went into effect, Ryan predicted, "A kid will make a hit in a couple of movies and then you'll never hear from him again. There'll be a continuous turnover and a lot of temporary fame."[4]

By 1956, Ryan seemed to be permanently imbedded between character actor and leading man. Writer Joe Hyams classed him among the "Hollywood standbys—those who work constantly, turn in superior performances, and enjoy substantial incomes."[5] According to Philip Yordan, by the mid-fifties Ryan was making about $125,000 per picture, but he continued to be plagued by Hollywood's desire to keep him in a limited acting category.

When writer Philip French wrote about the Western genre, he noted that "a small, tight-knit group of familiar faces won the West,"[6] led by heroes John Wayne, James Stewart, Henry Fonda, and Gary Cooper. It was almost inevitable that French should place Ryan's name at the head of the villain's column, with Richard Boone, Arthur Kennedy, Dan Duryea, Robert Wilke, John Dehner, and Claude Akins.

One avenue which Ryan had not fully explored concerned working on films made on location overseas, and he and Jessica often discussed the feasibility of location work. They were both aware of the strains on the family unit when parents and children separated, and decided to wait until Tim, Cheyney, and Lisa had grown sufficiently before either left home for a long period.

Also, Ryan felt a keen emotional distance when he left Jessica for any length of time, and he depended on her companionship almost exclusively when he wasn't working. Arvin Brown had been struck by the strength of commitment he saw in Ryan and Jessica's marriage, and that they sought comfort in each other in many ways.

Brown retained a strong impression that although Ryan may have been more dependent on Jessica in later years, earlier it may have been the opposite. Brown believed that their dependencies complemented one another, and reflected, "Bob depended on Jessica for her critical attitudes and he took into account what she had to say about his performances.

"Actually," emphasized Brown, "in any discussion, Bob considered very seriously everything Jessica contributed." When Brown talked about working with Ryan versus the issue of wives who "interfere with productions," he never had a doubt about Ryan's autonomy regarding how he should conduct himself.

John Houseman recalled that Ryan looked to Jessica for her opinions on most matters of importance, and that she had provided the impetus for much of their involvement with activist groups. "Bob thought Jessica was more intelligent and more educated than he was, and he greatly admired her writing talents," said Houseman.

In social situations, though, Brown remembered that "Bob was always the star," and that because of it, Jessica expressed jealousy at times. Usually, Brown said, the envy took the form of joking references about Ryan's attractiveness to other women. "Jess sometimes talked about feeling as if she was in the back seat at parties, and that she had gotten sick of it in the old Hollywood days," said Brown.

When Ryan was shooting a film at home, after work he often occupied his time in solitary activities. In the fifties, he bought a pool table and whiled away hours in his game room, listening to whatever music happened to be on the hi-fi. Or reading Maugham, Brecht, Scott Fitzgerald, or Hemingway.

Small-talk conversations bored Ryan, and during the times when he filmed pictures away from home, he apparently did little to divert himself other than reading. Lisa Ryan recalled her father's passionate interest in literature, and commented that his yearly regimen of rereading Joyce's *Ulysses* might have been something he would do on location. Since many of his films were shot in out-of-the-way places, Ryan often ended up in a mountain cabin or in a nondescript hotel somewhere.

"The Proud Ones" (20th Century–Fox), 1956. Ryan's Marshal Cass Silver receives a dutiful kiss from Virginia Mayo in one of his last romantic roles.

He once lamented, "I'm fated to work in faraway, desolate places," and said, "I envy Cary Grant because he makes all his pictures in Monte Carlo, Paris, or the Riviera, while I make mine in deserts with a dirty shirt, a two-day growth of beard, and bad food."[7]

On the rare occasions when Ryan traveled overseas prior to Jessica's joining him, the sights and sounds of other lands passed his view with scarcely a nod from him. Without Jessica there with whom to share his feelings, that which might have grabbed his interest became mere scenic diversions. Thus, he spent much of his time in his hotel room, occupied with his thoughts.

Robert Wallsten speculated that Ryan would have had little to say to people other than something having to do with the particular job and the standard amenities. Ryan's children spoke of their father's shyness in ordinary social situations, but said he was able to turn it on and off when necessary. Lisa Ryan had affectionate feelings in her voice, remembering times she spent with Ryan during filming, when the diffidence disappeared and the smile reappeared. She talked about "loving being with Dad when he was making a movie," because she saw a much more at ease person. Lisa said, "Dad rose to the occasion."

But she also talked about Ryan's darker side, which had become magnified in her mind as she grew up seeing his taciturn film portraits. When she vacationed in Ireland in her twenties, Lisa traveled to the section in which the Ryan ancestors had lived, and discovered that the people exhibited an emotional demeanor similar to her father's. She concluded that the happy-go-lucky Irish stereotype was a fallacy, and that her father's spare manner was incidental to the fantasy suggested by his screen persona.

The discomfort Ryan felt initiating conversations seemed to concern whether he thought the subject in discourse was important enough to talk about. Having grown up learning the value of words, he believed in thinking about a conversation's subtle implications before committing himself to a conversation. It was as if he rigidly interpreted the maxim, "Better to say nothing, than something unimportant." He may also have sustained a monastic effect from his Roman Catholic training, in which silence was one of the Golden Rules.

Ryan was not religious in the usual sense of the word, and after he met Jessica, he leaned heavily toward humanism. By his mid-forties, his spirituality was a mixture of dogmatic Catholic stringency and liberal Quaker tolerance. Thus, when he came up against the inevitable dilemma concerning movie star morality, he had to answer to a strong conscience.

A friend, John Springer, had met Ryan in the forties, when stars' offscreen escapades stole backstage gossip, and had seen Ryan fight his impulses. As a press-book writer for one of the studios, Springer was in the position to learn much about what celebrities did behind closed doors. Later, he moved to New York City and started his own public relations firm, while writing many articles and a few books about the movie industry.

Springer had a strong recollection of one night's events, when he witnessed Ryan draw up the fortitude to turn away a high-priced call girl who had been sent to his hotel room to "cheer him up."

Ryan told Robert Wallsten a similar story about an actress who once propositioned him during a movie. "She told Robert that it was her customary practice to bed down her leading man," said Wallsten, "and that she was just checking with him before she went ahead." Wallsten believed that Ryan was surprised more than anything else by the woman's nonchalant manner, and related "Robert told her in one sentence, 'I'm married and have two kids.'"

If Ryan encountered similar tests of fidelity at other times, whether he ever faltered amid the fantasy of trembling flesh seems academic. One friend stated pragmatically that being human, Ryan must have fallen at least once.

But one of his closest friends, screenwriter and author Millard Lampell, remembered talking with Ryan about values such as marital fidelity, and came away convinced that he had kept his promise to Jessica. One conversation took place one morning in the mid-sixties, as Lampell and Ryan were taking a walk on the beach at Martha's Vineyard.

"Bob and Jessica had taken a house for the summer, and had invited me and my first wife, Elizabeth, to stay with them for a few days," recalled Lampell. "That was the first time I really got to know Robert." Lampell knew that Ryan felt comfortable talking with him when the conversation turned toward personal things. "It was hard for Robert to talk to other people, but we did talk, and I remember that was the time I really learned that Robert had never been unfaithful to Jessica."

Ryan told Lampell about a number of passes that had been made toward him by actresses, among whom were powerful sex symbols, such as Joan Crawford and Rita Hayworth. But Lampell noted that Ryan seemed to have feelings about women that were "a mixture of naiveté and boyishness, and a kind of old-fashioned sense of integrity and faithfulness to his wife."

Arvin Brown testified to his effect on women, confirming, "they were tremendously attracted to Bob, much more than his screen presence would ever have led you to believe." Brown felt that his magnetism concerned something more intimate than looks. "It did start physically, since Bob was a strikingly handsome man, especially in his younger years, and very well built. But he also had a pretty lethal mixture of repressed energy and violence, combined with a real sweetness." Brown believed that the paradox Ryan presented increased his appeal to women. "The key thing was that Bob had this wonderful gentleness which was a real powerful attraction in a guy who seemed like he was maybe a dark force."

In his book, *No Pickle, No Performance*, Harold J. Kennedy wrote a chapter about his relationship with Ryan over the years. Describing an incident in which Ryan's sexual magnetism overwhelmed one actress's common sense on a transatlantic crossing, Kennedy related, "The lady, who was not only very glamorous but very big, had been making subtle passes at Bob during the whole trip, and on the last night she finally collared him on deck. Apparently deciding this was her last chance, she leaped on him, knocked him down, then either fell or jumped on top of him, ending up in a position she apparently found attractive." Ryan told Kennedy in a slightly embarrassed tone how he gently extricated himself from the panting woman's grasp, just as her husband came up. After profusely apologizing to Ryan, the irate man blackened both of his wife's eyes.

Kennedy thought Ryan "whetted the appetite of more than one lady star," because he "represented one of the last in a line of unassailably virile leading men." But Kennedy was always strongly aware of Ryan's "unavailability," and that he "basically was just not interested" in the pursuit.

9. Television and Other Diversions

In Ryan's final RKO film, *Back from Eternity*, the studio again delved into the remake category, casting him as a burned-out alcoholic pilot, withdrawing from society. But at the time RKO made the picture, its two new studio stars, Rod Steiger and Anita Ekberg, seemed to take over much of *Back from Eternity*'s main interest; Steiger, with his aggressive, eccentric style, Ekberg, with her voluptuous physique. Amid such circumstances, and a script which shifted the focus away from Ryan, the new version elevated the dramatics while lowering credibility.

The picture ended up as a curious swan song for Ryan, since his world-wise character, Bill Larnigan, finds that life begins at 50. In real life, Ryan was being threatened by the opposite.

With the rise of independent producers in Hollywood, actors were gaining more control over what they appeared in. Some produced, directed, and oversaw the screen writing, assuring they would get the largest piece of the action, and the most exposure. But Ryan continued to detest business matters which would have furthered his career, and was determined to do nothing but act.

By 1956, two other factors affecting his career were his advancing age in a medium which exalted youth, and a reduction in Hollywood's output of films. One of his best vehicles for expression, the *film noir*, was at the end of its cycle, leaving a big gap in what he did best. But television was slowly gaining ground as a viable option, just when he needed it.

At age 47, Ryan's face showed definite signs of premature aging, even though he kept in good physical condition with regular gym workouts and punching bag sessions. The lines on his forehead and around the eyes were becoming more pronounced, giving him the appearance of having been exposed to the sun too many times. His weathered look was finding a ready market, however limited, in television Westerns, such as Dick Powell's *Zane Grey Theatre* and *Wagon Train*.

By default, Ryan began to see the necessity of having more involvement in the direction of his career, and in 1957, he took a chance with a new television concept, the dramatic repertory series. The weekly anthology *Alcoa Theatre* featured Ryan and a rotating cast of stars, including Jack Lemmon, Charles Boyer, Jane Powell, and David Niven. Together they formed Dayton Productions, and presented a wide range of programming, from light comedy to serious drama.

The debut episode, entitled "Silhouette of a Killer," featured Ryan as an amnesiac suspected of murder. Other episodes, such as "On Edge" and "The Face of Truth," continued to explore his penchant for suspenseful stories and themes dealing with loyalty.

As he made his niche in television, Ryan found quality material in a number of other programs, as the medium vied for viewers' attention. Alternating with the *Alcoa Theatre*, he also appeared in several tense vignettes on the *Goodyear Theatre*, such as "The Crowd Pleaser" and "The Seventh Letter," which dealt with the fight game and police business, respectively.

In subsequent installments of the *Zane Grey Theatre*, other familiar themes cropped up. "To Sit in Judgment," for instance, cast Ryan as a sheriff hunted by vengeful killers, while in "Trial by Fear," he played a man unjustly tried for murder.

Throughout the fifties, Ryan had kept his eye on the theater, hoping to find something locally produced in the Los Angeles area, preferably in the classics. In early 1957, he got the chance when Harold J. Kennedy asked him to star in Giraudoux's *Tiger at the Gates*, which Kennedy hoped would make a mark on the West Coast stage.

After a quick reading of the play, Ryan replied, "Now you're talking my language. I would pay *you* for the privilege of reading beautiful words such as these. When do we start rehearsals?"

Kennedy lined up a top cast including John Ireland, Mary Astor, Marilyn Erskine, and Ray Danton, all of whom were willing, like Ryan, to work for the Actors' Equity minimum of $40 per week. The miniscule salary may have caused everybody to savor even more Christopher Fry's lyrical translation of Giraudoux. Ryan had already been privy three years earlier to the plight of stage performers who work for a pittance to express their art.

Kennedy decided to open the play for a week at the Sombrero Theatre in Phoenix, Arizona, which he said "was almost our undoing." His hindsight was 20-20 as he recalled the first night's show to an unsophisticated crowd who "were probably expecting something like *The Detective Story*. The audience responded as if to a bad comedian on the Borscht Belt. During the first act they left in droves and fled to the bar, which set a new liquor record for the night," said Kennedy. "Those few who bothered to come back for the second act brought double scotches and double bourbons with them."

Kennedy continued, "The celebration supper after the show looked like a

"Back from Eternity" (RKO), 1956. From left, Rod Steiger, Ryan and Anita Ekberg discuss their impending fate at the hands of South American head-hunters.

wake. The theatre manager told Bob and me it was the worst show they had ever had there, and that the theatre might have to close down because of it.

The next morning a discouraged Ryan appeared at Kennedy's hotel room door, sweating profusely. Kennedy asked, "Why are you perspiring so?"

"Flop sweat," answered Ryan.

Kennedy reassured him that the play was meant for a Hollywood audience, and he was certain it would go over well there. At that moment the morning newspaper thudded against his door to punctuate his prediction. He was right, the critics raved about the play, and Ryan's sweat cleared up a little.

When *Tiger at the Gates* opened at the Ivar Theatre in Hollywood as a benefit for the Oakwood School, audience reactions equaled the glowing reviews. Kennedy reported sellout box-office receipts for the entire engagement, and thought the play could have run indefinitely. But he believed that Ryan was the only member of the cast who was irreplaceable, and when he left the play because of a prior film commitment, Kennedy closed the show on schedule.

One peculiar incident occurred during the play's run. Howard Hughes stirred from the depths of his reclusiveness for the final time in his odd relationship with Ryan, to attend a performance one Saturday night. Finding no available seats, he dispatched his chauffeur to solicit four tickets, offering $50 each to arriving patrons. Hughes got the seats, saw the play, and left.[1] He may have been expecting *The Detective Story*. Ryan and Hughes never met.

Ryan's sole film of 1957 reunited him with director Anthony Mann, and was the first of several collaborations with producer Sidney Harmon and screenwriter Philip Yordan. *Men in War* placed Ryan in the grip of psychological warfare as a weary Army lieutenant, leading a ragtag platoon to an anonymous hill in Korea. His Lieutenant Benson reflected a radical change toward pacifism, compared with his gung-ho paramarine in 1943's *Marine Raiders*, perhaps analogous to his own maturation over the years.

Men in War tried to make a statement about the illogicality of war in its rationale that lives must be lost so as to save others. When Ryan's character says disgustedly to Aldo Ray's warrior, Montana, "God help us if it takes your kind to win the war," it is an uneasy alliance with conduct that is, at root, inhumane.

The picture received better-than-average reviews, and Anthony Mann included it among his four best films, with *Winchester '73*, *El Cid*, and *God's Little Acre*. In her book about Mann, Jeanine Basinger applauded *Men in War* as a superior argument against war. She wrote that its final "eloquent scene," in which Ryan tosses a handful of silver stars into the earth, "illustrates the futility of war better than 400 speeches in the United Nations."

As part of a three-picture agreement with Sidney Harmon, Ryan's contract called for a flat salary plus a percentage of the profits. He would have preferred taking a percentage only, but he was skittish about a possible box-office failure. Harmon described his and Ryan's first effort as "a nice deal."

Upon completion of *Men in War*, Ryan experienced a decline in movie offers from the major studios, which coincided with his fear of "never making another film." Fortunately, his corporate film venture agreement with Sidney Harmon forestalled his sharing the fate of numerous forties stars. Even so, Ryan was aware that working for Harmon was still a risk. Being a relatively new independent producer who made films on shoe-string budgets, Harmon's modest pictures had a high probability for equally modest success in a market dominated by the grandiose.

Philip Yordan believed Ryan's lack of egotism was his saving grace at that time, and that he never complained about the material he was given. Noting that Ryan worked on a lot of films which actors of the same caliber would have rejected as beneath their dignity, Yordan said, "It didn't bother him."

Ryan had plenty about which he could feel fulfilled outside of motion pictures, Yordan added, since by then the Oakwood School had forged ahead, and Ryan had become more involved in social activism and in doing stage work.

"Men in War" (United Artists), 1957. Ryan's Lieutenant Benson berates Montana (Aldo Ray) for killing a Korean soldier. (At right is L.Q. Jones.)

Yordan described Ryan's attitude toward the acting profession: "It was a job, and whether he liked a role or not, he put everything into it." Ryan's friend, director John Frankenheimer, reflected similar sentiments when he defined a professional as "someone who does a job even when they don't want to, and Bob certainly belonged in that category."

Ryan sat out the rest of 1957.

Sometime during that year, Ryan volunteered to narrate segments of a documentary for the United World Federalists, entitled "Eight Steps to Peace." The series, which consisted of eight themes drawn around a central point, the

"God's Little Acre" (United Artists), 1958. From left, Michael Landon, Vic Morrow, and Ryan finagle with a divining rod prior to an upcoming scene.

establishment of world peace, featured, besides Ryan, Henry Fonda, Tyrone Power, Raymond Massey, Vincent Price, and Vanessa Brown.

The film was written from a strong pro–United Nations viewpoint, and reflected upon history to support its contention that justice throughout the world could be realized only by a joint effort between countries. In his narration, Ryan chronicled world events during the twentieth century alone, citing abuses of power in Germany and Indochina, the development of the nuclear arms race, and depictions of the inevitable outcome of war: world poverty and chaos. He concluded with a reminder that if events continued on their present course, "We shall be turned to a world of airless gloom."

Toward the end of 1957, Sidney Harmon offered Ryan the role of Ty Ty Walden in God's Little Acre, to be directed by Anthony Mann. It was an out-of-character role, but one which Harmon pointed toward Ryan, knowing his wish to take on unusual portrayals, and escape stereotyping. On the advice of his agent, however, Ryan turned down the role, explaining to Harmon that he "wouldn't be believable."

Harmon next gave the script to Jackie Gleason. The day after reading it, Gleason invited Harmon to lunch and had memorized nearly his entire part. As Harmon sat in amazement, Gleason announced, "Don't you think I would make a wonderful Ty Ty? Tell you what I'll do. I'll do the picture for $200,000 and 50 percent of the profits." Harmon recalled that Gleason "said this with a straight face."

Looking at a budget that "wasn't anything near that figure," Harmon said, "I couldn't even consider it." After casting the rest of the picture, which included Mann "regulars" Jack Lord, Vic Morrow, and Aldo Ray, he still hadn't found a Ty Ty. Retracing his steps, Harmon admitted, "I had thought about many fine actors, but none of them were right for the role, and Ryan was still my number one choice."

In one final try Harmon asked Ryan, "Why don't you just make a test? You don't have to make the picture. Just do a test of a few scenes and judge for yourself if you think you're right for it."

"Bob accepted my offer, and about 20 minutes into the test he smiled and said, 'Sidney, I have to tell you that the part is a breeze. I'll do the picture.'"

Philip Yordan recollected, "When Bob informed his agent that he had accepted the part, the guy was dead set against it. The image his agent saw was a 50-year-old man playing a 70-year-old man, and he told Bob, 'They're going to typecast you as a doddering old man, and it'll ruin your career.'" At that point Ryan may have felt that age was academic.

After God's Little Acre earned glowing reviews, Harmon boasted, "Bob was wonderful in the role, and the picture was voted one of the best films of the year." Philip Yordan added a postscript: "Bob made a quarter million dollars off of it, twice his normal salary."

With the financial success of his last two pictures, Ryan saw what the art of bargaining could do for his career. At that point, he had become disillusioned with his agent's lack of effort in his behalf, realizing that as a species, agents were loyal only to the dollar bill.

Millard Lampell verified that especially during the heaviest welter of the McCarthy period, and for a time afterward, "agents were not of much use to any of us who were blacklisted, nor to liberals such as Robert." Throughout the fifties, Lampell had been blacklisted and was "working underground." Refusing to be beaten by the House Committee on Un–American Activities, he used other names and he continued writing screenplays for films and television programs. In the sixties he resumed using his real name on his work.

When Tim Ryan began his own acting career, he soon shared Lampell's opinion about the vagueness of agents after experiencing them as "misty people off in the corner."

To have made it big, Ryan would have had to ally himself with powerful filmmakers such as Hal Wallis, John Ford, Stanley Kramer, Harold Hecht, or Edward Lewis, to name a few. Ryan's only screen venture with Wallis in *About Mrs. Leslie* failed due to his stereotyped image, as reflected by Leonard Maltin's comments in *T.V. Movies*. Maltin called the picture's casting of Ryan and Shirley Booth "a forgivable illogical coupling." Likewise, Ryan's powerful portrait in John Sturges' *Bad Day at Black Rock* ought to have led to further important work with the director. Yet Ryan's only other effort for Sturges met short shrift in 1967's *Hour of the Gun*. Also, producer Edward Lewis's *Executive Action* served as Ryan's epitaph. Kirk Douglas and Burt Lancaster made several pictures with Wallis, which put a lot of money in their pockets and sent their names flashing across Technicolor film credits. The closest Ryan would come to such circumstances was his work with Sidney Harmon and Philip Yordan.

Millard Lampell believed Ryan had different ambitions from those that drove other actors and said, "Bob wasn't ambitious in the sense of pushing his career. He was ambitious as an actor, he wanted to stretch himself, and he wanted to see what his potential was. But as far as the kind of hustling that goes on in Hollywood was concerned, it was against his character to do anything like that."

Tim Ryan had a strong memory of his father saying, "You do one thing, and you do it very, very well." But Ryan's continued resistance against going after the big parts reflected several levels besides his belief in developing an expertise in a single talent. Having thought a lot about his father's seeming indifference toward achieving stardom, Tim Ryan speculated that his upbringing had much to do with it. Because Ryan had been raised in a well-to-do family, at least until the Depression, Tim believed he may not have needed to develop the hunger that propelled other stars to fight for better roles.

"Dad didn't have the kind of drive that somebody like Kirk Douglas had. Money was something he was kind of used to," Tim Ryan said. Recalling talks he had had with actors regarding what he called the "survivalist sense," Tim related a comment he once heard from Tony Curtis: "When you grow up on the Lower East Side, that puts you in a different position."

Ryan got another opportunity to do something unusual when he starred as Jay Gatsby in one of television's early live productions of classic novels. The Playhouse 90 presentation of *The Great Gatsby* was directed by Franklin Schaffner, and also starred Jeanne Crain, Rod Taylor, Barry Sullivan, and Kim Hunter in a lavish rendition of a piece that has rarely been adequately presented.

Broadcast on June 26, 1958, Schaffner's efforts to transfer the novel to television received mixed reviews. In the *New York Herald-Tribune*, critic John Crosby discussed an inherent problem in David Shaw's teleplay, and wrote, "The characters acted like people in a sort of grown-up dancing class whose wishes, habits, and lives don't resemble anything in my experience."

Schaffner's expressionistic direction included long tracking shots up and down marble staircases, and great overhead shots of Gatsby's opulent mansion, reminiscent of the best of Max Ophuls' films. However, critic Crosby called Schaffner's direction "profligate extravagance," creating a feeling that Gatsby's house was "a setting and not a home at all," and that "Ryan's Gatsby was a puzzlement, although I don't know that any other actor could have made it less so."

Ryan followed *The Great Gatsby* with a dynamic portrayal in a troubled, underrated film, *Lonelyhearts*. Based on Nathanael West's vitriolic novel of emotional turmoil and shattered dreams, the film emerged a convincing facsimile of the book. When producer Dore Schary approached Ryan to star in *Lonelyhearts*, he was immediately drawn to the part.

Playing a cynical newspaper editor who places man's baser instincts up for discovery by an idealistic reporter, Ryan carried the part keenly. He invested it with a bitter believability to restore the edge Dore Schary had dulled when his screenplay opted for a "miracle" ending.

Starring opposite Ryan was Montgomery Clift, then a virtual basket case from his self-destructive life-style, and exuding a moribund air which seemed to cast a pallor over *Lonelyhearts*. Thus, the downcast tone which followed the film to an uncomfortable reception at theaters seemed fated.

In author Patricia Bosworth's biography on Clift, she wrote about Ryan's contact with the tortured actor during filming of *Lonelyhearts* and in the following years. Bosworth first met Ryan when she interviewed him for an article she was writing for the *New York Times* in 1969, entitled "Robert Ryan: In Search of Action."

Through their conversations then and later, Bosworth sought out answers to the very personal questions about Ryan which he generally avoided in his quest for privacy. She learned much about his less publicized accomplishments as a committed social activist: "He didn't just *spout* politics—he actually *did*

"Lonelyhearts" (United Artists), 1958. Ryan's cynical newspaper editor William Shrike and wife Florence (Myrna Loy) return home to continue their conflict.

something constructive—by heading the SANE Committee in Hollywood, and by founding the Oakwood School." Later, Bosworth called Ryan a "compelling, brave human being," in the wake of his own sequence of trials.

On the set of Lonelyhearts, reported Bosworth, the production schedule was dominated by Clift's obvious problems. Most days he was well enough to work only in the mornings, and by afternoon he would be high on drugs, alternating amphetamines with barbiturates. He was also a hopeless alcoholic on the verge of a total breakdown.

Clift's near helplessness sparked the nurturing natures of his female costars, Myrna Loy, Maureen Stapleton, and Dolores Hart, who vainly tried to comfort him. Of the male cast, Clift confided in Ryan, drawn to his paternalistic presence and willingness to listen to his shattered remnants of brilliance.

Ryan was a "striking, complex man," said Bosworth, and his handsome physicality and diffident intelligence struck a note of attraction in the androgynous Clift. Clift was the type of man who could engage in small talk in social situations, but who reserved his intellectual side for those he felt were equal to it.

At that time Ryan was facing his own trouble with alcohol and empathized with Clift. Ryan understood Clift's inner pain, and may have been attracted to his frustrated artist's attitude, as well as to the tragedy written in his face (the message imprinted on Clift's face was not figurative. In 1956, he suffered a near-fatal auto accident which permanently marred his aquiline, almost perfect features). Ryan and Clift also mutually admired each other as professionals who had begun their careers on the stage and who remained tied to it even now.

Over and above the shooting delays caused by Clift's inability to complete a full day in front of the camera, one incident taxed not only director Vincent J. Donehue's patience but Ryan's as well. During numerous retakes of a fight scene between Clift and Mike Kellin, Clift became so disoriented that he failed to pull a punch and sent Kellin reeling. Clift burst into tears and was unable to finish the scene. In the final take Ryan came to the rescue by donning Clift's shirt and jacket, and it was his arm appearing in the final close-up.

Lonelyhearts opened at theaters to mixed reviews, meeting a fate similar to other Ryan films dealing with downbeat topics. The picture enjoyed better success in cosmopolitan circles, where its depiction of fragile relationships met wider acceptance. In *New Republic*, critic Stanley Kauffmann stated, "Robert Ryan, a player of resonances, does his best work with the character of Shrike, as directed by Vincent Donehue," and Leonard Maltin noted in *T.V. Movies*, "A superior cast in an interesting adaptation of Nathanael West's novel.

Shortly after completing *Lonelyhearts*, Ryan put into action his long-held ambition of doing legitimate theater in Southern California. One night in 1958 he dropped in at Sidney Harmon's house to chat. Harmon and a friend, New York theater entrepreneur Eddie Cook had been discussing starting a professional theater group, using local talent.

Harmon knew Ryan shared their interest, and asked him for suggestions about how to do it. He got the immediate reply, "There's only one thing to do. Get somebody to pay the rent." This simple answer was also the best, and after thinking it over that night, Harmon phoned Ryan and announced, "I think I can get U.C.L.A. to pay the rent."

They called on Abbott Kaplan, head of the University Extension, who was immediately interested. As Kaplan warmed to their idea, Harmon explained, "We must present a certain kind of theater, not compete with Broadway. And we need a justification for asking the state to support us." Ryan and Harmon had agreed beforehand that the plays should be "experimental plays, not necessarily commercial fare," thus qualifying for subsidized educational funding.

Kaplan agreed, adding, "We need someone who can talk to local actors, and inspire them enough so they'll act for scale" (the Equity minimum was $103.40 a week). After some thought as to how and where to make such a sales pitch, Kaplan volunteered the university's seminar facility at Lake Arrowhead.

Lee Strasberg was hired as a keynote speaker before perhaps 150 actors,

"Day of the Outlaw" (United Artists), 1959. Blaise Starrett (Ryan) and Helen Crane (Tina Louise) avoid each other's glances.

and gave push to the idea. Jubilant over the support they found at the Lake Arrowhead meeting, Ryan, Harmon, and Kaplan returned to Hollywood to solidify their plans. Since Harmon had been associated with the Group Theatre in New York, he suggested reversing the name of their company to the Theatre Group.

Kaplan agreed, and shortly thereafter, they held a weekend meeting on the campus to discuss their plan. In attendance were Lee Strasberg, Dore Schary, Delbert Mann, Anthony Quinn, Paul Newman, Joanne Woodward, Eva Marie Saint and others.

With an austere budget in mind, Ryan, film producer Milton Sperling, Kenneth MacGowan, chairman of the Theatre Arts Department at U.C.L.A., and a few others chose plays without much scenery, such as Dylan Thomas' *Under Milkwood*, and Bertolt Brecht's *Mother Courage*.

Lamont Johnson directed the first play. Ryan had called him up one day and asked, "What would you do if you had $1,000 to do a play?" Johnson replied immediately, "I can do a hell of a lot with $1,000." Remembering the exciting success of the staged readings he and Ryan had done as fund raisers for the Oakwood School, Johnson felt confident.

During its first year of productions, the Theatre Group of the U.C.L.A. Extension had enormous success, selling out all of its performances. In the second year, Abbott Kaplan hired John Houseman as the Theatre Group's artistic director, hoping his extensive stage training would encompass more ambitious pieces.

In the interim between seasons, Ryan made two more films to close out the fifties, neither of which were box-office smashes, for different reasons. The first, *Day of the Outlaw*, became a victim of circumstances when its director, the normally talented André de Toth, demonstrated the personal problems he was having through plodding direction. Ryan's next and last film of 1959, Robert Wise's grim, insightful *Odds Against Tomorrow*, caused some audiences to react in the negative because of its realistic treatment of racial bigotry, and its nihilistic ending.

One thing the two films had in common which helped *Odds Against Tomorrow*, but hindered *Day of the Outlaw*, was a low budget. Philip Yordan called the script he wrote for *Day of the Outlaw* "one of the best I've ever written," but attributed part of the film's failure to its limited budget of $400,000, and to several unfortunate errors and incidents.

Yordan recollected, "Everybody was on the bum with that picture." De Toth's private difficulties caused confusion as to where the film would be shot. Most of it had been written to take place indoors, but de Toth insisted on changes that sent the cast on location in the mountains. Ryan caught pneumonia which held up shooting for a week, then snowstorms caused further delays, and finally the money ran out.

Still retaining a tone of incredulity, Yordan said, "They came back, and there was no picture. So we just wrapped it up with a few days shooting in Hollywood, and nothing happened." Speaking with a resignation resulting from seeing many films fail from human error, Yordan lamented, "It could have been a real winner. Everybody worked for nothing."

On the other hand, the low-budget quality of *Odds Against Tomorrow* sharpened its appeal while making its story of race hatred emotionally shocking. Filmed on location in a small town in the Hudson River Valley, in New York City, and at the old Gold Medal Studios in the Bronx, *Odds Against Tomorrow* surfaced as one of the best and final pictures of the *film noir* cycle.

The film's last scene, in which the characters of Ryan and Harry Belafonte perish in an oil refinery explosion, left an indelible metaphor about the inevitable result of racism. But its message, while expressing a candor rarely heard in the cinema at that time, hit too close to home for some audiences. Nevertheless, the critics were nearly unanimous in their approval of *Odds Against Tomorrow*, and lauded Ryan's seething portrayal of bigotry.

Robert Wise felt that Ryan was the best casting choice as the loser from the South, ex-convict Earle Slater. "Bob was a dream to work with," said Wise. "He was a very real person, and had no phoniness." Over the years, like any director, Wise ran into problems dealing with insecure stars who needed coaxing through scenes, and he could always depend on Ryan's patience in those moments.

"Odds Against Tomorrow" (United Artists), 1959. Top: In the climactic shoot-out at an oil refinery, Ryan's Earle Slater prepares to fire at his enemy. Bottom: (From left) Ed Begley, Kim Hamilton and Ryan off camera during the filming.

There were respect and affection in Wise's voice when he said, "Bob was definitely one of the very best. He was always helpful with the other actors, and if I ever had a problem with one of them, he would always be patient." Wise recalled that on many occasions, "Bob worked with people whom other stars of his caliber would have had great trouble dealing with."

Echoing the intensity of Ryan's and Wise's triumph a decade earlier in *The Set-up*, *Odds Against Tomorrow* brought a sound conclusion to their work together in films, while expanding on the motivations of the type Ryan played in 1947's *Crossfire*.

After Ryan left Hollywood in 1962, he and Wise saw each other when Ryan came west to make a movie, and when they were both members of the Academy of Motion Picture Arts and Sciences. For a period of time, Ryan was a vice-president of the Academy, and appeared at the ceremonies as a presenter in 1966. He made the supreme effort of wearing tail and cummerbund as part of improving his image.

In 1959, Ryan and Jessica moved the family from the San Fernando Valley to Beverly Hills. The uprooting may have been a symbolic effort to recapture the past or to stave off the inevitable. The switch occurred at a time when, although Ryan's career was going well in financial terms, physically, he had arrived at a crucial age, the 50-year mark. Traditionally, Hollywood existed as a validator of beauteous youth forever etched on celluloid, and Ryan was in danger of being cast off.

Moving to chic Beverly Hills from a much smaller, ranch-style house, the Ryans were subject to a naturally higher visibility which Lisa Ryan described as "extravagant by comparison. It was sort of a shock because suddenly we were living in this very grand style."

When Lamont Johnson talked about a party he had attended at Ryan's house one night, he remembered being surprised at its incongruity to Ryan's house in the Valley. "I thought, 'Oh, Jesus, Bob is really going over the edge, he's buying it, he's falling in love with this elegance stuff.'" But Ryan's momentary lapse into the Beverly Hills lifestyle was short-lived. Johnson reported that things quickly went back to "grab-bag family style."

"It was a very informal kind of prairie home. You could practically still see the kids' sleeping bags laying on the floor under a kind of battered old piano, and a big billiard table where there should have been a dining table." Johnson tried to pinpoint what Ryan's home reflected, and felt, "It wasn't like the home of a movie or theatre star, or, after Bob moved to New York, that of a wealthy, retired man, or any of the things that he was."

Owning a house in Beverly Hills was the closest Ryan would come to its artificiality, for which Millard Lampell stated, "Bob had great contempt." Ryan once told an interviewer that "the striving for recognition involves a certain amount of ruthlessness," and confessed to "not being entirely purged of the envy that goes with it."[2]

Shortly after the move, Ryan became involved with the National Committee for a Sane Nuclear Policy (SANE), which had been founded in 1957 by Norman Cousins, Norman Thomas, and Clarence Pickett. Ever since the early fifties when he joined the United World Federalists, also begun by Cousins, Ryan's fears about the global nuclear buildup had increased, and he was getting more pessimistic about the future.

A great number of people in Hollywood shared his concerns about living in a safe world, and in September 1959, Ryan and Steve Allen were named co-chairmen of the Hollywood for SANE branch. The group advertised itself as nonpolitical, stressing that "radiation poison has no politics." Indeed, another SANE pioneer, Sanford Gottlieb, described SANE as "neither religious nor pacifist, but pragmatic."[3]

On September 26, Allen and Ryan hosted a huge buffet banquet at the Beverly Hills Hotel for nearly 200 show business people. In a Hollywood still feeling the effects of the blacklisting days, it was the most significant display of public interest in a cause in nearly a decade, and far removed from the usual publicity grabbing so often identified with Hollywood off-the-set junkets.

The speakers for the evening delivered in succinct terms their vision of what the future held in store for the world if the nuclear arms race continued on its intensified course. Guests heard Bertrand Russell, via a recording, Cal Tech geochemist Harrison Brown, and a Japanese scientist reporting on Strontium 90 contamination, predict a grim picture of the days ahead.

Doctor Brown, who had worked on the first atomic bomb project at the University of Chicago, accurately perceived a "world bristling with warhead missiles in attack-proof concrete nests, pointing in various directions and waiting for the push of a button."[4] Several films released in the four or five years after SANE made its push reflected the concern over panicky fingers: On the Beach (1959), Dr. Strangelove (1964), Fail-Safe (1964), The Bedford Incident (1965).

The Beverly Hills event began a major effort in Hollywood toward shocking people into awareness. A week later, Ryan and Allen placed an ad in both of the film trade papers, urging the reading of Albert Schweitzer's book, Peace or Atomic War, and asking for contributions or time.

On October 17, Ryan held a second dinner at his house, where over 150 actors, writers, directors, and producers gathered to hear Norman Cousins speak about the imminent dangers facing everyone. Cousins, whom one writer described as a "leading Eastern analyst of current mores,"[5] was the editor of The Saturday Review as well as a writer during his association with SANE.

Soon after the Hollywood for SANE gatherings, in an editorial for The Saturday Review, Cousins wrote, "Old methods for protecting life have now become the fuse points for exploding it," and that "the nation is no longer the outer ring of security, but it is now a flailing unit of anarchy."

Underlining his concerns from a humanistic viewpoint, Cousins entreated man to "think about his uniqueness, about his place in the universe, about the meaning and preciousness of life, about his values . . . about the rights of the next generation."[6]

Among the first to offer their support for Hollywood for SANE were Keenan Wynn, David Niven, Inger Stevens, Stan Freberg, James Whitmore, Mercedes McCambridge, Fletcher Markle, Jayne Meadows, Ray Bradbury, Rod Serling, Rod Steiger, and many others. One observer of the affairs at the Beverly Hills Hotel and at Ryan's house commented, "I've never met so many thinking people at one gathering in Hollywood since the late 'troubles.'"

From then on, on a yearly basis Hollywood for SANE threw star-studded fund-raising performances, while in the interim numerous committed actors gave speeches in support of SANE at local organizations, and appeared on radio and television spots. The first to take the podium besides Ryan and Allen included James Whitmore and Lee Marvin.

In the early days of Hollywood for SANE, Ryan and several others took up the cudgel night after night at the SANE office on Robertson Boulevard to set up an executive board and a policy-making committee. Among them were Philip Dunne, Phil Turetsky, Maxine and Sy Gomberg, Arthur Ross, Peter Charlton, Max Youngstein, Esther Lewin, Adele Davidson, Marianna Newton, and Barbara Belfor.

In January 1960, Ryan and Dunne drafted a letter to be sent to all leading presidential candidates, in the hope of persuading them to make a clear and firm statement on the issues of nuclear policy and disarmament. The two men had become friends in the late forties during the time when the Committee for the First Amendment gathered in defense against the House Committee on Un–American Activities.

Dunne, then a highly regarded screenwriter (*The Count of Monte Cristo* [1934], *Stanley and Livingstone* [1939], *How Green Was My Valley* [1941], and *Pinky* [1949]), who later directed many of his own screenplays (*Ten North Frederick* and *Blue Denim* [1959]), recalled meeting Ryan one night at Jane Wyatt's house, and being struck by a sense of "like appealing to like."

Ryan and Dunne agreed with each other politically, were both of Irish extraction and had Episcopalian mothers, came out of Ivy League colleges, and had both rejected organized religion. On an intellectual basis they related well and had long conversations exchanging ideas on a variety of subjects, from the intricacies of the movie business, to the classics of literature and of the theater, to their mutual interest in the act of thinking.

Ryan loved to hear Dunne tell stories about his father, writer and political humorist Finlay Peter Dunne, who had created the theatrical "Mr. Dooley" character when he was an editor at the turn of the century. On a deeper level, though, he probably liked Dunne's outlook on life, which provided a much sunnier side to his own less hopeful slant. As much as Ryan identified with Eugene O'Neill, Dunne was enamored of Thornton Wilder.

Dunne described Ryan as a "man with a very elegant mind who was fastidious in his associations. The people you might meet at Bob's house would be teachers, writers, and physicists. He was an old-fashioned liberal, a Constitution and Bill of Rights man."

In preparation for SANE speaking engagements and meetings, Ryan actively sought information and had numerous conversations with Norman Cousins. Cousins recalled Ryan's "very searching knowledge" of any situation, and in the Eisenhower and Kennedy years, he participated in developing strategies to cope with administration arguments against nuclear disarmament. "Bob could tell you who could do what, and not much time was wasted. He was a superb listener," said Cousins.

At preliminary hearings before the Democratic national platform, Ryan, Steve Allen, and Harry Belafonte represented SANE, and later, Ryan recorded a series of conversations, "The Voice of Man," with Norman Hunt of the Committee for Friendly World Broadcasting.

In early 1960, Ryan volunteered to work on a live television production for the American Friends' Service Committee, entitled "Which Way the Wind?" During the planning stages for the piece, he made contacts with CBS regarding production costs, and agreed to donate his salary to the Friends. Around that time he also appeared in a show which his friend, actress Marsha Hunt, had organized on behalf of the Southern California Committee for Refugees.

Initially, Steve Allen and his wife, Jayne Meadows, Don Murray, and Hugh and Kathryn Beaumont showed interest in assisting the Friends project, but outside commitments forced the Allens and Murray to bow out. Next, a joint effort between the Friends and SANE was explored, but a fundamental difference in ideology ended in a deadlock.

Ryan and Allen politely but firmly informed the Friends that the script for "Which Way the Wind?" was "not in line with the SANE philosophy. It is erroneously believed that SANE is a pacifist group. They cannot accept the unilateral idea."[8] Before the Friends finalized arrangements for the production, Ryan got the call for a film.

In the midst of working for SANE and the Friends, Ryan sometimes became a target of public enmity, as evidenced by a well-composed letter, dated July 6, 1960, which lies in the SANE archives as a reminder:

To Messrs. Steve Allen and Robert Ryan:

Friends:
    Enclosed herewith my contribution to be used by members of your organization/cell as evidence of the thinking of us Decadent War-Mongering Wall Street Reactionaries. We prefer freedom to slavish subservience to the obscene anti–Christ conspiracy that you and your comrades apparently hold so dear.
    You two gentlemen, I must admit, are first-rate toothpaste hucksters. Stick to your "Hollywood tradition," boys. After all, some toothpaste contains a deadly poison—fluoride.

To critics who implied that his liberal activism was motivated by a desire for personal gain, Ryan retorted that "Most actors play it safe, and will only support bleeding heart charities and the American flag." Indeed, more astute observers viewed Ryan differently compared with most show business figures. In the *New York Sunday News*, writer Bob Lardine reported that Ryan's "outspoken comments have singled him out as a particularly courageous man in a business that thrives on the noncommittal utterance."[9]

The Red-baiting scare of the McCarthy era had left a residue of polarized loyalties in which people were labeled either right or left wing. People close to Ryan knew that his sentiments about world issues came from a strong set of traditional values. Robert Wise carefully described Ryan as "very, very concerned about crucial issues," and, "liberal in the best sense, not a radical, and certainly not a Communist."

Millard Lampell remembered that Ryan was "outraged from a feeling that the committees investigating so-called un–American activities were attacks on the very spirit and backbone of what we felt was the American tradition, and what made America a country we loved."

Ryan's outspoken support of SANE, the ACLU, and most civil rights organizations was increasing at the same time that a tide of complacency existed in America and in other modern countries. Newspaper articles about his activities carried provocative titles: One emphasized him as "No Armchair Liberal,"[10] while another asserted, "This Dove Is a Tough Bird."[11]

Yet one critic accused him of being a mouthpiece for the liberal rhetoric of others, such as in Dore Schary's recent *Lonelyhearts*, for which Schary had written the screenplay. In one line of dialogue, Ryan's character states sardonically, "By tomorrow our world diplomats will have so carefully managed our affairs, we may all be disappearing in atomic clouds," while in another he intones, "The bombs keep bursting, the stockpiles keep growing, and two billion souls don't know what's going on in the world, and couldn't care less."

Authors Ian and Elisabeth Cameron discussed Ryan's persona from a slightly different angle, and saw it as authentic. In their book, *The Heavies*, they wrote, "Robert Ryan is almost alone among Hollywood stars known for their liberal activities in looking as if he might personally be a genuine liberal." The Camerons also noticed the paradox that had followed his career: "His kindly, rather worried face and tired eyes are sometimes seen in completely sympathetic parts, but the emotion that Ryan conveys most effectively on the screen is hate."

10. Entering the Sixties

The arrival of John Houseman as the artistic director of the Theatre Group at U.C.L.A. provided the impetus for the company to move from staged readings to full-scale productions. In his book *Final Dress*, Houseman described his plan for the second year's debut piece, and his decision to ask Ryan to star in it.

Because of their past stage success with *Coriolanus* on the New York stage, and Ryan's role as one of the Theatre Group's founders, Houseman felt it "appropriate that he appear in our first production, for which I chose T.S. Eliot's *Murder in the Cathedral*." Ryan was to play Beckett.

The difficulties he had encountered training his voice for the stage had diminished with practice; Houseman, however, recalled that limitations still existed. But Houseman believed that "Bob's vocal weakness was offset by his physical presence, his intelligence, and his personal experience of this profoundly Catholic play," and called him "a real Chicago Catholic."

Houseman arranged a production that was "deliberately simple so as to clarify Eliot's thought and to emphasize the theatrical quality of the text." The auditorium to be used was Schoenberg Hall, the university's 500-seat amphitheater, which was "ideally suited for theatrical production."

In addition to having excellent acoustics, the orchestra pit could be raised and lowered hydraulically, which allowed Houseman to use height and depth optimally, and had a variety of exits and entrances. The cast included film actors Richard Hale, John Hoyt, Alan Napier, and Pippa Scott.

Before Houseman began rehearsals, a meeting was held at the university to decide important matters having to do with future Theatre Group efforts. On the advisory board were Ryan, Houseman, Lamont Johnson, Sidney Harmon, and several members of the Theatre Arts Department. Over the next five or six years, they collaborated on many plays, which Johnson called "truly astonishing things that people still talk about."

Murder in the Cathedral opened on January 19, 1960, to excellent reviews. Critics called it "a masterpiece of drama," and Ryan won applause for his "almost homely simplicity that points up heroism as heroics would never do."[1]

The Theatre Group eventually moved to the Mark Taper Forum, in Los Angeles, where Sidney Harmon said proudly, "It is now one of the country's most prestigious regional theatres, which grew from an idea first discussed in my home with Robert Ryan and Eddie Cook."

Lamont Johnson continued as a board member, and though he felt that its later director, Gordon Davidson, had done "great work," something was lacking. "I don't think it has the spirit or the texture that we were able to achieve when we had no money at all," stated Johnson. "Instead of money and a beautiful theater downtown, we had to do it with imagination and everybody's mutual enthusiasm."

Considering Ryan's proud feelings from establishing the Theatre Group, the decade of the fifties ended on an upbeat note. He was to find more trials, however, in the sixties. The optimism he had demonstrated through his progressive activities would be tested to the limit, and would run concurrently with a prolonged career crisis.

In 1960, Ryan appeared in one motion picture and one television special, each portraying him differently in terms of character. In the former, it was energetic hope, while in the latter, pessimism won over.

Warner Bros.' *Ice Palace* cast him as a trusting Alaska fisherman, whose goodwill toward costar Richard Burton is repaid by avarice and lust. Ryan took the role of the tough but kind Thor Storm because of the film's box-office potential. Things seemed to go a little bit better when large budgets were involved. Or at least, there was an illusion that things were better.

Adapted from a novel by Edna Ferber, whose past works (George Stevens' *Giant*) had done well financially if not critically, *Ice Palace* followed its predecessors. Reviews were average to good. Paul V. Beckley, of the *New York Herald-Tribune*, wrote, "A sprawling, three-generation story of garrulous but rarely defined emotionalism ... pays a metaphorical tribute to Alaska...."

On the other hand, *Variety* stated, "The pacing is consistently good and the many dramatic wallops are developed logically," while asserting, "Robert Ryan is a standout. He's rugged, yet compassionate."

Ryan didn't like his first experience working for Warners, and felt that the studio treated its employees like factory workers. Another annoyance occurred to sour his Warners experience. During one of the outdoor scenes, he got a particle of artificial snow in his eye, which required a trip to the hospital. The eye was swollen for a week.

Next, Ryan starred in the Buick Electra Playhouse's live television special of Hemingway's *The Snows of Kilimanjaro*, but the only snow he faced was in the background set, which simulated the white-capped mountains of northeastern Tanganyika. Landing the lead as Harry Walters in Hemingway's autobiographical foray into disillusioned regret, Ryan was proud of the results, which aired on March 25, 1960. The combination of director John

Katharine Hepburn with Ryan, rehearsing at American Shakespeare Festival, Stratford, Connecticut, in 1960.

Frankenheimer's acute eye for the dramatic, plus Ryan's understated technique, brought out the melancholic subtleties that infused Hemingway's work.

Frankenheimer recalled that the production went through confusing changes, at first being set for videotaping. At the last minute, 20th Century–Fox, which had already made a movie of it, would only allow it to be done live. Then, the shooting was switched from New York to California, making things "very, very difficult," said Frankenheimer.

Through all this, Ryan's patience and professionalism impressed Franken-heimer greatly, and the director came to regard him as one of the best in the business. "Bob gave a terrific performance in the show," he said. When Frankenheimer was asked if he felt that Ryan was drawn to Hemingway's soul, he said, "I don't think so," but as an afterthought he added, "Bob was a very withdrawn man." Indeed, the two men shared several similarities: they were both born and raised in Chicago, showed prowess in boxing, and were enamored of Shakespeare, Fitzgerald, and Joyce.

Much of the work Ryan was finding belonged out of the mainstream of typical show business fare, and artistically, it required more initiative. Over the past few years, as the veneered glitter of Hollywood had become less and less appealing, and worthwhile film work had slowed down drastically, Ryan had more leisure time. And more time to think.

Ryan's Theatre Group activity had keenly aroused his interest in the stage and in Shakespeare, and in early 1960, Katharine Hepburn contacted him to costar with her in Shakespeare's *Antony and Cleopatra*, which was to be staged at the American Shakespeare Festival in Stratford, Connecticut.

Ryan jumped at the chance to play Shakespeare again. "Still licking my wounds" from what he called "the purgatorial bloodbath of the opening night of *Coriolanus* six years ago," he was ready to "once more dip my toes into the icy waters of audience exposure."[2]

When the festival commenced that summer, Ryan and Jessica brought the children with them to New England, and Tim began a friendship with Hepburn which developed in the following years. (Tim and Vickie Ryan named their daughter Katharine, in honor of Hepburn.) Tim recalled Hep-burn telling him that his father was "a damn fine actor," and that she had asked him to do the play because he was one of the few American actors who knew how to do Shakespeare, and that he "knew how to move around on the stage."

Having logged in countless hours talking into a tape recorder to improve his speech, Ryan felt ready to challenge not only his own resources, but also England's possessive hold on Shakespearean drama. He had vaulted the first hurdle separating the stage from screen acting when he learned not to depend on props to help him through a scene, and once quipped, "You can't walk around with your hands in your pockets, you can't light a cigarette, and you almost never sit down."

Ryan also knew that Shakespeare was "an almost total reversal of the realistic, slice-of-life acting"[3] that had earned him his reputation in films. He needed to find a way to give it full poetic value and yet keep it real. He felt that to play Shakespeare, one must love him not only for his poetic genius, but also for his excellent stories. From his previous work in *Coriolanus* and other classics, he knew he possessed the physical authority to command atten-tion and to enhance the quality of his performances.

"The Canadians" (20th Century–Fox), 1961. From left, Jack Creley, John Dehner, Richard Alden, Ryan, Torin Thatcher. Royal Canadian Mounted Policemen Gannon (Ryan) and McGregor (Thatcher) confront outlaws who massacred an Indian village.

Moreover, Ryan had seen British actors play Shakespeare, and believed that "American actors can offer different and possibly better portrayals." He believed the English were "too formal in their Shakespeare."[4] As in all of his past stage work, Ryan worked for the Equity minimum.

Antony and Cleopatra opened at Stratford on July 31, 1960, to generally favorable reviews. Lewis Funke, of the *New York Times*, reported:

> Under Jack Landau's sensitive, though on occasion, spotty, direction, it sparkles more than it splutters, and its defects are outshone by its virtues . . . considering the pitfalls that beset this sprawling play, it is no mean feat.

And on Ryan's Antony:

> Mr. Ryan is a robust Antony, a picture of a soldier. He has the physique for the role, and the attributes of a man who would succumb to the wiles of Cleopatra. There is a charm about him, too, and the grace of a well-proportioned football player.

Funke had one criticism, however, of Ryan's performance. Not surprisingly, it was in the area of speech:

> The flaw is a failure with the verse. Ryan's knowledge of the emotion in the role is evident, and also the ability to project that emotion. What is lacking is the ability to wed these to the verse.

When Hepburn had first considered asking Ryan to play Antony, she was aware that he had grappled with and partially overcome his difficulties with verse, but she felt that "physically, Robert was very well suited for the part."

Hepburn remembered being "thrilled" when Ryan agreed to do the play, and that as he progressed in his performances, "he became more interesting every day." At the end of the summer, Ryan had come to terms with the role of Antony so well that Hepburn felt he was "brilliant." She left Stratford with the sense that Ryan was a "good, true friend, and a good, true actor."

Working with Hepburn, Ryan learned a professional tip about not reading reviews. She told him that she never even glanced at the critics' comments, good or bad. In an article in *Cue* magazine, Ryan recounted, "If a reviewer wrote that Kate was wonderful in a scene, she asked herself, 'I wonder in what way was I great?' Then she would try to capture it that night—and absolutely kill it."

Ryan concluded that rather than worrying about pleasing the critics as he stood in the wings at a theater nervously awaiting his curtain call, he should instead "just go out and do the play."[5]

Shortly after the Shakespeare Festival ended, Ryan went to 20th Century–Fox in a starring role. The film, *The Canadians*, repeated a series of events that were emerging as a pattern in his career, that of success followed by failure. In 1954, he had done *Coriolanus*, then, the mediocre *Alaska Seas*; now, his fulfilling work in *Antony and Cleopatra* was being overshadowed by an even poorer film.

The same erratic trend had also hounded him in several pictures: *The Set-up*, followed by a string of average films; *Bad Day at Black Rock*, succeeded by *Escape to Burma*, and so on. Ryan was on the verge of a prolonged dry spell which would test his endurance to the limit.

In the sixties, motion picture making suddenly decreased. At the same time, Hollywood producers turned toward Europe where they could make less expensive films. Moguls such as Dino DeLaurentiis had begun the practice of going abroad in the fifties, and in 1961, Samuel Bronston followed suit with Nicholas Ray's epic, *King of Kings*.

When Ryan was called in to read for a part in the film, he feared his reputation had followed him: "I was sure they'd ask me to play Judas. I almost fell down when they offered me John the Baptist." Later, he admitted a fondness for his latest role because "it allowed me to shed my history of being perhaps the most hated actor in Hollywood by audiences."[6]

Having recently returned from location shooting in Saskatchewan for *The Canadians*, accepting the *King of Kings* part would mean again leaving home, this time to Madrid. There were few alternatives, so he agreed.

Besides Ryan's John the Baptist, *King of Kings* was an out-of-character picture for director Ray and writer Philip Yordan as well, which perhaps accounted for its widely discrepant reviews. Others who seemed similarly cast against type included Jeffrey Hunter, Harry Guardino, Rip Torn, and Royal Dano.

Since some critics had been accusing Hollywood of "cashing in on Biblical spectacles,"[7] Nicholas Ray's unorthodox interpretation naturally came under fire. Also, due to its large cast of experienced actors, much press surrounded the making of *King of Kings*.

In *Films and Filming*, writer Peter Banks described his visit on location with those who made the film. After watching Ray direct, Banks saw why he had been called an "actor's director": "He is infinitely patient, always ready to try the actor's way before the actor tries *his* way."[8]

Ryan and Ray shared the same opinion about working on a film like *King of Kings*. Once they became involved with it, it turned into a work of intense commitment. When *King of Kings* was released, Ryan was on hand to defend it from detractors. He believed in its value as art, and compared it with other religious epics which he termed "pornographic." He also felt that the film was "a much more honest attempt at accuracy than the Cecil B. DeMille epics."[9]

In *The Saturday Review*, Arthur Knight discussed the three holy characters, Christ, Mary, and John the Baptist, regarding the tone they were to create. Referring to their "sense of predestination and awareness of their roles to mankind," Knight stated, "Robert Ryan comes far closer to this mystic spirit."[10]

Others were not so accepting of Ryan's bid to change, and his stereotyped status became a hex that year. His John the Baptist was reduced to parody when Harvard University conducted its annual lampoon of the film industry, and inflicted on him the Worst Actor of the Year award. It is unknown whether Ryan ever found out about this dubious honor.

Philip Yordan remembered the critics' confused reactions to *King of Kings*, and said, "It was a strange thing that *Life* magazine panned the picture, but said it was a magnificent screenplay. Nick Ray knocked his brains out on that picture." Then cynically, Yordan added, "Some wise guy panned it because he said it starred a 'teen-aged Jesus.'"

After the one week's work on *King of Kings*, for which he earned $50,000, Ryan was idle for the remainder of 1961. The only film work that came his way occurred at the end of the year, but again, the contract involved another cameo role, this time as a general in the acclaimed treatise on World War II, *The Longest Day*.

"The Longest Day" (20th Century–Fox), 1962. Ryan's cameo as General Gavin was the first in a long list of brief appearances.

Once more, it was off to Europe alone, but Ryan felt some consolation from working on a quality piece with quality actors (including Robert Mitchum, Henry Fonda, Rod Steiger, Robert Wagner, Roddy McDowall, Eddie Albert, Edmond O'Brien, Alexander Knox, Richard Burton, and many others). In *The New Republic*, Stanley Kauffmann wrote of the film, "In several ways, *The Longest Day* is an extraordinary piece of filmmaking . . . its complex job of exposition is clear, fast, and exciting, and many of its battle scenes are excellent."[11]

During filming, an incident occurred stateside which followed Ryan to Europe. Shortly after going on location, he got an emergency message from Jessica at their Holmby Hills address. The previous day she had been menaced with a bomb threat from an anonymous phone caller, who warned her that their home would be blown up if her husband did not desist from airing a controversial radio broadcast. It was February 5, 1962.

The disputed program concerned the John Birch Society, and to prove his threat should be taken seriously, the phone assailant told Jessica that the homes of two local ministers had been bombed the week before for their defiance of a vigilante order. The police verified that the clergymen had indeed been victimized, but were unwilling to provide guard protection.

Tim Ryan talked about his mother's increasingly concerned entreaties for assistance to the West Los Angeles police, as she listened with incredulity to their indifference to her plight. Tim recalled sardonically, "They told my mother, 'Well, if you get bombed, give us a call.'"

As soon as Ryan learned of Jessica's jeopardy, he prepared to fly home immediately, but she urged him to complete his work on *The Longest Day*, after calling in a private security agency.

The respect which John Wayne felt for Ryan was validated when Wayne, who was starring in *The Longest Day*, volunteered to come home with Ryan to battle the enemy. Though Wayne may have shared some of the views put forth by the ultra-conservative John Birch Society, it was a question of loyalty to a friend.

"The Duke was sore as hell about the bomb threats," said Ryan, and joked about their friendship, "We get along fine, even though he considers me an awful New Deal son of a bitch. He figures I ought to wear horn-rimmed glasses, and be five feet four inches." Noncommittally, Ryan added, "The Duke is fairly conservative, and I'm fairly liberal, whatever that means."[12]

After some discussion, Ryan decided to go ahead with the scheduled radio programs on station KPFK, in North Hollywood, and no reprisals followed their airings. According to the show's producer, Jim Wilcox, the programs consisted of a series of readings from the Blue Book of the John Birch Society's founder, Robert Welch, and were intended to be neither pro– nor anti–Birch. Besides Ryan, other Hollywood personalities who participated in the readings included Rita Moreno and John Raitt.

The terroristic threats did not appear to greatly bother the Ryans' sense of security, but an incident came out of it which they preferred to keep from public knowledge and which seemed to have sparked their exodus from Hollywood and the West Coast. Philip Dunne validated the occurrence in his autobiography, *Take Two, A Life in Movies and Politics*.

Shortly after the John Birch affair, as Ryan and Jessica pulled into their driveway one night, their car's headlights pierced through the darkness to outline a large man brandishing a rifle near the front door of their house. Ryan slammed on the brakes and began to back out when the man stepped forward, revealing none other than John Wayne, returned from Europe to stand by his friend, politics be damned.

Ryan was grateful for the strength of Wayne's protective gesture if not for its implied vigilantism, but it incited paranoid visions of the real thing happening, and neither he nor Jessica felt safe any longer where they were living. In the aftermath of the bomb scare, armed men guarding his home, and Ryan's career slowdown, their chauffeur, Solomon Smith, suddenly fell ill with cancer and died.

"Billy Budd" (Allied Artists), 1962. Master-at-Arms Claggart (Ryan) threatens henchman Squeak (Lee Montague), and orders him to betray Billy Budd.

As if to symbolize an ascent, Ryan moved the family to the mountain resort of Ojai, where they stayed for several months. Solomon's widow, Williana, accompanied them. The move, instead of clearing things up, crystallized Ryan's dilemma. Tim Ryan remembered a greater feeling of distance pervading the move, and that there was a sense of "where do we go from here?"

The hour and a half drive north seemed to increase Ryan's sense of alienation toward Hollywood, and it toward him. Worthwhile roles, even cameos, came to a sudden halt. During the rest of 1962, he starred in one television show, *Wagon Train*, and lucked into one film role, by personally contacting its producer and director, Peter Ustinov.

Word had gotten to Ryan that Ustinov was about to make a film of Herman Melville's novel *Billy Budd, Foretopman*, so he telephoned Ustinov in London to contract for the part of Master-at-Arms John Claggart.

It is unclear as to why Ryan pursued the Claggart role, since it could only reinforce an image he had been trying to counteract. Conversely, the part was a choice one which he could milk for all the creativity it was worth, and it was tailor-made for the gloomy side of his persona. He landed the role, and although he was one of only two Americans in the cast (Melvyn Douglas being the other), he easily transcended the cultural limitation.

Billy Budd received nearly unanimous critical raves, but suffered a dismaying fate at the box office when two other sea epics, Mutiny on the Bounty and Damn the Defiant, appeared in theaters at the same time. The latter two films were shot in color, had higher production values, and featured several "name" stars in their casts. (Mutiny on the Bounty starred Marlon Brando, Trevor Howard and Richard Harris; Damn the Defiant starred Alec Guinness, Dirk Bogarde, and Anthony Quayle.) They were also promoted and released by major American distributors, while Billy Budd ended up haphazardly in the lap of Allied Artists.

Robert Wallsten recalled that Ryan was on hand at the New York premiere of Billy Budd, and that it was one of the few times he ventured to the movie theaters to see himself. Among the critics who noted Ryan's sterling performance, Pauline Kael also commented on his status in the industry in her book I Lost It at the Movies:

> Robert Ryan gives a fine performance in the difficult role of Claggart. He has had so few chances at anything like characterization in his movie career that each time he comes across, it seems amazing that he could have retained such power and technique.... Considering that he is a very specialized physical type – the tall, rangy American of Western mythology – his variety of characterizations is rather extraordinary. Perhaps just because he is the type who looks at home in cowboy movies, critics rarely single out his performances for commendation.

Kael's observations hit the mark fairly accurately, in that Ryan had much less success than his contemporaries in landing the really great parts in major productions. Her last statement, however, about "critics rarely singling out his performances for commendation," is erroneous.

Given the potential for Ryan's creativity in the role of Claggart, as well as its being the first attempt to bring Melville's demon to the screen, his interpretation may have gained an added dimension of intensity, having occurred during a period of personal frustrations.

Sufficient pessimistic circumstances existed in Ryan's life of late to suggest a parallel with Claggart's grim picture of the world. In delivering the Master-at-Arms' acerbic dialogue he evoked a ring of truth that seemed to come from deep within, and defined the themes of loneliness and inner pain with total honesty. Within that context, Pauline Kael remarked on Ryan's interpretation of evil versus its antithesis:

> His Claggart has the requisite Satanic dignity: he makes evil comprehensible. The evil he defines is the way the world works, but it is also the self-hatred that makes it necessary for him to destroy the image of goodness.

In *A Story of Cinema,* David Shipman echoed the consensus on Ryan's performance:

> Nothing else in the film is quite as good as the night-time conversation between Budd and Claggart, where the purity of the one and the evil of the other are beautifully balanced, with Claggart's strange psychology only implied.

Between the time *Billy Budd* was completed in early 1962 until its release that fall, Ryan had plenty of time to think about his future as an actor. He was feeling more and more that what he had been doing in films had given him few challenges, and the stage was tugging at him much harder than before.

While filming *Billy Budd,* Ryan spent long hours talking with costars John Neville and Paul Rogers about the theater. The two Englishmen were impressed by his knowledge of Shakespeare, and struck by the incongruity between his stage work and his screen stereotype. The animated conversations they shared about their past stage experiences and their future aspirations seemed to have prompted Ryan to make several bold career decisions. A few years later, Neville and Rogers would encourage him to truly stretch not only his acting ability, but also his physical limits.

11. A Move to New York

The half-year time spent in Ojai was a limbo for Ryan, until he got an unusual offer from New York playwright Howard Lindsay regarding a new musical he was currently casting for a fall opening. Katharine Hepburn had recommended Ryan to Lindsay, knowing of his secret desire to do a musical, and the play was scheduled for Broadway.

It was a grand opportunity for a dramatic change, so Ryan agreed to audition for the lead role as the President of the United States in the musical, *Mr. President*. Before director Joshua Logan, he sang "Always" and "White Christmas," and did well enough to get the part. His singing voice, although untrained, was carried by his enthusiastic delivery and his presence in the role.

Ryan had a great deal of anxiety over some imminent decisions. He was uncertain about taking on a completely different image in a singing part, and nervous about the idea of leaving the family for the length of *Mr. President*'s run. There seemed to be no alternative other than a temporary move East for the whole family.

The move was the hardest on the children, and the third displacement in three years. To ease their transition from laid-back California to frenetic New York City, Ryan and Jessica searched for a comfortable suburb where things were still safe. They landed in the upper-middle-class community of Bronxville, about a half hour from Manhattan. Williana Smith, still in mourning over the loss of Solomon, went with the family, as if to grasp at a semblance of continuity in her life. The change was too much for Williana, and shortly after the move, she returned to the comfort of her relatives in Los Angeles.

As it happened, Ryan and Jessica benefited emotionally from the move to New York. They had been eager to leave Hollywood and to be among more sophisticated surroundings. Culturally, Jessica could further her growth in writing and in art, and Ryan could branch into legitimate theatrical pieces that he would never find in California.

They rekindled friendships from the old days, such as Robert and Cynthia Wallsten, Millard and Elizabeth Lampell, and made many new acquaintances. Among them were people whom Ryan met through his activism, such as

"Mr. President"—Playbill advertisement for 1962 critical flop. Nanette Fabray and Ryan on stage.

Benjamin Spock, James Earl Jones, Paul Simon and Art Garfunkel, Alan Ginsberg, and Bob Dylan.

Ryan also saw socially a contingency of Hollywood expatriates that included screenwriter Albert Hackett, Ring Lardner, Jr., and a few others. But even then, the group of his more intimate friends remained small.

Unhappily, the pleasant surface appearance of Bronxville obscured a strain of underlying intolerance, which Ryan and Jessica discovered after having settled in. By then it was too late to change things as he had leased their home for a year, and everybody was compelled to accept a living situation in which they never felt comfortable.

During the run of Mr. President, the short commute became increasingly lengthy, and by its finish Ryan had decided that what dangers New York possessed were more palatable than the cold distance of Bronxville. His children had few words for the hypocrisy they encountered in Bronxville, but Lisa Ryan strongly recalled that "people were very bigoted. They didn't like blacks, Jews, or Catholics."

Although several great talents collaborated on Mr. President, Ryan was edgy about it from the start. With some hesitation, he had signed on at the urging of friends who had seen the play's advance credits, which included music and lyrics by Irving Berlin, production numbers by Leland Hayward, and choreography by Peter Gennaro.

Ryan had misgivings because his part was not completely written yet, but he was offered only vague replies when he asked about it. Robert Wallsten was among those convinced that Mr. President "couldn't miss." Just before the musical began its six-month run, Ryan talked to him about his concerns. "When Robert persisted with the people in charge," Wallsten recollected, "they told him, 'Musicals are never written, they evolve during rehearsals.'" Or when he expressed misgivings about the quality of some of the writing, he was mollified with words to the effect that "everything will be better once things get going."

Wallsten and his wife, Cynthia, were in Boston for the tryouts of Mr. President. When the show ended, he noticed looks of worry and exhaustion on the faces of those responsible for it. "They knew they had a failure on their hands," Wallsten said, "and there was a mad scramble to correct the unfixable."

Theater critic Cyrus Durgin wrote in the Philadelphia Bulletin on August 28, 1962:

> Mr. President is cemented to a certain extent with show biz clichés . . . the total is a show which never settles into a unified style, which is amusing in part and to my taste, is sometimes cornily dull, and never quite believable. . . . As President Stephen Decatur Henderson, Robert Ryan has dignity and is handsome and credible in the part.

The play underwent emergency alterations, as the writers desperately tried to enliven its innocuous theme. The usual methods of changing the order of scenes and rewriting of songs seemed strangely perfunctory, since when a play bombed during tryouts its fate was often sealed.

One song, "The Secret Service Makes Me Nervous," which was sung by the President's daughter (Anita Gillette), bothered Ryan's sense of propriety. He told Robert Wallsten that "In essence, the song is about a girl who can't get laid because the Secret Service is around."

The biggest problem with *Mr. President* had to do more with content than with style, as its mild treatment of life in the White House seemed to be an easy way out for lyricist Irving Berlin. At a time when tensions between the United States and Cuba were increasing, *Mr. President's* trite tale seemed inappropriate. Thus, it was guaranteed to please the masses while leaving serious theatergoers with a saccharin aftertaste.

Perhaps in an attempt to increase its favor prior to a New York opening, *Mr. President* next played on September 26, in Washington at the National Theatre, before an audience that included President and Mrs. John F. Kennedy, and an entourage of political and diplomatic personalities.

By the time it premiered a month later at the St. James Theatre, *Mr. President* had been improved enough to secure its shaky premise, aided by a heavy advanced ticket sales campaign. The results pleased the less discriminating while disappointing those who expected further wonderful things from its creators.

Critics were split in their assessment of *Mr. President*. The comments of Howard Taubman of the *New York Times* on October 22 were in the negative:

> Has there ever been as dull a president as the man occupying the White House in *Mr. President?* . . . The musical has been patched together out of lame topical allusions, pallid political jokes, and stab gags based on White House tribal customs. . . . Robert Ryan, who plays Mr. President as uninflectedly as written, shows some fervor as he cries that "the biggest roadblock to national progress is Congress."

On the same day, however, Norman Ladel of the *World-Telegram and Sun*, reflected the consensus of most observers:

> A musical about the President of the United States would seem to invite a sharper, more brilliant story treatment than was provided. I don't think the playwrights were necessarily unable to write such a script, but that they preferred this milder, more homey treatment.

Of Ryan's performance Ladel declared:

Let's face up to the fact that tall, lean, handsome, idealistic, dutiful and dedicated President Henderson, as portrayed by Robert Ryan, could poll more votes than any chief executive we've had since FDR. . . . Ryan never demeans his role, nor does he let himself be tempted by theatrics . . . he makes a good musical comedy president. His greatest political and stage assets are personality, warmth, and dignity.

Mr. President finished its scheduled run without any regrets from those who made and starred in it. Director Joshua Logan felt badly enough that he spoke little of it in subsequent conversations about his career, and avoided it totally in one of his books of memoirs. Likewise, Ryan left the play in an embarrassed state, feeling that patrons had been cheated.

Ironically, the Cuban missile crisis occurred during the musical's run, thereby emphasizing its anachronistic story. As the Cold War intensified and a global nuclear buildup continued, Ryan may have felt like a hypocrite, having taken part in a well-meaning, inoffensive work which at the end may have approached a grotesque parody on life.

Sometime during his stay in Bronxville, Ryan's mother died suddenly of a heart attack. She had remained in Los Angeles when the family traveled East, as the move was supposed to be temporary. It was the same kind of shock that had hit Ryan when he was a young man punching cattle in Montana, and had gotten word that his father had died. The physical distance of not being with his mother at the last moment may have increased his sense of things left unresolved, and of feelings gone unexpressed.

Mabel Ryan had been a stately Victorian presence in Ryan's life, and possessed a kind of old-country authority and calm reserve. However, she never quite approved of her son's being a movie star. She came from an era in which to be an actor or actress was to invite a certain amount of decadence and immorality, and when Ryan first told her of his desire to be an actor, she was against it.

"You can't earn a living that way," she demurred, "but it's a nice hobby." She also told him that he "couldn't act,"[1] and when he proved he could, she accepted it with difficulty, saying his "tough-guy roles" offended her. Ryan told one person, "She wants me to play a shaved fellow in a business suit, with a white shirt and gold cufflinks"; then, "I did a role like that once and she liked it. I didn't."[2]

Robert Wallsten got a brief phone call from Ryan the day his mother died, asking him to come out to Bronxville right away. When he arrived at the house, Ryan met him at the door, in tears and in his bathrobe. Wallsten described Ryan as "more distraught than I had ever seen him," and had a strong recollection of "Robert's arm around my shoulder, squeezing so hard that it hurt as he wept."

The funeral in Chicago was typically Irish, and its aftermath quietly endured. If Ryan shared his most private feelings about his mother's death wish with anyone, they went to the grave with Jessica.

In 1963, for the first time in his career, Ryan had no motion picture assignments. His fear about being unemployed was valid now, but nevertheless, he continued avoiding going after the big parts. By then, it seemed that his ambivalence about acting had as much effected his status between leading man and character actor as had the studios' and public's perception of him. (In one of Bing Crosby's last television interviews, with Barbara Walters, he discussed a pitfall accompanying epic stardom: an increased anxiety over failure. According to him, many actors, for fear of mandating lead billing in a film that might flop at the box office, settled for second or third billing. Crosby included Ryan in this group of stars.) His complaint of being "fated to work in desolate, faraway places" had turned into a self-fulfilling prophecy.

Throughout his career slowdown, Ryan coped silently, not wanting to "burden" people. To a few friends he talked generally, usually with a tone of stoic resignation. To Robert Wallsten, he sometimes referred to the "Hollywood pecking order," in which he felt certain he was never the first choice. When he was at home, Ryan maintained his practice of not bringing the job with him. Cheyney Ryan recalled that dinner conversations were often concerned with politics or education, and almost never about his father's films or roles.

Although Ryan tried to keep his career crisis hidden, his children felt that his silence about his inner feelings made them all the more conspicuous. There were periods when he occupied himself in his game room for hours at a time, methodically shooting pool. Tim Ryan believed that much of his father's closely guarded privacy was due to his upbringing in a family which clung to staid Victorian traits.

Millard Lampell observed that Ryan had "great loyalty toward his friends and enormous compassion, and that his family was the 'real center of his life.'" But Lampell also recalled that Ryan's greatest difficulty in relating to other people had to do with talking about personal things. Lampell said, "It just wasn't in Robert's past or in his tradition."

In referring to Ryan's temperament, Lampell recalled conversations he had with him regarding his childhood. "Part of Robert's introversion stemmed from his never having been terribly close to either his father or his mother," stated Lampell, and inferred that what drove Ryan was a throwback to a powerful ethnic strain. Attempting to describe Ryan's concept of happiness, Lampell emphasized, "With all that it implies, Robert was a Black Irishman, with a lot of dark, private moods."

Referring to Ryan's "solitary, lonely spells of drinking," Lampell said, "there were demons in Robert that I suppose he never talked about." Lampell's assessment of Ryan's spiritual force seemed to parallel the paradox of the Irish intellectual, precariously balancing the scales between hope and futility.

"Robert had a strange mixture of a belief in a better future, and at the same time a kind of black pessimism about the stupidity and foolishness of the way the world was being run," said Lampell.

Lampell first met Ryan in the late forties, after seeing him in *Crossfire*. "Robert really blew everyone away," said Lampell, recalling that "suddenly he was hot, and everybody knew who he was." They liked each other from the start, and became a little better acquainted in political surroundings, when they were involved with the Committee for the First Amendment.

Organized during the early period of the investigations by the House Committee on Un-American Activities, the liberal Committee for the First Amendment mounted two big broadcasts against it, both directed by Norman Korwin and written by Lampell. "Just about every major star in Hollywood appeared in the shows," said Lampell. (Ryan, Judy Garland, Fredric March, Cornel Wilde, Groucho Marx, Gregory Peck, Myrna Loy, Ira Gershwin, Lucille Ball, William Holden, Oscar Hammerstein II, Margaret Sullavan, Burt Lancaster, Burl Ives, Melvyn Douglas, and others.)

Ryan and Lampell had a few conversations at fund-raising parties for the Committee, one of which Lampell retained in his memory. One night at Ira Gershwin's house, Ryan approached Lampell and complimented him on a cantata he had written about Abraham Lincoln, "The Lonesome Train." Ryan expressed a wish to narrate the program, and told Lampell of his secret fancy of one day being able to be a singer.

"Robert knew most of the lyrics to 'The Lonesome Train' by heart, and he sang some of them that night," said Lampell, "and we both laughed about it." Thinking back, Lampell felt the spark for friendship grow from that interchange; however, his being blacklisted shortly thereafter interrupted the process.

The two next met in the mid-sixties at a show sponsored by the AFL-CIO in favor of Medicare. Their reacquaintance happened at an opportune time for Ryan, who was facing a work slowdown. Lampell was able to answer a proposition Ryan made to him 15 years earlier, by sending a narrator's part his way.

Lampell had written a screenplay for a documentary feature film called *The Inheritance*, and had recommended Ryan to its producer, Harold Mayer. An early innovator in documentary filmmaking, Mayer organized his own production company in 1961, and has since made many television series and film specials for public television. In addition, his theatrical documentary features have won worldwide acclaim.

Mayer's wife, Lynne, the associate producer of *The Inheritance*, remembered feeling initially tentative when she contacted Ryan for the part. He joked to her, "Of course I'll do it. Who do you think I am, Charlton Heston?"

Ryan was an ideal choice for the narration, not only in the tenor of his voice, but because *The Inheritance* reflected a cultural perspective about which he understood a great deal. Told through the eyes of immigrants who came to America by the thousands in the early 1900s, the film traced the growth of the labor movement from Ellis Island, through union participation in the civil rights struggles of the sixties.

Harold Mayer felt that Ryan was "spot on." "Bob's voice was slightly gruff and not totally cultured, but it was very well modulated," said Mayer, adding that the best aspect of Ryan's reading was his "great understanding of it."

In their brief time working together, Mayer's honest manner put Ryan at ease. Mayer reported that Ryan "seemed honored" to have been asked to do *The Inheritance*, though Mayer could only pay him the Actors' Equity minimum. "He did it for $1,000, which was next to nothing for a star of his caliber," said Mayer.

In one of the film's most hopeful statements, wherein Ryan intoned, "The message was written in fire, for better or for worse, man was in it together," his words were shortly afterward fulfilled in the negative. Between his completion of *The Inheritance* in late 1963 and its release in May 1964, John F. Kennedy was assassinated. Kennedy's death presented depressing proof of man's propensity for destruction, and was more alarming in the aftermath of the optimistic message of *The Inheritance*.

Ryan had admired Kennedy's courage and independence, and had identified with his background, Irish-Catholic and Democrat. Lisa Ryan said that Kennedy's death "devastated" her father, who had placed his faith in Kennedy to "save the world." She recalled a vivid memory of him coming by taxicab to pick her up at school on the afternoon of November 22, 1963. When she got into the back seat, he was sitting there, in full tears. It was one of the few times she saw him cry.

Other than his work on *The Inheritance* in 1963 and 1964, Ryan was relegated to television. Several factors, within his control and outside of it, were complicating matters, such as his physical distance from Hollywood, the filming of many motion pictures in Europe, and age.

Sometime in 1963, Ryan and Jessica decided to permanently relocate the family to New York City. They had gained a new sense of themselves moving to the East Coast, and they felt they belonged there more than anywhere else. Ryan knew that opportunities to do legitimate stage work were much better in New York, and despite what he considered a failure in the recent *Mr. President*, it had raised his confidence in his stage ability.

As soon as their Bronxville lease expired, Ryan moved into a spacious ten-room apartment at 88 Central Park West, which was located in the middle of the theater district and bordering Central Park.

The Ryans' apartment was one of the largest in their building, but it was furnished without pretention, downplaying the implied grandeur of its large, high-ceilinged rooms. Much of their furniture had been passed down through Jessica's family, and reflected an elegant yet austere simplicity.

Ryan and Jessica's tastes were eclectic. Several pieces were made of teak and were of Chinese origin, and the rooms were decorated with art objects from around the world.

Ryan's television work of 1963 and 1964 concerned psychological themes. His first program of the year, in an episode of the Kraft Suspense Theatre, cast him as a harried father whose daughter is involved in a hit-and-run auto accident in which a pedestrian is killed.

Next, Ryan appeared in two "psychiatrist" programs and another "Wagon Train" episode. In "The Breaking Point," starring Eduard Franz and Paul Richards, Ryan played an author-adventurer whose wife seeks mental help for him when he becomes accident-prone. "The Eleventh Hour," starring Ralph Bellamy and Jack Ging, gave him a departure from his usual tension-filled roles, as an effusive country politician, victimized by his criminal brother. Finally, in "Wagon Train," he played an ex-lawman with a score to settle.

During the time when Ryan wasn't doing a film, he intensified his activist work with SANE and the ACLU. Both organizations, as well as the United World Federalists, had given him a frightening slant on world issues. Being prone to obsessive ruminating about the state of things, he centered his attention on the civil rights struggles of the sixties, and on "Ban the Bomb" efforts.

The New York opening of The Inheritance at the Carnegie Hall Cinema in May 1964 was a special occasion for Ryan, as he had become deeply involved in the spirit represented in the film. Its statement of man's eternal striving for freedom and dignity, expressed in the American tradition he so loved, happened at a time in his life when he needed something emotionally uplifting.

Ryan volunteered to appear as one of the guests at the showing of The Inheritance, which included folk singers Judy Collins, Pete Seeger, and others. The night was a huge success, and critics lauded the film. The New York Times called it, "Memorable ... with shattering pictorial effects," while author Kenneth Tynan wrote, "This nightmare record of sweatshops and strike breakers explains more vividly than any book the spirit of idealistic rage in which American unions were founded."[3]

Overseas, the picture won several film festival awards in Germany, Italy, and Scotland, and at home it served as a symbol of the upsurgence of new-wave sixties thinking. Ryan was proud of his work on The Inheritance, and his final words in it, "We got to work for it, fight for it together," seemed appropriate for the consciousness that began in the middle of the decade.

Ryan's guest appearance for The Inheritance was one of the few times he roused himself into the limelight of the publicity game. Shortly thereafter, in a ritual that was performed about twice a year, his public relations agent convinced him to throw a party in order to get mentions in movie columns, and perhaps some work.

Ryan and the family had just moved into the Dakota, which would suit the ostentation in which stars were expected to indulge. Although he agreed to have the affair, Ryan left the entire handling of it to his agent. For name-dropping purposes, the agent usually drew up the guest list with celebrities half of whom Ryan didn't know very well or at all. On this occasion, the invited guests included several friends and acquaintances, such as John Houseman, Robert Mitchum, and Henry Fonda, as well as a number of personalities who came to promote their own publicity.

On the day of the party, Ryan and Lampell's friendship was cemented when a silent confrontation occurred between Lampell and director Elia Kazan, who had been a "friendly witness" during the blacklisting period. After 15 years of ostracism from the Hollywood community, Lampell had just emerged from the underground arena of pseudonymous screen writing to accept an Emmy award for a Hallmark Hall of Fame program, entitled "Eagle in a Cage." At that time he publicly announced that he had been blacklisted.

On the Emmy awards night of 1966 in New York, when Lampell walked to the podium amid enthusiastic applause and a brass band trumpeting, the music's triumphant tone took on added meaning in light of Lampell's acceptance speech moments later. After a few disarming comments which brought laughter from the audience, Lampell's diffident smile and dry humor turned serious. "This is my last remark," said Lampell. "I suppose everybody ought to know here," and without taking a breath to savor his words or the expectant faces in front of him, he continued, "I was blacklisted for ten years. Thank you."

Years later, Lampell commented that he had not planned to announce his ten-year exile on stage that night, but was prompted by a feeling of absurdity as he stood there before his peers, some of whom had probably turned their backs on him. "I had no idea I was going to say it, but when I heard my name, suddenly it seemed ridiculous to be standing there and acting as though nothing had happened in those ten years."

As Ryan circulated among the guests, he noticed Lampell's conspicuous indifference toward Kazan, and attempted the role of peacemaker between the two after Kazan asked him to be the intermediary. "The guy pleaded with Robert, and said that I had treated him unfairly when I published my blacklist diaries," Lampell recalled, "but Robert understood quite well my reasons for refusing to talk to Kazan." Although the director had proclaimed his innocence of betrayal again and again in the years since the blacklisting days, his entreaties seemed to invite a quote from Hamlet: "the man doth protest too much, methinks."

After The Inheritance, Ryan completed two other narrations for television that year, and conveniently, both programs were made in New York City. In the documentary series "World War I," which aired on CBS during the 1964–65 season, Ryan made daily trips to the network's Manhattan studios for a few months.

One wonders whether his work on the program stirred up any anxiety, as the series analyzed not only the war's physical destruction, but also its emotional damage. Robert Wallsten saw Ryan often during that time, and reported that he talked of not having much to do, but did not appear unhappy.

Next, Ryan narrated a locally made NBC documentary, entitled "The City of Ships," which aired in December 1964. In outlining the history of the Port of New York, Ryan earned high marks for his authoritative voice. The *New York Times* affirmed, "Robert Ryan, the actor, caught the thrill and emotion of harbor doings."[4]

From his local work, Ryan became well-known in the New York media, and was featured in a number of newspaper interviews and on talk shows. His outspokenness made good press, and gained impetus because the issues he was raising were appearing as a more immediate threat than before. SANE had been gaining a stronger foothold, while the other liberal groups he supported, in particular the ACLU, were pushing more vehemently than ever for social reform.

During the civil rights marches of 1964 and 1965, Ryan viewed the inflamed racial tensions with sadness for the "shameful way"[5] blacks and other minorities had been, and were still being, treated. He believed America's greatest domestic problem was its failure to grant blacks full citizenship, and contributed large sums of money to the ACLU's efforts toward guaranteed rights.

In an effort to fight the racial discrimination in Hollywood, Ryan helped organize AHAB (Artists Help All Blacks), with several other actors, including Bill Cosby, Robert Culp, and Sidney Poitier. Although the group failed to stay intact long enough to be truly viable, it may have triggered the mid-sixties recognition of black performers.

In times when Ryan caught flak for his viewpoints, they only served to strengthen his purpose. His critics seemed to forget that he was supporting ideals first set forth by the founding fathers, but never equally served. He blamed much of America's trouble on public apathy, and commented paradoxically on the ignorance of people who would rather listen to what actors had to say about issues, than to those who really knew the information.

Although he had attracted attention for his activist work, Ryan kept a low profile around New York. In his sprawling, 11-room apartment at the Dakota, he and Jessica kept much of their well-worn furniture from California, defying the ambience of the chic Manhattan address.

"Robert and Jessica's place was elegant, but not lavish," said Millard Lampell, "and they wanted very much to keep a warm, homey atmosphere there. Of all of the apartments at the Dakota I've visited, I think Robert's was probably the most comfortable."

The central meeting place at Ryan's was the game room, in which his huge, professional pool table occupied a prominent position, and a piano, game table, and stereo. Along the walls were posters and pictures from his plays and films, as well as three very significant photographs of D.W. Griffith, Douglas Fairbanks, Sr., and Charlie Chaplin. Ryan believed that the three men were the primary force behind the development of the motion picture industry.

Many conversations took place around the pool table, as Ryan and friends traded ideas in between shots. Millard Lampell remembered having "great discussions with Robert," and that Cheyney sometimes joined in.

From listening to their parents' lively conversations with writers and other intellectuals over the years, Ryan's children created their own talents and strengths. "There was always this sense of art and self-expression around the house," Tim Ryan said. He put a high value on his elementary grade years at the Oakwood School, and said, "It was my only real education. The teachers there taught me *how* to learn, how to find things out."

Tim wanted to be an actor, and in the fall of 1964 he returned to California, headed toward a degree in Theatre Arts at Pomona College. Cheyney was planning on Harvard and a career in education, while Lisa had shown early promise as an artist, and was attending the Nightingale-Bamford School in New York.

As 1964 ended, Ryan still had no major work in progress. Friends were aware that he was bothered by the inactivity, and that he went through periods of depression over it. Even when he had been making three or four pictures a year, it only added up to a few months' steady activity, and several months left to his own devices. Boredom often set in.

Tim Ryan remembered his father visiting a pool hall on Broadway from time to time, where he could forget his situation for a few hours. "Some of the great pool players used to hang out there, and Dad felt like it was a mutual honor playing with them," Tim said.

As Ryan and the various pool hustlers and onlookers were outlined in semi-shadow under overhead lights, to passersby they may have looked like ominous characters from a gangster movie. Inside, each person around the table seemed to be acting out an unconscious role reversal, Ryan, embodying one of his screen portraits and briefly escaping to another life, the others, treating him as they might a Willie Mosconi.

Living in mid–Manhattan, Ryan was close to the best and worst of life in New York City. Nearby was the well-bred theater area and the swank East Side, flanked by the tenderloin district which radiated from Broadway and Times Square. Among the countless, anonymous cut-rate concessions, X-rated movie houses, trendy boutiques, and chic restaurants, in which there was something for everyone, Ryan spied a few places that invited his acquaintance.

At Gartner's Hardware Store and the Tip-Top Shoe Store, on 72nd Street, Ryan picked up odds and ends, and the old-timers' views on the world situation. An out of the way delicatessen or a walk-in pizza parlor served as well as a fancy restaurant.

During the interim of his documentary work and the end of 1964, it was clear to Ryan that his acting career was in imminent danger of ending. Nearly three years had gone by since his last motion picture, and there were no prospects in the works. Philip Yordan related, "It was hard on Bob when he found out that people in Hollywood have short memories."

12. Cameo Appearances

In early 1965, Ryan mobilized, and went looking for work minus his agent. His core group of friends brought him out of unemployment when Philip Yordan and Sidney Harmon gave him a role in Warner Bros.' *The Battle of the Bulge*, to be shot in Spain. Ryan took the job more as a way of keeping his name and face alive, than as an acting challenge.

Yordan remembered being a little surprised when Ryan approached him in search of work, knowing he wanted to stay away from war films and Westerns. "Bob called me and said he had to come back with something, and that he couldn't wait any longer for the right part," said Yordan.

"Bob normally made about $150,000 per picture, but he was desperate and would have worked for short money just to come back," Yordan said. Knowing this, Yordan went directly to Jack Warner and bargained for Ryan. "When I told Jack I wanted to pay Ryan his full salary, he looked at me and exclaimed, 'But it's a very small part,' and I shot back, 'Look, I see no reason to cut his salary, and besides, his name will help the picture.'" The cigar-chomping Yordan, whom Lisa Ryan affectionately called a "lovable wheeler-dealer," had enough clout to get his way, and Warner finally agreed.

The Battle of the Bulge earned respectable box-office figures mainly because of its epic stature and highly regarded cast, which included Henry Fonda, Robert Shaw, and Dana Andrews. But most critics agreed that its script and direction rarely hit the mark, thus it joined a growing number of mediocre war stories made in Europe in the sixties. Ryan could at least say that he was cast as sympathetically as possible for a military figure, in that his role was a fictionalized portrait of General Omar Bradley.

Shortly thereafter, Ryan changed agents, who informed him that he wasn't getting parts because he wasn't asking for enough money. That news, plus Philip Yordan's gesture, gave him confidence in his marketability, and from then on he got his full salary, even in cameo roles.

Yordan speculated that Ryan made more money in the last eight years of his life than in the previous 25, though most of them were either cameos or in pictures that wasted his talents. "It really didn't bother him at all," Yordan maintained.

"The Professionals" (Columbia), 1966. Maria (Claudia Cardinale) "huddling" from the desert chill as Ehrengard (Ryan) thinks about their situation.

Millard Lampell believed that Ryan regarded his film work pragmatically now, as a means of supporting his family. By accepting his lot without complaint, Lampell said, Ryan kept the doors to future offers open. Moreover, the gloss of stardom had been forever dulled by the reality of experience.

Thinking back to his father's career in the mid-sixties, Tim Ryan observed, "After 25 years, things tend to get boring." He drew a pattern, beginning with his father's rapid rise after Pat O'Brien took him under his wing, to a long maturing process as an actor. Tim believed that his father had struggled a great deal and had felt a lot of uncertainty along the way, and that the cause of it was "a degree of temperament and insecurity."

"Part of what Dad had to deal with was that, relatively speaking, he was an overnight success, compared to what most actors go through," Tim said. Thus, the three difficult years that had just passed mixed uneasily with Ryan's fatalistic Irish-Catholic sense of gloom.

His next film of 1965, *The Crooked Road*, did nothing to diminish his pessimism, much less his visibility. Shot in black-and-white on a small island villa in Yugoslavia, and distributed by a minor studio, Seven Arts, the picture quickly made the circuit and disappeared. When Ryan reviewed the quality of his films over the years, he knew he was not alone in having appeared in

"The Dirty Game" (American-International), 1966. Ryan as General Bruce, advising Henry Fonda.

more than his share of forgettable ventures. Indeed, he believed that the secret to success as an actor depended on "a degree of talent and a large degree of luck."[1] He also thought that actors had limited judgment about the quality of a film, and that even in their best films, they often came away dissatisfied with themselves.

In the midst of all the ocean-hopping, Ryan flew to Washington to take part in a celebration of the centennial of Abraham Lincoln's second inaugural address. It was March 4, 1965, and on the east steps of the Capitol building, there stood Ryan in frock coat and false beard, delivering Lincoln's address. As he stood before the television cameras and a crowd of 30,000 people, he underscored Lincoln's words, "With malice toward none; with charity for all."

In contrast to his proud Washington appearance, later in 1965, Ryan was off to Europe again, in a mélange of cold-war intrigue, *The Dirty Game*. His interest in the picture had been sparked because it had been conceived as a pilot for a television series. The mediocre efforts of the film's three directors put an end to his fantasy when it bombed at theaters.

Ryan's sole consolation from such films was the money he earned. If people asked him why he gave his talents so often to inferior material, he had a stock answer for them which he borrowed from John Barrymore: "We Barrymores can survive anything that pays."[2]

Ryan's perseverance paid off when his next film, *The Professionals*, brought him back to prominence as one of the Western's symbols of the rugged American cowboy. In the company of costars Lee Marvin, Burt Lancaster, Jack Palance, and Woody Strode, he showed that at age 55 he could still handle the company and the desiccated terrain of the Death Valley location.

His role as a tough but gentle horseman and adventurer seemed to have been written to fit his temperament. Yet it was a paradoxical casting that perfectly exemplified the "Hollywood pecking order" he talked about. The roles of Marvin, Lancaster, and Palance had meat to them, while Ryan and Strode seemed to exist mainly as silent backup. Though he appeared in all of the scenes, Ryan's spoken part was barely 20 lines.

Philip Dunne remarked, "I always thought Bob was totally wasted in *The Professionals*. Everybody else had something to do, and even at the end when he had what should have been his great moment..." and his voice trailed off. Looking on the brighter side, though, *The Professionals* was one of the best Westerns in the sixties, of a stature of symbols remembered. It depicted symbols of bravery and glory buffeted by suffering and the passage of time, and of the wisdom that comes from doing things the hard way.

In her book *The Private Eye, the Cowboy, and the Very Naked Girl*, Judith Crist referred to Ryan and several actors who had become larger-than-life personalities. In describing the cast of *The Professionals*, Crist noted, "They fulfill themselves because they are professionals in the fullest sense."

In early 1966, Ryan took another shot at a television series when he starred in an episode of the Bob Hope Chrysler Theatre, entitled "Guilty or Not Guilty." Filmed in New York City, the 60-minute pilot cast Ryan as an assistant district attorney trying to fight vigilantism and urban crime, aided by his young, idealistic colleague, Richard Beymer.

The show excited no enthusiasm, however, possibly because several other "lawyer" series had already exhausted the formula. The most successful among them included "The Defenders," with E.G. Marshall and Robert Reed, "Slattery's People," starring Richard Crenna, and "Sam Benedict," featuring Edmond O'Brien.

Ryan traveled to England in April 1966, after signing up for a small role in Robert Aldrich's much debated war film, *The Dirty Dozen*. Again, it was a cameo in which his character, Colonel Breed, was reduced to a pompous martinet in a picture which ill-used the talents of other high caliber actors, Ernest Borgnine, Richard Jaeckel, Ralph Meeker, George Kennedy, and Robert Webber.

The Dirty Dozen's producers succeeded in their casting gimmickry, and the film broke box-office records, while its far-fetched premise and flagrant violence outraged some critics. The idea that the military would recruit capitally convicted G.I.s to embark on a suicide mission behind enemy lines aroused incredulity on moral grounds.

When Ryan returned to the States, he found a few jobs awaiting him, but none were a challenge. In his first comedy, Paramount's *The Busy Body*, he stayed in character as a syndicate head in director William Castle's spoof on gangster films. Opposite comedians Sid Caesar, Jan Murray, Dom DeLuise, Bill Dana, and others, Ryan did little other than collect his paycheck. He had the company, however, of dramatic veterans Anne Baxter and Charles McGraw with whom to share his discomfort.

Sometime in 1966, Ryan took inventory of his assets since a lot of money was coming in from his films, television work, and business interests. Friends remembered that his financial status was more secure now than it had ever been, despite appearing mostly in cameos recently. He was still making his full salary, and in 1966–67, he earned well over $350,000.

By the end of the year, Ryan's Hollywood career was revived, although his comeback had been in pictures which demanded little creativity in two very familiar categories, Westerns and war films. In John Sturges' *Hour of the Gun*, he was cast in a walk-through cameo as Ike Clanton, the murderous gunman and cattle rustler from the O.K. Corral days. It was a situation similar to what had happened in *The Professionals*, in that his part was greatly underwritten compared to those of costars James Garner and Jason Robards.

Having finished *Hour of the Gun* in Mexico, Ryan's next two films sent him to Europe again, with a vacation included. Tim Ryan was in California at Pomona College, Cheyney was a student at Harvard University, while Lisa was out of school for the summer of 1967 and could accompany her parents overseas.

At the same time that he signed to appear in *A Minute to Pray, A Second to Die* and *Anzio*, Ryan set his goals as an actor on a different course. Although he had successfully made a comeback in movies, he felt very ambivalent about being offered the same kinds of roles year after year.

After a five-year recuperation from what he considered "a total disaster,"[3] *Mr. President*, Ryan acted on an earlier suggestion from friends Paul Rogers and John Neville. On the set of *Billy Budd* in 1962, he and the two Englishmen had debated the idea as to whether American actors could do justice to Shakespeare. In the fall of 1967, Ryan took the opportunity to prove his belief in the strength of the American style of acting.

Ryan contacted Neville, then artistic director of the Nottingham Playhouse in Nottingham, England, and proposed staging O'Neill's *Long Day's Journey into Night* in England. The idea was a natural and logical progression of his identification with the playwright's soul. Ryan knew that the play had never been presented in England with an Irishman playing James Tyrone, and he had been disappointed with the most recent interpretation of the tortured patriarch by Anthony Quayle.

Ryan bore remarkable similarities not only to O'Neill, but to the character of James Tyrone. In the play, Tyrone is an aging, half-debauched actor lamenting his ruined health and his wasted youth. When Ryan took on the Tyrone

"Hour of the Gun" (United Artists), 1967. Ike Clanton (Ryan) draws his gun in final shoot-out with Wyatt Earp.

role, he stepped closer to O'Neill's personality, while seeming to make a symbolic ethnic gesture.

In their book *Interpretations of Life*, authors Will and Ariel Durant wrote about O'Neill in terms which seem applicable to Ryan, stating that O'Neill's undying ancestral identity brought him "poetry, fantasy, and alcohol," and that he "never ceased to be Irish, never learned to bear Anglo-Saxons cheerfully."

Ryan and O'Neill shared other characteristics. In comparing much of Ryan's work with that of O'Neill, the latter whose works the Durants called "autobiographical tragedies of lifelong suffering," the parallels grow. O'Neill had been raised by a hard-working father who had sent him to the best schools, and in his twenties, he had been a seaman on vessels sailing around the world. The Durants wrote, "Those laborious days and mysterious nights toughened his spirit and language, let him see life from the stoker's room or near the top of a mast."

Neville readily accepted Ryan's suggestion of *Long Day's Journey into Night*, but needed time to think about his second choice of *Othello* for the Playhouse's repertory company. He concluded that since Shakespeare had conceived the Othello character as a foreigner, Ryan's American accent would not be a deficit.

Ever since *Coriolanus* and *Antony and Cleopatra*, Ryan had been preparing for his next encounter with Shakespeare. A few years before, he had written an article in the *New York Times* in response to the often debated subject of "proper speech" in acting. Having read theater critic Howard Taubman's recent review of a New York performance of *Dr. Faustus*, Ryan had an immediate reaction.

Taubman had asserted, "One of the hazards of braving Shakespeare is that precious few actors in the United States command the proper speech to encompass the language." A bit defensively, Ryan acknowledged in his article that "the English are not interested in adding any American to their product, although on their stage they willingly accept Irish, Welsh, Scotch, Midland, and Cornish English."

Ryan realized that the few American actors capable of doing the classics possessed what Alistair Cooke termed in *One Man's America*, "middle Atlantic speech." Having wrestled for years with his own Illinois intonation, Ryan concluded with the admission that "If we are to have an American classic theater we will certainly have to move far in from the mythical Middle Atlantic."[4]

The three months Ryan spent in Nottingham went by quickly, as the grueling repertory schedule left little time for anything but acting and sleeping. Matinees were the most taxing, with a half hour between performances of the two massive plays, and Ryan's cold-water flat provided slight respite.

Other than the beautiful, 950-seat Nottingham Playhouse which Ryan loved more than any other theater he had worked in, he found the rest of the city unattractive. Though at the end he had paid most of his $140-a-week salary to his dresser, and had lost 28 pounds, he declared, "I wouldn't have missed it for the world."[5] The experience revitalized his goals, and sent him back to the stage as a second career.

His instincts about the success of *Long Day's Journey into Night* had been correct. "The British had never seen it done the way it should be done, with an American-Irishman playing Tyrone," Ryan said later. Having felt a deep intimacy with the Tyrones, he affirmed, "These are the people I came from, so I understand them."[6]

The critics who came up from London to praise *Long Day's Journey* were not as pleased with *Othello*, although audiences filled the theater nearly every night. One evening, after *Othello* had received six curtain calls, Ryan poured himself a tankard of beer backstage as he wiped the pancake makeup from his face. To an observer standing nearby he explained his reasons for such an extraordinary career move. "There isn't any place in the States where you can do this kind of work," he said. "If I had tried to do this in America," he continued, "it would take eight lawyers, five accountants, and six tax men. This way, all I needed was a work permit." Then, with a wink he added, "I came here for me and me alone."[7]

Just prior to his work in Nottingham, Ryan went on an extended vacation through Europe with Jessica and Lisa. During the trip, he had arranged his two film assignments as both were to be shot in Italy. Neither picture earned significant critical note, although the first, *A Minute to Pray, A Second to Die*, gave him more of a role than he had seen in years. But in *Anzio*, his only film for director Edward Dmytryk in 20 years, he again fell into cameo status as a dispassionate general.

While traveling through Italy, and then Spain, Ryan got the chance to repay a favor to his friend Philip Yordan. Yordan was producing a Western near Madrid, *Custer of the West*, and was trying to cast the movie when Ryan called him up. The picture, lasting just over two and a half hours, was an epic production, and one of the best accounts of the last days of George Custer.

Even so, with a small budget, Yordan had trouble getting the most for his money. When he asked Ryan to play a cameo as a grizzled Irish cavalry sergeant hanged for desertion, he immediately consented and volunteered to do the part for nothing. Yordan recalled that Ryan's agent unsuccessfully advised against it. "Bob could have demanded his full salary," said Yordan. "It was a magnificent gesture, because I had been looking for a minor character actor."

The time Ryan spent in Europe that year was the beginning of the happiest period of his life, some friends believed. "Bob grew tremendously as an actor when he went to Nottingham," said Millard Lampell. "It would have been so easy for him to just go on playing in war films and adventure stories."

When Ryan returned to New York in late 1967, he had a firm belief in the

"A Minute to Pray, a Second to Die" (Cinerama), 1968. Governor Lem Carter (Ryan) and gunman Clay McCord (Alex Cord) defend themselves against marauding bounty hunters.

viability of the classics on the contemporary stage. He still saw himself as a film actor, however, and Lisa Ryan remembered his good spirits on the set of *Custer of the West*. "Dad was so open when he was making a movie, I used to love being with him at those times," she said.

In 1968, Ryan became more involved than ever with political issues. As a critic of American intrusion in Vietnam, he guested on several local talk shows, such as New York's "The Scene." That year he also appeared on the *Johnny Carson Show*, and when he was asked his opinion of Ronald Reagan's bid for the governorship of California, he gave a reply that was ironically prophetic. Turning to the audience, he stated with certainty, "Ronald Reagan should be the governor of California like I should be the president of the United States."

During the hotbed of controversy over Vietnam, Ryan's views crystallized as his sons struggled with the issue themselves. "Cheyney and I talked to Dad a lot about Vietnam and how crazy the whole thing was, and he began to question things even more," Tim Ryan said. Politically, both sons were to the left of their father, but he supported them all the way.

By that time Cheyney had been an active member in Students for a Democratic Society at Harvard, while Tim had registered as a conscientious objector. When Cheyney's SDS activities threatened to get him expelled, Ryan and Jessica advised him not to compromise himself. In 1969, Cheyney was expelled from Harvard for taking part in antiwar demonstrations. Undaunted, he finished his studies at Boston University, and went on to earn a Ph.D. in philosophy.

The changes occurring in Ryan's life that year were part of what Tim Ryan called, a "current-consciousness-raising period." In January 1968, Ryan joined Millard Lampell and other celebrities in a grand Carnegie Hall tribute to folk-hero and musician Woody Guthrie. Lampell had been asked to put together a memorial concert which needed two narrations, so he offered them to Ryan and actor Will Geer.

Carnegie Hall was sold out two hours after tickets went on sale, and people mobbed the streets, trying to get closer to the ticket booths or to grab a scalper. An electric atmosphere surrounded the event, which grew into more than just paying respect to Guthrie. The emotional climate in America in those days was ripe for the spirit of the concert, whose message was built on the theme of peace and equality.

Lampell lined up a group of folk singers and musicians, including Arlo Guthrie, Pete Seeger, Richie Havens, Odetta, Lee Hayes, and Bob Dylan. Dylan's appearance, in particular, struck a note of faith because he had dropped out of the scene two years previously, after a near-fatal motorcycle accident. When he showed up at the concert, alive and well, he revived the symbols of revolution and change he had preached in his music.

On the evening of the concert, Carnegie Hall was filled to capacity as people came together in a spirit of brotherhood. Some likened the event to a minor Woodstock minus the alienation. Closing the generation gap for a night at least, those from the Depression era joined with flower children of the counter-culture and sang folk songs having no age barrier.

"It was a wonderful time for everybody," said Lampell. "Bob was in his glory at the rehearsals, and then at the concert. He loved folk songs and had always admired all of the singers who appeared." The concert was a shoving-off point for singer Judy Collins, and for Bob Dylan's backup band, which everyone called simply, The Band. The group formally adopted the name, and went on to a long and successful recording career.

After the concert, Ryan threw a party for the cast at his Dakota apartment. "Everybody was there, Will Geer, Dylan, Alan Ginsberg, and all of the singers," Lampell said. "I think that was about the happiest I've ever seen Bob. He provided food and drinks, and sat on the floor with his kids around him, singing and listening to the music until two or three in the morning."

Ryan followed the Carnegie Hall engagement with two public appearances, one at the Lincoln Center Broadway for Peace show, the next in

Washington, as a narrator at the reopening of the Ford's Theatre. The building had just been restored to its condition on the night Lincoln was shot, and was going to be the new home of the National Repertory Theatre. Among those who worked on the Washington affair were old friends of Ryan's, John Houseman, Henry Fonda, Fredric March, Helen Hayes, and Harry Belafonte. The singing entourage included Belafonte's male chorus, Carmen de Lavallade, and the United States Marine Band.

John Houseman had been contracted to direct the show, which was to be televised on CBS and attended by the president of the United States. Preparations for the show went fairly smoothly, Houseman reported; however, a few minor incidents overshadowed the project.

During rehearsals, Secret Service and FBI men showed up everywhere, since the affair was to be seen by a distinguished audience. On the night of the show, Ryan, March, Hayes, Odetta, and several cast members were kept waiting in the rain until they were properly identified. Finally, Secretary of the Interior Stewart Udall's memorial dedication to Abraham Lincoln was counterpointed by the nonappearance of the president, and by a shaky speech from an obviously unprepared vice president.

The next day's news brought a strange conclusion to the story when it was learned that Lyndon Johnson had been called away to receive news that the North Vietnamese had just launched the Tet offensive.

As the Tet offensive signalled an increase in the dying overseas, in the States one domestic tragedy followed another, contradicting the efforts of the peace movement. First, Martin Luther King, Jr., then Bobby Kennedy, were felled by assassins, wiping out two more who had fought for a cause. "It was a hard period for Dad when his important political idols were killed," said Tim Ryan.

Shortly thereafter, Ryan gave his full support to Eugene McCarthy's bid for the presidency, believing that the Republican Party's endorsement of Richard Nixon would only mean further embroilment. Ryan liked McCarthy's courage to run unendorsed, and in May, he traveled to the New Hampshire primaries in his behalf.

Next, he attended the Democratic National Convention in Chicago as the alternate delegate from New York, and came face-to-face with the sort of anarchy he had described in his political documentaries. The riots there jogged his awareness considerably, and he understood better his sons' militant stand on issues.

In the summer of 1968, Ryan accepted a role in director Sam Peckinpah's apocalyptic Western, The Wild Bunch, and flew down to Parrass, Mexico, the hell-hole of location shooting. He had not been there since 1955, and never would have missed it. The place was hot and desolate, with little to do but work, eat, and sleep.

Ryan had given little thought to the importance of The Wild Bunch when

"The Wild Bunch" (Warner Bros.–Seven Arts), 1969. Amid bloody carnage, Deke Thornton (Ryan) stands over bodies of Pike Bishop (William Holden) and Dutch Engstrom (Ernest Borgnine).

he had accepted the part. At first glance, it was just another Western to him until he arrived on the set and saw what Warner Bros. were planning. The cast featured a gallery of Western icons, including William Holden, Ernest Borgnine, Edmond O'Brien, Ben Johnson, and Warren Oates.

In supporting roles, Peckinpah chose an equally impressive list of character actors, including Emilio Fernandez, Albert Dekker, Jaime Sanchez, L.Q. Jones, Strother Martin, Dub Taylor, and Rayford Barnes. Fernandez was hired as a standby director for Peckinpah, because of his extensive work as a director of Mexican cinema.

With a $6,000,000 budget, a three-hour-plus running time, and a heavy promotional campaign on the table, producer Phil Feldman bet a large ante on Peckinpah. The gamble paid off, and *The Wild Bunch* became one of the most debated films of the decade.

Owing to its then unsurpassed carnage, early previews of *The Wild Bunch* excited revulsion for some and fascination for others. Director Paul Schrader examined the intense criticism leveled at Peckinpah's seeming glorification of

"The Wild Bunch." In-between scenes on location in Parrass, Mexico.

violence, and concluded it was cathartic and necessary to the story. In *Cinema* magazine, Schrader wrote:

> Peckinpah uses violence the way every dramatist does, to make the plot turn. Then he applies vicarious violence . . . to satiate our appetites. At the final most difficult level, he goes beyond vicariousness to superfluity. Violence can then either become gratuitous or transcend itself.[8]

For his own part, Ryan thought Peckinpah went too far with his choreographed, slow-motion violence, but he saw the new levels of screen aggression as a reflection of modern times. In trying to resolve his moral dilemma concerning the issue, he considered the pro and con viewpoints. One side presumed that films such as *The Wild Bunch* incited violence, while the opposite opinion held that people could find the cinema as a safe release. Ryan found no acceptable middle ground.

Before its final release in the summer of 1969, the picture went through extensive editing and was seen at four different lengths. There was a sad footnote to *The Wild Bunch*: on the night of May 5, 1968, a member of the cast, veteran character actor Albert Dekker, was found suffocated in his Hollywood apartment. His death was believed to be suicide, but was ruled an accident.

13. Stage Satisfactions

Shortly after completing *The Wild Bunch*, Ryan started work on one of his biggest projects, the formation of his own repertory theater company. He had discussed the subject sometime earlier with Henry Fonda, and formally decided to give it a try when he made a sudden financial windfall from an oil-drilling venture.

Fonda was as interested as was Ryan in the idea of reviving some of the better American classics in a repertory setting, but like Ryan, he also abhorred the business side of setting up such an enterprise. A friend, actress Martha Scott, had connections in the theater, and after listening to Ryan and Fonda's proposal, she volunteered a troupe of young actors then studying in New York under director Leo Brady.

Ryan named the company the Plumstead Playhouse, and chose as its first production, Ben Hecht and Charles MacArthur's *The Front Page*. His plan was to dust off plays that went to the heart of America, such as the works of William Saroyan and Thornton Wilder, but which had lain undisturbed for years. This was in response to his failing interest in the contemporary American stage, in which a new order of playwrights was modernizing the medium to appeal to what he thought was the lowest common denominator, nudity and sexuality on stage for its shock value. At the time, Lincoln Center was doing a lot of experimental theater, which Ryan felt was trendy and obscure in value.

Ryan wanted to present a topical piece that would be easy to identify with, and chose *The Front Page* after enduring the recent Democratic Convention in Chicago. Considering the chaotic events occurring there, and its allusions to law, order, the Reds, and the mayor, he saw the play as an appropriate corrosive anecdote on society.

Besides Ryan and Fonda, the Plumstead Playhouse featured several veteran actors also interested in doing legitimate repertory, including John McGiver, John Beal, Estelle Parsons, and Anne Jackson. The Playhouse's initial plan was ambitious, alternating *The Front Page* with *Our Town*. If the concept worked, Ryan talked about doing *J.B.*, *The Time of Your Life*, with Gene Kelly directing, and possibly *Idiot's Delight*, starring Lauren Bacall.

Ryan returned a compliment to his friend Harold J. Kennedy, after the latter contacted him for a part in *The Front Page*. Kennedy had received fine notices for his performances in earlier productions of the play, and was a natural for the role of the hilarious hypochondriac, Bensinger. Ryan immediately promised him the part, but a few days after notifying Martha Scott of the addition of Kennedy, he got a return call from her.

Leo Brady already had the cast set, she told him, and he didn't think Kennedy was right for Bensinger. Ryan told her, "Well, maybe Leo wouldn't think I was right either. Why don't we just forget about it." And he hung up.

Two minutes later, Ryan got a call back from Scott. She had just talked to Brady, who had apologized, saying he had made a mistake. He said he had been thinking of a different Harold Kennedy, and on second thought, this Harold Kennedy would be perfect.

The Plumstead Playhouse's three weeks of rehearsals at the Mineola Playhouse, in Mineola, Long Island, were an annoying experience for Ryan and the other veterans. The problem was in the cast, which mostly consisted of recent graduates from Brady's acting classes at Catholic University. They not only looked too young, but they also behaved unprofessionally throughout rehearsals. Harold Kennedy recalled fearing that Ryan and Fonda were going to walk out when several members of the cast still hadn't learned their lines after four days of rehearsing.

Though Ryan and Fonda were incensed that many in the cast seemed not to take their roles seriously, neither was driven to have a direct confrontation. Kennedy watched the two seethe silently for a time as their anger slowly increased. One interchange between Ryan and another actor, Anthony George, happened during a lively part of the second act. Kennedy recalled: "On came Bob, without a script, delivering each line with machine-gun precision. And each line was a bullet in Hildy Johnson's heart. George, who was playing Hildy, just slumped down breathless on the floor when they finally called 'curtain.'" Even with that, Brady did nothing to correct matters.

Finally, after one of the actors missed his call four times in a row (because he was in the basement watching the World Series), Ryan walked directly to the front of the stage and told Brady, "If that boy is one second late for one more entrance, I am walking out of this play."

Brady gave the young man a brief scolding, he no longer missed his curtain call, but the indifferent atmosphere continued. Ryan still worked hard on the play, but he was furious that he had been forced to confront someone with his irresponsibility.

Due to last-minute changes in the agenda, *Our Town* opened the Plumstead Playhouse's season at the Mineola Playhouse on September 24, 1968. The final product survived the earlier problems and earned excellent reviews. Of Ryan's performance, *New Yorker* theater critic Edith Oliver commented, "There is true Yankee humor and fiber in Robert Ryan's fine editor Webb."

The Plumstead players repeated their success when *The Front Page* began its two-week run on October 5, 1968. Kennedy recalled that the play pleased Ryan immensely, and that he especially liked the performances of John McGiver and Charlie White. "Bob would stand in the wings, howling with laughter as he watched John and Charlie vigorously go through their roles as the pompous mayor and his inept sheriff," Kennedy said.

In the *New York Times* on October 20, 1968, Clive Barnes lauded the play and cast, and noted Ryan's total command of the mercurial newspaper editor, Walter Burns:

> Better still was Robert Ryan as Burns. With a pencil-thin mustache and a manner suggesting that he kept a spittoon in his dressing room, Mr. Ryan very clearly would have virtually run any other paper out of town. I am told that the character Burns was based on once planted an editorial in a rival newspaper. Mr. Ryan looked and behaved as if he could and would be just that.

When the engagement ended, Martha Scott wanted to bring the show to City Center in New York for a special two-week run, but Ryan was firmly against it. The cast discrepancies had tainted his and Fonda's experience. There was a wrap-up party at a local restaurant, and Kennedy remembered Ryan tossing down a clams casino, chasing it with a slug of beer, and saying, "Well, that buried that."

Shortly after the Plumstead venture ended, David Lowe, who owned the Millpond Theatre in Roslyn, Long Island, asked Ryan to star in his production of Saroyan's *The Time of Your Life*. Having seen Ryan in the Mineola production, Lowe knew he was right for the philosophical Irishman part.

When the show opened, the critics called it the best work from Lowe's company in its two years of existence. Local theater reviewer Robert Coleman commended Ryan's spirited portrayal:

> There's a corking performance by Robert Ryan as the Irish, poetic, philosophic, understanding barfly who frequents a waterfront dive, gabbing with its down-at-heel habitués and giving them a hand when he can. Saroyan would like Ryan. He makes the mystic benefactor a human, regular guy. He plays him simply.

A week after *The Front Page* closed, Ryan telephoned Harold Kennedy at the Franconia Hotel, and asked him to come over to the Dakota. When Kennedy arrived, he recalled the silent vastness of Ryan's place, which exuded the privateness he kept well-guarded. "When I got there you would have thought he lived alone," Kennedy said. "There was no trace of Jessica or the children."

Ryan got right to the point. He wanted to stage *The Front Page* in New York City, with Kennedy directing and setting up all the arrangements. Ryan would star in the play, On or Off Broadway, he would do it for free, and he wanted a first-rate, disciplined actor in every part. From the original cast he wanted all new members, except for John McGiver, Charlie White, and Kennedy. At the end of their meeting, Ryan's last words to Kennedy were, "Give me a call in a few days and tell me how we can do it."

Kennedy knew that the idea of reviving a 41-year-old play with a cast of 24 was not the sort of thing investors would leap at. Off Broadway would not work, and Broadway could succeed only if the play had established stars in every part. For that to happen, the cast would have to work for the Equity minimum of $167.50 a week.

Knowing that no agent would listen to a job paying the Equity minimum, Kennedy did the hiring himself. When he approached people, his initial pitch, that Ryan was working for $167.50 a week, became his chief selling factor. The Hildy Johnson part gave Kennedy the most difficulty. He offered it to several people, including Peter Falk, George Segal, and Jason Robards, but for various reasons none of these worked out.

Benjamin was willing to take second billing to Ryan, but wanted no other stars (including his wife, Paul Prentiss) billed above the play's title, so he was out. Falk at first agreed to do Hildy, but a film came up during negotiations. The same problem happened with Jason Robards, who said yes at first, but then accepted a film assignment.

Kennedy was elated when George Segal called him about the part; Segal, however, insisted on top billing above Ryan. "George would have made a great Hildy,"said Kennedy, "but his stipulation was out of the question." The last choice, Bert Convy, was also the best choice, Kennedy said in retrospect. The rest of the cast was made up of familiar faces from the New York show business scene and from Hollywood, including Doro Merande, Peggy Cass, Arnold Stang, Don Porter, James Flavin, Conrad Janis, and Val Avery.

Kennedy had less trouble coming up with the money to back the project. He called on theatrical producer Charles Woodward, who, with Edward Albee and Richard Barr, headed the Theatre 69 organization, which sponsored funding for new playwrights' works. Kennedy came out of the meeting with an agreement for a four-week run at the Ethel Barrymore Theatre, with profits going to Theatre 69's Playwrights Unit.

While Ryan was waiting to begin the play, he flew to England for a quick role as the world-weary Captain Nemo, in *Captain Nemo and the Underwater City*. He didn't particularly like the script, but felt as if he needed something to pad his Equity scale.

Lisa Ryan recalled returning home late one night and hearing her father muttering to himself, "something like 'Oh, Jesus, Captain Nemo and the Underwater City?'" as he went over the script in the kitchen. It was the only time Lisa heard her father voicing displeasure with a role. After the previous year's satisfying work on *The Wild Bunch*, appearing in an inferior version of Jules Verne's dark fantasy may have given him a sinking feeling in his stomach.

The Front Page opened at the Ethel Barrymore on Saturday night, May 10, 1969. In the *New York Times* on Sunday morning, Clive Barnes proclaimed, ". . . It remains one of the funniest and most exciting of all American plays. No other play in my experience so vividly conveys the feel, scent, and most of all the excitement of newspapers. . . ."

Ryan's performance won unanimous critical acclaim. Barnes confirmed, "Robert Ryan, a shaggy bear of a man, gives Walter Burns a determined core of cynicism nonetheless corrosively funny for being so intense," while another reviewer asserted, "Robert Ryan's dazzling characterization of Walter Burns is a standout."

Local theater critic Richard Watts, Jr., summed up the consensus on Ryan's complete immersion in his role: "He is simply immense as the brutally single-minded Walter Burns. The highest compliment I can pay him is that he made me hardly miss Osgood Perkins' memorable creation of the part."

On Monday morning Kennedy got a phone call from Ryan, who was downstairs in the lobby, urgently waiting to see him. When Kennedy opened his door, there stood Ryan with a package wrapped in newspaper with Clive Barnes's review showing. He sat Kennedy down and told him, "I didn't want to tell you this before, but everybody, my agents, my business manager, my press agent, all told me I was crazy to let you direct this play. It was nothing against you personally, but they all thought we needed a big-time director. But I was adamant. Now, of course, they're all on the phone, telling me how right I was, and that they agreed with me all along."

He handed Kennedy the package and said, "Open it."

Kennedy unwrapped it to reveal "one of the most delicate and exquisite figurines I had ever seen. Bob said, 'Max Reinhardt gave it to me on my wedding day, and now I want you to have it.'"[1]

The Front Page had been scheduled for a limited run of four weeks, was extended for four more, and closed in the midst of its momentum. Some theater observers were puzzled by the show's abrupt end, since according to one source, "it never had a losing week, and word of mouth was good."[2] Happily, Off Broadway producer Jay Fuchs saw plenty of life in the play, and took up the banner for its extension.

While Ryan waited for the play's fall resumption, *The Wild Bunch* opened at theaters amid a storm of controversy. *Cue* magazine's William Wolf found "little justification for discussing this ugly, pointless, disgustingly bloody film," while *Newsweek*'s Joseph Morgenstern contended that "several hundred senseless frontier killings don't add up to enlightenment. They only add up to several hundred senseless frontier killings."

Many critics, however, called the picture brilliant. In the *Washington Post*, Gary Arnold declared, "the most fascinating and explosive American movie to come along since *Bonnie and Clyde*," and hailed Peckinpah as "the most talented American director of his generation."

Ryan was elated about the film's success, and despite the deletion of some footage involving him, he was happy with his part. His reputation with the critics had always carried plenty of weight through thick and thin, but the durability of 66 pictures had spread to more serious acclaim.

In *An Anthology by the National Society of Film Critics*, Penelope Gilliatt discussed Ryan's role in *The Wild Bunch* from the perspective of his unrecognized artistry:

> Better even than William Holden and Ernest Borgnine, *The Wild Bunch* has Robert Ryan, one of the very best actors of his generation in America, and someone who would have been playing the big classical parts for years in most other countries.

Gilliatt noted ironically that Ryan's best scenes in *The Wild Bunch* involved actor Albert Dekker, whose career as a dependable character actor bore similarities to Ryan's: "The exchanges between Ryan and Dekker are written with again ten times more perception than the dialogue in most of the studiously high-class movies made here."

As the sixties drew to a close, Ryan had gone through several personal and professional crises, and had survived intact. He felt more in control of his life than ever, and declined television and film offers when he extended his stay in *The Front Page* until January 1970.

When the play reopened in October 1969, it had undergone eight cast changes. The newcomers, however, only added to its vitality. Replacing Julia Meade, Helen Hayes enlarged upon a small role which she had seen countless times since the late 1920s, when her late husband, Charles MacArthur, cowrote *The Front Page* with Ben Hecht.

The only outburst of anger during the life of the play occurred between Ryan and Hayes, in an argument having to do with the star's dressing room. Hayes maintained that Ryan was the star of the play, and that he should have the star's dressing room. Ryan disagreed, saying that he was not about to take a ground-floor dressing room, while the first lady of the stage climbed the stairs. Their discussion turned into a heated exchange before Harold Kennedy solved the problem. A set of drapes was strung to divide the disputed room in half, and both stars then used it.

In its last extension, the show again received excellent reviews. Clive Barnes reiterated in the *New York Times*: "The present performance, happily and authentically staged by Harold J. Kennedy, is beautiful. Robert Ryan as the rascally Walter Burns goes from strength to strength. He is marvelous. . . ."

Harold Kennedy had the best of memories of his association with Ryan, and referred to him as "the spark plug of *The Front Page*. Bob got to deliver one of the most famous curtain lines in the American theater, which was, 'The son of a bitch stole my watch.'"

Helen Hayes agreed that he was the best choice ever for Walter Burns, and when he left the play in January 1970, the cast threw a farewell party for him in the basement of the Ethel Barrymore Theatre. From the ceiling hung a huge banner signed by everyone, which stated simply, "Robert Ryan—the son of a bitch stole our hearts."

Throughout the run of *The Front Page*, each night afterwards, Ryan and Kennedy retreated to the Gaiety Delicatessen to have a few drinks and to unwind from the excitement of the evening. The ritual was always the same, Ryan had two Lowenbraüs, Kennedy drank two scotches.

The two drinks they shared together represented a special time to Kennedy, but Ryan sometimes worried that Kennedy might be bored by the plain, low-key setting. The Gaiety was a far cry from the nearby theatrical haunts which Kennedy frequented. On the contrary, Kennedy recalled, "I enjoyed the quiet, intimate relaxation of those two drinks every night enormously." He also noted that Ryan never once asked anyone else in the cast to join them.

When Kennedy talked about Ryan, he had tremendous respect for the trust that had grown between them. But when he referred to the clear boundaries separating Ryan's professional and personal lives, his tone had a tinge of regret. He knew he had only been allowed into a small part of the life of the "most private person I have ever known."[3]

After *The Front Page* had run its course in New York, there was life for it elsewhere. Martha Scott arranged a television special of the play, telecast in early 1970, with George Grizzard as Hildy Johnson, and Estelle Parsons as Mollie Molloy. Several critics thought the interplay between Ryan and Grizzard came close to the spirit intended by Hecht and MacArthur. Next, Ryan and Kennedy had hopes of doing the play live in Hollywood that year, but life intervened before it came to pass.

The tremendous success of *The Wild Bunch* signalled a renewed interest in the Western in Hollywood, and encouraged Ryan to take another role in the genre. A new, young British director, Michael Winner, who was about to start filming *Lawman*, starring Burt Lancaster and Lee J. Cobb, contacted Ryan for an interesting character study as a weary, weak-willed marshal.

When Winner came to New York to talk to him about the part, Ryan was at first taken aback. At his front door appeared a fair-haired Englishman with shoulder-length locks, ready to challenge an American institution. Ryan soon learned that Winner had his ideas clearly in mind, and that the technical skills he had learned from doing British television transferred well to the motion picture medium.

In addition, the literate screenplay was laconically written, and the cast boasted many superb character actors, including Joseph Wiseman, Robert Duvall, Sheree North, Albert Salmi, J.D. Cannon, John McGiver, Ralph Waite, and Robert Emhardt. Since many of these had appeared in scores of Westerns collectively, *Lawman* became a celluloid tintype of the Old West.

Ryan flew to Durango, Mexico, for the shooting. Since his last time there in 1955, the place hadn't changed much, but it was a cut above Parrass. During production, Ryan was impressed by Winner's direct, sure way of filming, and admired his radical approach.

Most directors used a technique involving a series of master shots with all of the actors, and then moving to medium shots and close-ups. Winner liked the method often used by John Ford, called cutting with the camera, which maintained a sense of continuity in the scenes. It also left little room for error.

Though for the most part Winner's instinctive flair brought a visually realistic sense to *Lawman*, his habit of using the fast zoom to convey urgency bothered some critics. That one technical blunder aside, however, Winner, who also produced the picture, came up with an anti–Western of inspired thinking.

In the *New York Times*, Howard Thompson wrote, "the picture is long on sting, as sharply directed by England's Michael Winner and cynically turned by the writer, Gerald Wilson,"[4] while *Playboy* noted, "Robert Ryan, Burt Lancaster, and Lee J. Cobb project magnitudes of star power."[5]

Despite fine reviews, though, *Lawman* came to theaters and left relatively quickly, perhaps due to its grim conclusion. Audiences still responded best to films which ended optimistically. Movie critic Leonard Maltin reflected, "an intriguing thought-Western ... [whose] unsatisfactory resolution mars an otherwise compelling story," but declared, "Ryan gives one of his finest performances as a timid sheriff."

Overseas, Ryan's portrayal gained wide attention on the heels of his superb turn two years previously in *The Wild Bunch*. Lisa Ryan was in Paris in the summer of 1971 when *Lawman* was playing at a theater on the Champs-Elysées. She happened to pass by the theater one day, and was surprised by what she saw: A long line of patrons waited impatiently for admission, and buzzed excitedly among themselves as if they were about to witness a major event.

The occasion was a Robert Ryan Film Festival, at which many of his by then classic dramatic studies were being showcased. In *Cahiers du Cinéma*, critics had reserved a special category for him since the fifties, while in London, cinema enthusiasts had recently reprised several of his pictures.

Ryan's modest appraisal of his work was meeting with enough evidence to the contrary that he began to take himself and his movies less for granted. Arvin Brown had become acquainted with Ryan at that time, and remembered his change in attitude.

"Bob was aware of the recent European acclaim, but it was a revelation for him to see that people in the profession were taking him *very* seriously as an actor," said Brown.

"It meant a lot to Bob because he never looked at his movies as worth anything. He was like many other professionals who came into films at about

"Lawman" (United Artists), 1971. "Bought and paid for" Marshal Cotton Ryan (Ryan) delivers recent information to Vince Bronson (Lee J. Cobb).

the same time, like Mitchum or Lancaster," Brown continued, "guys who were dedicated to their craft without really understanding how important what they did was.

"In Bob's mind, it was only his stage acting that gave him an entitlement in any way to be taken seriously as an actor. But the films were catching up to him, and people were seeing more and more what a damn fine actor he was, and how difficult it was to do what he did." Brown concluded, "Everyone around him appreciated his movies long before he did."

After completing *Lawman*, Ryan and Jessica went up to their home in New Hampshire for a much needed vacation. Ryan had liked the state since his Dartmouth days, and had traveled there several times since moving East. In the late sixties, he had a pleasant, A-frame house built on the side of a mountain.

During the summer of 1970, Ryan received news which made his newly found recognition ironic. The fatigue and weakness he had attributed to the location work in Durango continued even after a period of rest at his mountain home. One morning while cooking breakfast, he burned his foot with hot grease from a pan, and went to a local hospital for treatment.

During the doctor's routine questions, Ryan disclosed his recent lassitude, and as a safeguard, X-rays were taken. When the doctors told him the results, he was stunned: he had lymphosarcoma, cancer of the lymph glands, and it was inoperable.

Ryan immediately began a draining four-month regime of cobalt treatments, knowing that his prognosis was only 50-50. After the first shock came the reconciliation. He had several things to think about having to do with mortality. The current cancer theory at that time talked of arresting a malignancy, not curing it, and physicians grasped for an arbitrary stay of the inevitable by giving Ryan a five-year postponement in which to do what he had to do.

The answer to one of Ryan's questions to doctors, about giving up smoking, might have given him further cause for alarm. He had been a heavy smoker all his life, but was told that at that stage of his illness, "It won't make much difference, so go ahead."

Years earlier, he had tried unsuccessfully to quit for three months, and then he switched from nonfiltered to filtered to low tar cigarettes, but eventually he crept back to his usual quota.

"It caught up with Bob, just like it did Duke Wayne and Tony Mann," said Philip Yordan. He related how the three men used to come to work fortified with enough cigarettes to see them through any situation. A heavy smoker himself, Yordan declared with conviction, "Cigarettes killed all three of them."

When the debilitating chemotherapy ended in late 1970, the creases had deepened and the leanness became thinness. Other than going out of circulation for several months, Ryan kept his illness a private affair. He phoned Harold Kennedy to cancel plans to do *The Front Page* live in Los Angeles, but made no mention of his illness.

In varying terms, he talked about his feelings to a few friends. To Millard Lampell, he "accepted it with a kind of stoic courage, a sort of, 'What will happen, will happen.' He figured he had five years to live."

Robert Wallsten knew about Ryan's illness only through phone conversations, because shortly after Ryan began his treatments, Wallsten went through his own personal trial: his wife, Cynthia, was diagnosed with cancer, and underwent chemotherapy. The next time Wallsten saw Ryan at a party at Albert Hackett's house, no mention was made of illness, although the tone of their warm greetings to each other carried a tinge of consolation.

14. Long Day's Journey

When Ryan went back to work in early 1971, he was anxious. He knew that the word "cancer" carried a stigma, and that studios were always wary of any illness that might delay a film's progress. Before hiring him for a part in his first film post-diagnosis in the embarrassing *The Love Machine*, Columbia Pictures dispatched people to verify his state of health. He informed them that "nobody with lymph cancer ever drops dead in the middle of a movie."[1] (At that time, author Jacqueline Susann, on whose novel *The Love Machine* was based, was undergoing treatment for cancer. She died in 1978.)

After completing the film, Ryan talked with Jessica about his displeasure with it. In light of his ominous pathology, he felt that he had compromised his standards, and that every minute was crucial. When X-rays indicated the malignancy had been arrested, he and Jessica felt that he had been given a reprieve in which to do something special.

He decided to go back to the stage, and chose O'Neill's *Long Day's Journey into Night*, to be presented in New York. At that point in his life, the choice of O'Neill's familial tragedy made it a moot question as to whether art was imitating life or vice-versa.

A friend suggested Arvin Brown to Ryan as a possible director, based on his earlier production of *Long Day's Journey*, with Frank Langella and Mildred Dunnock. In addition, Brown had worked successfully on another Irish play, *The Whistle in the Dark*, by Tom Murphy, and seemed to have the experience and the sensitivity to the Irish temperament that Ryan wanted.

When Brown and Ryan met for the first time, Brown felt the "intense shyness" Ryan presented to people, and he recalled being intimidated by it. Moving past his own self-doubts about working with an actor of Ryan's stature, the two men quickly became close friends.

Brown tried to explain why he was able to gain access to Ryan's normally difficult to reach inner self. "I think that Bob's own proximity to death allowed him to express an emotional vulnerability he hadn't ever found that easy to talk about. But on the other hand, it became harder and harder for him to acknowledge a physical vulnerability.

"He had a great sense of modesty about his skills as an actor," Brown noted, "but one of his last remaining vanities was his physical strength. Bob was an extremely strong man, and proud of the fact that he had done a lot of his own stunts in his films.

"Bob also had a tremendous sense of himself as a survivor, and he talked about all of his past problems as things he had, in fact, survived." Brown speculated, "I think it was heartbreaking for him to discover that, to a certain extent, I had to plan rehearsals around him." Brown added that he had worked with many actors in the theater who had much less energy than Ryan, but that "compared to what he was used to in himself, it was a hard adjustment to reality."

Most of Brown's perceptions about Ryan's struggle with his illness came through inference, and despite the closeness that developed between them, Ryan never discussed his fears directly. "It was always in the air, but it was never really talked about," said Brown.

Through conversations with Jessica, though, Brown learned to what extent Ryan was affected. "It never occurred to Bob that he would be seriously ill, and he was hit harder by it in certain ways than Jessica ever expected. He was very needy of her from the time he became ill to the time we started working together."

During preparations for *Long Day's Journey*, Ryan gradually regained his strength, and played a part in selecting the rest of the cast. The first choice for Mary Tyrone was Kim Stanley, at that time having her own share of personal difficulties. Knowing that her interview needed to be done delicately, Ryan volunteered. "Bob felt that he could talk to her as someone who had been where she was at the moment," said Brown. "He said he would level with her, and find out what she felt about herself emotionally, and whether she could undertake the rigors of the part and the play." The meeting never came to pass, since after missing several appointments, Stanley backed away.

The final choice for Mary Tyrone, Geraldine Fitzgerald, became a powerful enough force in the play's exposition to shift the balance slightly from James Tyrone to Mary. At first, Ryan was intimidated by the Mary Tyrone interpretation as planned by Brown and Fitzgerald because it differed from the controlled version he had seen in England in 1967.

Brown called Fitzgerald's style "a strong, earth-connected approach which was a little too big for Bob at the beginning. Geraldine took chances with the role that made him nervous." Ryan had difficulty adjusting his sense of Mary Tyrone to accommodate Fitzgerald's "instinctual, spontaneous technique," said Brown. "Bob came from a school in which he planned things and rehearsed until he felt absolutely comfortable with what he was doing."

By tuning into Brown's idea of the dynamics between James and Mary, Ryan grew as an actor. He learned that the economy necessary for film acting needed a degree of extravagance to work best on the stage. In comparing this *Long Day's Journey* with the 1967 English version, he felt that the British didn't truly understand the Tyrones. He told one person that the Tyrones were "a 'Jewish' family—they say terrible things to one another, but it isn't meant the way people might take it."[2]

Ryan also got more in touch with how strongly his background related to O'Neill's characters. During conversations with Brown, Ryan brought back stories from childhood, such as his grandfather telling him about the "No-Irish-need-apply" signs, which marked immigrants' entry into the United States. Such connections helped him to comprehend the Tyrones' miserliness and insecurity.

Under director Brown's watchful eye, Long Day's Journey speedily went through rehearsals, and opened at the Promenade Theatre on April 21, 1971, to outstanding reviews. In the New York Times on April 23, Clive Barnes offered his perceptions:

> It is remarkable how well we get to know this family...we see not only people at that moment in time, but also the past that made these people. ...Arvin Brown's staging is scrupulously accurate and manages to get the feel of a family essential to the play.
> The actors talk to one another as if they had been talking for years—they interrupt one another, they shout over one another, and when they listen, they listen with ears seemingly attuned to past voices. The room is full of ghosts of past conversations, threats, and promises.

Of Ryan's James Tyrone, Barnes accurately noted:

> "It is a great part, and Robert Ryan moves into it with care, love and understanding. He shows us the character, little by little, and finally creates a picture of a man, neither good nor bad, but understandable. None of the other characters is perhaps quite so complex...."

In the New York Times on May 2, Walter Kerr reflected on the stoic honesty that Ryan invested in Tyrone:

> Mr. Ryan seems to have been waiting, through three lingering and vaguely shaped acts, for just this midnight postmortem on four aborted lives, for a time of reckoning that will solve nothing but say everything.... The portrait, in its all-of-a-piece complexity, is beautifully composed, and Mr. Ryan explores the mea culpa in which no forgiveness is asked with admirable, leather-tough control.

The four-month run of Long Day's Journey may have been a cathartic experience for Ryan. Though he felt he understood the Tyrones' emotionalism, the family's open display of anger had been a dynamic foreign to his own past. In his upbringing and even now, anger had been an emotion he kept under control, thus Lamont Johnson's allusion to his "fizzing anger" gains relevance.

In letting loose and baring his soul on stage in a situation resembling issues in his own life, Ryan may have come closer to a few realizations about himself.

Arvin Brown related that Ryan had provided the main impetus in setting up the production, and in suggesting Geraldine Fitzgerald for the Mary Tyrone part. He recognized that her ability to suggest barely controlled hysteria was an essential trait for the interpretation of Mary. Having become emotionally invested in the play, Ryan's involvement took on paternalistic qualities, which he expressed in different ways to Brown and to actors Stacy Keach and James Naughton (James, Jr. and Edmund Tyrone).

Toward Brown, Ryan behaved almost like a surrogate father, due partly to differences in age (30 years) and experience, but also because Ryan felt pride in having chosen Brown to direct the play. The play's critical success was a large stepping-stone in furthering Brown's career.

But Brown recalled that despite Ryan's gestures toward assertiveness, it remained difficult for him to express his feelings, expecially complimentary ones, toward those he cared about. Ryan had worked closely with James Naughton to help the young actor grapple with his part as Edmund, but he was reticent in complimenting Naughton's progress.

After Ryan observed Naughton in rehearsals one day, he took Brown aside and whispered, "The kid's getting pretty damn good, but I don't want to tell him because he might get a swelled head. Keep this between you and me." Brown believed that "Bob's almost painful shyness may have caused him difficulties with those he loved."

Following the success of *Long Day's Journey into Night*, Ryan enjoyed several months of what some friends felt was the most relaxed period in his life. In August 1971, he and Jessica vacationed at their home in New Hampshire, and invited Arvin Brown and his wife, Joyce, to stay with them.

"After his illness, New Hampshire represented a great retreat for Bob and the family," Brown reminisced. "It was wonderful to see them all being open with each other, and not kind of edgy." He noted ironically that the calm he noticed may have been due to Ryan's cancer diagnosis. "I think it changed him a lot, and made him less covered to other people and less demanding.

"One of the things I loved about Bob was his lack of vanity about his emotional trials in the past. He was more than willing to talk about his bouts with drinking, and that he had been through hard times," Brown said. Though it never became a confessional situation between the two men, Ryan made reference to bleak periods of despair when he drove around for hours at a time, "not knowing where he was," Brown confirmed.

The degree of closeness that grew between Brown and Ryan happened much faster than it had with most of his friends who went back much further in the past. He may have felt more comfortable relating to Brown because there was no history to talk about, and only the future to consider.

15. The Loss of Jessica

Publicly, Ryan seemed not only to have arrested his illness, but to have mentally risen past the supreme crisis that threatened him. As if to convince others and perhaps himself that he was coping with his feelings, he gave stock answers to inquiring people. There were signs, however, of his acceptance of his mortality.

He told one person, "Look, I've had a good shot at life. In the first place, I'm not a kid, so what the hell do I have to complain about?" He also spoke of "having a different feeling about life, of seeing trees and flowers and pretty girls." Fatalistically, he added, "life is much better enjoying it day to day."[1]

As a metaphor, the title and content of Ryan's next film, 20th Century–Fox's *And Hope to Die*, seemed to contradict the notion that he was getting well. Directed by René Clément in and around Montreal, Canada, the film placed Ryan in a familiar mold again, as a gang boss involved in a caper doomed from the start. Working with Clément, he added another European cinema notable to his repertory, while providing an intriguing contrast in style to that of costar Jean-Louis Trintignant (in his first English speaking role).

The producers took Ryan for granted during filming, and asked him to do his own stunt work in some physically demanding scenes. Though he was annoyed by their presumption, he agreed, as if to prove he had really conquered his disease.

Just as Ryan appeared to have gotten a second wind in his life, the harbinger of death made a whimsical turn and handed its message to Jessica. In May 1972, she suddenly became ill and was diagnosed with terminal cancer of the liver. The only choice left was whether she would die in the hospital or at home. She chose the latter.

The shock of the news totally stunned the family, and events from then on became cloudy for everybody as they tried to grasp for a reason. Ryan set about preparations for the end, which came quickly. Harold Kennedy bumped into him at a newsstand where Ryan was buying every magazine on the rack. In a few words, he informed Kennedy that Jessica was sick but that it was "nothing serious." Ten days after her diagnosis, Jessica died on May 22, at the age of 57.

Jessica approached her demise in a final conscious act of caring for her family. She knew how fulfilling Ryan's stage work had been, and she urged him to continue on that path. She wanted him to pursue a plan they had talked over before, of working again with Arvin Brown, who had recently become the director of the Longwharf Theatre, in New Haven, Connecticut.

"Jessica didn't want Bob to go back to the Hollywood scene, and she was afraid he would take anything, just to be working," said Brown. "She wanted him to follow through in himself as a serious actor. Bob broke down when he told me that.

"The heroic thing about Jessica's death is that it was such a conscious thing on her part. She had a private meeting with each member of the family in which she confronted head-on that she was dying."

There was a simple Quaker memorial service afterward, in which everybody held hands in silence for a few minutes. "It was a very touching ceremony, and all of us felt very close together. Then Tim and Cheyney sang a song in memory of Jessica," Millard Lampell said. Her ashes were mulched into the ground around a pear tree on the New Jersey farm owned by Lampell and his second wife, Ramona.

Ryan made no attempt to conceal his grief over the loss of Jessica, and often stayed at Lampell's place, just over the bridge from New Hope, Pennsylvania. "Bob went into a really black funk, and started drinking again," said Lampell. Having made an effort to avoid hard liquor since the fifties by substituting beer, he fell off the wagon and returned to scotch.

He drew close to Arvin Brown and his wife, Joyce, after Jessica's death, and confided some of his regrets about things he hadn't done for her. "Bob blamed himself for having put her through lots of tough times. I got the sense that his marriage had its problems and traumas, but that it was a strong, devoted marriage," said Brown.

Unable to tolerate the memories of life at the Dakota, Ryan moved across the street to another large and equally lonely apartment. Lisa Ryan was living nearby, and spent a lot of time at her father's place as they helped each other through their mourning period and became closer than before.

"Dad and I used to sit around and tie one on, and it broke down some of his barriers of shyness," Lisa related. "I think Mother's death loosened him up a little bit."

After a few months of idleness in which his thoughts gave him no peace, Ryan geared himself for one more round. Shortly before Jessica's death, he had passed up a role in MGM's *Lolly Madonna XXX* because they had been planning a European vacation. The part was still open, so he flew down to Knoxville, Tennessee, for the filming.

On location, director Richard Sarafian nicknamed him "One-take Ryan," and thought he was a "fabulous" actor. "When Bob came into the picture, he was great with the young actors (Jeff Bridges, Scott Wilson, Gary Busey, Ed

Lauter, and Kiel Martin), and they were ready to adopt him as a father," said Sarafian.[2]

Ryan's appearance in *Lolly Madonna XXX* had a lack of energy which some critics noticed. Jeffrey Lyons wrote, "Ryan looks far older here, and is more subdued than in his last film."[3] Indeed, the strain of Jessica's death had left him shattered, and his serious bouts with alcohol further ravaged his weakened condition.

Albert Hackett recalled seeing him around that time, and that he was "puffy in the face and didn't look well. I used to meet him passing in Central Park, and he always gave the impression of being very robust, but after Jessica died, all that ended."

On his next trip to Hollywood, Ryan stayed at Philip Dunne's house, and lamented about his loss and all of the things he had wanted to do with Jessica. "What the hell did I make all that money for?" he asked Dunne.

Ryan had only one goal at that point, to provide for his family. "All of a sudden, Bob realized that he had these two very large apartments to pay for, and despite his accumulated wealth, he felt he needed to replenish his coffers," said Arvin Brown.

His next film, however, had nothing to do with money and was a labor of love. (Ryan's salary for *The Iceman Cometh* was $25,000, as were the salaries of costars Lee Marvin and Fredric March.) John Frankenheimer was about to direct the film version of O'Neill's *The Iceman Cometh*, and was casting for the picture with executive producers Henry Weinstein and Edward Lewis. "Henry asked me who I would like to have for the Larry Slade part, and I decided that Robert Ryan would be perfect," said Frankenheimer.

"Bob had a deep sadness inherent in most of O'Neill's characters, he had the depth, and he was a fabulous actor," declared Frankenheimer. "Also, he looked to me just like Larry Slade should look."

Frankenheimer believed that one of Ryan's great strengths was that he was "in touch with his inner self such as very few people are," and that he was a "terribly honest actor. There was never any subterfuge in anything that Bob did."

It was appropriate that Ryan should work on his last released film with a director of Frankenheimer's temperament and artistic caliber. Since Frankenheimer's early triumphs with *Birdman of Alcatraz* and *The Manchurian Candidate* in 1962, his work has often dealt with intense themes, especially in *The Train* (1964), *Seconds* (1966), and *The Gypsy Moths* (1969). Over the years, he has proven his nerve as a director by delving into existential themes, while delivering highly crafted and consistently entertaining pictures, notably *The French Connection II* (1975), *Black Sunday* (1977), and *52 Pick-up* (1986).

By the time the three weeks of rehearsals for *The Iceman Cometh* began in January 1973, Ryan had regained most of his mental fortitude. When he arrived on the set, he gave no indication of being sick, and plunged into the

"And Hope to Die" (20th Century-Fox), 1972. Charley Ellis (Ryan) threatens
Froggy (Jean-Louis Trintignant) before the climactic scene.

production with energy that belied his condition. He told Frankenheimer that
he "had the cancer licked, but he couldn't get over the irony that Jessica had
died before him."

"As before, Bob was always on time, he knew his lines cold, and he was
there even on days when he wasn't working." Frankenheimer reported that the
large cast, headed by Lee Marvin and Fredric March, and Jeff Bridges, Bradford Dillman, Moses Gunn, Sorrell Booke, John McLiam, and George
Voskovec, was totally committed to making the project perfect.

Frankenheimer had recently returned from Europe where he had lived for
a period of time, and had brought back a custom he had seen practiced by
European production companies. On Fridays after shooting was completed,
he brought out a huge spread of food and drink to share with the cast and
crew.

Frankenheimer's wife, Evans, who also appeared in *The Iceman Cometh*
as Cora, recalled that everyone developed a togetherness unlike the climate on most movie sets, and that it became like an "extended family experience."

Ryan was ecstatic about *Iceman* because it was being shot in sequence,
which was almost unheard of in films, but which Frankenheimer stipulated to
the producers before he accepted the assignment. Evans Frankenheimer
reported that the cast members had all been attracted to working on the

picture because most had been stage actors at some point in their careers. "Since the whole cast was there almost all the time, and most of us appeared in every scene, the feeling was exactly like being in a play," she said.

Evans recalled how her and John's friendship with Ryan went further than the camaraderie that had begun on the set. One night while she and John were relaxing at home in Malibu, there was a knock at their door, and Evans answered it to find Ryan standing there, looking a little forlorn. Away from the familiarity of the set, conversation still flowed easily between Ryan and the Frankenheimers. The visits became more frequent until Ryan asked to stay at their house on weekends.

Curiously, though the Frankenheimers had a need for privacy which was as strong as was Ryan's, their friendship had an intangible pleasure precluding that need. As if to underscore the trust and respect that existed between her husband and Ryan, Evans commented, "John doesn't open up to everybody."

Ryan and Frankenheimer had several things in common, in their backgrounds as well as in their personalities. "They were both very professional, and very masculine," Evans said. "They were also both raised as Catholics and John is half Irish, so they had a lot to talk about."

"One of the things I liked most about Robert was his sense of humor," Evans recalled. "Even when he was portraying a villain, he often came across as having a sense of humor." She said that she thought his version of Larry Slade was "absolutely incredible," because having seen the play a few times before, her old sense of Larry had been that he was "very unattractive" as a character.

Prior to seeing Ryan's interpretation of Slade, Evans had watched other actors attempt without success to suggest the passion which had existed between Slade and Parritt's mother. Though Ryan had visibly aged, he retained a presence that brought his character to life the way O'Neill probably would have wanted it played, Evans speculated. "Robert was still such a handsome man even in the ruined state he was playing, that he gave it another dimension which was wonderful," she said.

Though Frankenheimer had carefully selected a high quality cast, most of the performers were in the less visible category of veteran character actors. Thus, there was an unspoken deference to the three main stars, Ryan, Fredric March, and Lee Marvin.

Frankenheimer said that two of Ryan's assets, his gentleness and his patience, were of great importance in working with members of the cast. Most of Jeff Bridges' one-to-one dialogue involved Ryan, and at age 23 then, Bridges was understandably anxious. Frankenheimer believed that Ryan helped Bridges to the extent that "Parritt was one of the best things Jeff has ever done."

Ryan also helped Lee Marvin a great deal, since at that time, Marvin was

"The Iceman Cometh" (American Film Theatre), 1973. A drawn and weary Larry Slade, flanked by tarts Pearl and Margie, philosophizes about the pipedreams of men.

going through a personal crisis. Moreover, Marvin's tough-guy image tended to intimidate others, and Ryan instinctively knew how to reach him.

"Lee had tremendous respect for Bob, and the two of them worked very well together," Frankenheimer recollected. "I think that Bob gave Lee a lot of confidence, and Lee knew that when he was in a scene with Bob, everything was going to be okay. Bob kept telling him how good he was in the part of Hickey."

In the past, Marvin's bouts with alcohol had sometimes followed him during filming. Evans Frankenheimer observed that Marvin seemed very conscious of Ryan's presence, and of wanting to be totally together on the set.

Ryan had his hero to worship as well, in Fredric March, and talked excitedly with friends about working with him. Several times during filming he phoned Arvin Brown and "in typical Bob Ryan fashion, he was more delighted with Freddy March than he was with himself."

"The Iceman Cometh." In a scene at Last Chance Saloon, owned by reclusive Harry Hope (Fredric March, at left), Larry Slade (Ryan) and Harry trade philosophies concerning the pipedreams of men.

Lamont Johnson sat and talked with Ryan on the set of *The Iceman Cometh*, and recalled that he was "euphoric about the film." Years earlier, they had discussed doing the play with the Theatre Group at UCLA, but "it wasn't to be," Johnson said. Then, with relief he added, "Thank God he did it on film."

Ryan gave Johnson some indication that he was aware of the significance of his doing *The Iceman Cometh*, and he touched on the subject of death. Johnson recalled, "With his good gallows kind of humor, Bob remarked, 'You know, I've played so much O'Neill, from *The Hairy Ape* to *Anna Christie*, it's funny that I wind up playing in *Iceman* just as the Iceman is staring me in the face.' Then he said, 'I almost believed the old wives' tale that if you are a good boy, you'll get what you want for Christmas, and Santa Claus will be kind to you.'"

After the 35 days of shooting, Ryan saw the final cut and "absolutely loved it," John Frankenheimer said. "Of all the films he had done, Bob was proudest of *Iceman*."

But Ryan never made it to *The Iceman Cometh*'s national release and astonishing critical acclaim. In *Newsweek* on November 12, 1973, Paul Zimmerman wrote:

John Frankenheimer realizes perfectly the objectives of this experiment in subscription cinema and filmed theater. It is a great movie of a great play, rich in the kind of profound, multi-level performances that movies rarely have time to develop, intimate yet majestic in a way that is special to film. . . .

Robert Ryan, his face a wreck of smashed dreams, provides a tragic dimension that makes this *Iceman* a moving, unforgettable experience.

In her book *Reeling*, Pauline Kael wrote down her considerable thoughts on Ryan's long, torturous road in preparation for the apotheosis of his career and life:

Robert Ryan brings so much understanding to Larry's weakness that the play achieves new dimensions. In the most difficult role he ever played on the screen Ryan is superb. He becomes O'Neill for us, I think. George Jean Nathan said that O'Neill carefully selected photographs of himself that were to be published, and always "made sure they were not lacking in that impressive look of tragic handsomeness which was his. . . ."

Ryan has that tragic handsomeness here and O'Neill's broken-man jowls, too, and at the end, when Larry is permanently "iced" – stripped of illusion – we can see that this is the author's fantasy of himself: he alone is above the illusions that the others fall back on; he is tragic, while the others, with their restored illusions, have become comic. . . .

Ryan brought to this role the craft that he had perfected, which he certainly knew he might never be able to exercise to its fullest again. The man who had tested himself against such uncompromisingly difficult roles on the stage as Coriolanus and the father in *Long Day's Journey into Night*, and on the screen as the depraved Claggart of *Billy Budd*, got a chance to show his stature, and he was ready. He is so subtle he seems to have penetrated to the mystery of O'Neill's gaunt grandeur – to the artist's egotism and that Catholic Cassandra's pride in tragedy which goes along with the fond pity for the foolish clowns lapping up their booze.

After *The Iceman Cometh*, Ryan made two more films, perhaps as an afterthought or as a last minute reprieve.

16. Final Days

A ray of relief glimmered through the pall of depression and loneliness overshadowing Jessica's death and Ryan's indefinite future. In late 1972, he attended a dinner party in New York at which actress Maureen O'Sullivan was one of the guests, and shortly afterward, they were being seen everywhere.

Robert Wallsten speculated that the formula for their chemistry consisted of a few uncomplicated elements and one important one. "Maureen was wonderful for Robert because she was warm, sensible, Irish, and she understood his dark moods and how to cope with them."

Their relationship grew from companionship to something more and Ryan seemed to gain a second wind. "Maureen fell madly in love with Robert, and I think they were going to be married," said Albert Hackett, "but Robert wanted to wait a respectable period of time after Jessica died before getting married."

Other friends, however, felt that Ryan's future was too indefinite for marriage, and that he was living for the moment. Philip Dunne ventured to say that Ryan was putting on a brave front, and that deep down his heart was rent beyond repair. "I think Robert lost the will to live when Jessica died," said Dunne.

Yet it is difficult to know for certain what he was thinking since he gave conflicting impressions of his state of affairs. Recently, he had been asked by the Max Reinhardt Archives in New York to write a short tribute to the late director's genius. The six-paragraph paper Ryan submitted expressed in emotional terms the creative energy he had learned over 30 years earlier, but its tone was weighted with a hint of mortal self-awareness that appeared to be in its final chapter.

In the piece he referred several times to the words "life" and "spirit," while reflecting thoughts about Reinhardt's artistry that alluded to himself. His last two paragraphs might have been applied to his own soon-to-arrive eulogy:

> Reinhardt's own obsession was the inner life of man, the mysterious spirit that both flickers and flames in all of us. How to release and reveal it was his artistic dedication and the creative purpose of his life. Two people sitting in a hovel

served his purpose as well and often better than a giant stage jammed with battalions of actors and Everests of scenery.

I last saw him 30 years ago, just before his death, and I have noted ever since the efforts of conscientious but pedestrian artisans to reshape theater into "contemporary" forms. If he were alive he could well instruct them. But I can only hope that they are ploughing through a dull morass that will finally lead them back to the life, joyous, vital and profound that I first saw in those years and have never seen since.

After *The Iceman Cometh*, Ryan worked on two more movies and one television special. In MGM's *The Outfit*, he reprised one final time the morose criminal type he had played so well. The picture might also have been a relic for many in the cast, whose inclusion seemed to reflect an adamant MGM wish to enter the film as a last dying entry in the *film noir* genre.

The large number of supporting players, culled from gangster movies of the forties and fifties, and combined with the appearances of several sports figures in bit parts, bears mentioning: Timothy Carey, Richard Jaeckel, Marie Windsor, Jane Greer, Henry Jones, Elisha Cook, Jr., Roy Roberts, Emile Meyer; and Archie Moore, Roland LaStarza, Tony Traebert, Phil Kenneally, and Carl Eller.

Curiously, on the last day's shooting for *The Outfit*, a party was held in Ryan's honor, and the mayor's office presented him with an award of appreciation for his contributions to the arts. In retrospect, a cynical observer might have commented that the affair mimmicked a low-budget Oscar ceremony celebrated too late for Ryan to enjoy its significance.

Film critic Charles Champlin of the *Los Angeles Times* was present at the party and observed Ryan's withheld manner toward the proceedings: "Ryan arrived late for the party in his honor and stood unobtrusively at its edges for quite a while, taking in the scene—the vivid, ambitious ladies and the circling men—with what seemed an amused, affectionate detachment."

In response to Ryan's self-effacing comment that most of his pictures were "dogs," Champlin wrote in the *Times*, "It would at that be hard to think of another major American actor who had so often lent dignity and the sureness of great craft to inferior material," and that he was "so consistently and unassertively good that it was too easy to take him for granted."

After *The Outfit*, Ryan appeared as a defense attorney in the acclaimed television movie *The Man Without a Country*, directed by Delbert Mann, opposite Cliff Robertson, Beau Bridges, Peter Strauss, and Sheppard Strudwick. As one of Ryan's last films, *The Man Without a Country* attracted him due to its story, which served as an allegory for granting amnesty to men who rejected the Vietnam War. In the *New York Times*, reviewer John O'Connor wrote, "It emerges with a significance for today that may not have been anticipated," and in the *Washington Post*, critic John Carmody declared, "It is good to see old pros like Ryan helping to move the story along."

Before making what was to be his last film, Ryan returned to New York, and spent an enjoyable period visiting friends and being with Maureen O'Sullivan. At a dinner party at Albert Hackett's place, he seemed happy and did a song and dance for people. "Robert was in a joyous mood," said Hackett. "It looked like he was getting ready for the big moment when the year was up, and he and Maureen would be married."

In May, Ryan's doctors assured him that his malignancy was still in remission, and that he could safely sign on to do the upcoming Broadway musical version of the 1965 film *Shenandoah*. Next, it was off to Hollywood again, after producer Edward H. Lewis hired Ryan to star in the political thriller *Executive Action*.

The offer to appear in *Executive Action* came at a timely moment to deflect Ryan away from his own circumstances. He became intensely interested in its premise at a time when he had all but ceased active involvement in social-minded issues.

Initially, Ryan was skeptical about *Executive Action*, but after reading Dalton Trumbo's script and material he used in its creation, he was convinced that the Kennedy assassination had not been a one-man operation.

The film was shrouded in secrecy and surrounded by controversy at a time when political cabal was rocking the United States, and traditional institutions were being challenged. The Watergate scandal had just made headlines, thus *Executive Action*'s bold assertion, that the assassination of John F. Kennedy was a conspiracy mounted by wealthy American industrialists, had the reality of past malfeasance to back it up.

Having been in a minority as a spokesman for unpopular causes, in *Executive Action* Ryan shared company with people having convictions similar to his own. When producer Lewis approached director David Miller to work on the film and gave him Trumbo's script to read, Miller immediately signed on. Ryan, Lewis, and Miller all believed the picture was socially significant because the official investigation of the Kennedy assassination had been hurriedly concluded at the order of Lyndon Johnson.

From then on, the cast and crew worked together toward completing it as an artistic team. As *Executive Action*'s producer, Lewis took no fee, and the creative artists worked for the Equity minimum scale. This allowed much of the economical budget to be used to give the film the finest production values money could buy.

Heading the cast with Ryan were Burt Lancaster and Will Geer, and Dalton Trumbo's screenplay, adapted from a story by Donald Freed and Mark Lane, resulted in a chilling indictment of the elite minions who govern affairs from the sanctity of suburban estates.

Trumbo and Geer had a legitimate axe to grind in working on a film which stirred up suspicion toward right-wing factions, having both been blacklisted. Their involvement on *Executive Action* was symbolic retribution, and was

"Executive Action" (National General), 1973. Co-conspirators in the John F. Kennedy assassination, Foster (Ryan) and Harrington (Burt Lancaster) stand by prior to scenes in a railroad car.

validated by facts reported by Freed and Lane in their book about the Kennedy assassination.

The two most important points the authors dealt with concerned who actually assassinated Kennedy and whether there was a conspiracy behind it. In researching their best-selling book on which the film was based, Freed and Lane relied on information contained in the Warren Commission Report.

Ryan and Geer had first become friends in 1954, after John Houseman ignored Hollywood executives who warned him not to hire Geer to play in *Coriolanus*. Houseman employed Geer during a time when he had been out of work for three years. Throughout the rest of the fifties, Geer remained unemployed in Hollywoood.

In 1960, Ryan and Geer worked together on *Antony and Cleopatra*, but it wasn't until 1962 that Geer returned to Hollywood. After that, he alternated his film work with a minstrel-like existence, taking to the road in a converted bus and traveling around the country. He developed a one-man show, staging Shakespeare, Walt Whitman, and other types of theater.

Working on *Executive Action*, Ryan seemed to have absorbed some of Geer's nomadic spirit, and he became excited about the idea of going on a trip around the country. His sense of wanting to travel also arose from working in one of the props in *Executive Action*, which was a well-heeled caboose equipped with a pool table.

When Ryan stayed at John and Evans Frankenheimer's home in Malibu during filming of *Executive Action*, they discussed renting a caboose in which they would all take a rambling vacation, up through the Smoky Mountains into West Virginia. The Frankenheimers began to make plans for the near future, but time ran out.

In a matter of a few weeks from completion of *Executive Action* to the time when the Frankenheimers saw Ryan in New York, he had gone from looking "marvelous" to "very sick," said Evans. It was the end of June.

David Miller was shocked when he learned that Ryan had taken a turn for the worse, because on the set of *Executive Action*, he had demonstrated a tremendous amount of energy. "Bob came in early every day during filming, and he always checked with me before he left for the day," said Miller, and called Ryan a "marvelous actor."

"Bob and Burt Lancaster were very close, which made their performances more natural," recalled Miller. Before Ryan returned to New York after completing shooting, he said to Miller, "Not only do we respect each other now, but we've become good friends."

On July 3, Ryan entered New York Hospital shortly after complaining about a back pain that wouldn't go away. While he lay there, Maureen O'Sullivan was at his bedside almost constantly to comfort him. Cheyney was the first to be notified that his father had gone into the hospital again, and came down from Boston to see what could be done.

As is the wont of the medical profession, Ryan's doctors were typically noncommittal about the true state of affairs, stubbornly holding out on their prognosis, as if it were their ace-in-the-hole. Tests had been conducted to determine whether the cancer had spread, and Cheyney had been told that it would be a few days before the results would return to confirm or deny.

At that time, everybody was going along as if things would get better, including Ryan, but there was a slight awkwardness in the doctors' attitudes that gave Cheyney pause. Hope was still the main thought in everybody's consciousness, though, and Cheyney related that he and his father stayed clear of talking about specifics.

Toward the end of the week, the inevitable worst conclusion came back from the doctors, who told Cheyney and Maureen O'Sullivan that the cancer had returned and had spread to Ryan's lungs. Before making a decision as to whether or not to continue the fight with further chemotherapy, Cheyney phoned Tim in Los Angeles and Lisa in Newport, Rhode Island. Time became telescoped as they packed a hurried bag and came home.

By that time, Ryan had tubes running into his nostrils to help him breathe, and he was a gaunt figure perilously submitting to the invasion. On the afternoon of July 11, he had a breathing attack, but help was nearby and he came through it after a rapid series of emergency measures.

Cheyney, Lisa, and Maureen, all saw Ryan that day, and considering his extreme condition, they were torn with the conflict of holding back what the doctors had reported. Late in the afternoon, when Maureen came back to Ryan's apartment, in tears and anxious about the care he was getting in light of the crisis that day, she asked Cheyney to alert the hospital staff.

That evening, Tim got in from Los Angeles and all three children discussed the grave question confronting them of how and when to tell their father that the end was close by. They considered further treatment, but Ryan's life at that point was bordering on indignity and prolonging it by chemical means approached an insult. He had arrived at his ultimate existential dilemma.

While the children grappled with feelings that tore at them, Ryan's crisis happened suddenly and impersonally. Sometime in the late evening, he suffered a hemorrhage of the lungs which backed up into his throat, cutting off his breathing. At that hour of the night in the silent corridors of the hospital, help was too far away and came too late. In an agonized denouement as lonely as in any of his films, Ryan choked to death near midnight.

Tim Ryan took the telephone call from the hospital.

Ryan's children were the least prepared of anyone for his death, partly because he gave no sign that he was ill, partly because his condition was overshadowed by Jessica's death. Millard and Ramona Lampell took care of final arrangements, a simple, very private memorial service, and a small Irish wake afterward at the Dakota. Among those in attendance were the Lampells, Evans Frankenheimer, Joyce Brown, the Albert Hacketts, Dore Schary, and Jason Robards.

Though Ryan had not been a practicing Catholic in years, one final irony slipped into the picture when a relative from Chicago who was a monsignor, came forth to conduct the service at the Blessed Sacrament Church on July 17. It seems that the priest, advanced in years and steadfastly adhering to the old school of clergymen who still conducted their rituals in Latin, became confused during the service and began to stumble until the affair finally approached parody.

Later on, Evans Frankenheimer recalled someone commenting that Ryan, with his "gallows sense of humor, would probably have laughed his head off watching the poor man's embarrassment."

Millard and Ramona Lampell brought Ryan's ashes to their New Jersey farm, and sprinkled them into the ground under the pear tree to mingle with those of Jessica.

Part II
Creative Output

Chronological Filmography
with Selected Criticism

Each film is rated on a scale of one (poor) to five (excellent), based on a consensus of film reviewers and the author's analysis of each film. Some pictures have increased in interest over the years because of their style and or content, or if viewed within the context of an "auteur." A few warrant consideration based on Ryan's performance or on the quality of the cast. The rating appears in parentheses following the title.

The College Widow (1927). Warner Bros. *Director* Archie L. Mayo. *Cast* Delores Costello, William Collier, Jr.

Ryan was an extra.

Strong Boy (1929). Fox Film Corp. *Director* John Ford. *Cast* Victor McLaglen, Leatrice Joy.

Ryan played a baggage man.

Golden Gloves (2) (1940). Paramount, 69 min. *Director* Edward Dmytryk. *Associate Producer* William C. Thomas. *Story* Maxwell Shane. *Screenplay* Maxwell Shane, Lewis R. Foster. *Art Directors* Hans Dreier, William Flannery. *Music Director* Sigmund Krumgold. *Camera* Henry Sharp. *Editor* Doane Harrison. *Cast* Richard Denning (Bill Crane), Jeanne Cagney (Mary Parker), J. Carrol Naish (Joe Taggarty), Robert Paige (Wally Matson), William Frawley (Emory Balzer), **Robert Ryan** (Pete Wells), James Seay (Jimmy), Sidney Miller (Sammy Sachs), Johnny Morris (Jerry Kolker), Frank Coghlan, Jr. (Kid Lester), Alec Craig (McDonald), John Gallaudet (Folger), Abner Biberman (Torsovitch), Byron Foulger (Hemingway), James Millican (Bob).

Ryan played one of the young boxers.

Queen of the Mob (2) (1940). Para-mount, 61 min. *Director* James Hogan. *Based on the book* Persons in Hiding *by J. Edgar Hoover. Screenplay* Horace McCoy, William R. Lipman. *Art Directors* Hans Dreier, Ernst Fegte. *Camera* Theodor Sparkuhl. *Editor* Arthur Schmidt. *Cast* Ralph Bellamy (Scott Langham), Jack Carson (Ross Waring), Blanche Yurka (Ma Webster), Richard Denning (Charles Webster), James Seay (Eddie Webster), Paul Kelly (Tom Webster), William Henry (Bert Webster), Jeanne Cagney (Ethel Webster), J. Carrol Naish (George Frost), Hedda Hopper (Mrs. Emily Sturgis), Pierre Watkin (Stitch Torey), Billy Gilbert (Caterer), John Harmon (Pinky), John Miljan (Pan), Russell Hicks (Judge), William Duncan (D.A.), Raymond Hatton (Auto Camp Proprietor), Neil Hamilton (Murdock), **Robert Ryan** (Jim), Lloyd Corrigan (Photographer), James Flavin (F.B.I. Chief), Paul Fix, Brooks Benedict (Men).

Ryan played a young staff worker.

Ghost Breakers (1940). Paramount, 82 min. *Director* George Marshall. *Cast* Bob Hope, Paulette Goddard, Richard Carlson, Paul Lukas, Anthony Quinn, Willie Best, Paul Fix, Lloyd Corrigan, Virginia Brissac, James Flavin, **Robert Ryan.**

Ryan and James Flavin played extras.

179

Northwest Mounted Police (2) (1940). Paramount, C-125 min. *Producer* Cecil B. DeMille. *Associate Producer* William H. Pine. *Director* Cecil B. DeMille. *Based on the book* Royal Canadian Mounted Police *by* R.C. Fetherston-Haugh. *Screenplay* Alan LeMay, Jesse Lasky, Jr., C. Gardner Sullivan. *Art Directors* Hans Dreier, Roland Anderson. *Set Decorators* Dan Sayre Groesbeck, Joe De Yong. *Assistant Director* Arthur Rosson. *Costumes* Natalie Visart, Joe De Yong. *Makeup* Wally Westmore. *Dialogue Supervisor* Edwin Maxwell. *Technicolor Consultants* Natalie Kalmus, Henri Jaffa. *Technical Advisors* Major G.F. Griffin, R.C.M.P., Sergeant George A. Pringle, N.W.M.P. *Music* Victor Young. *Sound* Harry M. Lindgren, John Cope. *Special Effects* Gordon Jennings, Farciot Edouart. *Camera* Victor Milner, W. Howard Greene. *Editor* Anne Bauchens. *Cast* Gary Cooper (Dusty Rivers), Madeleine Carroll (April Logan), Paulette Goddard (Louvette Corbeau), Preston Foster (Sergeant Jim Brett), Robert Preston (Constable Ronnie Logan), George Bancroft (Jacques Corbeau), Lynn Overman (Tod Croft), Akim Tamiroff (Dan Duroc), Walter Hampden (Chief Big Bear), Lon Chaney, Jr. (Shorty), Montagu Love (Inspector Cabot), Francis McDonald (Louis Riel), George E. Stone (Johnny Pelang), Regis Toomey (Constable Moore), Richard Denning (Constable Thornton), **Robert Ryan** (Constable Dumont).

Ryan played a mounted policeman.

Texas Rangers Ride Again (2) (1941). Paramount, 68 min. *Director* James Hogan. *Screenplay* William R. Lipman, Horace McCoy. *Camera* Archie Stout. *Editor* Arthur Schmidt. *Cast* Ellen Drew (Ellen "Slats" Dangerfield), John Howard (Jim Kingston), Akim Tamiroff (Mio Pio), May Robson (Cecilia Dangerfield), Broderick Crawford (Mase Townesly), Charles Grapewin (Ben Caldwalder), John Miljan (Carter Dangerfield), William Duncan (Captain Inglis), Anthony Quinn (Joe

Yuma), Harvey Stephens (Blair), Eva Puig (Maria), Harold Goodwin (Comstock), Eddie Foy, Jr. (Mandelin), Joseph Crehan (Johnson), Monte Blue (Slide Along), Tom Tyler (Gilpin), Charles Lane (Train Passenger), **Robert Ryan** (Eddie — boy in car).

Bombardier (2) (1943). RKO, 99 min. *Director* Richard Wallace. *Producer* Robert Fellows. *Story* John Twist, Martin Rackin. *Screenplay* John Twist. *Music Director* Constantin Bakaleinikoff. *Music* Roy Webb. *Songs* M.K. Jerome and Jack Scholl. *Art Directors* Albert D'Agostino, Al Herman. *Set Decorators* Darrell Silvera, Claude Carpenter. *Assistant Director* Edward Killy. *Montage* Douglas Travers. *Sound* Bailey Fesler, James G. Stewart. *Special Effects* Vernon L. Walker. *Camera* Nicholas Musuraca. *Editor* Robert Wise. *Cast* Pat O'Brien (Major Chick Davis), Randolph Scott (Captain Buck Oliver), Anne Shirley (Burt Hughes), Eddie Albert (Tom Hughes), Walter Reed (Jim Carter), **Robert Ryan** (Joe Connors), Barton MacLane (Sergeant Dixon), Richard Martin (Chito Rafferty), Russell Wade (Paul Harris), James Newill (Captain Rand), Bruce Edwards (Lieutenant Ellis), John Miljan (Chaplain Craig), Harold Landon (Pete Jordan), Margie Stewart (Mamie), Leonard Strong (Japanese Officer), Abner Biberman (Japanese Sergeant), Neil Hamilton (Colonel), Kirby Grant (Pilot), Hugh Beaumont (Soldier).

Ryan's career at RKO was signaled without fanfare in *Bombardier*, a standard WW II exploitation film which chronicled, semi-documentary style, and with considerable fictitious rhetoric, the development of the modern bombsight. Major Davis (Pat O'Brien) was the low-key man whose invention became the film's focus, and the story was embellished in typical Hollywood style, making it a showcase of numerous war stereotypes.

Besides O'Brien's good-guy stereotype, Randolph Scott costarred as Captain Oliver, in a competition which appeared to be a proof of bravery. Director Wallace could tell a story, and when he stuck to the facts he did a good job; when he exaggerated, he did it with a theatrical vengeance, possibly aided by *Bombardier*'s screenplay, which forced nearly the entire cast to verify their heroism.

The mundane plot concerns a friendly feud between Davis and Oliver about the merits of dive-bombing from fighter planes versus high-altitude bombing from bombers. Interspersed with training footage of the Army's bombardier school, RKO's script employed usual character types (Ryan played an unwilling recruit).

Joining Ryan, Eddie Albert, Barton MacLane, and Walter Reed portrayed gung-ho trainees eagerly awaiting a combat opportunity. In the stateside scenes, the recruits beamed with gleeful abandon in mock bombing runs; however, in the war sequences, their carefree confrontation with death seemed dated.

Ryan was sixth-billed as the initially recalcitrant Airman Joe Connors, who early on in the film proves his loyalty by entrapping an espionage agent, but whose enthusiasm goes down in flames when his airplane is shot down by the enemy. The final shot of Connors is an interesting martyr image to compare with Ryan's early portrayals. When Connors' B-17 takes a direct hit and the crew bails out, he stops for a moment to fire his pistol into his bombsights, to prevent the enemy from retrieving anything. As he takes aim, an anti-aircraft shell explodes outside his turret, mortally wounding him with shards of shrapnel. In a last dramatic gesture, Connors fires several rounds into the bombsights, and slumps lifelessly atop them as the plane crashes in an intense explosion.

Reviews: "*Bombardier* is a salute to the Norden bombsight ... and its generally muscular tone compares favorably with that of such weak, routine productions as *Aerial Gunner*. But it must compete with no less beautiful flying sequences in at least a half-dozen other U.S. films, and

compared with the British minor masterpiece, *Target for Tonight*, most flying films before and since seem superfluous." (*Time*, 6/21/43.)

The Sky's the Limit (2) (1943). RKO, 89 min. *Director* Edward H. Griffith. *Producer* David Hempstead. *Associate Producer* Sherman Todd. *Based on the story* A Handful of Heaven *by* Frank Fenton, Lynn Root. *Screenplay* Frank Fenton, Lynn Root. *Songs* Johnny Mercer, Harold Arlen. *Choreography-Stager* Fred Astaire. *Music Director* Leigh Harline. *Art Directors* Albert S. D'Agostino, Carroll Clark. *Set Decorators* Darrell Silvera, Claude Carpenter. *Assistant Director* Ruby Rosenberg. *Sound* Terry Kellum, James Stewart. *Special Effects* Vernon L. Walker. *Camera* Russell Metty. *Editor* Roland Gross. *Cast* Fred Astaire (Fred Atwell), Joan Leslie (Joan Manion), Robert Benchley (Phil Harriman), **Robert Ryan** (Reg Fenton), Elizabeth Patterson (Mrs. Fisher), Marjorie Gateson (Canteen Hostess), Richard Davies (Lieutenant Dick Merlin), Clarence Kolb (Harvey Sloan), Freddie Slack and his Orchestra (Colonial Club Orchestra), Eric Blore (Jackson), Amelita Ward (San Francisco Girl), Neil Hamilton (Naval Commander), Peter Lawford (USAF Officer).

Ryan's second RKO role began to explore his potential for aggression, since he was cast as Fred Astaire's slightly obnoxious Air Force buddy. *The Sky's the Limit* differed from Astaire's usually pleasant musical comedies, because his character was a flyer troubled by WW II who goes on a soul-searching fling with Joan Leslie.

The picture was an interesting vehicle for Astaire, since his dance numbers involved the breaking of champagne glasses as part of his choreography. As Astaire's best friend, Reg Fenton, Ryan stepped into the role with the type of forward behavior which Ginger Rogers must have noticed and disliked when she previewed his performance prior to casting *Tender Comrade* with David Hempstead. (See biography.)

In one scene, Ryan threatens to expose Astaire's true identity to Leslie, unless Astaire performs a dance on a restaurant table. As Astaire hops to his bidding, Ryan pounds the table in mock anger, almost as if he were in a cowboy movie. *The Sky's the Limit* is a curiosity piece for Ryan and Astaire enthusiasts.

Reviews: "Fred Astaire is a Flying Tiger, home from the war and being much made over. . . . Trying to keep his identity hidden and achieve the lady of his heart keeps him leaping over the plot like fury . . . the settings are much too elaborate for plain working people, but the music, the gaiety, the wonderful blues dance performed by Fred in a bar, give the film a lift and a dash that put it over." (*Photoplay,* 7/13/43.)

Behind the Rising Sun (3) (1943). RKO, 89 min. *Director* Edward Dmytryk. *Based on the book by* James R. Young. *Screenplay* Emmet Lavery. *Assistant Director* Ruby Rosenberg. *Art Directors* Albert S. D'Agostino, Al Herman. *Set Decorators* Darrell Silvera, Claude Carpenter. *Music* Roy Webb. *Music Director* Constantin Bakaleinikoff. *Sound* Terry Kellum, James G. Stewart. *Special Effects* Vernon L. Walker. *Camera* Russell Metty. *Editor* Joseph Noriega. *Cast* Margo (Tama), Tom Neal (Taro), J. Carrol Naish (Publisher), **Robert Ryan** (Lefty), Gloria Holden (Sara), Don Douglas (O'Hara), George Givot (Boris), Adeline Reynolds (Grandmother), Leonard Strong (Tama's Father), Iris Wong (Secretary), Wolfgang Zilzer (Max), Shirley Lew (Servant), Benson Fong, Philip Ahn, Richard Loo, William Yip (Japanese Officers), Mike Mazurki (Japanese Wrestler), H.T. Tsiang (Policeman), Nancy Gates (Sister), Abner Biberman (Inspector).

Working on *Behind the Rising Sun* gave Ryan a better chance to demonstrate his boxing skills than did *Golden Gloves*, and to again work with Edward Dmytryk. In *Behind the Rising Sun*, the pugilistic prowess which Ryan intimated in *Golden Gloves* got a rousing ten-minute reprise.

Behind the Rising Sun dealt with the ethical issues of World War II, told from two perspectives, American and Japanese, and the film's bicultural narrative set it apart from other war pictures. Although the picture was doubtless conceived to stimulate patriotic fervor, its story was based on actual incidents reported from the Orient before the war.

Since many films of the war era sensationalized their stories to the point of hysterical propaganda, *Behind the Rising Sun* barely avoided entrapment because of the caliber of its cast. The main characters, Tom Neal, J. Carrol Naish, and Margo, poignantly reflected the film's conscience, while Dmytryk elicited performances from the Japanese characters which achieved an ominous tension, avoiding parody.

As the American athlete, Lefty, Ryan attracted favorable critical notice, and though in a supporting role, he was involved in some of the film's best scenes. Since he performed his own stunt work in the exciting fight sequence with a huge Japanese judo wrestler (Mike Mazurki), the scene became intensely realistic.

Most critics lauded Ryan's athletic agility, but one writer condemned the fight scene. In *Commonweal* magazine, Philip Hartung stated, "It is the most brutal and needlessly long exhibition I have ever seen in films." Ryan's final scene in *Behind the Rising Sun*, being tortured and then crucified by demon-like Japanese captors, succeeded as a penetrating religious symbolism. It was also an interesting progression of his beginnings as a tragic screen presence.

Reviews: "The actors have done well with the material. . . the minor characters have all come to life, and among them, Robert Ryan, as the taciturn but tough boxer, gives a plausible, accurate performance." (Otis L. Guernsey, *New York Herald-Tribune,* 10/14/43.)

"The boxer versus jiu-jitsu expert symbolizes the U.S.-Japanese War. . . .

Their boxer-wrestler battle is as savage as anything in the history of screen roughhouse." (*Time*, 8/9/43.)

"A gripping, fascinating story that clutches the imagination and interest and holds on until the final reel . . . the entire cast, including Robert Ryan (brilliant in the fight scene) is splendid." (*Photoplay*, 10/43.)

Gangway for Tomorrow (3) (1943), RKO, 69 min. *Producer-Director* John H. Auer. *Story* Aladar Laszlo, Arch Obeler. *Screenplay* Arch Obeler. *Music* Roy Webb. *Music Director* Constantin Bakaleinikoff. *Art Directors* Albert S. D'Agostino, Al Herman. *Set Decorators* Darrell Silvera, William Stevens. *Assistant Director* Lloyd Richards. *Sound* Terry Kellum, James G. Stewart. *Special Effects* Vernon L. Walker. *Camera* Nicholas Musuraca. *Editor* George Crone. *Cast* Margo (Lisette), John Carradine (Wellington), **Robert Ryan** (Joe Dunham), Amelita Ward (Mary Jones), William Terry (Bob Nolan), Harry Davenport (Fred Taylor), James Bell (Burke), Charles Arnt (Jim Benson), Alan Carney (Swallow), Wally Brown (Sam), Erford Gage (Dan Barton), Richard Ryen (Colonel Mueller), Warren Hymer (Pete).

Gangway for Tomorrow offered Ryan a quiet performance in a compact little film lasting a mere 69 minutes. Yet the quality of its story and direction warranted a better fate than dismissal to the lower half of a double bill at an RKO theater. Producer/Director John H. Auer had been educated in Vienna and had done a number of low-budget features for Republic Pictures, after having first worked in Mexico as a producer. To *Gangway for Tomorrow* he brought a European texture that mixed well with the film's rougher spirited American counterpart.

In the war film category, *Gangway for Tomorrow* contained the same patriotic messages as did other films of the period; however, Arch Obeler's screenplay kept the melodramatics at a minimum while telling five poignant vignettes. The story

begins as five defense workers ride to work one morning with a plant executive (Charles Arnt) who subtly intimates that they have chosen the easy way to fulfill their duty.

As the three men and two women recall the circumstances that have brought them together, their stories are as fascinating as they are disparate. Ryan's character, Joe Dunham, again depicted him in the mold of the patriotic, ruddy-faced male of that period. Just prior to enlistment in the Army Air Corps, Dunham, a race car driver, wants to make his mark by winning the Indianapolis 500. Although in the lead for most of the race, in the final laps Dunham is severely injured in a crash, and loses his chance to fight for democracy. As he lies in a hospital bed, swathed in bandages, he tells his recently enlisted friends, "You guys fly 'em, I'll build 'em."

Of the five tales, Ryan's was one of the most idealistic in its heroic aspects, while the other stories were more concerned with the pain of war. James Bell's former prison warden best suggested the anxiety of the times, while Margo's French Resistance fighter stressed courage and nationalistic pride. John Carradine and Amelita Ward effected sympathetic portraits as a redeemed hobo and a faded starlet, respectively.

Besides Nicholas Musuraca's somber, expressionistic photography and realistic sets from Darrell Silvera, director Auer also used *montage* to compress the action and to unite the individual sequences. Of the films that Ryan appeared in before Jean Renoir's *The Woman on the Beach* (1947), *Gangway for Tomorrow* seemed to most reflect a conscious artistic expression of a director.

Reviews: "The screen as a medium for useful propaganda is well illustrated by *Gangway for Tomorrow*. . . . Turning in the best performances are Margo . . . John Carradine . . . and Robert Ryan." (Frank Quinn, *New York Daily Mirror*, 12/16/43.)

"An unpretentious little film, running

just 69 minutes, *Gangway* is nevertheless fresh and bright in treatment and provides an interesting story of five factory workers. . . . The members of the cast, in particular, Margo and Robert Ryan, handle their assignments well." (*Brooklyn Daily Eagle*, 12/16/43.)

The Iron Major (3) (1943). RKO, 85 min. *Director* Ray Enright. *Producer* Robert Fellows. *Based on the story by* Florence S. Cavanaugh. *Screenplay* Aben Kandel, Warren Duff. *Art Directors* Albert S. D'Agostino, Carroll Clarke. *Set Decorators* Darrell Silvera, Al Fields. *Technical Advisors* William Joy, Ernest E. La-Blanche. *Music* Roy Webb. *Music Director* Constantin Bakaleinikoff. *Assistant Director* Edward Killy. *Sound* Terry Kellum, James G. Stewart. *Camera* Robert de Grasse. *Editors* Robert Wise, Philip Martin, Jr. *Cast* Pat O'Brien (Frank Cavanaugh), Ruth Warrick (Florence Cavanaugh), **Robert Ryan** (Father Tim Donovan), Leon Ames (Robert Stewart), Russell Wade (Private Manning), Bruce Edwards (Lieutenant Jones), Richard Martin (Dave Cavanaugh), Robert Bice (Coach), Virginia Brissac (Mrs. Ayres), Lew Harvey (Lieutenant), Bud Geary (Sergeant), Walter Brooke (Lieutenant Stone), Louis Jean Heydt (Recruiting Sergeant), Frank Puglia (Nurse), Victor Kilian (Francis Cavanaugh), Ian Wolfe (Professor Runnymead).

Ryan's role as Father Tim Donovan in *The Iron Major* was in line with the wholesome image for which RKO was grooming him, and also related strongly to his background. In his second film with Pat O'Brien, God, country, and family were the patriotic messages, told in the biography of World War I hero and legendary football coach Frank Cavanaugh.

Although *The Iron Major* focussed on Cavanaugh's struggles as a driven workhorse, in an effort to relate to World War II, its screenplay also depicted his war record and injuries. The tight screenplay plus sincere direction from Ray Enright resulted in an above-average biography.

Ryan's Father Donovan had more than enough strength to support O'Brien's characterization of the dynamic coach who brought victory to several Ivy League colleges, including Dartmouth and Fordham.

Reviews: "A typical Pat O'Brien role just about sums up this life story of Major Frank Cavanaugh . . . Robert Ryan, as Father Donovan, is outstanding." (*Photoplay*, 10/25/43.)

Tender Comrade (3) (1943). RKO, 101 min. *Director* Edward Dmytryk. *Producer* David Hempstead. *Associate Producer* Sherman Todd. *Story-Screenplay* Dalton Trumbo. *Art Directors* Albert S. D'Agostino, Carroll Clark. *Set Decorators* Darrell Silvera, Al Fields. *Music Director* Constantin Bakaleinikoff. *Music* Leigh Harline. *Sound* Roy Meadows. *Special Effects* Vernon L. Walker. *Camera* Russell Metty. *Editor* Roland Gross. *Cast* Ginger Rogers (Jo), **Robert Ryan** (Chris), Ruth Hussey (Barbara), Patricia Collinge (Helen Stacey), Mady Christian (Manya), Kim Hunter (Doris), Jane Darwell (Mrs. Henderson), Mary Forbes (Jo's Mother), Richard Martin (Mike), Richard Gaines (Waldo Pierson).

Ryan's first romantic lead opposite one of Hollywood's most glamorous stars, Ginger Rogers, was also his first exposure to the ideological controversies stirred up by the House Committee on Un–American Activities, despite some accusations that *Tender Comrade* was pablum.

Tender Comrade was the second collaboration between Rogers and screenwriter Dalton Trumbo, whose work on the 1940 film *Kitty Foyle*, had won an Oscar for Rogers and healthy profits for RKO. With success in their corner, Rogers and Trumbo approached the studio with an average wartime potboiler. Four years later, however, both the picture and Trumbo were brought up for intense congressional scrutiny.

The story of *Tender Comrade* dealt with the trials and tribulations of Rogers, who, as a defense plant worker, weds a young soldier (Ryan) who is killed in action shortly afterward. When Ryan's Chris marches off to war, Rogers' feisty Jo meets the challenge by setting up a cooperative living situation with three other women. While rallying for the cause, Jo discovers she is pregnant, and the story shifts from melodrama to message.

From such innocuous circumstances, a case was built against Trumbo, especially after Rogers' mother, Lela, viewed the film. A staunch flag waver, Lela called Trumbo's screenplay subversive, and leveled numerous criticisms toward the script which bordered on the ridiculous. A few examples of Trumbo's "propaganda": In one scene, Rogers declares angrily to one of her housemates, "You sound like a Fifth Communist"; in another sequence, after Jo and her three housemates (Hussey, Collinge, and Hunter) "accept" their newly hired cleaning woman even though she is German, she gains their trust by a symbolic pledge of allegiance: "Once, in Germany, we had a democracy, but we let it be murdered."

When the House Committee on Un-American Activities gathered steam in 1947, Lela Rogers was among the first to take the stand, citing *Tender Comrade* as a film in which her daughter had been given dialogue espousing a Communist ideology. Her testimony led to Trumbo's eventual blacklisting.

Although *Tender Comrade* hardly warrants attention as propaganda, its direction by Edward Dmytryk and better than average production values elevated it to the level of an interesting curiosity piece. It is also worth a look to see Ryan playing a romantic figure back in his beginnings as an RKO hopeful. His earnest portrait of a handsome young man in love, who heroically goes off to war and is killed, could have steered him toward a career predominated by dashing, romantic types. As fate or luck-of-the-draw would have it, he ended up with a more substantial bill of fare.

Reviews: "A poignant, merry, and at times heartbreaking story. . . . There are spots that climb the heights of emotional appeal but there are many flat surfaces in between . . . on the other hand, we have some delightfully tender and amusing scenes between Rogers and her young husband, Robert Ryan. Seldom has marriage of an average young couple been more honestly played. Ryan is one of the finds of the year in our opinion." (*Photoplay*.)

Marine Raiders (3) (1944). RKO, 91 min. *Director* Harold Schuster. *Producer* Robert Fellows. *Story* Warren Duff, Martin Rackin. *Screenplay* Warren Duff. *Assistant Director* Edward Killy. *Art Directors* Albert S. D'Agostino, Walter E. Keller. *Set Decorators* Darrell Silvera, Harley Miller. *Music* Roy Webb. *Music Director* Constantin Bakaleinikoff. *Sound* James S. Thomson. *Special Effects* Vernon L. Walker. *Camera* Nicholas Musuraca. *Editor* Philip Martin, Jr. *Cast* Pat O'Brien (Major Steve Lockhard), **Robert Ryan** (Captain Dan Craig), Ruth Hussey (Ellen Foster), Frank McHugh (Sergeant Leary), Barton MacLane (Sergeant Maguire), Richard Martin (Jimmy), Edmund Glover (Miller), Russell Wade (Tony Hewitt), Robert Anderson (Lieutenant Harrigan), Martha Vickers (Sally).

Ryan's steel-nerved paramarine image is indelibly etched in one's mind, especially in a couple of riveting war sequences in this above average World War II film, in which he costarred with Pat O'Brien and Ruth Hussey. Director Harold Schuster churned out the story in a straightforward manner, but allowed his players to expand and create depth in their parts.

The dilemma bothering Ryan's Captain Craig in *Marine Raiders* was similar to what he encountered in many of his roles, that of the noble soul brought to an abrupt truth. His emotional crisis occurs when he experiences the inhumanity of war, and discovers it is not played by rules of fairness. Along his journey of self-awareness, he learns the true meaning of heroism.

Craig also learns to love when he

meets a nurse while on furlough in Australia, where his commanding officer (O'Brien) sends him to recuperate from battle fatigue. Sitting in an officers' club, despondent and alone, Craig has a chance encounter with a beautiful Army nurse (Hussey), who senses his unhappiness and helps him to get in touch with his feelings.

In several scenes, the chemistry of all three stars blended to achieve a natural atmosphere, such as in the hand-to-hand combat of jungle fighting, and in the meeting and developing relationship between Ryan and Hussey. Ryan created something believable out of what could have been a stereotyped caricature, in a portrait of romantic nuances versus hardened masculinity.

Reviews: "Robert Ryan is particularly well-cast as the case-hardened paramarine, and Miss Hussey adds up to a charming, starry-eyed Australian waif." (*New York Times,* 7/1/44.)

"A formula war movie which mildly transcends its formula through bits of truer-than-average dialogue, studio combat, acting, and direction, and an occasional flexibility of insight or camera work which seems to distinguish RKO pictures as political decency distinguishes those made by Warners ... Robert Ryan, if he is allowed to forget about Gary Cooper, may become one of the few good leading men." (Manny Farber, *Nation,* 7/8/44.)

"It is at its best when it is celebrating the South Pacific war ... these sequences are very good indeed. ... Both O'Brien and Ryan are splendid as leaders of the coordinated units which turned the tide against the Nipponese ... the film builds up a considerable emotional burden in its quiet description of a romance between a paramarine captain and an Australian girl whom he meets during a brief furlough ... Ryan is convincing as the parachuting lug who is too nervous to think straight after going through a bad time on Guadalcanal." (Howard Barnes, *New York Herald-Tribune,* 7/1/44.)

Trail Street (1947). RKO, 84 min. *Director* Ray Enright. *Executive Producer* Jack Gross. *Producer* Nat Holt. *Based on the novel* Golden Horizons *by* William Corcoran. *Screenplay* Norman Houston, Gene Lewis. *Art Directors* Albert S. D'Agostino, Ralph Berger. *Set Decorators* Darrell Silvera, John Sturtevant. *Music* Paul Sawtell. *Assistant Director* Grayson Rogers. *Sound* John L. Speak. *Montage* Harold Palmer. *Special Effects* Russell A. Cully. *Camera* J. Roy Hunt. *Editor* Lyle Boyer. *Cast* Randolph Scott (Bat Masterson), **Robert Ryan** (Allen Harper), Anne Jeffreys (Ruby Stone), Gabby Hayes (Billy and Brandyhead Jones), Madge Meredith (Susan Pritchett), Steve Brodie (Logan Maury), Billy House (Carmody), Virginia Sale (Hannah), Harry Woods (Lance Larkin), Phil Warren (Slim), Harry Harvey (Mayor), Jason Robards (Jason).

Ryan's first film after returning from the Marines was a mixed blessing, in a costarring part opposite Randolph Scott, Anne Jeffreys, and Gabby Hayes. Veteran director Ray Enright did his usual workmanlike best with this average horse opera, but its script lacked credibility in its exaggerated staginess and in its high falutin dialogue.

Land agent Allen Harper was one of Ryan's more eager portrayals, as an earnest Easterner brimming with hope, gazing wide-eyed over the clear, breezy wheat fields of Kansas in the 1870s. Second-billed to Randolph Scott's Bat Masterson, Ryan was given a role contrasting radically with a part he played in a similar low-budget RKO oater, *Return of the Badmen,* which he made for Enright in 1948. However, his psychopathic Sundance Kid in *Return* was a much more intriguing characterization.

Unfortunately for both films, the ubiquitous Gabby Hayes, whose buffoonish presence was on hand too often in both films, guaranteed that realism would be replaced by slap-stick. Thus, *Trail Street's* story of rampant land-grabbing and assorted crimes, masterminded by the devious, swaggering Logan Maury (Steve Brodie), and his rotund accomplice Carmody (Billy House), became tedious and irrelevant.

Additionally, the fictitious situation that pits Masterson against hordes of faceless gunmen fails to save the picture from being viewed as a curiosity piece. Although there is some technical expertise from cameraman J. Roy Hunt (the scenes involving bad-guy-dressed-in-black Lance Larkin [Harry Woods] are interesting), the inevitable ending gun battle fails to ignite sufficient excitement. As in many Westerns of that era, the impact of *Trail Street*'s final shoot-out was lowered by its having been shot in semidarkness.

Trail Street was the epitome of contrast compared with Ryan's next two films of 1947, and is only useful to think about if viewed in retrospect to his career. It was the last example of his exuberant boy-next-door image that was easily forgotten when his intensity was cut loose in serious drama.

Reviews: "On Trail Street in Liberal, Kansas, where the law just doesn't have a chance, lots of things are going on. Robert Ryan is a land agent who hopes to get the farmers to farm. ... Scott comes riding in, gets a few sly boys behind bars, subdues some big mobs single-handed, and makes everything all right for Ryan and his lady fair, Madge Meredith." (*Photoplay.*)

The Woman on the Beach (5) (1947). RKO, 71 min. *Director* Jean Renoir. *Executive Producer* Jack Gross. *Associate Producer* Will Price. *Based on the novel* None So Blind *by* Mitchell Wilson. *Adaptor* Michael Hogan. *Screenplay* Frank Davis, Jean Renoir. *Art Directors* Albert S. D'Agostino, Walter E. Keller. *Set Decorators* Darrell Silvera, John Sturtevant. *Technical Advisor* Charles H. Gardiner, Lt. Cmdr. USCGR. *Music* Hanns Eisler. *Music Director* Constantin Bakaleinikoff. *Orchestrator* Gil Grau. *Dialogue Director* Paula Walling. *Assistant Director* James Casey. *Sound* Jean L. Speak, Clem Portman. *Montage* Harold Palmer. *Special Effects* Russell A. Cully. *Camera* Leo Tover, Harry Wild. *Editors* Roland Gross, Lyle Boyer. *Cast* Joan Bennett (Peggy), **Robert Ryan** (Scott), Charles Bickford (Todd), Nan Leslie (Eve), Walter Sande (Chief Wernecke), Irene Ryan (Mrs. Wernecke), Glenn Vernon (Kirk), Frank Darien (Lars), Jay Norris (Jimmy), Hugh Chapman (Young Fisherman), Harry Harvey (Dr. Smith), Charles Pawley (Barton), Martha Hyer (Mrs. Barton).

Ryan's second film after returning from the Marines was his first *film noir*, a dark melodrama which explored fully the *noir* themes of isolation and alienation. Working with director Jean Renoir on *The Woman on the Beach* gave Ryan an opportunity to work with one of Europe's masters of impressionism. The subdued acting style Ryan had learned at Max Reinhardt's acting school balanced perfectly with Renoir's understated technique, but unhappily, *The Woman on the Beach* was Renoir's last American film, and the only picture he made with Ryan.

In Renoir's moody, atmospheric production, the director painted a dreamlike scenario for his conflictual romantic tryst involving Ryan, Joan Bennett, and Charles Bickford. A blustery New England seaside village provided an appropriate setting for the characters to struggle with their dark, disturbed passions.

Ryan portrayed a young, shell-shocked coast guard lieutenant sent on leave to recuperate mentally after the torpedoing of his ship by a German U-boat. Scott Burnett (Ryan) meets the beautiful but wanton Peggy (Bennett), and her blind, bitter husband, Todd (Bickford). Todd, once a famous artist, and Peggy, used to live the glamorous life in New York, but after she blinded him in a drunken argument, the resulting anger has made their marriage a quiet siege. All three are searching and in pain, thus their meeting is ripe for trickery, adultery, and attempted murder.

The film's climatic locale accurately suggested the emotional isolation of the characters, underlining the solitude they sought as well as fled from. Their emotions resembled the sea near which they slept, ever changing, calm then tumultuous. Preoccupied with loneliness, the encounter between Scott, Peggy, and Todd provoked a crisis that set them free from their fetters of despair.

Renoir's use of natural landscapes and climatic extremes created a mood of intimate yet eerie surrealism, and his brilliant allegorical dream sequence involving Scott and his fiancée, Eve (Nan Leslie), exemplified the best of his impressionistic influence. To heighten the ethereal quality of the dream sequences, other highly stylized outdoor scenes included an adulterous encounter between Scott and Peggy inside the hulk of a shipwreck, and a breathtaking scene of Scott on a white stallion, galloping along the beach with the crisp wind licking at his stirrups, and an intense gleam in his eye.

Renoir was assigned to direct *The Woman on the Beach* by RKO producer Jack Gross (one of his few true allies among the studio establishment). After reading Mitchell Wilson's novel, *None So Blind*, on which the film was based, and being offered the services of Joan Bennett, Renoir agreed to collaborate on the screenplay with Gross and to direct it.

Shortly after they began writing the script, Gross died, leaving the bulk of the work to Renoir, who then hired Frank Davis to help finish it. Renoir encountered difficulties adjusting to the film's theme, which nearly suffocated him with its preoccupation with isolation.

In his autobiography, *My Life and My Films*, Renoir wrote, "It was a story quite opposed to everything I had hitherto attempted. In all my previous films, I had tried to depict the bonds uniting the individual to his background ... now, I was embarked on a study of persons whose sole idea was to close the door on the absolutely concrete phenomenon which we call life."

After *The Woman on the Beach* met disappointing previews, RKO returned it to the editing room to trim a commercially unsalable property down to a grade 'B' running time (thus, its abbreviated 71-minute length). Although several critics applauded the film's complexities, Renoir's unpopular status at RKO hastened its brief run, after which it was quickly shelved.

To the indifferent public reaction toward *The Woman on the Beach*, Nathan Norman Weiss commented in the *Hollywood Quarterly*: "It is no commonplace affair. . . . One recognizes Mr. Renoir as one of the practitioners of enlightenment who have come and gone with the suddenness of spasm in RKO Radio's constant reorganization. . . . It may be that the picture is too complexly conceived for mass audiences; yet there is a nicely calculated design over the semiprofundities within, and a great many persons will not be inclined to peek."

In Renoir's book, he shared his frustrations about the picture's failure to gain wide notice, but he was nevertheless proud of it. He also felt a perverse pleasure knowing it reinforced his maverick director status in Hollywood. Ryan considered Renoir one of the "most remarkable" men he had ever met, and humbly said of Renoir, "He opened my eyes to the subtlest aspects of character." Renoir repaid the compliment when he wrote of Ryan's Scott Burnett, "The admirable Robert Ryan subtly enabled us to share in his suffering."

Reviews: "The skilled principal players interestingly suggest real people; notably good is Robert Ryan, as a competent but unsophisticated man who gets involved with some very bad companions." (*Time*, 6/2/47.)

"*The Woman on the Beach* is an unusual, taut drama . . . the picture is shot through with moments of emotional intensity, arresting photography, and an expressive score... Robert Ryan is a properly stalwart, confused lover." (A. Weiler, *New York Times*, 6/9/47.)

"Enough of the unusual in film drama has been injected into this offering via

Jean Renoir, to garner it interesting responses from the adult audiences. . . . The performances of Ryan, Bickford, and Bennett, are of the better variety." (*Filmgoers' Daily*, 5/15/47.)

"Its individual scenes are done in powerful cinema which carries a fascination beyond surface meaning. . . Renoir has directed his cast well, and at least two of the many scenes that quiver with nervous tension rise to a brief pitch of excitement." (Philip T. Hartung, *Commonweal*, 6/27/47.)

Crossfire (5) (1947). RKO, 86 min. *Director* Edward Dmytryk. *Executive Producer* Dore Schary. *Producer* Adrian Scott. *Based on the novel* The Brick Foxhole *by* Richard Brooks. *Screenplay* John Paxton. *Art Directors* Albert S. D'Agostino, Alfred Herman. *Set Decorators* Darrell Silvera, John Sturtevant. *Music* Roy Webb. *Music Director* Constantin Bakaleinikoff. *Assistant Director* Nate Levinson. *Sound* John E. Tribby, Clem Portman. *Special Camera Effects* Russell A. Cully. *Camera* J. Roy Hunt. *Editor* Harry Gerstad. *Cast* Robert Young (Captain Finlay), Robert Mitchum (Sergeant Keeley), **Robert Ryan** (Montgomery), Gloria Grahame (Ginny), Paul Kelly (The Man), Sam Levene (Samuels), Jacqueline White (Mary Mitchell), Steve Brodie (Floyd Bowers), George Cooper (Mitchell), Richard Benedict (Williams), Tom Keene (Detective), William Phipps (Leroy), Lex Barker (Harry), Marlo Dwyer (Miss Lewis), Harry Harvey (Tenant), Jay Norris, Robert Bray (M.P.s), Kenneth MacDonald (Major).

Landing one of the lead roles in RKO's *Crossfire* was a stroke of luck for Ryan, as it placed him at the forefront of Hollywood's exciting new stars. Although his intensity had been tapped initially in two earlier films, *Marine Raiders* and *The Woman on the Beach*, *Crossfire* was pivotal.

Ryan believed that success in show business often happened when one was in the right place at the right time. In the case of *Crossfire*, luck found an unlikely

setting at Camp Pendleton's separation center. While waiting to be mustered out of the Marine Corps, Ryan met Richard Brooks, then a successful screenwriter, who had recently finished writing a novel, *The Brick Foxhole*. After reading it, Ryan asked to be considered for the role of Montgomery if it ever became a movie, and Brooks consented. That hope became fact two years later, when *Crossfire* was developed from Brooks's novel.

Several brilliant, controversial minds came together on *Crossfire*, in the persons of producer Adrian Scott, director Edward Dmytryk, screenwriter John Paxton, and executive producer Dore Schary. The film is socially significant for its courage to explore the previously hidden problem of anti-Semitism, and is cinematically successful as a thought-provoking, suspenseful melodrama in the best tradition of *film noir*.

Those who made *Crossfire* were initially faced with a problem in Brooks's original story, since it involved three soldiers who murder a fourth when they discover he is a homosexual. That issue was still a taboo topic in America, but Scott, always daring in his choices of subject matter, proposed to alter the central theme from hatred of homosexuals to hatred of Jews. Dmytryk concurred with him, but Schary was at first against the idea. Although he was known for his "message" films, as a producer he was also concerned with box-office earnings, and thought the venture was unsalable.

The reasons for Schary's skepticism were not entirely monetary in nature. There was also political trouble in Hollywood, as the "Red Menace" was said to have "infiltrated" show business, and the House Committee on Un-American Activities was casting an accusatory glower toward anyone with liberal sentiments. Schary believed a treatment on anti-Semitism would invite undue scrutiny, and possible recrimination.

Moreover, the Holocaust was still a painfully recent tragedy toward which the United States wished to remain mute.

Though part of Schary's savvy was in taking risks with socially conscious issues, his wariness with *Crossfire* was due to an audience research poll indicating that only eight percent of those polled would be interested in seeing the film.

Despite Schary's qualms, Dmytryk and Scott hired John Paxton, who had written a number of excellent screenplays during the forties, to adapt a script from the novel. RKO's head of production, N.P. Rathvon, was impressed by the final script, and gave Scott and Dmytryk the go-ahead.

Crossfire's moderately high production costs were due to Schary's choice of several "name" actors to enhance its box-office draw. But it was economically shot in 20 days to offset the stars' salaries, and to compete with Paramount's *Gentleman's Agreement*, also about anti–Semitism. RKO's urgency in releasing it paid off, and it became the studio's biggest moneymaker of the year, and was voted the best picture of the year by the National Board of Review.

As a penetrating example of the *film noir* genre, the thematic elements of alienation, isolation, and loneliness were given the grand treatment in *Crossfire*, as all its characters are depicted in a state of flux, in limbo. The soldiers and civilians alike are portrayed as tired, bored, frustrated souls, trying to pick up the pieces of their lives, victims of the emotional turmoil of World War II. All are searching, waiting for something to happen, and as depicted by the professionals from RKO, the performances were superb, even down to the bit parts.

The choice of the three leads in *Crossfire* was a stroke of genius, and validated Schary's sagacity in casting and in public relations. Besides Ryan, the starring roles of Robert Young, as the tired but patient police captain, and Robert Mitchum, as the dour Army sergeant who helps him, provided a good balance of acting styles. They were aided by a supporting cast of equal efficiency, most notably by Gloria Grahame, as a pathetic B-girl, Paul Kelly,

as her dishonorably discharged ex-husband, and Sam Levene, in a thoughtful profile as the man who is murdered because of his ancestry.

The plight of returning soldiers gained added dimension from performances by Steve Brodie, who sweated and strained admirably as a witness to the murder of the Jew, and George Cooper was appropriately confused as the man mistakenly charged for the crime.

In accepting the unsympathetic role of the sadistic bigot, Montgomery, Ryan took a big risk in career terms, since a failure of the movie might have short-circuited his advancement. He always viewed his role in *Crossfire* as a mixed blessing, and believed it contributed to his being cast as a perpetual heavy.

Although today he is often remembered for that part alone, in a larger sense it served him well, since from his Best Supporting Actor nomination in 1947, he became a major contender for stardom. Moreover, it was a statement, albeit inadvertent, of his and everyone else's conflicts and ambivalences as human beings. His friend Henry Fonda once said that acting was therapy for him, a way of expressing the positive and negative aspects of being human, but with a constructive purpose. Ryan seemed to have shared these sentiments.

Reviews: "Ryan's role as the anti–Semitic G.I. in *Crossfire* is an extraordinary performance; full in terms of the character he was playing, of concealment, with a thin coating of restless charm covering a cancerous malignancy that threatened to break out and shatter everything." (John Cutts, *Film and Filming*, 7/61.)

"Much of the movie is as effective as a series of kicks to the solar plexus. Robert Ryan turns in the scariest performance of the season as the over-talkative, pathological Jew-hater. It is gruesome to watch such a character as Ryan." (*Time*, 8/4/47.)

"Mr. Dmytryk has handled most excellently a superlative cast for the drama.

Robert Ryan is frighteningly real as the hard, sinewy, loud-mouthed, intolerant and vicious murderer." (Bosley Crowther, *New York Times*, 7/25/47.)

"*Crossfire* is a savage melodrama which keys the problem of race hatred into an unusual murder story . . . vivid, revealing direction by Edward Dmytryk. . . . The story's force lies in the supreme hatefulness of a really noxious villain. As portrayed by Robert Ryan in a thoroughly believable performance, this killer is an overbearing ignorant smart aleck who refers to his victim as "The Jew boy" . . . Ryan's and Dmytryk's contributions are combined here in a stark portrait." (Otis Guernsey, *New York Herald-Tribune*, 7/23/47.)

"Dmytryk builds up terrific tension through his portrayal of a postwar atmosphere in which there is a lot of fight and hatred with no place to go . . . *Crossfire* is definitely a picture to see with assets like Dmytryk's thoughtful direction and the good cast in which Ryan, Paul Kelly and Gloria Grahame excel. . . . Its point that murder grows out of minor hatreds (for which we might all be to blame) should be taken seriously." (Philip T. Hartung, *Commonweal*, 8/1/47.)

"*Crossfire* is a gruesomely exciting story about some soldiers, one of whom murders a Jew. . . . It is extremely well-played by Roberts Young, Mitchum, and Ryan, very notably Ryan; by Sam Levene and Paul Kelly, and by practically everyone in the cast. It is excellently written and directed by John Paxton and Edward Dmytryk, respectively." (Manny Farber, *Nation*, 8/2/47.)

Berlin Express (4) (1948). RKO, 86 min. *Director* Jacques Tourneur. *Executive Producer* Dore Schary. *Producer* Bert Granet. *Assistant Producer* William Dorfman. *Story* Curt Siodmak. *Screenplay* Harry Medford. *Art Directors* Albert S. D'Agostino, Alfred Herman. *Set Decorators* Darrell Silvera, William Stevens. *Music* Frederick Hollander. *Music Director* Constantin Bakaleinikoff. *Assistant*

Director Nate Levinson. *Makeup* Gordon Bau. *Costumes* Orry-Kelly. *Sound* Jack Grubb, Clem Portman. *Special Effects* Harry Perry, Russell A. Cully, Harold Stine. *Camera* Lucien Ballard. *Editor* Sherman Todd. *Cast* Merle Oberon (Lucienne), **Robert Ryan** (Robert Lindley), Charles Korvin (Perrot), Paul Lukas (Dr. Bernhardt), Robert Coote (Sterling), Reinhold Schunzel (Walther), Roman Toporow (Lieutenant Maxim), Peter Von Zerneck (Hans Schmidt), Otto Waldis (Kessler), Fritz Kortner (Franzen), Michael Harvey (Sergeant Barnes), Tom Keene (Major), Charles McGraw (Colonel Johns), Gene Evans (Train Sergeant).

After a resounding success in *Crossfire*, Ryan made an about-face in character by playing an American agriculturalist sent to post–World War II Europe to implement a nutrition program for war victims. Executive producer Dore Schary's preference for using the cinema to examine issues found a proper setting in one of the worst affected cities in Europe, Frankfurt.

Much of *Berlin Express* takes place within the rubble and curiously monolithic shells of countless bombed-out buildings that riddled Berlin for many years after the war had ended. Combining *film noir* and documentary styles, *Berlin Express* is atypical, because although the themes of alienation and isolation are much in evidence, the story also contains a sociopolitical message.

Being geared toward the repairing of people's sundered lives, *Berlin Express*'s setting among the ruins provided an almost garish backdrop in which to present the film's philosophical statement. Director Jacques Tourneur, who had a successful track record in the mystery genre, validated his reputation by coming up with the same feeling of suspense as in his earlier works.

Lucien Ballard's clearly defined cinematography used the destruction leveled on Germany to increase the picture's visual impact. His work on *Berlin Express* was a creative challenge in that he needed to adapt his equipment for overseas portability. What resulted was location photography equalling the quality of his superior studio production work.

Part of *Berlin Express* takes place on a train traveling through Europe, and focusses on the developing relationship of several passengers. Not coincidentally, they represent the major powers involved in World War II, the United States, Russia, Germany, and France, and their journey is a metaphor for change and progress. The characters move from mutual distrust to a growing awareness of their respective humanity, and by the film's end their enmity is diminished.

When an important diplomat, Doctor Bernhardt (Paul Lukas), is kidnapped by a Nazi underground group while en route to a peace conference, Ryan's Lindley leads the search to find him. At first, his comrades join him with little commitment, but a sense of commonality slowly unites them as they comb the nighttime haunts of Frankfurt. Traveling down the city's darkened alleys and abandoned streets to an inner sanctum of off-limits cabarets, their search becomes an odyssey of realization.

The story's suspense is heightened since each of the passengers is suspect in the kidnapping. Before Doctor Bernhardt is rescued, several dramatic conflicts take place on the train and in the ruins of Frankfurt. When a passenger, Perrot (Charles Korvin), tries to strangle Bernhardt, Lindley sees the attack through a window reflection and notifies the M.P.s. Perrot is killed, and *Berlin Express* concludes with a tenuous rapprochement between Bernhardt's rescuers.

In the film's final minutes, the characters reach their destination and exchange awkward good-byes. Lindley makes a point of pursuing further friendship when he gives his address to the most antagonistic of the group, the Russian Lieutenant Maxim (Roman Toporow). Lindley represents the hope offered by America, and when Maxim lets his address fall to the ground, the symbolic

rejection disheartens everyone. At the last minute, Maxim retrieves the address, and the group parts company with encouraged hearts. Lindley's gesture of understanding and tolerance galvanizes everyone's hope for a better future.

Ryan landed second-billing to Merle Oberon, above Paul Lukas, and exhibited a quiet warmth which contrasted sharply with the image he had recently created in *Crossfire*. His part as Robert Lindley was a healing role.

Reviews: "Under the executive producership of Dore Schary, the RKO studio has once again combined a constructive treatment of a contemporary problem with vivid dramatic entertainment... Tourneur's direction, with quick cuts and rapid pacing of excellent dialogue, maintains the suspense from the opening scenes of violence on a fast moving train to the climax in the cellar of a ruined brewery... Robert Ryan, in another excellent portrayal following upon the heels of *Crossfire*, plays a tall, talkative, self-confident agricultural expert." (Otis L. Guernsey, *New York Herald-Tribune*, 5/21/48.)

"Jacques Tourneur's direction has kept the action unflagging and the identity of the ringleader a well-kept secret ... however, it is the panoramic view of life amid the "war architecture" of Frankfurt and Berlin ... which gives the adventure the authentic impact of a documentary ... Robert Ryan, Merle Oberon, Charles Korvin, Paul Lukas, and Robert Coote, turn in equally solid delineations." (A. Weiler, *New York Times*, 5/21/48.)

"Ryan establishes himself here as a first-rate actor, conclusively demonstrating that his brilliant performance in *Crossfire* was no one-shot affair. He has ease, quality of sincerity, and polish." (*Variety*, 4/7/48.)

Return of the Badmen (3) (1948). RKO, 89 min. *Director* Ray Enright. *Executive Producer* Jack Gross. *Producer* Nat Holt. *Story* Jack Natteford, Luci Ward. *Screenplay* Charles O'Neal, Jack

Natteford, Luci Ward. *Art Directors* Albert D'Agostino, Ralph Berger. *Set Decorators* Darrell Silvera, James Altwies. *Music* Paul Sawtell. *Music Director* Constantin Bakaleinikoff. *Assistant Director* Grayson Rogers. *Makeup* Gordon Bau. *Costumes* Renie. *Sound* Jean L. Speak, Terry Kellum. *Special Effects* Russell A. Cully. *Camera* J. Roy Hunt. *Editor* Samuel E. Beetley. *Cast* Randolph Scott (Vance), **Robert Ryan** (Sundance), Anne Jeffreys (Cheyenne), Gabby Hayes (John Pettit), Jacqueline White (Madge Allen), Steve Brodie (Cole Younger), Tom Keene (Jim Younger), Robert Bray (John Younger), Lex Barker (Emmett Dalton), Walter Reed (Bob Dalton), Michael Harvey (Grat Dalton), Dean White (Billy the Kid), Robert Armstrong (Wild Bill Doolin), Tom Tyler (Wild Bill Yeager), Lew Harvey (Arkansas Kid), Walter Baldwin (Muley Wilson), Minna Gombell (Emily), Warren Jackson (George Mason), Jason Robards (Judge Harper), Harry Shannon (Wade Templeton), Bud Osborne (Stagecoach Driver), Kenneth MacDonald (Colonel Markham), Earle Hodgins (Auctioneer).

Although Ryan was star-billed in many of his films, his time onscreen was often less than that of his costars. *Return of the Badmen* is a good example of this trend, as well as being a standard treatment of the formula Westerns which Hollywood churned out during the forties. Excepting Ryan's performance, *Return of the Badmen* offered little for audiences to think about.

RKO advertised *Return of the Badmen* as a "big budget epic," and intended to attract audiences for the spectacle of a large scale production. Unfortunately, neither the action nor the story supported the film's promotional hype, and matters were further complicated by the clownish Gabby Hayes, whose antics detracted from scenes having potential dramatic value. In addition, Anne Jeffreys' glamorously made-up appearance and corny dialogue lessened the realism of her part. But a gallery of RKO studio stalwarts,

including Steve Brodie, Tom Keene, Robert Bray, Lex Barker, Walter Reed, and Robert Armstrong, galloped out of the corrals to lend some credence to an otherwise ordinary horse opera. Although Randolph Scott was *Return of the Badmen*'s main star, his wholesome portrait seemed too pristeen, thus Ryan's Sundance Kid emerged as a more interesting character.

Ryan's Sundance was no hero, but rather, he was a sadistic killer whose psychopathic behaviors included several cold-blooded murders, delivered with a fervor that was subtly compelling. The sum and substance of *Return of the Badmen* was only average, but those who stay up late at night to catch a glimpse of Ryan doing what he does best might be advised to include it on their list.

Reviews: "*Return of the Badmen* has enough badmen in the cast to stock a year's output of Westerns.... Most of these villains, though fairly well cast and reasonably picturesque, merely get in the way of each other's villainy.... The only heavy who throws his weight around to any effect is the Sundance Kid (Robert Ryan, a thoroughly hissable villain). He kills a good Indian in cold blood, murders a reformed she-bandit when he can't convince her to switch back to banditry, and finally meets his match in a protracted bare-fisted bout with the marshal." (*Time*, 8/16/48.)

"Robert Ryan has managed to come through unscathed with a cool, expert performance as a prairie sadist." (Howard Thompson, *New York Times*, 8/5/48.)

"Robert Ryan, as the murderous Sundance Kid, comes off best in the film, duplicating the viciousness of his portrayal in *Crossfire*." (James Barstow, *New York Herald-Tribune*, 8/5/48.)

Act of Violence (4) (1948). MGM, 82 min. *Director* Fred Zinnemann. *Producer* William H. Wright. *Story* Collier Young. *Screenplay* Robert L. Richards. *Art Directors* Cedric Gibbons, Hans Peters. *Set Decorators* Edwin B. Willis, Henry W.

Grace. *Music* Bronislau Kaper. *Music Director* André Previn. *Assistant Director* Marvin Stuart. *Makeup* Jack Dawn. *Sound* Douglas Shearer, Charles E. Wallace. *Camera* Robert Surtees. *Editor* Conrad A. Nervig. *Cast* Van Heflin (Frank Enley), **Robert Ryan** (Joe Parkson), Janet Leigh (Edith Enley), Mary Astor (Pat), Phyllis Thaxter (Ann Sturges), Berry Kroeger (Johnny), Taylor Holmes (Mr. Gavery), Harry Antrim (Fred Finney), Connie Gilchrist (Martha Finney), Will Wright (Pop).

Act of Violence was one of director Fred Zinnemann's first efforts, and it succeeded as an exciting cat-and-mouse tale of revenge, and as an example of low-budget filmmaking expertise. The picture has never attracted as much attention as have other more ambitious Zinnemann films, such as *High Noon* or *From Here to Eternity*, but it deserves mention for its clarity in dealing with sensitive issues.

In its story of the consequences of wartime collaboration with the enemy, *Act of Violence* explored several *film noir* motifs. MGM borrowed Ryan from RKO to play the film's heavy, the mostly silent, menacing ex–G.I., Joe Parkson. Beginning in classic *noir* style, our first glimpse of Parkson tells us he is different from others because he has a limp, and as he shuffles up a darkened street, his gait carries a pronounced urgency.

Cut to his tall, trench-coated figure and hat pulled low, then to his face, broken out in a slight sweat. He hurries up the steps of a sleazy hotel to his room and heads straight for his bureau, from which he pulls a .45 caliber pistol. As he slams a clip into the gun and looks off, perhaps setting his purpose in motion, the film's title flashes in bold letters across the screen to underscore Parkson's mission.

Zinnemann wastes no time getting to his point. The next scene cuts to a sunny California town where Frank Enley (Van Heflin) is busy receiving an award from the town council. Shortly thereafter, Parkson arrives in town, and it becomes evident he is searching for Enley. At this point, one's sympathies lie with Enley, who is apparently a pillar of the community, while Parkson seems to be a borderline psychotic. But there is a twist to the story, since Enley is hiding a past transgression for which Parkson has come to exact retribution.

During the war, Enley and Parkson were both held prisoner of war by the Germans, and in an escape attempt, several of Enley's men were killed. Parkson learns that Enley had warned the Germans about the escape, and further, Parkson's lameness is a result of being bitten by attack dogs while escaping.

Enley has recently married Edith (Janet Leigh), and has been living quietly for three years, but when Parkson comes to his house to kill him, Enley's peaceful existence turns into a tarnished self-exposure and a tragic end. As Enley endures his final hours, Zinnemann's taut direction sends him on an anxiety provoking series of encounters with some of his town's less respectable citizens.

The technical aspects of *Act of Violence* account for much of its excitement, as cinematographer Robert Surtees tails Enley down lonely streets and alleyways, fleeing in terror from Parkson. Most of the film takes place at night in familiar *noir* territory, underscoring the shame Enley feels, while indoors, Surtee's effective use of nighttime interiors emphasizes the loneliness of Enley's dilemma. In particular, the scenes at Enley's house while he awaits Parkson, and the clandestine haunts where he meets three people of shady backgrounds, have a solitary nature that emphasizes the picture's existential theme. Although we see two images, the middle-class, suburban setting, versus the low-brow urban cellar, those who occupy space there share similar feelings of futility.

After Enley falls under the influence of a B-girl, Pat (Mary Astor), a jack-of-all-schemes, Mr. Gavery (Taylor Holmes), and a petty crook, Johnny (Berry Kroeger), in desperation he hires Johnny to kill Parkson. At the film's climax, as

Johnny lies in wait for Parkson, Enley has a crisis of conscience, and in the midst of stopping Johnny, he is killed.

As Parkson kneels above Enley's corpse in the rain, he realizes that Enley has sacrificed himself, and concludes his odyssey of revenge. The tragic ending, in which death is the sole means of expiation for Enley, is essential *film noir*, especially since Parkson is left with a measure of guilt. Moreover, there is irony in Enley's past transgression when it is revealed that he had informed on his comrades in the belief that he was saving their lives.

Ryan's emerging pattern of characerizations dealt with the recurring themes of pain and isolation, set against a backdrop of betrayal of friendship. In *Act of Violence*, Parkson is depicted as having been friends with Enley until the trust between them was broken, but at least in the end they have a spiritual reconciliation.

Act of Violence was one of Hollywood's early explorations of the antihero picture, and Ryan could have played Parkson in several ways. The portrayal he chose initially inspired both repugnance and dread, but these eventually gave way to a feeling of pity for the man's suffering. In their book, *The Heavies*, Ian and Elisabeth Cameron referred to Ryan's "kindly, worried face and tired eyes that are sometimes seen in completely sympathetic parts." Thus, when the shock of Parkson's menacing demeanor wears off, one sees that he has also been baring his soul. Since the role was similar in some respects to his characters in other late forties films, Ryan was becoming so firmly established in the mold of the "sympathetic heavy" that audiences were not going to accept him as otherwise.

Reviews: "Strong meat for the heavy drama addicts, tellingly produced and played to develop tight excitement. Robert Ryan and Van Heflin deliver punchy performances. Ryan is relentless as the would-be killer." (*Variety*, 12/22/48.)

"Mr. Zinnemann has pictured a visual setting for terror and violence, and has kept the pursued and the pursuer going at a grueling pace.... As Van Heflin's relentless pursuer, Ryan is infernally taut." (Bosley Crowther, *New York Times*, 1/24/49.)

"*Act of Violence* is sharpened up with extra-special direction and performances by Robert Ryan as the hunter and Van Heflin as the hunted ... Ryan's inexorable nemesis and Heflin's remorseful weakling are effective and make one wish they had played a scene together." (Otis L. Guernsey, *New York Herald-Tribune*, 1/17/49.)

"Although *Act of Violence* does not have a great deal of violence in it, it is chock-full of scary situations thanks to the direction of Zinnemann. It isn't so much *what* happens to these people but *how* it happens, that makes the film so exciting. The acting is good throughout and Zinnemann has used his actors and settings to work up an atmosphere of terror.... You may even get as frightened as Heflin when he flees from Ryan through the streets of Los Angeles." (Philip T. Hartung, *Commonweal*, 2/4/49.)

The Boy with Green Hair (4) (1948). RKO, C-82 min. *Director* Joseph Losey. *Executive Producer* Dore Schary. *Producer* Stephen Ames. *Based on the story by* Betsy Beaton. *Screenplay* Ben Barzman, Alfred Lewis Levitt. *Art Directors* Albert D'Agostino, Ralph Berger. *Set Decorators* Darrell Silvera, William Stevens. *Music* Leigh Harline. *Orchestra* Gil Grau. *Music Director* Constantin Bakaleinikoff. *Technicolor Consultants* Natalie Kalmus, Morgan Padelford. *Makeup* Gordon Bau. *Costumes* Adele Balkan. *Assistant Director* James Lane. *Sound* Earl Wolcott, Clem Portman. *Camera* George Barnes. *Editor* Frank Doyle. *Cast* Pat O'Brien (Gramp), **Robert Ryan** (Dr. Evans), Barbara Hale (Miss Brand), Dean Stockwell (Peter), Richard Lyon (Michael), Walter Catlett (The King), Samuel S. Hinds (Dr. Knudson), Regis Toomey (Mr. Davis), Charles

Meredith (Mr. Piper), David Clarke (Barber), Dwayne Hickman (Joey), Charles Arnt (Mr. Hammond).

In terms of advancing Ryan's career, *The Boy with Green Hair* did little to give it forward motion, yet he got involved with it more as a personal statement than anything else. Filmed at the outset of the investigations by the House Committee on Un–American Activities, executive producer Dore Schary's liberal message, that war must be avoided, fell into a precarious position that might have aroused scrutiny.

Although *The Boy with Green Hair* had a definite antiwar theme, it didn't tread on anyone's toes. Instead, it was a sincere, inoffensive vehicle for Pat O'Brien's standard father-figure type, and Dean Stockwell's curly haired precosity in the starring role.

As director Joseph Losey's first feature film, *The Boy with Green Hair* was a much tamer version of his later films having to do with peace, such as *The Damned* (1962) and *King and Country* (1964). Having been shot in Technicolor made it more visually interesting (Dean Stockwell's hair turns a vivid green), but otherwise, the picture was too innocuous to be of great merit.

Ryan's cameo as a kindly court psychiatrist who examines Dean Stockwell required him to appear briefly at the film's beginning and end. He remained humble despite his recent rise to fame in *Crossfire*, *The Woman on the Beach*, and *Act of Violence*.

Reviews: "Produced under the Dore Schary regime at RKO, its subject matter jumps out of the well-worn groove of Hollywood productions and tries to speak out against war in a sentimental fantasy about an extraordinary child. ... It comes to town bearing a reasonable share of honor for its makers and entertainment for its audiences." (Otis L. Guernsey, *New York Herald-Tribune*, 1/13/48.)

Caught (5) (1949). MGM, 88 min. *Director* Max Ophuls. *Producer* Wolfgang Reinhardt. *Based on the novel* Wild Calendar *by* Libbie Block. *Screenplay* Arthur Laurents. *Art Director* Frank Sylos. *Set Decorator* Edward G. Boyle. *Music* Frederick Hollander. *Music Director* Rudolph Polk. *Assistant Director* Albert van Schmus. *Makeup* Gus Norin. *Wardrobe* Louise Wilson. *Technical Advisor* Dr. Leo Morton Schulman. *Sound* Max Hutchinson. *Montage* Michael Luciano. *Process Camera* Mario Castegnaro. *Camera* Lee Garmes. *Editor* Robert Parrish. *Cast* James Mason (Larry Quinada), Barbara Bel Geddes (Leonora Eames), **Robert Ryan** (Smith Ohlrig), Ruth Brady (Maxine), Curt Bois (Franzi), Frank Ferguson (Dr. Hoffman), Natalie Schaefer (Dorothy Dale), Art Smith (Psychiatrist), Sonia Darrin (Miss Chambers), Wilton Graff (Gentry).

Director Max Ophuls' *Caught* was a great vehicle for Ryan to showcase his repressed power. Although he was third-billed to James Mason and Barbara Bel Geddes, his Smith Ohlrig was a much more complex portrayal, and his understated playing of the neurotic, obsessed millionaire made it grimly believable. His interpretation registered on a visceral level, making Ohlrig into a fearful presence rather than a hypochondriacal sissy.

The story of *Caught* concerns a rags-to-riches woman, Leonora Eames (Bel Geddes), who believes that marrying into wealth is the road to happiness. She meets and marries the phenomenally affluent but equally disturbed Ohlrig, a neurotic who must own and dominate everything. After a year of barren existence as a figurine in Ohlrig's sterile mansion, Leonora breaks away long enough to become involved with Ohlrig's antithesis, the friendly, caring pediatrician, Dr. Quinada (James Mason).

After learning that she is to give birth to a child by Ohlrig, she returns to him, driven by her illusion that money will lessen her feelings of desolation. As punishment for her affection for Quinada, Ohlrig becomes fanatically possessive of Leonora, and by the film's climax, she is on the verge of a nervous breakdown.

When Ohlrig is stricken with an angina attack, she refuses to aid him, and though he recovers, his grip on her is severed. Regaining her emotional equilibrium, Leonora is reunited with Quinada in the closing scenes.

The moral of *Caught*, that money cannot buy happiness, has been told countless times before, thus the value here is in its telling. Ophuls' ever-searching camera did much to convey the sterility of the opulent. The dark, immense study, the huge marble staircases, the cold, clear lights of the crystal chandeliers in Ohlrig's mansion, are central to the film's symbolism, and underscore the emptiness often exacted as the price of wealth.

While *Caught* delved into typical *film noir* elements of loneliness, desperation and greed, Ophuls' expressionistic style belied *noir* conventions. This was evident in the film's luxurious, baroque sets, suggesting a timeless European atmosphere in its vast, expansive interior scenes shot in subdued tones, and in its sweeping music score by Frederick Hollander.

Ophuls was a leading proponent of the mise-en-scène style of directing, whose talent for mood and setting combined with Arthur Laurents' perceptive screenplay, resulting in a melodrama of esthetic texture. Ophuls' reputation had been built more on *how* he expressed rather than *what* was expressed.

James Mason, appearing in his first American picture, gave a sincere performance in a difficult role, and Barbara Bel Geddes was touchingly pathetic as the poor-little-rich-girl who came of age the hard way. As Ohlrig's fawning lackey, Franzi, Curt Bois injected a telling irony into his role.

Of all the characters in *Caught*, Ryan's Ohlrig was the most complex, and achieved center stage by its subtle force. At the beginning of the film, Ohlrig's emotional problems are first revealed when, during an abrasive conversation with Leonora, he becomes anxious and dons his captain's cap in an unconscious ritual. This seemingly innocuous act sets the stage for the events to follow.

When Ohlrig lures Leonora to his mansion and she resists his invitation to "have a nightcap," he demands, "What's the matter, don't you think *I* like you?" rather than, "Don't *you* like me?" His choice of emphasis indicates his narcissism.

Ohlrig's need for power is again depicted when he visits his psychiatrist, and argues with him about the origin of his angina condition. When the good doctor speculates that his attacks are "all in your head," Ohlrig becomes angry, fires the doctor, and in a final gesture of defiance, vows to marry Leonora.

As in many Ryan films, *Caught* was ahead of its time, but it was an artful enterprise that drew an intriguing psychological picture of having either too little or too much money. In her book, *Kiss, Kiss, Bang, Bang*, Pauline Kael wrote of *Caught*: "This little publicized movie was a financial failure, but I think it is the most interesting and emotionally complex of Ophuls' four American films."

Reviews: "A generally interesting, engrossing adult entertainment with many effective, highly dramatic moments ... Robert Ryan, as the psychopathic spouse, plays with tremendous power the role of the Napoleonic multi-millionaire with a demoniacal hatred of his wife." (*Cue*, 2/18/49.)

"The performances are top-notch and consistent, as is the direction and physical production. . . . As the tall, dark man of many business interests, odd hours, playboy tendencies, and a reluctance to wedlock, Robert Ryan plays him to the hilt." (*Variety*, 2/22/49.)

"Robert Ryan and Barbara Bel Geddes dominate most of the sequences in *Caught*. Ryan is the central character in these proceedings and he knows it. His portrait of a spoiled tycoon is terrifying." (Howard Barnes, *New York Herald-Tribune*, 2/18/49.)

"As the husband, Robert Ryan is cruel and relentless, without any redeeming qualities, but the forcefulness of his

characterization makes it stand out."
(*Showmen's Trade Review.*)

"Robert Ryan is dynamic as the arrogant, neurotic spouse." (Bosley Crowther, *New York Times*, 2/18/49.)

The Set-up (5) (1949). RKO, 72 min. *Director* Robert Wise. *Producer* Richard Goldstone. *Based on the poem by* Joseph Moncure March. *Screenplay* Art Cohn. *Art Directors* Albert S. D'Agostino, Jack Okey. *Set Decorators* Darrell Silvera, James Altwies. *Music and Music Director* Constantin Bakaleinikoff. *Technical Advisor* John Indrisano. *Makeup* Gordon Bau. *Sound* Phil Brigandi, Clem Portman. *Assistant Director* Edward Killy. *Camera* Milton Krasner. *Editor* Roland Gross. *Cast* **Robert Ryan** (Stoker Thompson), Audrey Totter (Julie), George Tobias (Tiny), Alan Baxter (Little Boy), Wallace Ford (Gus), Percy Helton (Red), Hal Baylor (Tiger Nelson), Darryl Hickman (Shanley), Kenny O'Morrison (Moore), James Edwards (Luther Hawkins), David Clarke (Gunboat Johnson), Philip Pine (Souza), Edwin Max (Danny), Dave Fresco (Mickey), William Green (Doctor), Abe Dinovitch (Ring Caller), Herbert Anderson, Jack Raymonds, Helen Brown, Constance Worth (Married Couples), Archie Leonard (Blind Man), Jess Kirkpatrick, Paul Dubov (Gamblers), John Butler (Blind Man's Companion), Bernard Gorcey (Tobacco Man), Donald Kerr (Vendor).

The Set-up was a gritty, grim look at the violent sport of boxing, and a hard-hitting, uncompromising depiction of the lot of the small-time boxer in countless matches, in sordid, anonymous honky-tonks, before uncaring faces. As told in *The Set-up*, pugilism emerged far from glamorous; instead, it was sober and depressing.

Told in concise terms with nary a wasted word by director Robert Wise, *The Set-up* was an economical work of art. Yet it was released in 1949 as a routine programmer, ignored during the shuffle of personnel at RKO after Howard

Hughes took over. Although Dore Schary was the film's original producer, when he left RKO after an argument with Hughes, Richard Goldstone replaced him. From these confused circumstances a magnificent picture was created, succeeding as a powerful message about the sport of boxing, and as a symbolic example of society in microcosm.

The *film noir* world of *The Set-up* emphasized realism over star attraction, heightened by authentic sets to create its quasi-surreal atmosphere. In light of the film's austere budget, Robert Wise used character actors Audrey Totter, George Tobias, James Edwards, Percy Helton, and Alan Baxter.

Their work helped create a motion picture that justifiably rivals Mark Robson's *Champion*, and Robert Rossen's *Body and Soul*, as the best film ever made about boxing. In *Hollywood in the Forties*, authors Charles Higham and Joel Greenberg asserted that *The Set-up* had "all the savagery of a Daumier or a Gillray," and wrote of the "agony and despair of Ryan's great performance."

Art Cohn's script subtly stressed the futility assailing the characters in *The Set-up* with dialogue reeking of the abject cynicism of of the *noir* genre. The viewer is introduced to the parasitic nature of the cast within three minutes, as the camera pans slowly over the teeming streets outside the Paradise City Arena, coming to rest to eavesdrop on the conversations of several patrons standing at the ticket window.

In a few terse lines their hardened attitudes are revealed as they impatiently wait for the spectacle to begin. Among them is a blind man whose companion doubles as his eyes, a woman who complains of being "dragged" to the fights but who shortly afterward shrieks for blood, and a milk toast husband whose wife watches amusedly as he vicariously compensates for his passive nature via the ringside mayhem.

The camera moves to two men standing under the marquee of the night's schedule of events, sarcastically joking about the "entertainment" to come.

One says to his companion, "What do you think about Stoker Thompson (Ryan)?"

The other looks at him and scornfully chuckles, "Is he still fightin'? I remember him when I was a kid."

As they walk away the first man retorts with a sneer, "Don't tell me you're *that* old."

Cut to the marquee as a match is struck across Stoker's name. The match travels to the cigar of Tiny (George Tobias), Stoker's manager, who asks Red (Percy Helton) with off-hand indifference, "Where's Stoker?"

Red replies, "He's over in the hotel gettin' some shut-eye."

"Don't that guy get enough sleep in the ring?" demands Tiny with a sneer.

"You oughta know, you're his manager," retorts Red.

The characters' feelings of futility and hopelessness are communicated mainly by their actions, rather than through dialogue. Milton Krasner's camera passes quickly but intimately over several rapt spectators, just long enough to reveal their depraved sensitivities. One is an obese man who eats throughout the entire night, and who chortles scornfully when Stoker slips and falls in the ring. Another has a radio to his ear, simultaneously listening to a baseball game as the fighters batter each other.

Before his own match, while Stoker watches another bout, a spectator in front of him screams over and over, "Kill 'im! Kill 'im! Come on, keep it up! Keep it up! Throw that right!"

Stoker is surprised by the crowd's fervor, but the insanity of it escapes him. He is a simple, uncomplicated man, and neither the scars on his face, the fuzzy feelings in his head, nor the rabid clamor of the spectators, convinces him that he is merely a pawn in a cruel contest.

The atmosphere of *The Set-up* is one of neon lights, dark alleys, lonely hotel rooms, and one-way tickets out of town.

Milton Krasner created an intensely stark setting by avoiding the use of filters which would have de-emphasized the picture's harsh, gladiatorial tone. The sweaty, smoke-filled confines of the arena, and the anxious noise of its denizens had an oppressive ambience, contrasted sharply with the dreamlike, surrealistic quality of the neon lights outside the arena, bearing names such as "Fantasyland" and "Dreamland." "Paradise City," the sleazy town in which *The Set-up* takes place, completes the film's irony.

Although the staging of *The Set-up* is deceptively simple, there is real craftsmanship in the crosscutting and quick cuts, while the close-ups of the spectators' faces, interspersed with those of the sweating pugilists beating each other to a pulp, graphically illustrate the savage voyeurism of boxing.

Ryan adopted a tired, pained demeanor as the aging Stoker, 35 years old and over the hill, yet stubbornly resisting the inevitable. His relationship with his wife, Julie (Audrey Totter), is also in jeopardy, because she has patiently endured seeing her husband getting his brains beaten out night after night, and has finally reached her limit. She tells Stoker that he is living in a dream, and as she sits in a barren, dimly lit hotel room, gazing at the clock, she feels hopeless.

Stoker's career comes to a violent end when he refuses to throw a fight and is punished by having his hand deliberately crushed by an angry mobster, Little Boy (unctuously played by Alan Baxter). Thematically, Stoker's resistance is a noble gesture in a predatory, venal world, and reunites him with Julie. His defeat becomes a triumph that reaffirms his dignity as a man.

Reviews: "The film is saved from complete nihilism by the small core of humanity in Robert Ryan's superb performance. He has little to say. He is as ignorant and ignoble as all the other boxers. His face looks appropriately tired and battered. He is defeated. Yet there remains a poetic sensibility in his eyes and his occasional tentative smile. His eyes are always watching, and we see him alternately hope and despair as he waits his turn in the ring. He has just enough human dignity left to blindly refuse corruption, and for it he suffers a bold, brutal beating that means the end of what little there was to his boxing career. At the end, he has enough self-pride left to be able to boast that he has won his fight and did not take the fall." (Eileen Bowser, *Film Notes*, Museum of Modern Art, 1969.)

"Stoker Thompson possesses an unarticulated nobility that is subtly projected by Robert Ryan. One of the most important *noir* actors, Ryan not only possesses the physical appearance of a fighter, but gives a beknighted dignity to Stoker that is necessary to make him an existential hero." (Blake Lewis, *Film Noir—An Encyclopedic Reference to the American Style*, Overlook Press, Woodstock, N.Y., 1979.)

"In *The Set-up*, the prizefighters aren't champions, but the derelicts, beginners, and old men who fight four-rounders in arenas that have more trash on the floor than seats. . . . It is a shocking movie, not only because it is often good, but because it is the grimiest, most brutal film in years. . . . The movie's honesty comes from the static performance of Robert Ryan, as a thoughtful preliminary fighter, one punch away from punch-drunk." (Manny Farber, *Nation*, 5/7/49.)

"As a detailed and unrelenting description of small-time prize fighting, *The Set-up* is an almost perfect job. . . Robert Ryan, in one of his best performances, plays a shabby, discouraged pug who has made a miserable living in the ring for 20 years. The film is reassurance that there are still craftsmen around the studios." (Robert Hatch, *New Republic*, 4/25/49.)

"The ugly aspects of the fight game are forcefully brought home in this movie. Robert Ryan turns in a noteworthy job as a small-time prizefighter. . . . You get to meet as motley an assortment of characters as ever appeared in one picture. . . . By the time the last savage punch is delivered, it's well-established that prizefighting, as depicted here, is an extremely sordid business." (*Photoplay*, 3/22/49.)

The Woman on Pier 13 (aka **I Married a Communist**), (4) (1949). RKO, 73 min. *Director* Robert Stevenson. *Executive Producer* Sid Rogell. *Producer* Jack Gross. *Story* George W. George, George F. Slavin. *Screenplay* Charles Grayson, Robert Hardy Andrews. *Art Directors* Albert S. D'Agostino, Walter E. Keller. *Set Decorators* Darrell Silvera, James Altwies. *Music* Leigh Harline. *Music Director* Constantin Bakaleinikoff. *Assistant Director* William Dorfman. *Makeup* W.H. Phillips. *Costumes* Michael Woulfe. *Sound* Phil Brigandi, Clem Portman. *Camera* Nicholas Musuraca. *Editor* Roland Gross. *Cast* Laraine Day (Nan Collins), **Robert Ryan** (Brad Collins), John Agar (Don Lowry), Thomas Gomez (Vanning), Janis Carter (Christine), Richard Rober (Jim Travis), William Talman (Bailey), Paul E. Burns (Arnold), Paul Guilfoyle (Ralston), G. Pat Collins (Charles Dover), Fred Graham (Grip Wilson), Harry Cheshire (Mr. Cornwell), Jack Stoney (Garth), Lester Mathers (Dr. Dixon), Marlo Dwyer (Evelyn), Erskine Sanford (Clerk), Bess Flowers (Secretary).

When *I Married a Communist* was shown at a sneak preview in September 1949, RKO president Ned Depinet demurred on its national distribution. After perusing the preview cards, he wrote to his department heads, "I do not believe it will be wise for you to send a complete set of preview comments to our branch and district managers."

The film returned to RKO's operating room, and was released several months later as *The Woman on Pier 13*, having undergone numerous additions and deletions, and a thorough bowdlerizing at the hands of Howard Hughes. The ominous sneak preview had convinced RKO heads that the public had little interest in anti–Communist films, one of Hughes's fixations, but he doggedly insisted on running it through the mill.

Robert Hardy Andrews's final screenplay sensationalized the Communist ideology, while depicting the party as a repository for criminals and murderers. However, the film's message is not overly reactionary if viewed from a contemporary perspective, in which radical political groups allow psychopaths to masquerade as freedom fighters.

As melodrama and *film noir, The Woman on Pier 13* concerns the problems of Brad and Nan Collins (Ryan and Laraine Day), when a leering Communist named Vanning (Thomas Gomez) extorts union-busting services from Collins in exchange for keeping his mouth shut about Collins' earlier days as a union enforcer.

Collins refuses at first, but when Vanning threatens to turn him in for an earlier crime, he is forced to work for him. Eventually, Collins confronts Vanning in a dramatic waterfront shoot-out in which both are killed. Along the way, other unfortunates who lose their lives are John Agar, run down by a car, Janis Carter, thrown out of a hotel window, and Paul Guilfoyle, drowned in the river.

Robert Stevenson's sturdy direction moved *The Woman on Pier 13* past Howard Hughes's protracted meddling to result in an intriguing, if overdone, melodrama. Ryan fell naturally into his role as the misguided young man, lured by idealistic dogmas who later "comes to his senses."

Reviews: "*The Woman on Pier 13* is a right smart sampling of melodrama, fast paced and attractively padded with action and violence... Robert Ryan carries the story on his sturdy shoulders as vice-president of a shipping company... Ryan gives a good, solid performance." (*New York Times,* 6/16/50.)

"*The Woman on Pier 13* alternates brutality and sex in a story about a shipping boss whose Communist past catches up with him. Robert Ryan is in the center of things, giving another of his hard-as-nails performances as a rising young executive who at one time was a stevedore and a cardholder." (Otis L. Guernsey, *New York Herald-Tribune,* 6/16/50.)

"*I Married a Communist* is a celluloid bullet aimed at the U.S.S.R. ... Robert Ryan's appearance in a film (*Crossfire, The Set-up*) has almost come to mean a low-budget picture with a future. He gives this movie some unexpected authenticity because he is capable of crossing black and white traits in a role, without showing his hand." (*Time* magazine reviewed the film before its title was changed.) (*Time,* 10/17/49.)

1. The first draft of a screenplay entitled *I Married a Communist* was submitted by journeymen screenwriters George Slavin and George W. George, on 19 April 1948. They were paid $450 per week. Script revisions lasted another five weeks, from 3 May–7 June.

2. The title *I Married a Communist* was owned by Eagle-Lion Pictures and was formally purchased by RKO pictures on 27 August 1948, for $15,000 plus 25 percent of the profits of the picture.

3. RKO personnel discussed the "enormous exploitational value" of using the then well-known Communist turned informer, Elizabeth Bentley, in a brief prologue to the film.

4. The Slavin-George treatment was sent to RKO, but it was decided that script revisions were in order. On 31 August 1948, screenwriter Art Cohn was hired to revise the script, and a week later James Edward Grant joined him.

5. Cohn and Grant submitted a revised estimated script on 29 December 1948. They were paid $16,375 and $24,166.67 for their work.

6. Director Nicholas Ray had been hired to do the film, but requested the services of Herman Mankiewicz for further script revisions. Mankiewicz exacted minimal changes on the script during his six weeks of work from 10 December 1948 to 29 January 1949. He was paid $16,500.

7. Screenwriter Charles Grayson was paid $6,000 for the third treatment of the revised version produced between 7 February and 19 March 1949.

8. RKO personnel were still concerned with the script's basic message (low-budget melodrama versus anti–Communist propaganda). Screenwriter Robert Hardy Andrews began revisions on 18 March– 30 April 1949. He earned $6,333.33 for producing a second revised final script and a third revised final script.

9. Nicholas Ray cancelled his commitment to direct the film and John Cromwell had also declined. Robert Stevenson was borrowed from the Selznick organization in February 1949. Final screenplay credits were given to Charles Grayson and Robert Hardy Andrews, with the story being attributed to George W. George and George J. Slavin.

10. Principal shooting of I Married a Communist lasted 25 April–25 May 1949. Two additional days of shooting were required after Howard Hughes initially screened the picture and was dissatisfied with several scenes. The film was ready for release in mid–August.

11. The initial sneak previews of the film were not favorable and on 14 October 1949, Hughes and RKO announced a delay in the national release of the film. RKO executives hurriedly set about the task of marketing the picture with a different title.

12. At the end of October 1949 production head Sid Rogell sent Hughes a list of 19 replacement titles such as Waterfront at Midnight, Shadow in the Dark, Where Danger Lives, Incident on Pier 13, etc.

13. The title The Woman on Pier 13 first appeared on an anonymous handwritten memo that was sent to Hughes dated 16 December 1949. On 4 January 1950 Sid Rogell announced: "Hughes authorizes use of The Woman on Pier 13 replace communist. Willing to go ahead with original shameless, nameless woman campaign..."

14. On 16 January 1950 RKO formally announced that The Woman on Pier 13 is the final title for I Married a Communist, which was announced as the

final title on May 13, 1949.

15. The Woman on Pier 13, as of 30 December 1950, had a final certified cost of $891,360.34 and was estimated by two historians at RKO to have finished its run with a box-office deficit of $650,000. (How Red Was My Valley: Hollywood, the Cold War Film, and I Married a Communist, Daniel J. Leab, Journal of Contemporary History, [SAGE, London, Beverly Hills, and New Delhi], Vol. 19 [1984], 59-88.)

The Secret Fury (2) (1950). RKO, 86 min. Director Mel Ferrer. Producer Jack Skirball. Story Jack R. Leonard, James O'Hanlon. Screenplay Lionel House. Art Directors Albert S. D'Agostino, Carroll Clark. Music Director Constantin Bakaleinikoff. Camera Leo Tover. Editor Harry Marker. Cast Claudette Colbert (Ellen), **Robert Ryan** (David), Jane Cowl (Aunt Clara), Paul Kelly (Eric Lowell), Philip Ober (Kent), Elisabeth Risden (Dr. Twining), Doris Dudley (Pearl), Dave Barbour (Lucian Randall), Vivian Vance (Lea), Percy Helton (Justice of the Peace), Dick Ryan (Postman), Ann Codee (Tessa), Joseph Forte (Martin), Edit Angold (Flora), Adela Towland (Mrs. Palmer), Aileen Babs Cox (Woman), Howard Quinn (Bellhop), John Mantley (Hotel Clerk), Abe Dinovitch (Man), Wheaton Chambers (District Attorney), Bert Moorhouse (Assistant District Attorney).

When RKO decided to make The Secret Fury, it was banking on the talents of Ryan, Claudette Colbert, and a cast of character actors to make something important out of an implausible screenplay. Colbert, who co-owned the Loving Theatre Corporation, originally proposed the making of The Secret Fury, and produced the film in conjunction with RKO.

In the director's chair on The Secret Fury sat actor and sometime director Mel Ferrer, who turned out a slightly interesting, but puzzling and ultimately disappointing, product. The picture was his second directing effort, and he demonstrated an ability for building mood and suspense; however, his static direction failed to sustain enough credibility to overcome glaring loopholes in the storyline.

The Secret Fury falls into a hazy category because it has *noir* aspects in its photography and in its use of shadow detail; however, its story of bigamy, murder, and insanity lacks a crucial thematic ingredient: alienation. The characters in The Secret Fury are too wholesome, and the setting, in a middle-class California town where life is generally pleasant, is too stable an environment to warrant a *noir* classification.

The film's title refers to the malady afflicting Colbert's Ellen after she experiences a series of dismaying mishaps. First, on her wedding day, a man appears at the church, claiming that she is already married. When the man vanishes, Ellen and her fiancé, David (Ryan), set out to find him and uncover the truth. While attempting to discredit allegations of Ellen's bigamy, David begins to doubt her when several witnesses claim she is indeed married to another man.

When David and Ellen finally track down the man who is supposedly her husband, he is mysteriously murdered, and Ellen is arrested for the crime. At her trial, she has a nervous breakdown and ends up in an insane asylum. David goes sleuthing and finds the church witness as well as a hotel maid (Vivian Vance), both of whom are willing to tell the truth for a price. Before the witness and the maid present their statements to the police, however, they are killed, and Ellen is left with no alibi.

As David mulls over his next move while walking on the beach one day, he discovers clues indicating Ellen's innocence. In the film's climax, Ellen escapes from the asylum after concluding that her uncle (Philip Ober) is responsible for her troubles. When Ellen confronts him with the truth, he attempts to kill her, but David arrives in the nick of time. David and the uncle have a fight, and a

huge mirror falls on the uncle, killing him instantly. In the final scenes, David and Ellen collapse in a lachrymose embrace, presumably to live happily ever after.

Although The Secret Fury began with an intriguing premise, its script went astray shortly after the beginning, as the plot contrivances became increasingly absurd. Ryan played David well enough, but his character was poorly conceived, depicting him one moment as reticent and ineffectual, while in the next, he is transformed into an assertive, resourceful amateur detective. The Secret Fury became one of numerous modest features in which RKO stranded Ryan with the hope that he could draw audiences.

Reviews: "The new film at the Paramount is little more than a catalogue of melodramatic devices. It runs wild through a series of almost humorous contrivances, and hacks away at a fairly good idea until there is not much left of it on the screen." (Otis L. Guernsey, *New York Herald-Tribune,* 6/22/50.)

"The major performers expend more energy than intelligence on this wantonly unintelligible tale.... To lay the blame on the cast for the nonsense that takes place on the screen would be an obvious injustice." (Bosley Crowther, *New York Times,* 6/22/50.)

Born to Be Bad (4) (1950). RKO, 94 min. *Director* Nicholas Ray. *Producer* Robert Sparks. *Based on the novel* All Kneeling *by* Anne Parrish. *Screenplay* Edith Sommer. *Art Directors* Albert S. D'Agostino, Jack Okey. *Music Director* Constantin Bakaleinikoff. *Camera* Nicholas Musuraca. *Editor* Frederick Knudtson. *Cast* Joan Fontaine (Christabel), **Robert Ryan** (Nick Bradley), Zachary Scott (Curtis), Joan Leslie (Donna), Mel Ferrer (Gobby), Harold Vermilyea (John Caine), Virginia Farmer (Aunt Clara), Kathleen Howard (Mrs. Bolton), Dick Ryan (Arthur), Bess Flowers (Mrs. Worthington), Joy Hallward (Mrs. Porter), Irving Bacon (Jewelry Salesman).

Born to Be Bad was a better movie than the critics would have led people to believe, but their cool reception of it seems more a result of circumstances rather than the assertion that it was a bad movie. In fact, *Born to Be Bad* was well-written, fast paced, and convincingly played; however, the timing was not right for the glossy soap opera, since the genre had exhausted its inventiveness as a Hollywood formula.

RKO, which was notorious for doing eccentric, perplexing things, matched a number of talents in *Born to Be Bad*, hoping to come up with a winner. Working with Ryan for the first time was director Nicholas Ray, while stars Joan Fontaine, Zachary Scott, Joan Leslie, and Mel Ferrer labored earnestly to make a worthwhile project of the film.

Since Howard Hughes had been orchestrating all RKO productions like an enigmatic mad hatter, the picture's shaky history might have served as a premonition. Originally scheduled for production in 1946, *Born to Be Bad* was put on hold twice and underwent cast changes before it was laid on Ray's lap in 1950. Ray, Ryan et al. did a creditable job with their task, and created a diverting melodrama out of Anne Parrish's novel, *All Kneeling*.

The title *Born to Be Bad* refers to Joan Fontaine's vain and venal Christabel Caine, who schemes her way into millionaire Curtis Carey's (Scott) mansion. Cloaked under a thin layer of innocence, she quickly steamrolls over Curtis's fiancée, Donna (Leslie), while offending nearly everyone she meets. She first digs her claws into Nick Bradley (Ryan), a writer whose intuition about her opportunism is temporarily overcome by her seductiveness. After an early confrontation with her selfishness, Nick begins to suspect her true motives, and accurately describes an art portrait of Christabel as a "cross between Lucretia Borgia and Peg-o-my-heart." When she coolly informs another would-be suitor, Gobby (Ferrer), that he could never support her on an

artist's wages, her mercenary intent becomes clear.

Having wed Curtis for his money rather than for love, Christabel quickly loses interest in him, and tries to form a love tryst with Nick, who has just reached prominence with his first novel. When Curtis confronts Christabel about her seeming indifference toward him, she mollifies him by going on a vacation with him. However, on a supposed mission of mercy for her ailing Aunt Clara, Christabel approaches Nick once more, but he knows her game and rejects her proposition.

When Curtis learns of Christabel's clandestine visit with Nick at his hotel, he finally divorces her. Nick and Curtis emerge from their tangled emotions with their integrity intact, while Christabel is last seen leaving with a stack of fur coats and a barely flustered countenance.

Although *Born to Be Bad* was a soap opera, in Nicholas Ray's perceptive hands, it emerged as a morality play. Perhaps the serious attitudes of the film's stars accounted for its elevation from a light but sophisticated tale of mores to a commentary on the tendency of money to corrupt. Besides Ryan's growing reputation as a tragic figure, Joan Fontaine and Zachary Scott had also distinguished themselves previously in roles of dimension, while Mel Ferrer, Joan Leslie, and Harold Vermilyea gave accurate portrayals as people involved in the world of artists, writers, and book publishers.

Considering its cast, direction, and screenplay, *Born to Be Bad* should have attracted attention, but many critics were nonplussed by the shortened, stilted ending, which depicted Curtis's realization about relationships as he is flying his airplane. This was awkwardly conveyed by a few perplexing grimaces from Curtis as he surveys the horizon, and a hurried reconciliation with Donna, who has come chasing after him.

In the *RKO Story*, authors Richard B. Jewell and Vernon Harbin noted that the film's ending was changed to satisfy the censors, and they described the result as "sentimental and self-righteous." While their criticism bears consideration, it seems secondary to the film's other merits. Amid the multitudes of worthwhile pictures churned out of Hollywood during the heyday of the double bill, *Born to Be Bad* deserves more than a cursory look.

Ryan's role as Nick Bradley resembled the kind of character he wistfully spoke of having missed too often, and was the romantic, clever, sophisticated city type he believed was earmarked for actors like Cary Grant and Clark Gable. As in many of his roles, his part was a throwback to his past, when he had entertained aspirations of becoming a writer. Ryan never included *Born to Be Bad* among his slim list of personal favorites, thus the picture stands as almost mute testimony to a less known, but nevertheless intriguing, entry in his filmography.

Reviews: "Mr. Ryan gives the kind of warm consideration in his scenes with Joan Fontaine which suggests that the director was principally concerned with spicing *Born to Be Bad* with boiling romantic clichés." (*New York Times*, 9/29/50.)

"*Born to Be Bad* is a dull little story... RKO Pictures hasn't spared the horses for this one. Such 20-game winners as Robert Ryan, Joan Fontaine, Zachary Scott, and Joan Leslie, are in there pitching." (Joe Pihodna, *New York Herald-Tribune*, 9/29/50.)

Best of the Badmen (2) (1951). RKO, C-84 min. *Director* William D. Russell. *Producer* Herman Schlom. *Story* Robert Hardy Andrews. *Screenplay* Robert Hardy Andrews, John Twist. *Art Directors* Albert S. D'Agostino, Carroll Clark. *Music Director* Constantin Bakaleinikoff. *Camera* Edward Cronjager. *Editor* Desmond Marquette. *Cast* **Robert Ryan** (Jeff Clanton), Claire Trevor (Lily), Jack Buetel (Bob Younger), Robert Preston (Matthew Fowler), Walter Brennan (Doc Butcher), Bruce Cabot (Cole Younger), John Archer (Curly Ringo), Lawrence Tierney (Jesse James), Barton MacLane (Joad), Tom Tyler (Frank James), Robert Wilke (Jim Younger), John Cliff (John Younger), Carleton Young (Wilson), Byron Foulger (Judge), Harry Woods (Proprietor of Trading Post), Everett Glass (Doctor).

In this RKO sequel to 1948's *Return of the Badmen*, Ryan's character, cavalry officer Jeff Clanton, gave him a switch toward the good, and more development than his Sundance Kid found in *Return*. Nevertheless, Robert Hardy Andrews' overblown screenplay and director William D. Russell's exaggerated maneuvering of his players rendered this Technicolor horse opera a cut below its predecessor. Since Andrews was responsible for scripting *The Woman on Pier 13*, the results of *Best of the Badmen* were in line with not only Hollywood's, but RKO's particular penchant for repeating failures.

The story of *Best of the Badmen* concerned the post–Civil War era, and the United States government's amnesty proposal for outlaws. In this case, it is the James and Younger brothers, as well as other assorted criminals who turn themselves in after Jeff Clanton assures their safety. Crooked detective Matthew Fowler (Robert Preston) has a grudge against Clanton, however, and after violating Clanton's promise of amnesty, Fowler has him arrested on a false murder charge.

After escaping from jail and bitterly rejecting the law, Clanton joins the James-Younger gang and follows them into a life of crime. Fowler's wife, Lily (Claire Trevor), falls in love with Clanton and persuades him to give himself up. In the obligatory final shoot-out between Clanton and Fowler, the crooked cop gets it in the back, the outlaws are again granted amnesty, and Clanton and Lily ride off into the sunset.

There is not a great deal more to say about *Best of the Badmen* or about Ryan's role in it, other than that he looked credible in the part, and that it was one of his first "wronged man" roles.

Reviews: "An unusually fine cast is thrown into the hopper this time, but it's ground up with a painfully unoriginal story. Robert Ryan, Claire Trevor, Robert Preston, and Walter Brennan put up a fine struggle to lend some credibility to the mixture, but they are overwhelmed by a double dose of standard ingredients. Director William D. Russell has kept things moving as fast as possible in front of the Technicolor cameras." (James S. Barstow, *New York Herald-Tribune*, 8/10/51.)

Flying Leathernecks (4) (1951). RKO, C-102 min. *Director* Nicholas Ray. *Producer* Edmund Grainger. *Story* Kenneth Gamet. *Screenplay* James Edward Grant. *Art Directors* Albert S. D'Agostino, James W. Sullivan. *Music Director* Constantin Bakaleinikoff. *Camera* William E. Snyder. *Editor* Sherman Todd. *Cast* John Wayne (Dan), **Robert Ryan** (Griff), Don Taylor (Cowboy), Janis Carter (Joan), Jay C. Flippen (Clancy), William Harrigan (Dr. Curan), James Bell (Colonel), Barry Kelley (General), Maurice Jara (Shorty), Adam Williams (Malotke), James Dobson (Pudge), Carleton Young (Captain McAllister), Brett King (Lieutenant Stark), Gordon Gebert (Tommy), Lynn Stalmaster (Lieutenant Castle), Hugh Sanders (General), Pat Prest (Greta Malotke).

The teaming of Ryan and John Wayne was a strong factor in the success of Nicholas Ray's Technicolor war saga of Marine Corps fighter pilots battling the Japanese in the Pacific during World War II. This Ryan-Ray outing was a solidly made, if at times maudlin picture, aided by several lengthy combat scenes using actual war footage.

Flying Leathernecks presents the dilemma of Major Dan Kirby (Wayne), who, as commanding officer of a squadron of pursuit fighter pilots, bears the onus for split-second combat decisions which may end in death for someone in his command. His second-in-command, Griff (Ryan), initially respects and admires Kirby; however, after the deaths of several pilots and Kirby's seeming callousness about them, Griff's loyalty turns to enmity.

When Griff gets his own command and has to make the same kinds of decisions for which he earlier condemned Kirby, he realizes the burdens of leadership and the two men have a reconciliation.

Ryan and Wayne provided the spark needed to raise the drama above the ordinary, and in two scenes in which they faced off in angry confrontation, one wished they would have taken a poke at each other just to see who would win.

Nicholas Ray did a good job making the inevitable stateside scenes in most war films of that period believable. Especially in the scenes between Wayne and his wife (Janis Carter), Ray used his camera well to avoid sentimentality. Miss Carter, best known for her vampish roles, came out of character and was credible in a role that is always difficult to carry off, that of the patiently waiting and attentive wife.

Ryan's Griff was reminiscent of his driven paramarine Dan Craig, in *Marine Raiders*. In both films, his character was troubled by the ambiguities of war, an idealistic soul playing by the rules who rudely discovers that in war fair play is suspended. Moreover, in *Flying Leathernecks*, Kirby's stance toward Griff is paternal, while in *Marine Raiders*, Pat O'Brien was the father figure. In the end, the prodigal son returned.

Reviews: "Since this new war drama is a Howard Hughes presentation from RKO, and costars those battle stalwarts, Robert Ryan and John Wayne, any customer can rightly assume that he'll get his money's worth in the way of uniformed virility and battle casualties." (Howard Thompson, *New York Times*, 9/20/51.)

"*Flying Leathernecks* uses Technicolor photography of fighting in the South Pacific and a good cast to show our fighting Marines in action. The conflict between Ryan and Wayne compares well with the situation we have seen in several modern war movies." (Philip T. Hartung, *Commonweal*, 11/2/51.)

The Racket (4) (1951). RKO, 89 min. *Director* John Cromwell. *Producer* Edmund Grainger. *Based on the play by* Bartlett Cormack. *Screenplay* William Wister Haines, W.R. Burnett. *Art Directors* Albert S. D'Agostino, Jack Okey. *Music Director* Mischa Bakaleinikoff. *Camera* George E. Diskant. *Editor* Sherman Todd. *Cast* Robert Mitchum (Tom McQuigg), Lizabeth Scott (Irene Hayes), **Robert Ryan** (Nick Scanlon), William Talman (Bailey), Ray Collins (Welch), Joyce MacKenzie (Mary McQuigg), Robert Hutton (Dave Ames), Virginia Huston (Lucy Johnson), William Conrad (Turck), Walter Sande (Delaney), Les Tremayne (Chief Craig), Don Porter (Connolly), Walter Baldwin (Sullivan), Brett King (Joe Scanlon), Richard Karlan (Enright), Tito Vuolo (Tony), Howard Petrie (Governor), William Forrest (Governor's Aide), Howland Chamberlin (Higgins), Ralph Peters (Davis), Milburn Stone (Foster the Assistant), Max Wagner (Durko), Richard Reeves (Leo the Driver), Don Beddoe (Mitchell), Harry Lauter, Art Dupuis (Cops).

When Howard Hughes bought RKO, one of his first announcements was a remake of *The Racket*. He had first produced the film in 1928, when he owned the Caddo Company, and 20 years later, he was still intrigued by the underworld and its machinations. Typically, it took three years after Hughes bought RKO before *The Racket* went into production.

Samuel Fuller was the first to work on the screenplay, then Nicholas Ray was consulted, but Hughes's script-tampering penchant led to rewrites by William Haines and director John Cromwell, and finally by W.R. Burnett. Moreover, midway through production, Hughes decided to shoot extensive retakes, costing $500,000. The results were disappointing.

Though the dramatics of the film were first-rate, its plotline remained grounded in a 1928 time frame that was anachronistic. RKO editors labored arduously trying to piece things together, and came up with a generally coherent narrative.

The Racket fell into *film noir* status because it dealt with gangsterism and political corruption, depicting them as insidious and universal, indeed, existential. Alienation threatens from all sides. Gangster Nick Scanlon (Ryan) rules his henchmen with brutality, gaining their loyalty through intimidation. In turn, he distrusts the syndicate heads above him, and safeguards his status by trampling over those who oppose him.

Scanlon's chief enemy, police captain Tom McQuigg (Robert Mitchum), also suffers from alienation, as he watches while various public officials fall under the syndicate take. The district attorney (Ray Collins) as well as a state inspector (William Conrad) are working for the syndicate, run by a faceless person known only as "the Old Man." Having been shuffled from precinct to precinct over the years, McQuigg has become almost as cynical as those he is out to stop.

In the end, though, at least a few cogs are broken off the wheel of corruption, when Scanlon is killed by the syndicate and the state crime commission arrives, armed with arrest warrants for the district attorney and the state inspector.

Ryan's Scanlon was one of his most vicious roles, and may have set the mold for his future more than his frightening portrait in *Crossfire*. He played Scanlon with a cagey abandon that made him into a compelling, yet repulsive, character.

We are introduced to Scanlon being shaved by his barber, whose hand is shaking over impending news. Scanlon watches, then responds the only way he knows, with aggression. Later, he calmly watches as an informer is executed, beats his brother and a henchman, has McQuigg's house bombed, and kills a policeman. In one of Ryan's best scenes, in which he eats an apple while talking to McQuigg, he demonstrated writer Gary Carey's reference to the "sublime meeting between actor and prop."

Reviews: "The remake has been refurbished for timely exploitation values, has good masculine star names, and can be pushed to good overall grosses. The plot ideas for *The Racket* are certainly not new to films, but this version comes over with a fresh touch ... Robert Ryan and Robert Mitchum dominate the picture with forceful, credible performances that add a lot of interest." (*Variety*, 10/17/51.)

"An unusual *film noir* with strong performances, especially Ryan's, and a bizarre ending." (Leonard Maltin, *TV Movies*, 1985–86.)

"Rough, tough action with a couple of rugged leads on opposite sides of the law ... Robert Ryan is the murdering hoodlum ... the rather outmoded plot attempts to show the link between criminals and politicians in an effort to bring the film up-to-date. Somehow the attempt falls flat but the action leaps along in high gear." (*Photoplay*, 1/52.)

On Dangerous Ground (5) (1951). RKO, 82 min. *Director* Nicholas Ray. *Producer* John Houseman. *Based on the novel* Mad with Much Heart *by* Gerald Butler. *Adaptors* A.I. Bezzerides, Nicholas Ray. *Screenplay* A.I. Bezzerides. *Art Directors* Albert D'Agostino, Ralph Berger. *Music Director* Constantin Bakaleinikoff. *Music* Bernard Herrmann. *Viola Work* Virginia Majewski. *Camera* George E. Diskant. *Editor* Roland Gross. *Cast* Ida Lupino (Mary), **Robert Ryan** (Jim Wilson), Ward Bond (Brent), Charles Kemper (Bill Daly), Anthony Ross (Pete Santos), Ed Begley (Captain Brawley), Ian Wolfe (Carrey), Sumner Williams (Danny), Gus Schilling (Lucky), Frank Ferguson (Willows), Cleo Moore (Myrna), Olive Carey (Mrs. Brent), Richard Irving (Bernie Tucker), Pat Prest (Julie), Ruth Lee (Helen Daly), Vera Stokes (Mother), Steve Roberts (Running Man), Vince Barnett (Waiter), G. Pat Collins (Sergeant

Wendell), Jimmy Conlin (Doc Hyman), Joan Taylor (Hazel), Nestor Paiva (Gabbanierri), A.I. Bezzerides (Gato), Nita Talbot (B-girl).

On Dangerous Ground was an esoteric masterpiece, which Nicholas Ray and screenwriter A.I. Bezzerides adapted from the British novel *Mad with Much Heart* by Gerald Butler. Ryan may have given one of his subtlest portrayals in the film, which was short on dialogue, high on visual expression, and augmented by a dramatic musical score. His character, Detective Jim Wilson, was a *noir* type with which he was familiar, a man so tormented by what he sees in the line of duty that he is driven to commit brutal acts, but who is redeemed in the final analysis.

Created at the height of the *film noir* era, *On Dangerous Ground* is a superb example of the genre. As depicted in the seedy nighttime setting of Los Angeles's tenderloin district, corruption and degradation prevail, punctuated by random violence. The role of Wilson delineates the conflict of the story, that of a cop turned cynical and rancorous from dealing with the dregs of humanity. He feels that the public fears and distrusts the police, and begins to alienate his fellow officers. He has become a loner, an essentially good man gone sour, and although his conscience bothers him, he is trapped.

Feelings of frustration and futility are intertwined in the actions of many of the characters in *On Dangerous Ground*. A rummy tells Wilson, "I had one of my spells. I thought I was gonna die." Then he gulps down a shot of liquor. Wilson's partner, Pop Bailey (Charles Kemper), carries an old news clipping of his son in a football uniform and has eight children. He talks of the old days.

The police, especially, are depicted routinely responding to numerous grim situations. The problem that initially brings Wilson into notice is the murder of a policeman, and we see the unorthodox tactics he uses to catch the killer. The deviance infecting him is of the sadistic sort, and he has come to enjoy catching criminals and punishing them himself. Stooping to the level of those he detests, he has incorporated their self-destructiveness into his own actions.

One scene, with the blonde, vampish Myrna (Cleo Moore), indicates the extent of his frustrations, as masochism and sexuality are tied together. As Myrna shows Wilson the bruise her boyfriend recently gave her, she directs his hand, holding an unlit cigarette, into her mouth. The music in the background synchronizes with a shot of Wilson turning toward Myrna, who says, "You'll *make* me talk, you'll *squeeze* it out of me with those big, strong arms, *won't* you?" He softly replies, "That's right, sister." The next fade-in shows Wilson slowly descending the dark staircase of her building in deep thought, leaving one to ponder whether he has left Myrna safe or sorry.

Another spare, yet graphic, scene depicting Wilson's impulses occurs in an eerie *film noir* setting, appropriately named the Harbor Hotel. A stool pigeon has tipped off Wilson and his partner about a murder suspect, Bernie Tucker, and the two cops pay him a visit. Accompanied by the rising crescendo of Bernard Herrmann's magnificent score, Wilson loses control of himself and snarls, "I *always* make you punks talk! Why do you make me *do* it? *Why? Why?*" He appears on the verge of a total breakdown as he responds to Bernie's masochistic entreaty, "*Hit* me, *hit* me, *hit* me!" by nearly beating him to death.

The pangs of conscience that erupt when Wilson returns to his apartment that night are acted out symbolically. Frowning as he shuts the door and switches on the bare, overhead light, Wilson's face contorts into a desolate mask of anger and hopelessness. As he gazes despairingly at the trophy resting on his dresser, it is the sole remnant from his optimistic past. To blot out the world he jerks down the window shade, walks

to the sink, and while a trombone insinuates a somber melody in the background, he is compelled to wash his hands of his recent dirty work. It is an unconscious "undoing" act, but as he anxiously wipes his hands with a towel, the guilt remains.

The story behind the creation of *On Dangerous Ground* is unusual for several reasons, not the least of which concerns its tepid critical reception in 1952. Artistically, the film was ahead of its time, and is probably Nicholas Ray's most profound picture. But the disparity in its exposition, from the chaotic, violence-ridden corruption of the city, to the relatively bucolic setting of the country was too much of a stylistic difference to be appreciated by the mainstream.

Though it is difficult to know for certain, the displeasure that Ray and producer John Houseman felt upon seeing the initial critical reviews of *On Dangerous Ground* may have helped lower the film in their esteem. Yet today it is recognized as a powerful study in terms of style, technique, and content, and has been given proper acclaim by serious film scholars, such as Cahiers du Cinéma.

In addition to Ray's high artistic talent, cinematographer George E. Diskant's expertise in low-key, high contrast lighting situations, and Bernard Herrmann's beautiful musical score, counterpointed the drama as it unfolded. Virginia Majewski's virtuoso viola work perfectly complemented his orchestration, which Herrmann regarded as the best composition of his career.

It is difficult to decide whether it was those in front of or behind the camera that made *On Dangerous Ground* such a fascinating study. Its cast of character actors was impeccable, headed by Ward Bond, as a vengeful father whose daughter is murdered, Ed Begley, as Wilson's tough commanding officer, and Charles Kemper and Anthony Ross, as weary veteran officers. In smaller roles, Cleo Moore, Gus Schilling, Richard Irving, Nita Talbot, and Nestor Paiva were either brazen or pathetic as various denizens of the night.

The conflictual setting of *On Dangerous Ground* was a challenge for Ryan, as its dramatic changes in mood, from the dark tension of the city to the pristeen snow-covered countryside, required a different kind of acting technique. Though the film's first half was a well-told version of the police drama, its second, more eccentric half contained much less dialogue, and communicated mainly through the actions and facial expressions of the characters, while emphasizing its moodiness with expressionistic settings.

Underscoring the characters' dark emotions, George Diskant's high contrast film took full advantage of the Colorado mountains sequences, especially apparent during the chase involving Wilson, Brent (Bond), and Danny (Sumner Williams).

Working within Ray's unconventional story, Ryan and costar Ida Lupino brought the whole piece together by making their scenes together into intimate conversations. In the interior scenes at the home of the blind woman, Mary (Lupino), Ray mainly used close-up shots of Ryan and Lupino, establishing their feelings for each other through action rather than dialogue. Although Wilson and Mary's romantic involvement is shown only briefly in the final frames, their embrace possesses real emotional power.

In the book *Film Noir: An Encyclopedic Reference to the American Style*, writer Robert Porfirio seems to have accurately perceived the merits of *On Dangerous Ground* and of Ryan's performance:

Reviews: "Nicholas Ray's visual treatment of despair and salvation is one of the most moving in *film noir* . . . the central character of Wilson is conceived and delineated with great impact. The structural division of the film is in two parts, city and country, and creates a narrative framework of a journey that is literally from city to country, and subtextually,

an inner journey of self-realization. . . . Above all, there is the mesmerizing presence of Robert Ryan and Ida Lupino. Ryan's face expressed the motif of alienation that pervades Ray's work better than any dialogue could. As played by Ryan, Wilson's violent interrogation of a suspect asking "Why do you punks make me do it?" is one of the most neurotic and self-destructive actions in *film noir*, so that the character's return to his apartment later that night becomes a gripping vision of loneliness. Wilson looks for a moment at his sports trophies, which are the only positive symbols left in his life and bitterly asks, 'Who cares?' Few actors could give this line as evocative a reading.

"Robert Ryan is excellent as the lonely, embittered detective—mostly silent, bent on catching criminals and seeing that they pay the penalty for their crimes." (*Showmen's Trade Review.*)

"Producer John Houseman and director Nicholas Ray have shot the metropolitan phases of the story in a city's shabby streets, catching in sleaziness and violence some sense of the rancor of the cop, in which role Robert Ryan does a straight, cold-eyed, stout-muscled job." (Bosley Crowther, *New York Times*, 2/13/52.)

"The story is told with a camera and a rather unorthodox one . . . the chief virtue of the film is the fascinating jumble of action that results when the two determined characters Ryan and Bond try to outlaw each other at the job of detecting." (Manny Farber, *The Nation*, 3/22/52.)

"The film is presented soberly—at times it is photographed in a mood of gray honesty that is beautiful; the actors, including Ryan, Bond and Lupino work hard and often to good effect, and the picture resorts to none of the tricks and mannerisms of commercial melodrama." (Robert Hatch, *The New Republic*, 1/28/52.)

Clash by Night (5) (1952). RKO, 105

min. *Director* Fritz Lang. *Producer* Harriet Parsons. *Executive Producers* Jerry Wald, Norman Krasna. *Based on the play by* Clifford Odets. *Screenplay* Alfred Hayes. *Art Directors* Albert S. D'Agostino, Carroll Clark. *Set Decorators* Darrell Silvera, Jack Mills. *Costumes* Michael Woulfe. *Music* Roy Webb. *Music Director* Constantin Bakaleinikoff. *Song* Dick Gasparre, Jack Baker, George Fragos. *Special Effects* Harold Wellman. *Camera* Nicholas Musuraca. *Editor* George J. Amy. *Cast* Barbara Stanwyck (Mae Doyle), Paul Douglas (Jerry D'Amato), **Robert Ryan** (Earl Pfeiffer), Marilyn Monroe (Peggy), J. Carrol Naish (Uncle Vince), Keith Andes (Joe Doyle), Silvio Minciotti (Papa D'Amato), Gilbert Frye (Man), Al Cavens (Guest), Mario Stiletti (Bartender), Frank Kreig (Art).

RKO's 1952 filmed version of *Clash by Night*, in which Ryan, Barbara Stanwyck, and Paul Douglas ably represented belabored souls chasing after happiness, matched and improved upon the melancholic play which Clifford Odets wrote in 1941. All three stars played their roles with total conviction, aided by Alfred Hayes' screenplay, which rang out with the hard-pressed desperation of those nearing middle-age but who are still searching.

Director Fritz Lang agreed to do *Clash by Night* at the request of RKO executive producer Jerry Wald and Barbara Stanwyck. Lang had a fascination with the idea of a world populated largely by maladjusted personalities, and his stories often intertwined deviant protagonists fighting the inevitability of fate. Since his previous works had been mostly in the action/mystery genre, he delved into a different realm in *Clash by Night*'s tale of adultery and marital discord.

Although *Clash by Night* had a violent nature to it, its mayhem was of the psychological variety, culminating at the film's end with a single physical action. Lang believed that brutality in films was necessary for dramatic development, and set about developing the concept within the confines of the marital setting.

The main characters in *Clash by Night* are disillusioned, lonely, and bitter, thus their plight is clearly a *film noir* dilemma. Mae Doyle (Stanwyck) returns to her hometown in the cannery district of Monterey, California, after being gone for ten years. Her past is clouded by the unhappiness of more than a few failed love affairs, and she is weary of her search. She meets Jerry D'Amato (Douglas), and sees in him the qualities of security and devotion which she has sought with increasing urgency as time has passed. Mae's longing for protection overcomes the truth that she doesn't love Jerry, but nevertheless, she marries him.

Enter Jerry's best friend, the sardonic Earl Pfeiffer (Ryan), who has just come out of a divorce. Earl pursues Mae, ignoring his friendship with Jerry, and the two have an affair. When Jerry discovers Mae's dalliance, he moves out of their house with their newborn child, and Mae goes to Earl.

Distraught over her actions and realizing that she has never committed herself to anyone, Mae leaves Earl and returns to Jerry. In the final scenes, Mae begs Jerry for forgiveness and the two have a reconciliation, while the pathetic Earl is back where he started, despondent and loveless.

The triangulation between Jerry, Mae, and Earl is an appropriate *film noir* scenario in which fate becomes a self-fulfilling prophecy. All three bear responsibility for their plight, which stems from varying degrees of alienation. Although Jerry is not as bitter as are Mae and Earl, he is afflicted with low self-esteem. Early in the film, when Jerry arranges a date with Mae through her brother, Joe (Keith Andes), he tells her, "I ain't much of anything."

Mae and Earl are not far behind Jerry. When Joe asks Mae about her long absence from home, she replies tersely, "What have I been doing? Here it is in four words: Big ideas, small results." When Jerry says self-effacingly, "I been takin' up a lot of your time, Mae," she retorts, "My time is not so precious."

Earl Pfeiffer's problems seem more deeply rooted, appearing in the form of self-hatred and misogyny. To Mae's question, "You don't like women, do you?" Earl declares angrily, "Take any six of 'em, and throw 'em in the air. The one who sticks to the ceiling, I like." His bitterness toward women is evidenced elsewhere: Speaking of his wife, he says, "Some day I'm gonna stick her full of pins, to see if blood runs out!"; of another woman, he carps, "I ought to cut up that celluloid angel a little bit, she'd look more interesting." Despite his negativity toward women, however, Earl is dependent on them. In one breath, he asserts, "A man without a woman is nothing," while in the next, he confesses, "I'm a glutton for punishment."

Alfred Hayes' perceptive screenplay fully explored the self-destructive aspects of adultery in the caustic verbal exchanges between Mae and Earl. One conversation takes place on a moonlit veranda outside of a dance hall, where a desperate Earl makes his first pass at Mae:

> Mae: (Referring to a former lover) "He's the only man I ever knew who gave me a feeling of security."
> Earl: "Which makes me what?"
> Mae: "A sparrow in the treetop."

Then:

> Earl: "Mae, what do you *really* think of me?"
> Mae: "You impress me as a man who needs a new suit of clothes, or a new love affair, but he doesn't know which."
> Earl: "You can't make me any smaller, I happen to be pre-shrunk."

There is a masochistic quality in the relationship between Mae and Earl, but Earl possesses an added degree of self-destructiveness. One evening after he gets drunk and passes out at Jerry and Mae's house, he wakes up the next morning and demands of Mae, "Why didn't you let me sleep it off in the gutter?" Then, a minute later, he declares angrily, "I drink that shellac to get unborn." Letting down his guard for a moment, Earl begs Mae to "save me from dying of loneliness," but his reprieve from the abyss of despair is destined to fail.

As the tortured odd-man-out who hides his pain behind a veneer of sarcastic masculinity, Ryan's portrayal of Earl Pfeiffer rivaled his best work, and was also one of his most important contributions to the *film noir* genre.

Reviews: "Robert Ryan, Barbara Stanwyck, and Paul Douglas are veterans who can handle a line of dialogue and an emotion with facility.... As the lover, Ryan is a natural in his depiction of a man groping for a way out of a lonely existence." (A. Weiler, *New York Times*, 6/19/52.)

"*Clash by Night* offers two good actors (Robert Ryan and J. Carrol Naish) and fluid, flexible direction that makes it worth your time. Ryan enacts a 'sort of imitation,' as the 'Kingfish of Buckman County,' run down and out of luck, a cynical guy who plays every word and gesture halfway into paranoia and with hard-bitten pathos. The role has been played by everyone from Mitchum to Widmark, but Ryan is the first one to give you the sense of an ordinary citizen being destroyed by a neurotic urge to act and admire himself at the same time. With pantomime that gives the sensation of a clock ticking away inside his skull, he is almost always caught in the process of observing himself while seeming to be observing and philosophizing about his friends." (Manny Farber, *Nation*, 7/26/52.)

"The drama revolves around the three principals, who play it for all it's worth.... Each contributes to the film the maximum of dramatic talent. The production owes much to the sincerity and earnestness of their performances.... Ryan plays the interloping lover with a cunning blend of strength and weakness." (Alton Cook, *New York World Telegram-Sun.*)

Beware, My Lovely (5) (1952). RKO, 77 min. *Director* Harry Horner. *Producer* Collier Young. *Based on the story and play by* Mel Dinelli. *Screenplay* Mel Dinelli. *Art Directors* Albert D'Agostino, Alfred Herman. *Set Decorators* Darrell Silvera, Al Oremback. *Music* Leith Stevens. *Music Director* Constantin Bakaleinikoff. *Camera* George E. Diskant. *Editor* Paul Weatherwax. *Cast* Ida Lupino (Mrs. Gordon), **Robert Ryan** (Howard Wilton), Taylor Holmes (Mr. Armstrong), Barbara Whiting (Ruth Williams), James Wilmas (Mr. Stevens), O.Z. Whitehead (Mr. Franks), Dee Pollack (Grocery Boy).

Adapting a movie from a play often poses problems for screenwriters, because the intangibles of the stage may elude their grasp. Fortunately, the screenplay for *Beware, My Lovely* was written by Mel Dinelli, who also wrote the play on which it was based. Billed as a suspense thriller, *Beware, My Lovely* succeeded in this regard, yet its abbreviated length sealed its fate as a routine programmer. Indeed, when the film opened in New York, it was featured along with eight vaudeville acts, as if to underscore its unimportant treatment by RKO. Nevertheless, among all of Ryan's 70-odd portraits, it may have been one of his most finely etched definitions of emotional pain.

A fascinating aspect of *Beware, My Lovely* was its ability to build tension from a modest structure. In addition to Ryan's schizophrenic handyman, Howard Wilton, the film's sole other major character was Ida Lupino, as the lonely widow in whose house the unsettling story unfolded. The unpretentious setting for the drama was a large, Victorian era house, replete with blind corners and mirrors in every room to startle.

The plot of *Beware, My Lovely* was uncomplicated. Mrs. Gordon (Lupino) needs help with her housework, and hires the diffident Howard, unaware of his psychosis. Howard is lucid when he arrives at her door one day, having forgotten his recent murder of a woman during one of his recurrent spells of violence.

Shortly thereafter, a taunting girl triggers a psychotic attack in him that alternates between menacing Mrs. Gordon with death, to withdrawing into insane mutterings and other paranoid states. The rest of the story concerns Howard's increasingly demented behavior, and Mrs. Gordon's desperate attempts to escape.

Director Harry Horner had won an Oscar for his art direction of *The Heiress* (1949), and his creativity showed strongly in *Beware, My Lovely*'s intricate, carefully laid-out set designs, and in the expressionistic camerawork by George E. Diskant. Using numerous and varied camera set-ups, Diskant often shot Ryan's character from a low angle to suggest him as a looming, ominous presence. Diskant's camera came in close to build tension by lingering on the players' faces. He caught Ryan running through a gamut of emotions, often capturing them through reflective surfaces and by superimposition.

A few examples of Diskant's artistry: Ryan's terror-stricken face, superimposed against the wheels of an advancing locomotive; and his image, reflected ominously in a bucket of water, in mirrors, and in Christmas tree ornaments.

Beware, My Lovely contained essential *film noir* elements of loneliness and alienation. The main characters are portrayed as indirect victims of war. Mrs. Gordon is depressed, having recently lost her husband in World War I, and Howard went over the edge when he was declared unfit for military service. Though both are isolated, fate draws them together for the purpose of freeing them from their different states of hell on earth. But paradoxically, Mrs. Gordon's exodus from her shell of seclusion results in the opposite for Howard, since at film's end he remains lost, bound for a ward in an asylum.

The role of Howard Wilton was a real challenge for Ryan because it required an implicit suggestion of violence. Within that context, he enacted a portrait which might best be described as one of persecuted impotence.

Although *Beware, My Lovely* allowed Ryan to demonstrate a small stroke of his acting skill in career terms it provided little impetus forward.

Reviews: "Those who have never seen a picture in which a crazy fellow holds a woman captive in her own house, while outside in the street children laugh and the sun shines, should by all means go to *Beware, My Lovely*, in which Ryan and Lupino enact precisely that little drama. Ryan makes a convincing, rather pathetic lunatic; Miss Lupino 'registers' fright to the last decibel." (Robert Hatch, *Theatre Arts*, 7/52.)

"Harry Horner's direction manages considerable emphasis on suspense, and the trouping of the two stars is excellent. Name importance is lent to the picture by the names of Ryan and Lupino." (*Variety*, 10/9/52.)

"Robert Ryan, as Howard, is a psychotic personality with intervals of lucidity, and his alternating phases of comparative reasonableness and savage intolerance are both used with disturbing effect to reduce Miss Lupino to ultimate quivering fear. Psychologically, *Beware, My Lovely* is a convincing study of one man's paranoia.... Mr. Ryan, as the homicidal psychotic, turns in a remarkably sensitive portrait.... Mr. Ryan's acting alone warrants seeing the film." (Paul V. Beckley, *New York Herald-Tribune*, 9/13/52.)

"Although Harry Horner's *Beware, My Lovely* is too short, his direction of the script is quite effective and frequently throws you into a cold sweat. Ryan gets convincingly mad and violent as the handyman, and Lupino is realistically terrified as the lonely widow." (Philip T. Hartung, *Commonweal*, 7/4/52.)

Horizons West (4) (1952). Universal, C-81 min. *Director* Budd Boetticher. *Producer* Albert J. Cohen. *Story-Screenplay* Louis Stevens. *Art Directors* Bernard Herzbrun, Robert Clatworthy. *Set Decorators* Russell A. Gausman, Joe Kish. *Music Director* Joseph Gershenson. *Sound* Leslie I. Carey, Herbert Pritchard. *Camera* Charles P. Boyle. *Editor* Ted J. Kent. *Cast* **Robert Ryan** (Dan Hammond), Julia Adams (Lorna Hardin), Rock Hudson (Neil Hammond), John McIntire (Ira Hammond), Judith Braun (Sally), Raymond Burr (Cord Hardin), James Arness (Tiny), Frances Bavier (Martha Hammond), Dennis Weaver (Dandy Taylor), Tom Powers (Frank Tarleton), Rodolfo Acosta (General Ecobar), John Hubbard (Sam Hunter), Douglas Fowley (Tompkins), Walter Reed (Layton), Raymond Greenleaf (Eli Dodson), Tom Monroe (Jim Clawson), Lillian Molieri (Teresa), Dan White (Dennis), Edward Coch, Jr. (Juan), Paulette Turner (Celeste), John Harmon (Deputy Sheriff Johnson), Robert Bice (Righteous Citizen), Dan Poore (Henchman), Frank Chase (Borden), Tom Riste (Al), Mae Clarke (Mrs. Tarleton), Peter Mamakos (Lieutenant Salazar).

Ryan provided a good deal of steely authority to Budd Boetticher's post–Civil War Western of turmoil in and around Austin, Texas. Made in 1952 at Universal-International, *Horizons West* has been overlooked by today's critics of the Western, but it is probably one of Ryan's better efforts in the genre. Within Boetticher's repertory, it outclasses his better known pictures, such as *Comanche Station*, *The Tall T*, and *Seven Men from Now*.

Several aspects of *Horizons West* rank it well above average as dramatic fare, not the least of which was Ryan's portrayal of a restless ex–Confederate major, Dan Hammond, who turns to a life of crime, and becomes drunk with power. Louis Stevens' screenplay built a solid story, and he injected the plot with subtle psychological undertones.

Returning home from the Civil War, Hammond is nursing a bitterness at having lost the war and three years of his life. After ominously announcing to his brother, Neil (Rock Hudson), "I guess I just can't stand losing, *anything*," he rides into Austin intent on making up for lost time and hurt pride. Shortly thereafter, he becomes a land grabber, a cattle rustler, and a murderer. Once a respected citizen, he alienates his family and the entire town of Austin.

Symbolically, the conflict that afflicts the Hammond family bears similarities to the Cain and Abel theme. Dan Hammond is a previously decent person whose selfish streak degenerates to megalomania as a side effect of the war. Despite his criminal actions, he is still capable of decency when he spares his brother's life, and he seems to feel a degree of guilt over his lawlessness.

Horizons West was beautifully photographed using the old Technicolor process and color consultants. Rich hues of blue, purple, and red complemented the sets and costumes, and the location settings gave it the scope of a larger scale Hollywood production, minus the hyperbole. Boetticher mounted his action convincingly, particularly in the fight scenes between Dan Hammond and one of his enemies, and in a few other sequences.

Also, the high quality cast delivered the realistic dialogue with a conviction that gave the film added impetus. On the side of good, the performances of John McIntyre, as the quietly strong Hammond patriarch, and Rock Hudson, as the stalwart Neil, were very good. Raymond Burr was unctuously arrogant as the cruel rancher who loses his life and wife to Dan Hammond. And Julia Adams' provocative portrayal as Hammond's paramour provided the right balance to tame his rebel nature. As former Confederate soldiers, James Arness and Dennis Weaver turned in sincere contributions.

Ryan's Dan Hammond conformed to his attraction to parts that portrayed him as a sympathetic heavy. Although by film's end Hammond has committed numerous crimes and has murdered one of his best friends, he possesses a conscience that helps to diminish his culpability. His relationship with Lorna (Julia Adams) is loving, and he saves his father from debt by paying off his mortgage. Revealing some insight into his flawed personality, Hammond admits to Tiny (Arness), just before killing him, "I guess I was driven too far by power and money." Thus, there is tragedy in his nighttime demise in Lorna's arms, after he is gunned down by a former friend (Walter Reed).

Reviews: "Ryan endows his character with a certain ruthless ruggedness ... Budd Boetticher's direction of the Louis Stevens story manages some good action sequences, and the lensing by Charles Boyle was well handled, providing pictorial beauty." (*Variety*, 9/24/52.)

"Ryan is a maladjusted Civil War veteran who wants to get rich quick and easy. He is tall and menacing as a Southern major who is too restless to return to ranching like his brother. The action in the struggle comes along with satisfying regularity under Budd Boetticher's direction. This is a perfectly acceptable Western, full of big ambitions, violence, and the visual color of a period production." (Otis L. Guernsey, *New York Herald-Tribune*.)

"It must be acknowledged that Mr. Ryan and Mr. Hudson, as two brothers on either side of the law, bring some gritty muscularity to the proceedings, particularly the former." (Howard Thompson, *New York Times*, 11/22/52.)

City Beneath the Sea (2) (1953). Universal, C-87 min. *Director* Budd Boetticher. *Producer* Albert J. Cohen. *Based on the book* Port Royal, the Ghost City Beneath the Sea *by* Harry E. Reisberg. *Screenplay* Jack Harvey, Ramon Romero. *Art Directors* Alexander Golitzen, Emrich Nicholson. *Camera* Charles P. Boyle. *Editor* Edward Curtiss. *Cast* **Robert Ryan** (Brad Carlton), Mala Powers (Terry McBride), Anthony Quinn (Tony Bartlett), Suzann Ball (Venita), George Mathews (Captain Meade), Karel Stepanek (Dwight Trevor), Hilo Hattie (Mama Mary), Lalo Rios (Calypso), Woody Strode (Kijon), Tommy Garland (Martin), Michael Dale (Kirk), Leon Lontoc

(Kip), Bernie Gozie (Maru), John Warburton (Captain Clive), Barbara Morrison (Mme. Cecile), Peter Mamakos
(Mendoza).

Ryan's second film for Universal Pictures ranked well below *Horizons West* as
adult fare, and had the lightness of a
Saturday matinée. Although Budd Boetticher directed, and the story moved
along at a brisk pace, it was little more
than an ordinary adventure, made attractive by good deep-sea photography
and Technicolor film. The film's main attraction was the performances of Ryan
and Anthony Quinn, who rose mightily
to the occasion of a pedestrian screenplay.

The two starred as happy-go-lucky
deep-sea divers hunting for a sunken gold
shipment in the Caribbean. Although
their talents were greatly underutilized,
their collective screen presence carried
one past the mundane plot. Besides Ryan
and Quinn, others in the cast fared less
well, including George Mathews as a
crooked speculator, and Woody Strode
as a sturdy servant.

Ryan had a bonafide romance in *City
Beneath the Sea* with Mala Powers, and a
few of their scenes depicted the kind of
lighter, less intense image that might
have suggested a Cary Grant movie. The
film's exotic locale had a freer feeling that
contrasted sharply with the atmosphere
of a number of Ryan's recent pictures.

As a routine adventure yarn, *City
Beneath the Sea* stands comfortably among
similar efforts; however, it deserves a
look to see Ryan waltzing through his
carefree part while appearing as if he is
genuinely having fun.

Reviews: "For those who like their
nautical-minded actors in the water,
there's *City Beneath the Sea*, in which
Robert Ryan and Anthony Quinn play a
couple of fun-loving but tough deep-sea
divers. The Technicolor in the undersea
scenes is very pretty." (Philip T. Hartung,
Commonweal, 3/27/53.)

"A two-fisted adventure about big
men in the big business of treasure

hunting beneath the sea. The plot is
predictable but Ryan and Quinn are convincing leads and carry the show."
(Steven H. Scheuer, *Movies on TV*,
1984–85.)

"Ryan and Quinn are well-cast as
two happy-go-lucky professional divers."
(*Theatre Arts*, 3/53.)

The Naked Spur, (5) (1953). MGM,
C-91 min. *Director* Anthony Mann. *Pro-
ducer* William H. Wright. *Screenplay* Sam
Rolfe, Harold Jack Bloom. *Art Directors*
Cedric Gibbons, Malcolm Brown. *Music*
Bronislau Kaper. *Camera* William Mel-
lor. *Editor* George White. *Cast* James
Stewart (Howard Kemp), Janet Leigh
(Lina Patch), **Robert Ryan** (Ben Van-
dergroat), Ralph Meeker (Roy Ander-
son), Millard Mitchell (Jesse Tate).

Ryan optioned his talents to MGM
in late 1952, and accepted the pivotal role
of the amoral murderer Ben Vandergroat,
in Anthony Mann's gem of a Western,
The Naked Spur. Since arriving in
Hollywood, Ryan had made six Westerns,
none of which were very good or very
successful. But Mann had directed several fine, economical pictures prior to
The Naked Spur, and with James Stewart
heading the cast, Ryan had confidence.

Mann had built his reputation in the
action/Western genre, but was a director
who concentrated on "feelings." He had
an instinctive sense for the visual expression of man's inner conflicts, and *The
Naked Spur* contained thematic elements
of greed, alienation, and frustration,
which made it appropriate as a *film noir*
Western.

The fatalistic story concerns five people cast together unwillingly, and a $5,000
bounty for Vandergroat is the mercenary
goal three of them have in mind. Stewart
plays Howard Kemp, a reluctant bounty
hunter chasing Vandergroat from Kansas
to Colorado. Kemp intends to use the
reward money to buy back his ranch,
which his fiancée sold while he was off
fighting the Civil War. Adding insult to
injury, she ran off with another man.

Kemp is an honest man who feels guilty about chasing men for money, and Vandergroat badgers him by reminding him of the stigma of bounty hunting. Vandergroat embarrasses him further by constantly referring to his fiancée's betrayal.

Kemp's sole receipt of the reward is threatened by the unwanted partnership of a morally unstable ex–Army lieutenant, Roy Anderson (Ralph Meeker), and a desperate, disillusioned prospector, Jesse Tate (Millard Mitchell, in his last film). During their journey to bring Vandergroat to justice, he plots to divide his captors by creating greed and jealousy among them.

The allure of Vandergroat's female companion, Lina Patch (Janet Leigh), becomes an added dynamic in his methodical plan when he uses her as bait to stir up competition between Kemp and Anderson. At film's end, the selfish ways of Ben, Roy, and Jesse spell their doom, while Lina provides the redeeming quality, love, that saves Kemp from sharing a symbolic fate with them.

Some observers have lauded *The Naked Spur* as one of the finest Westerns ever made, and it has often been studied by serious film scholars. In Lawrence Alloway's book, *Violent America: The Movies–1946 to 1964*, he commented on the rise of the Western as valid art, and on Mann's technical virtuosity on *The Naked Spur*: "The visual quality of the New Westerns is often marvelous; an intensified sense of space and light in outdoor settings; the alternations of long, patient pans and sudden flickering images of fast-cut gunfights, staged with a new rage and ingenuity...one must consider the inhabited landscapes of movies like *The Naked Spur*...every feature of landscape is assessed as a foxhole or vantage point, as an ambush for us or for them. Thus, the visual clarity and elegance of the photography increases the terrain's potential for threat, so that the landscape becomes the analogue of an ever more treacherous cast of characters."

Although *The Naked Spur* was not a costly epic, its collective elements registered high in gut-level emotions. William C. Mellor's Technicolor photography and Bronislau Kaper's moving score captured the intended mood of melancholy and foreboding which pervaded the film. Finally, Harold Jack Bloom's terse, insightful screenplay could not have been better written.

The Ben Vandergroat character fit in well with Ryan's growing portfolio of almost likeable psychopaths. Initially, he is presented as a victim of unfortunate circumstances, and one nearly feels sympathy for him. He recalls to his captors his transient, unhappy childhood, of how his mother "caught the fever and died on the way to Kansas," of running away from home, and of how his father unceremoniously "tied me up and throwed me in a wagon."

On his own at an early age after "Pa got gunned down in a saloon before we ever seen Kansas," Ben has become a societal misfit. His murderous streak is only proven in the last minutes of the film, when he kills Jesse in cold blood. Ryan portrayed Ben as a crafty, brutal villain, thinly disguised under a slyly cheerful veneer of innocence. The role allowed him to develop sufficiently the motivations behind Ben's actions, a liberty he did not have in a number of other pictures.

Reviews: "*The Naked Spur* is a bang-bang-up Western and the shootingest Hollywood horse opera in months.... Shot in the Colorado Rockies, the plot is unfolded almost entirely with the camera rather than with words. A striking exercise in violence, it is a Western with real form, rhythm and authentic style. Best sequence: a three-way shooting match between Ryan, Stewart, and Meeker, up and down a cliff jutting over a raging, impassable river." (*Time*, 2/2/53.)

"As the Western is a staple product that too often emerges as a banal treatment of standard situations and dialogue, it is a pleasure to report that *The Naked*

Spur is as refreshingly tough and taut as they come. . . . It is economical with words, generous in deeds, both dastardly and noble, and swiftly paced in settings that are superb and seemingly just created for Technicolor." (A. Weiler, *New York Times*, 3/26/53.)

"Director Mann, realizing the script's strong points are in its characterizations, wisely doesn't try to make the five pretty or nice. . . . The acting of Ryan, Stewart, Leigh, Meeker, and Mitchell, is uncommonly good; also, uncommon for a Western, the issues are not clearly defined in black and white." (Philip T. Hartung, *Commonweal*, 4/17/53.)

"Mann did a careful, artful job with the ingredients of *The Naked Spur*, (including) Ryan's oily Iago-type expressions of sneering evil." (Manny Farber, *Nation*, 3/28/53.)

Inferno (5) (1953). Twentieth Century–Fox, C-83 min. *Director* Roy Baker. *Producer* William Bloom. *Screenplay* Francis Cockrell. *Art Directors* Lyle Wheeler, Lewis Creber. *Camera* Lucien Ballard. *Editor* Robert Simpson. *Cast* **Robert Ryan** (David Carson), Rhonda Fleming (Geraldine Carson), William Lundigan (Joe Duncan), Larry Keating (Emory), Henry Hull (Sam Elby), Carl Betz (Mike Platt), Robert Burton (Sheriff), Everett Glass (Detective Mason), Adrienne Marden (Secretary), Barbara Pepper (Waitress), Dan White (Lee), Harry Carter (Fred Parks), Robert Adler (Ken), Charles Conrad (Man).

An inexpensive, compact film often has as much impact as a large scale epic, and such was the case with *Inferno*, a study of man versus man versus nature. The setting in which *Inferno*'s drama unfolds is the Mojave Desert of southern California, and its theme is greed inflamed by lust.

The film's plot centers around a familiar scenario, a conflict involving two men and one woman. Ryan, William Lundigan, and Rhonda Fleming are the people in question, and the object of the latter two's shenanigans is the murder of Ryan and control of his considerable wealth. David Carson (Ryan) is a spoiled, boozing millionaire with a selfish streak in his personality, who is left stranded in the desert with a broken leg by his wife (Fleming) and her lover (Lundigan). Their plan is that he should die "accidentally," leaving them with his fortune, but they have underestimated the willpower of their victim.

Ryan's Carson sits on the top rung of the ladder because of an inheritance, rather than through his won determination and inner strength. But after figuring out that his wife, Geraldine, and her accomplice, Joe Duncan (Lundigan), have no plans to rescue him, his anger builds a resolution to survive. He sets his broken leg himself and vows not to give up until he settles the score.

During his tortuous survival trek, he comes to grips with his alcoholism and selfishness, and begins to feel again. Alone for the first time in his life, he is compelled to think about the emotional distance toward others that he has created. The desert setting is allegorical to his existential struggle, and his brush with death brings him to a different awareness of his life. Metaphorically, Carson's self-discoveries arise from being abandoned in the desert: he sees life where he thought death prevailed, and hope amid despair.

As photographed by the great Lucien Ballard, *Inferno* exuded a stark, realistic feel; one could almost hear and sense the sun baking everything to a dessicated state. Also, having been filmed in 3-D and Technicolor added tremendously to the film's visual excitement. Artistically, *Inferno* is a solid example of the fare produced by many less known, but nevertheless competent directors. Though it was directed by an Englishman, Roy Baker, its style was typically American, utilizing a rugged individualist motif within a suspenseful thriller plot.

In their roles as the adulterers who ultimately betray each other, William

Lundigan and Rhonda Fleming were convincing, and Henry Hull, Larry Keating, and Carl Betz rounded out the small credible supporting players. The Carson part was tailor-made for Ryan, and he fit in naturally with the desolate wilderness of *Inferno*. Also, it challenged his ingenuity because his dialogue was mostly done in voiceover.

One particularly moving vignette depicted Carson, having used his last drop of water, conjuring a fantasy in which his parched surroundings suddenly became lush, verdant landscapes of refreshing coolness surrounded by cheerful sounds of a stream gurgling nearby. In helping to offset the string of bad guy images he had accepted lately, *Inferno* became one of his sentimental favorites.

Reviews: "It must be said right off that *Inferno* is the best of the 3-D pictures thus far. Its Technicolor of the Mojave Desert in three dimensions is stunning, and the story is more adult than most of the pap which the movies have been exhibiting in 3-D. Roy Baker has given the whole film an atmosphere of reality." (Philip T. Hartung, *Commonweal*, 9/4/53.)

"Ryan, under the deft direction of Roy Baker, portrays this role not only with his usual verisimilitude in the portions of rugged physical movement. He also visually reinforces the character's thought and feelings." (*Christian Science Monitor*.)

"The restrained treatment of Roy Baker turns a simple, grim story idea with conviction, irony and chilling crescendo. Mr. Ryan's portrayal of the gritty, determined protagonist, is, of course, a natural." (H.H. Thompson, *New York Times*, 8/12/53.)

"As a 3-D film *Inferno* has some interesting moments, especially those in which the color tones and soil formation of the desert are used to create the illusion of depth. The stratagems by which Ryan survives are plausible, and the will to live has in this case an inspiring exemplification. *Inferno* has another good virtue: good editing by Robert Simpson, especially in the cuts away from shots of Ryan's hunger and thirst to shots of food and drink being consumed by the wife and her lover." (Robert Kass, *Films in Review*, Aug.–Sept. 1953.)

Alaska Seas (2) (1954). Paramount, 78 min. *Director* Jerry Hopper. *Producer* Mel Epstein. *Based on the story* Spawn of the North *by* Barrett Willoughby. *Screenplay* Geoffrey Homes, Walter Doniger. *Assistant Director* C.C. Coleman, Jr. *Camera* William Mellor. *Editor* Artie Marshek. *Cast* **Robert Ryan** (Matt Kelly), Jan Sterling (Nicky), Brian Keith (Jim Kimmerly), Gene Barry (Verne Williams), Richard Shannon (Tom Erickson), Ralph Dumke (Jackson), Ross Bagdasarian (Joe), Fay Roope (Walt Davis), Timothy Carey (Wycoff), Peter Coe (Greco), Jim Hayward (Jailer), Aaron Spelling (Knifer), William Fawcett (Silversmith), Earl Holliman (Indian Boy), Richard Kipling (Croupier), Abel Fernandez (Rechie).

In a continuing bid to gain leading man status, Ryan returned to Paramount for the first time since 1941, when the studio had declared he "was not the right type." This time he was top-billed in a romantic triangle involving Jan Sterling and Brian Keith, but again, his role was a villainous one. It didn't matter, however, because the picture was a bogged-down melodrama, slackly directed by Jerry Hopper, which quickly disappeared from everybody's awareness after a brief run.

The story of *Alaska Seas* concerns two men, one good (Keith), one bad (Ryan, of course), who start out in a salmon-fishing partnership, but who end up at each other's throats for its ownership and the affections of Sterling. Ryan played his character, Matt Kelly, in his usual exuberantly mean way, undermining his former partner's engagement, sabotaging his boats, and trying to kill him. In the end, though, Kelly has a change of heart and leaves the scene, while Kimmerly (Keith) and Nicky (Sterling) are reunited.

Reviews: "As long as *Alaska Seas* sticks to its title and plies the salmon fishing grounds, this lightweight melodrama remains at least palatable. Unfortunately, Ryan, Sterling, and Keith do most of the leaping in a standard story that holds few surprises." (*New York Times*, 3/6/54.)

"Ryan plays the role for all it's worth." (*Variety*, 1/27/54.)

About Mrs. Leslie (5) (1954). Paramount, 104 min. *Director* Daniel Mann. *Producer* Hal B. Wallis. *Based on the novel by* Vina Delmar. *Screenplay* Ketti Frings, Hal Kanter. *Art Directors* Hal Pereira, Earl Hedrick. *Set Decorators* Sam Comer, Arthur Kram. *Music* Victor Young. *Costumes* Edith Head. *Special Camera Effects* John P. Fulton. *Process Camera* Farciot Edouart. *Camera* Ernest Laszlo. *Editor* Warren Low. *Cast* Shirley Booth (Mrs. Leslie), **Robert Ryan** (George Leslie), Marjie Millar (Nadine Roland), Alex Nicol (Ian McKay), Sammy White (Harry Willey), James Bell (Mr. Poole), Eilene Janssen (Pixie), Philip Ober (Mort Finley), Henry Harry Morgan (Fred Blue), Gale Page (Marion King), Virginia Brissac (Mrs. Poole), Ian Wolfe (Mr. Pope), Ellen Corby (Mrs. Croffman), Ray Teal (Barney), Isaac Jones (Jim), Maidie Norman (Camilla), Amanda Blake (Gilly), Percy Helton (Hackley), Jerry Paris (Mr. Harkness).

Ryan stayed at Paramount for his next film of 1954, *About Mrs. Leslie,* and vindicated his work in the tepid *Alaska Seas.* Pairing him with Shirley Booth was a strange casting choice; however, director Daniel Mann was hoping to capitalize on his successes two years earlier with *Come Back, Little Sheba,* which won Booth an Oscar as Best Actress. Unhappily, *About Mrs. Leslie* became the victim of viewer rigidity.

The film begins in the present, with Booth playing the owner of a Beverly Hills rooming house, having been left a large sum of money from a bequest. As she listens to the personal problems in her boarders' lives she reexperiences a deep pain from her own past.

Cutting to flashback, the story moves to her former life as a nightclub singer, and to her first meeting with a handsome, sincere man (Ryan) one night. Each sees a mutual need in the other, and when he asks her to be his companion on a vacation in California, she accepts with little hesitation. The man asks only that they appear to be married, as Mr. and Mrs. Leslie.

Their interlude develops into a peculiar, clandestine love affair that occurs once a year for six weeks during the summers, but which creates in each a yearning for their brief time together. The plot is inherently doomed, and progresses toward its inevitable tragic conclusion, when Mr. Leslie dies suddenly of a heart attack. Ironically, Mrs. Leslie learns of his death impersonally, via a teletype sign on the New York Times building during the celebration of Japan's surrender in 1945.

Overall, *About Mrs. Leslie* had the precision of director Mann's extensive stage work; however, scriptwriter Ketti Frings cluttered the story with tangential subplots, which diffused the romantic tension between Ryan and Booth. The supporting players, a young couple encountering rough spots in their lives (Alex Nicol and Marjie Millar), and an elderly pair (James Bell and Virginia Brissac), faced with the death of their daughter, worked well in their roles, and created an interest to support their addition to the story.

Ernest Laszlo's evocative black-and-white photography captured the story's pensive tone, with expert handling of contrast in the oceanside as well as in the interior sequences between Ryan and Booth. The most impressive scenes: the first meeting of Ryan and Booth at a crowded Greenwich Village cabaret; their morning gambols on a California beach; a twilight séance over wine.

Ryan's Mr. Leslie had as much pathos as any of his roles, while exploring more fully his captivity to play totally sympathetic characters. Curiously, a situation appeared in the Mr. Leslie role which paralleled Ryan's childhood. In one scene he admits to Mrs. Leslie, "I was one of those poor little rich kids who didn't have anyone to play with." Later, he confesses that his obsession with war history is "my personal war, since I bury myself in it to escape today."

Ryan had the vulnerability needed to carry off the part, but some observers felt it was incongruous to his established screen persona. The majority of the critics, however, applauded his portrayal and his attempt to move in a different direction.

Reviews: "...this quiet, attractive film ... has moments of insight and a civilized sympathetic quality rare in the contemporary American product.... Ryan is remarkably good." (James Morgan, *Sight and Sound*, July–Sept. 1954.)

"There have been films made about so-called back street wives, but few with the warmth, richness of color, character, incident and dialogue, nor for that matter, with the beauty and forthrightness of performances contributed by its stars Ryan and Booth." (*Cue.*)

"The company is superbly chosen. Shirley Booth is moving when allowed to be, and Robert Ryan is rock-ribbed and stalwart as the unhappy airman troubled by the things of this earth." (Lee Rogow, *Saturday Review*, 7/3/54.)

"Possibly Ryan's most complex and most successful screen characterization ... a performance of rare depth and beauty ... his playing met the flood of Shirley Booth's emotional pitch head-on to make for an entertainment of singular charm." (John Cutts, *Films and Filming*, July 1961.)

Her Twelve Men (2) (1954). MGM, C-91 min. *Director* Robert Z. Leonard. *Producer* John Houseman. *Screenplay* William Roberts, Laura Z. Hobson. *Art Directors* Cedric Gibbons, Daniel B. Cathcart. *Music* Bronislau Kaper. *Assistant Director* Al Jennings. *Camera* Joseph Ruttenberg. *Editor* George Boemler. *Cast* Greer Garson (Jan Stewart), **Robert Ryan** (Joe Hargrave), Barry Sullivan (Richard Oliver), Richard Haydn (Dr. Barrett), Barbara Lawrence (Barbara Dunning), James Arness (Ralph Munsey), Rex Thompson (Homer Curtis), Tim Considine (Richard Oliver, Jr.), David Stollery (Jeff Carlin), Frances Bergen (Sylvia Carlin), Ian Wolfe (Roger Frane), Ivan Triesault (Erik Haldeman), Peter Votrian (Alan Saunders).

In *Her Twelve Men*, Ryan continued his free-lance effort to break out of typecast status opposite Greer Garson, who was herself trying a new tack at the box office. Unfortunately, its screenplay tramped out all the clichés in a cut-rate piece of matinee fare, which clung to stereotypes rather than tackling the issues.

Greer Garson, in a sort of feminine Mr. Chips minus the bravado, struggled against a story whose characters' most difficult task was to accept a woman as the headmistress of a private school for spoiled rich kids. As her adversary-turned-suitor, Ryan stoically accepted a chauvinistic role and dialogue such as "People who can't do anything else become teachers," and "We offer students reality, not nonsense."

Coincidentally, a few aspects of *Her Twelve Men* related to Ryan's life: He is a teacher at the Oaks School, a man whom his colleagues admire and respect, and who promotes a philosophy of "progressive schooling." If nothing else, Ryan could testify that his role in the film went the furthest in the direction of good than most in his repertory, and that he, like costars Garson and Barry Sullivan, made the most of the lackluster material.

Reviews: "This pleasant little comedy-drama provides Greer Garson with an opportunity to exhibit warmth, charm, and understanding in her best Mrs. Chips tradition. Robert Ryan is excellent as the school master who really understands boys and enjoys his work." (*Photoplay.*)

Bad Day at Black Rock (5) (1954). MGM, C-81 min. *Director* John Sturges.

Producer Dore Schary. *Assistant Producer* Herman Hoffman. *Story* Howard Breslin. *Screenplay* Millard Kaufman. *Assistant Director* Joel Freeman. *Music* André Previn. *Art Directors* Cedric Gibbons, Malcolm Brown. *Set Decorators* Edwin B. Willis, Fred MacLean. *Color Consultant* Alvord Eiseman. *Camera* William Mellor. *Editor* Newell Kimlin. *Cast* Spencer Tracy (John J. Macreedy), **Robert Ryan** (Reno Smith), Anne Francis (Liz Wirth), Dean Jagger (Tim Horn), Walter Brennan (Doc Velie), John Ericson (Pete Wirth), Ernest Borgnine (Coley), Lee Marvin (Hector), Russell Collins (Hastings), Walter Sande (Sam).

Now considered a classic tale on the ills of prejudice and on the contagium of silence, *Bad Day at Black Rock* was Dore Schary's brainchild. By 1954, Schary, ever vigilant for using the cinema as a medium for social statement, decided to bring another skeleton out of America's closet. MGM executive Nick Schenk was initially against the project, but Schary pushed hard to get the film made. After deciding to produce it himself, he attracted John Sturges to direct, and Millard Kaufman, a former Marine Corps officer, to write the screenplay. Schary liked Kaufman's work, which combined toughness and hard intellectuality, and his finished script delivered the same qualities.

Schary calmed his own doubts about the film's success quotient by assembling a "name" cast, headed by Ryan and Spencer Tracy. In addition, Ernest Borgnine, Lee Marvin, Walter Brennan, and Dean Jagger contributed original portrayals under Sturges's comfortable direction. Of his nearly 20 Westerns, *Bad Day at Black Rock* was Sturges's only contemporary piece, but the picture retained enough of a 19th century tone to make it an unusual blend of social commentary and Americana.

Set in post–World War II Arizona, *Bad Day at Black Rock* concerned itself with prejudice toward Japanese-Americans during the war. The drama unfolds in a hole-in-the-wall town in the middle of the desert, Black Rock. When Spencer Tracy's John J. Macreedy arrives there from a train one day, his reception by the townspeople is as cool as the day is hot. Although his presence there seems harmless, the locals do their best to make him leave. Attempting to ignore their hostility, Macreedy explains his intentions: he is delivering a medal to the father of a friend killed in action during the war.

This news makes matters worse for Macreedy, because the man he is looking for is a Japanese farmer named Komoko, and the people of Black Rock dislike foreigners of any type. The town linchpin, Reno Smith (Ryan), nervously tells Macreedy that Komoko left town several years earlier, but Macreedy investigates further. He learns that after Pearl Harbor, Smith went into a rage, burned down Komoko's house, and gunned him down.

The dramatic conflict which ensues as Macreedy gradually unravels the mystery is concerned with collective guilt and emotional inertia. Both he and the witnesses to Smith's crime share a melancholy silence, but for different reasons: Macreedy, because of a war injury which has left his arm useless, they, because of Smith's tight grip on their consciences.

Life is pitted against death when Macreedy regains his will to live after witnessing the moribund state of the citizens of Black Rock. They are mirror images of what he has become, and he is sickened by what he sees. Driven to action, he jars the townspeople's sensibilities, and brings Smith to justice. The tragic murder of Komoko emerges as a sacrifice which serves to liberate Macreedy and the town.

Bad Day at Black Rock received unanimous critical acclaim, partly because of Schary's acumen in putting together the right ingredients. Sensing that the public would be attracted by the collective marquee value of the cast, he chose his stars carefully. He also knew he needed to capture audiences within the first few minutes of the picture, and though he had planned to present the film without music, a sneak preview indicated viewers were puzzled by the beginning, not knowing what to anticipate. Prior to its national release, Schary brought the picture back to the studio and hired André Previn to write a score, instructing him to make it loud, pulsating, and martial.

Bad Day at Black Rock has admirably withstood the test of time, which Pauline Kael noted in her book, *Kiss, Kiss, Bang, Bang*: "The title suggests a banal Western, but this 1954 film was the first to bring up the wartime outrages against Japanese-Americans . . . it is a very superior example of motion picture craftmanship. John Sturges is an excellent director—each movement is exact and economical; the cinematographer, William C. Mellor, uses composition and color intelligently."

Ryan's Reno Smith, although a murderer, evokes pity, because he is depicted as an insecure man driven by an inner deprivation. When Macreedy threatens his tenuous hold on the town, Smith becomes fearful like a caged animal, and in an effort to maintain power, he likens Macreedy's bravery to a disease, calling it "contagious." Smith is also a throwback to the Old West, who feels threatened by encroaching society. When he demands of Macreedy, "Why don't they leave us alone?" his convoluted reasoning implies that his territory has been invaded, and that his actions are a means of protection. Yet when he calmly murders his girlfriend (Anne Francis), only reprehensible feelings for him remain.

Reviews: "Considerable excitement is whipped up in this suspense drama, and with the names of Robert Ryan and Spencer Tracy hell-weathering the marquee values, it gives a good account of itself." (*Variety*, 12/15/54.)

"Practically the whole cast is first-rate. Robert Ryan, as the chief villain, has some fine scenes with Spencer Tracy." (*Time*, 1/17/55.)

"Dore Schary's production is excellent throughout, with stunning photography and an outstanding cast. John Sturges' direction is so good that you are never aware that these are actors being directed. It is amazing how a gentleman like Robert Ryan can play a bully to perfection." (Philip T. Hartung, *Commonweal*, 1/14/55.)

"*Bad Day at Black Rock* has a dramatic unity, an economy of word and action, that is admirable in an age of flabby Hollywood epics that meander on forever . . . Robert Ryan is the strong, thoughtful man who has bullied the town into obedience." (William K. Zinsser, *New York Herald-Tribune*, 2/5/55.)

"A tight, economical work, directed and staged with conviction, and it enlarges the stature of everyone connected with it . . . Robert Ryan, as always narrow-eyed and smiling, is a rancher who gives the orders in Black Rock, and is sturdily supported by Jagger, Brennan, Ericson, and Marvin." (Robert Hatch, *Nation*, 2/19/55.)

Escape to Burma (l) (1955). RKO, C-88 Min. *Director* Allan Dwan. *Producer* Benedict Bogeaus. *Based on the story* Bow Tamely to Me *by* Kenneth Perkins. *Screenplay* Talbot Jennings, Hobart Donavan. *Art Director* Van Nest Polglase. *Set Decorator* Fay Babcock. *Assistant Directors* Nate Watt, Lew Borzage. *Costumes* Gwen Wakeling. *Music* Louis Forbes. *Camera* John Alton. *Editor* James Leicester. *Cast* Barbara Stanwyck (Gwen Moore), **Robert Ryan** (Jim Brecan), David Farrar (Cardigan), Murvyn Vye (Malesh), Lisa Montell (Andora), Robert Warrick (Sawba), Reginald Denny (Commissioner), Peter Coe (Captain of the Guard), Alex Montoya (Dacoit).

Upon looking at the caliber of the people responsible for *Escape to Burma*, one wonders why things went so wrong. About ten minutes into the film, the inescapable conclusion is that rigor mortis was setting in at RKO. The deed completed, *Escape to Burma* would be a worthwhile addition to film study seminars on how collective competence can sometimes defeat itself.

The principal problems with *Escape to Burma* seem to be threefold, and in order of guilt they are: script, direction, and cinematography. Filmed on studio sets, it had the artificiality of a city zoo, and the few outdoor scenes seemed to have been shot in a nearby park. Moreover, the dialogue closely resembled a Technicolor *Bomba, the Jungle Boy*, and drew upon tried and true Middle East stereotypes to compound the film's failure potential.

Possibly, director Allan Dwan had fallen victim to the infirmities of age, as this was nearly his four hundredth feature film. However, producer Benedict Bogeaus's advertising hyperbole must have been a throwback to his days as a real estate dealer in Chicago, and before *Escape to Burma* was trundled off to the RKO vaults, it drew audiences to the theaters by hook and by crook. Bogeaus's hard-sell promotional campaign included an expensive and imaginative number of gimmicks, such as free vacuum cleaners to lucky theater owners, an *Escape to Burma* puzzle for patrons, and lofty advertisements proclaiming, "In the hot, green hell of Burma ... there's no escape from the sun ... the sin ... or the swift deadly chase."

As a Ryan vehicle, *Escape to Burma* exploited his romantic image without giving him much to do. His few intimate scenes with Barbara Stanwyck failed to validate the steamy passions suggested by the ads; in fact, the poster pictures depicting Ryan and Stanwyck in close embrace never actually happened. However, on paper, his role conformed to the Ryan penchant for playing the pursuer or the pursued, but without any excitement.

Reviews: "Stanwyck rides herd over a tea plantation—and a pack of wild animals—but doesn't know how to deal with a wanted man (Ryan) who seeks refuge. The cast does what it can with the pulp material." (Leonard Maltin, *TV Movies*.)

"Both experienced hands at melodrama, Robert Ryan and Barbara Stanwyck costar in a tale of danger and romance ... the picture goes into a pattern of chases, captures, and escapes through the jungle. Though no scenes were filmed on location, many of the sets and backgrounds are handsome, with plenty of wildlife." (*Photoplay*, 4/26/55.)

House of Bamboo (4) (1955). Twentieth Century-Fox, C-102 min. *Director* Samuel Fuller. *Producer* Buddy Adler. *Screenplay* Harry Kleiner. *Additional Dialogue* Samuel Fuller. *Art Directors* Lyle Wheeler, Addison Hehr. *Set Decorators* Walter M. Scott, Stuart A. Reiss. *Music* Leigh Harline. *Assistant Director* David Silver. *Camera* Joe MacDonald. *Editor* James B. Clark. *Cast* **Robert Ryan** (Sandy Dawson), Robert Stack (Eddie Spanier), Shirley Yamaguchi (Mariko), Cameron Mitchell (Griff), Brad Dexter (Captain Hanson), Sessue Hayakawa (Inspector Kito), Biff Elliot (Webber), Sandro Giglio (Ceram), Harry Carey, Jr. (John), Peter Gray (Willy), Robert Quarry (Phil), DeForrest Kelley (Charlie), John Doucette (Skipper), Teru Shimada (Nagaya).

Ryan and Samuel Fuller share a common distinction in that their films have always received more attention in Europe than in the United States. European tastes in cinema have been generally seen as more sophisticated than those of Americans, thus its success in the States was limited by its abstractness. Much of the appeal of *House of Bamboo* depended on stylistic devices, such as lighting, set designs, and cinematography.

On the surface, *House of Bamboo* belonged in the police drama genre, but underneath, it was a *film noir* laden with symbolism. Fuller delved into one of his preferred themes, the idea that opposing states, love and hate, loyalty and deceit, exist at the same time in everyone, and are held in precarious ambivalence. He decided that Tokyo was the most appropriate place for his conflict, and presented a clear cultural dichotomy which became enlarged within the context of the story.

Harry Kleiner's screenplay, to which Fuller contributed additional dialogue, offered an unusual story of an American Army sergeant (Robert Stack), sent undercover to catch a gang of robbers and murderers. The criminals, led military style by Ryan's Sandy Dawson, are a sociopathic group of ex–G.I.s, all of whom were convicted of crimes in the military and dishonorably discharged.

They are bound by a bizarre code of silence imposed by Sandy: If a gang member is wounded during a shoot-out, he is to be immediately killed by any other gang member. Sandy's reason for such measures is icily rational: The risk is too great that he would crack under police pressure and betray his comrades.

Fuller cleverly depicted his cultural juxtaposition. Amid the elegant icons of Japanese history, polite geisha girls, lotus blossoms, and honorable behavior among men, Western corruption is spreading. Sandy refers to the Japanese as the "politest people in the politest country in the world," an offhand compliment meaning they are easy prey for his gang. Ironically, having been the first American film to be made in Japan since before World War II lent a special realism to *House of Bamboo*.

Eddie Spanier (Stack) infiltrates Sandy's gang, and learns that Sandy is the killer he is looking for. Aided by Mariko (Shirley Yamaguchi), the wife of a gang member killed by Sandy, Eddie quickly gains Sandy's trust. Sandy's second-in-command, Griff (Cameron Mitchell), develops an intense hatred for Eddie, which climaxes when Sandy excludes Griff from a big heist.

Before the robbery, Sandy learns from an informant that the police have been tipped off. Believing that Griff is responsible, Sandy kills him, but then discovers that Eddie is the real informer. Sandy plans to have Eddie killed, but the scheme backfires, and in a dramatic shoot-out on a rotating carousel high above Tokyo, Eddie kills Sandy. In the film's final frames we see Sandy's lifeless arm hanging over the carousel railing as Eddie walks away slowly.

House of Bamboo was a *film noir* done in grand style. Fuller filmed the picture in Cinemascope and Technicolor because he wanted the gritty gangster element to contrast harshly with the beauty and serenity of Japan. In several scenes, Mount Fujiyama looms awesomely in the background, as a mute metaphor on the insignificance of man in comparison.

Alienation and ambivalence are integral to the story since within the ranks of Sandy's gang loyalty can only be guaranteed until the next job, when one's friend might become his assassin. Despite the predatory nature of Sandy's gang and his dispassionate killing of his own men, they are strongly drawn to him as a patriarchal figure. Yet it is the competition to be Sandy's "Ichi-ban," number one boy, that causes his downfall.

Fuller cast *House of Bamboo* with mostly silent but efficient henchmen, including DeForrest Kelley, Harry Carey, Jr., and John Doucette, while Brad Dexter and Sessue Hayakawa were steel-jawed and laconic as policeman. Likewise, Robert Stack and Cameron Mitchell gave terse performances, while Shirley Yamaguchi, in her first film, provided a gentleness to offset the roughness of the all male cast.

Though Ryan was top-billed in *House of Bamboo* and was the most interesting character in the picture, as in many of his films, one was left with a sense of not having seen enough of him. In some ways, the Sandy Dawson role was a difficult part because Ryan communicated his psychopathy through understatement. Although Sandy is a ruthless killer, he maintains a rigid self-control, even when he kills Griff.

Ryan also brought a dimension of demented kindness to Sandy, evident in the scene in which he murders Griff. Fuller vividly recalled the scene, and commented, "Bob's monologue to the man he shot in the water barrel was a troika of Hamlet's inability to know how to kill, and of his own regretful act of killing—and then explaining his act to the dead man he loved."

Reviews: "A well-made cops-and-robbers story filmed in Tokyo. ... It is enhanced by the petal-like beauty of the scenery ... Robert Ryan bosses a little band of thieves with a nice military precision.... They are 'briefed' on an 'operation,' they attack an 'objective,' and never make a getaway—they 'withdraw.' Ryan is smooth and businesslike." (*Time*, 8/1/55.)

"As the leader of the gang of big-time bandits and operators of cheap gambling halls, Robert Ryan does a lot to give the fiction a firm and suspenseful quality. His faint hint of psychopathic tension introduces a fine uncertainty, and his skill at subdued underplaying provides a sense of dread." (Bosley Crowther, *New York Times*, 7/2/55.)

"Ryan gives the film's most interesting performance. He is a quiet-spoken villain who plans robberies with the tactics and terminology of a military commander." (*Christian Science Monitor*.)

"Robert Ryan is the cold, canny gangster who runs a crime ring that specializes in robbing banks and hijacking trains. He is a suave villain who gets a sardonic pleasure from toying with his victims." (William Zinsser, *New York Herald-Tribune*, 7/2/55.)

The Tall Men (2) (1955). Twentieth Century-Fox, C-122 min. *Director* Raoul Walsh. *Producers* William A. Bacher, William B. Hawks. *Based on the novel by* Clay Fisher. *Screenplay* Sydney Boehm, Frank Nugent. *Music* Victor Young. *Songs* Ken Darby, Jose Lopez Alaves. *Costumes* Travilla. *Assistant Director* Stanley Hough. *Art Directors* Lyle R. Wheeler, Mark-Lee Kirk. *Camera* Leo Tover. *Editor* Louis Loeffler. *Cast* Clark Gable (Ben Allison), Jane Russell (Nella Turner), **Robert Ryan** (Nathan Stark), Cameron Mitchell (Clint Allison), Juan Garcia (Luis), Harry Shannon (Sam), Emile Meyer (Chickasaw),

Steven Darrell (Colonel), Will Wright (Gus), Robert Adler (Wrangler), Russell Simpson (Immigrant Man).

A big budget and a few name stars were the reasons for the initial box-office success of *The Tall Men*, but its spark quickly died when audiences discovered that the film's most important message had to do with Jane Russell's boots and bodice. Moreover, the deathless struggle between Ryan's Nathan Stark and Clark Gable's Ben Allison was so protracted that their confrontation at film's end is strangely anti-climactic.

The people at 20th Century–Fox attempted to rekindle the marquee value of Gable and Russell while Ryan's string of recent successes indicated he still had significant drawing power. One of the Western's most prolific directors, Raoul Walsh, was at the helm, but his steady hand seemed only stolid on *The Tall Men*. Since script weaknesses seemed to be the main problem, it is likely that Jane Russell was hired in the hope that her low-cut tops would distract attention away from the unconvincing plot.

The Tall Men concerns two brothers, Ben and Clint Allison (Cameron Mitchell), who attempt to rob Ryan's Nathan Stark of a large sum of money he is carrying, and are ready to kill him to get it. Stark bargains with them and proposes that they become partners in a cattle drive guaranteed to net them as much as will stealing from him. Ben agrees to the uneasy alliance despite Clint's protests, and the three embark on an enervating journey that, at film's end, leaves one with as much ennui as the weary players must have felt.

To make matters worse, the script includes several instances in which Miss Russell has difficulty taking off her boots, while Ryan and Gable are called upon at strategic moments to assist her. This, coupled with the voyeuristic appeal of Miss Russell's ample bosom, becomes a parody within the context of the story. Probably the best thing about *The Tall Men* was its Cinemascope and Technicolor photography, and its action sequences, but these were not enough to warrant the time or the effort.

Ryan verified his long-suffering attitude by accepting one of his more forgettable ventures. Clark Gable's character was so obviously built up in comparison that Ryan's Stark seemed to always be in a state of supplication. But on further analysis, the Stark character is revealed as a more respectable, kind, and sensible person than is the lawless, callous, impetuous Ben Allison.

Reviews: "Several times during this Western, Jane Russell makes occasions to get out of her tight boots, usually with the labored assistance of Clark Gable or Robert Ryan ... the spectacle of Miss Russell's being relieved of the pain in her pedal extremities is about the only novel excitement contained in this depressingly hackneyed horse opera.... Gable and Ryan go at it as though they were acting a deathless tragedy." (Bosley Crowther, New York Times, 10/12/55.)

"This big, amiable Western has Gable, Russell, and Ryan on a pioneering cattle drive from Texas to Montana. Tart-tongued Jane is set on marrying the ambitious Ryan, but it's obvious that she loves the not-so-ambitious Gable, for all their quarrels." (Photoplay, 12/55.)

The Proud Ones (3) (1956). Twentieth Century-Fox, C-94 min. Director Robert D. Webb. Producer Robert L. Jacks. Based on the novel by Verne Athanas. Screenplay Edmund North, Joseph Petracca. Music Lionel Newman. Orchestrator Maurice de Packh. Costumes Travilla. Assistant Director Ed Schaumer. Art Directors Lyle Wheeler, Leland Fuller. Camera Lucien Ballard. Editor Hugh S. Fowler. Cast **Robert Ryan** (Cass Silver), Virginia Mayo (Sally), Jeffrey Hunter (Thad), Robert Middleton (Honest John Barrett), Walter Brennan (Jake), Arthur O'Connell (Jim Dexter), Ken Clark (Pike), Rodolpho Acosta (Chico), George Mathews (Dillon), Fay Roope (Markham), Edward Platt (Doc Barlow), Whit Bissell (Mr. Bolton), Paul Burns (Billy Smith), Richard Deacon (Barber), Lois Ray (Belle), Jack Low (Guard), Ken Terrell (The Weasel), Don Brodie (Hotel Clerk), Jackie Coogan (Man on Make), Stanford Jolley (Crooked Card Player).

One should look a little more closely than a glance at Ryan's third release for 20th Century-Fox, since he again played a good guy. Moreover, his part as Sheriff Cass Silver was a well developed role, though his romantic involvement with costar Virginia Mayo lacked the youthful passion of his previous efforts.

The Proud Ones attempted to say something substantial about loyalty and justice, which may have attracted Ryan. His Cass Silver is a man with shame in his past, having been unjustly accused of a killing years earlier, and run out of town by a crooked saloon owner, Honest John Barrett (Robert Middleton). As the story unfolds, Silver meets up with Barrett again when the latter arrives in Cass's town, accompanied by his equally amoral entourage. Cass has been licking his wounds all this time, and is ready for an eventual confrontation with Barrett.

Matters get complicated when an angry young gunslinger, Thad (Jeffrey Hunter), drifts into town. It seems that Cass killed Thad's outlaw father in the line of duty, but Thad thinks it was murder and swears vengeance. The relationship between Cass and Thad progresses from distrust to uneasy admiration, and finally to genuine affection as Cass proves his innocence to Thad.

Besides his trouble with Barrett, Cass is also beset with physical ailments. He suffers from intermittent blindness from an earlier gunshot wound, and his spells come at crucial moments. Before the final dramatic shoot-out with Barrett and his hired guns, the town turns against Cass and city council demands his resignation. When he faces the people whom he used to call 'friends' but who have now deserted him, his character bears a similarity to one of Ryan's preferred motifs, that of the betrayed, righteous soul.

When he delivers his bitter diatribe toward the council for its hypocrisy, his orator's voice carries the scene to an emotional level.

In the tradition of the old-guard Hollywood director, such as Henry King or Henry Hathaway, director Robert D. Webb did a journeyman job of *The Proud Ones*. His style had a straightforward technique that relied on established principles, such as the long take and the short pause. Having been shot in Cinemascope and Technicolor by Lucien Ballard gave the picture a better-than-average sense of realism, while providing a sturdy visual spectacle.

One might describe *The Proud Ones* with the adjective 'sincere,' because its supporting cast included low-key Western regulars, Walter Brennan and Arthur O'Connell, as well as the dependable faces of Rodolpho Acosta, George Mathews, Whit Bissell, Edward Platt, and Richard Deacon. Although the film was not a masterpiece, it featured Ryan in a kindly, paternalistic role just as he was approaching that phase due to age.

Reviews: "Ryan is such a good actor that he makes *The Proud Ones* seem better than it is. With intense sincerity and skill he portrays the marshal of a small Kansas town who is beset with almost as many troubles as Job. . . . Robert Webb has directed the elements of the story well to keep his audience in a constant state of excitement, and his good cast manages to give conviction to the crowded and violent plot. Yet it is on fine upstanding Marshal Ryan that our interest centers." (Philip T. Hartung, *Commonweal*, 8/17/56.)

"Sheriff Robert Ryan has his hands full in this sprawling, brawling Western. He must keep ruthless Robert Middleton from taking over the town." (*Photoplay*, 6/12/56.)

"*The Proud Ones* is a fairly exciting story. The trouble is that you can confuse it with a good many other Westerns. The action, if not the suspense, is plentiful. Mr. Ryan and Jeffrey Hunter handle

their guns well. Walter Brennan's jailer is a delight." (*New York Times*, 8/11/56.)

"It is prettily done, with its Eastman color reconstruction on a Cinemascope screen of a Kansas town booming on the new cattle trails . . . the story is diffused, finding its chief quality in the developing relationship between the marshal (played in the strong, silent, true-as-a-rock style by Robert Ryan), and the younger man whose father was shot by the marshal. . . . More could have been done with the hero's attacks of blindness." (*Films and Filming*, 8/56.)

Back from Eternity (3) (1956). RKO, 97 min. *Producer-Director* John Farrow. *Screenplay* Jonathan Latimer. *Art Directors* Albert S. D'Agostino, Gene Allen. *Assistant Director* Emmett Emerson. *Music* Franz Waxman. *Costumes* Ann Peck. Camera William Mellor. *Editor* Eda Warren. *Cast* **Robert Ryan** (Bill Larnigan), Anita Ekberg (Rena), Rod Steiger (Vasquez), Phyllis Kirk (Louise), Keith Andes (Joe), Gene Barry (Ellis), Fred Clark (Crimp), Beulah Bondi (Martha), Cameron Prud'Homme (Henry), Jesse White (Pete), Adele Mara (Maria), Jon Provost (Tommy), Tris Coffin (Grimsby), Daniel Bernaduccio (Bartender), Rex Lease (Airport Representative), Charles Meredith (Dean), Alex Montoya (Police Sergeant).

In a last ditch effort to resuscitate itself from a demise in 1956, RKO studio heads had been trying to forestall bankruptcy with promises of exciting new ventures. The studio had lately been pulling out all the stops by hiring several stars, such as Anita Ekberg and Rod Steiger, and by touting itself as "the busiest lot in Hollywood." Ryan had often been RKO's saving grace in the past, and he was hired to star in a remake of a picture John Farrow had directed in 1939, named *Five Came Back*. As if to signify the lengths to which RKO was resorting, the new version was ironically entitled *Back from Eternity*.

The plot of *Back from Eternity* concerns a group of people whose airplane crashes in a remote section of the Amazon rain forest. Their plight is complicated by the impending menace of a tribe of headhunters intent on increasing their inventory of shrunken heads. Amid such dire circumstances, the mettle of the crew and passengers is put to the test with varying results, culminating in a poignant climax.

The incongruous group composing the passengers and crew respond realistically with bravery and cowardice to their dilemma. In the star role, Ryan brought a quiet resourcefulness to his worldly wise, burned-out airline pilot, Bill Larnigan, who leads everyone to safety. His understated portrayal was almost too low-key, though, compared with the film's other pivotal role, the convicted assassin, Vasquez (Steiger). Farrow had made a few changes in the remake to enliven the characters, but the new rendition seemed to shift their importance. Thus, *Back from Eternity*'s heroic emphasis moved from Larnigan to Vasquez, since the latter makes the final decision as to who will be saved.

Ryan and Steiger's parts were the best written of the cast, however, and the others labored earnestly to raise up the story's tension level. Among them, Fred Clark grimaced admirably as the reptilian Mr. Krimp, and Phyllis Kirk, Gene Barry, and Jesse White were notable as desperate passengers. Unhappily, the characters of Beulah Bondi and Cameron Prud'Homme emerged as unctuous stereotypes, while Anita Ekberg seemed too voluptuous as the vampish Rena. Finally, Keith Andes' profile as Larnigan's copilot was too eager, while Jon Provost's Tommy was cutely sincere.

At such times in *Back from Eternity* when the dialogue sagged and the players fell into stereotype, the film's technical aspects kept things interesting. Farrow, who also produced the film, did a yeoman's job of his task, while William C. Mellor's cinematography lent an atmospheric quality to the Brazilian jungle scenes, despite their having been obviously shot on a huge studio set. Finally, Franz Waxman's score, alternatingly spine-tingling and majestic, gave the drama an immediacy to overcome the melodramatics of the somewhat overblown screenplay.

The Larnigan role attracted Ryan because it was a positive character, but scarred with a few rough edges. Larnigan is a solitary man, a former hotshot pilot with a mysterious past, who is now an expatriate flying banana runs to and from South American countries. Although it is revealed that Larnigan is a heavy drinker, his fame and skill supersede his being disciplined by the airline.

Ryan's character bore a resemblance to other Ryan portraits: As written, Larnigan has become cynical about life. At the beginning of *Back from Eternity*, Larnigan informs Rena that he is retiring from the human race to a remote beach in South America, after being widowed several years earlier and moving aimlessly from job to job. But his brush with mortality and the love of Rena rekindle his interest in living.

Reviews: "*Back from Eternity* uses the tried and proven formula of gathering a group of people in one setting, and then letting them work on their destinies after a catastrophe brings out the best and the worst in them. Producer/director Farrow never lets our interest sag as he shows us what happens to the group led by cynical pilot Ryan." (Philip T. Hartung, *Commonweal*, 9/28/56.)

"The film generates good melodrama, and is sparked by the strong handling of the actors in a persuasively enacted situation. Ryan delivers a highly restrained performance." (*Variety*, 8/29/56.)

Men in War (4) (1957). United Artists, 104 min. *Director* Anthony Mann. *Producer* Sidney Harmon. *Based on the novel* Combat *by* Van Van Praag. *Screenplay* Philip Yordan. *Assistant Director* Leon Chooluck. *Music* Elmer Bernstein. *Art Director* Frank Sylos. *Camera* Ernest Haller. *Editor* Richard C. Meyer. *Cast* **Robert Ryan** (Lieutenant Benson), Aldo

Ray (Montana), Robert Keith (Colonel), Philip Pine (Riordan), Vic Morrow (Zwickley), Nehemiah Persoff (Lewis), James Edwards (Killian), L.Q. Jones (Davis), Adam Kennedy (Maslow), Scott Marlowe (Meredith), Walter Kelley (Ackerman), Race Gentry (Haines), Robert Normand (Christenson), Anthony Ray (Penelli), Michael Miller (Lynch), Victor Sen Yung (Korean Sniper).

The patchy hills of Korea provide a fittingly grim, desolate setting for the numerous physical and emotional struggles besetting the soldiers in Men in War. Led by Ryan, a platoon of battle-worn G.I.s wends a wearying journey toward relief that at film's end leaves the viewer similarly affected. Director Anthony Mann intended to create an intense physical experience from the outset of Men in War, and who but Ryan could have so aptly typified the generalized battle fatigue of his platoon, evidenced by his five-day growth of beard, furrowed brow, and heavily bagged eyes?

The story of Men in War is allegorical to one of Mann's favorite themes, the perpetual battle between good and evil, which he believed was a universal conflict. From the outset of the film, Ryan's Lieutenant Benson, an unwarlike soldier who thinks before shooting, clashes wills with the smart talking, aggressive Montana (Aldo Ray).

Montana is an instinctual soldier who responds to impending danger with the accuracy of a sixth sense. His seemingly unwarranted killings of enemy soldiers, set within a military situation, are charged with the ambivalence of war. Benson's implied humanity is presented as a deficit, while Montana's behavior makes the amenities of the Geneva Convention moot.

As in all of Mann's films, his acute visual sense and flair for staging extremely realistic action sequences guaranteed Men in War's success. Aided by Elmer Bernstein's plaintive score, the travails which Benson's platoon endures, plodding through the dusty, forbidding Korea

toward a hill made for Sisyphus, takes on an eerie texture. Cinematographer Ernest Haller shot Men in War using crisp tones of black and white from several vantage points, creating images that could also have been effective still-life studies.

One of Haller's best shots takes in a panorama of fields of long grass undulating in the sun, and focuses on fluttering tufts of wild daisies. The scene is hauntingly beautiful until the camera cuts to a twisted, smoldering piece of steel, and a soldier lying nearby with a knife in his back. The montage flaunts the contrasts of war, juxtaposing beauty and ugliness.

In Men in War, the soldiers' duress becomes tremendously psychological, since the enemy is often unseen, yet his presence and menace are always imminent. The North Koreans' use of psychological warfare incites constant paranoia and irrational behavior among Benson's men. As his platoon tiptoes its way through a leaf-covered mine field, Sergeant Lewis (Nehemiah Persoff) becomes a casualty when he loses his nerve, and is blown up by a land mine.

Another scene builds to a grim climax when Sergeant Killian (James Edwards) lets down his guard for a moment to savor a few daisies, while a faceless enemy creeps up on him. The last view of Killian is his feet, shaking spasmodically as a Korean bayonet runs him through, then disappearing as his body is slowly dragged into the underbrush.

Several vivid performances in Men in War reflected producer Sidney Harmon's casting wisdom. Chiefly, Robert Keith, Nehemiah Persoff, and Vic Morrow gave startling portraits of battle fatigue, while James Edwards and Philip Pine (who had both worked with Ryan on The Set-up) played sensitive G.I.s whose humanity brought them different destinies. Other familiar faces included L.Q. Jones, Victor Sen Yung, and Scott Marlowe.

Ryan's Lieutenant Benson seems to have been his statement about the distressing business of war, in which the survival of the fittest is the only rule.

According to Philip Yordan's screenplay, humaneness is of little value in wartime, since while Benson declares that men like Montana "fight alone and die alone," he must grudgingly admit to Montana's indispensability. Their opposing ideologies, Benson's representation of good versus Montana's epitome of ruthlessness, constantly vie for the upper hand.

When Montana kills four Koreans before he is certain of their identity, Benson can tolerate him no longer. In their final confrontation, Benson sends Montana away and says with contempt, "God help us if it takes your kind to win the war." Thus, the moral dilemma of *Men in War* is left unresolved, and it probably never could be. Ryan seemed to understand the paradox.

Reviews: "*Men in War* is a stark account of infantrymen in combat.... Director Anthony Mann has reduced war to its cruel basic terms ... death is constantly expected, but it comes in unexpected ways—from a rifleman in a tree, a thrown knife, an unseen land mine ... the tough and competent lieutenant who tries every trick in the book to get his men back is a type that Ryan plays with laconic skill." (William K. Zinsser, *New York Herald-Tribune*, 3/20/57.)

"From the beginning, *Men in War* is one long display of horror and misery as the soldiers, under the command of a tired and tormented lieutenant, try to slog their way back to their lines.... The lieutenant, as played by Robert Ryan, is a rugged and ruthless soldier by the rules of realism here laid down." (Bosley Crowther, *New York Times*, 3/20/57.)

"Robert Ryan is the platoon leader—and it should be noted what an unusually good actor he is when he gets his chances.... For the first half, the film is superb. There is remarkable camera work, magnificent realistic studies of men faced with an almost hopeless situation, and some stunning, quite harrowing suspense as one gets the idea that the platoon is surrounded by a quiet, remorseless enemy.... What puts the movie distinctly out of the ordinary is the direction, the believable way in which the men behave, the images, effective sheerly as images, and a notable music score by Elmer Bernstein. There are many first-rate acting jobs, including those by Robert Ryan, Aldo Ray, Philip Pine, and Vic Morrow. Philip Yordan wrote the screenplay, and Anthony Mann directed, both obviously very good men." (Hollis Alpert, *Saturday Review*, 2/16/57.)

God's Little Acre (5) (1958). United Artists, 118 min. *Director* Anthony Mann. *Producer* Sidney Harmon. *Based on the novel by* Erskine Caldwell. *Screenplay* Philip Yordan. *Music and Music Conductor* Elmer Bernstein. *Assistant Director* Louis Brandt. *Makeup* Maurice Seiderman. *Production Designer* John S. Poplin, Jr. *Set Decorator* Lyle B. Reifsnider. *Dialogue Coach* Janet Brandt. *Costumes* Sophia Stutz. *Sound* Jack Solomon. *Special Camera Effects* Jack Rabin, Louis DeWitt. *Camera* Ernest Haller. *Editor* Richard C. Meyer. *Cast* **Robert Ryan** (Ty Ty Walden), Aldo Ray (Will Thompson), Tina Louise (Griselda), Buddy Hackett (Pluto Swint), Jack Lord (Buck Walden), Fay Spain (Darlin' Jill), Vic Morrow (Shaw Walden), Helen Westcott (Rosamund), Lance Fuller (Jim Leslie Walden), Rex Ingram (Uncle Felix), Michael Landon (The Albino), Russell Collins (Watchman).

For its time, the film adaptation of Erskine Caldwell's bawdy novel was considered risqué, but by today's standards it seems tame. Although Philip Yordan's tight script toned down the book's more explicit sexual references, it retained a good measure of Caldwell's southern sassiness. (Since its publication in 1933, Caldwell's novel has periodically been vilified as obscene by the courts. In Philadelphia, Pennsylvania, the book was seized by police, and at various times, the Georgia Literature Commission has attacked it, recommending prosecution of dealers who sold it. *God's Little Acre* may not be published or sold in Massachusetts.

When Sidney Harmon sent scouts to Georgia to negotiate location sites for the filming of God's Little Acre, they encountered subtle resistance from the people there. Harmon was unable to lease shooting areas, and ended up filming God's Little Acre in Stockton, California.)

Accolades were due Ryan for skillfully tying together the disparate elements of his role as Ty Ty Walden, the poor Georgia farmer whose fantasy of finding hidden gold nearly causes the dissolution of his family. The role required rapid changes in mood, between comic and tragic, and depicted the kind of honest humor he would have liked to have done more often. It was also one of the best examples of his varied portraiture, while still being forced into an uneasy courtship with the bad-guy stereotype.

God's Little Acre is allegorical to man's quest for happiness and tranquility, illustrated by Ty Ty's mad scramble after what he sees as a better way of life. The opening scene gives the first evidence of Ty Ty's deluded vision. As the camera pans over his fertile Georgia land lying fallow while he feverishly excavates hole after hole, discontent is brewing among his offspring.

Several subplots highlight God's Little Acre. One involves Ty Ty's oldest son, Buck (Jack Lord), and his tormented relationship with his wife, Griselda (Tina Louise). Son-in-law Will Thompson (Aldo Ray) still has an eye for Griselda from an earlier romance, and trouble begins when he attempts to rekindle what he lost.

Director Anthony Mann accurately recreated Caldwell's sultry sense of languid summer nights and frustrated passions in two outstanding sequences. The first, shot at night under the expert camera guidance of Ernest Haller, depicts a nighttime rendezvous between Will and Griselda in the front yard of Ty Ty's house. The camera pans over shadow-drenched angles and objects as the shimmering, half-naked silhouettes secretly meet and grope for each other urgently.

Through a series of montages that speed up the action, Will and Griselda touch and feel, eyes searching. Underlining the sensuality of their encounter, a lyrical flute score, composed by Elmer Bernstein, plays a haunting melody in the background.

A second scene, again with Will and Griselda, proved Mann's skill in building romantic tension in a manner as ruggedly virile as he had shown in his Westerns. Combining one of God's Little Acre's principal scenes with a consummation of Will and Griselda's pent-up love, Mann created an image of lasting symbolism.

As Will attempts to buck the system one night by breaking into a local textile factory which closed down leaving hundreds of workers jobless, Griselda begs him to stop. He ignores her, methodically pulling switches as machinery surges to life. Mann incorporates Will's action of turning on the plant's power system with the physical union of Will and Griselda. As the factory lights cut through the night in Peach Tree Valley, Will's desperate move becomes a gesture of life and potency in a dying Southern town.

As in many Mann films, ever-present violence invades, truncating Will's success while making him a martyr. The scene ends as workers surge around the fallen man and carry him to his home in a candlelit procession. Poetically photographed by Ernest Haller, the scene had a texture reminiscent of a time period such as had been depicted by Steinbeck in Grapes of Wrath.

The climax of God's Little Acre, which takes place on Ty Ty's front porch, lasts a mere ten minutes but is a gripping piece of filmmaking that showcased Mann's strength in staging action sequences. Beginning with an argument between Buck and Griselda, the scene builds to a crescendo as Buck and a brother, Jim Leslie (Lance Fuller), explode into a death struggle.

When Ty Ty intervenes, Jim Leslie

strikes him in the head with a fence post, sending him to the brink of eternity, where he teeters for some moments. Writhing on the ground as blood trickles from his wound, Ty Ty laments over the damage done by his obstinate delusion, while a third son, Shaw (Vic Morrow), pleads with him not to die.

But the violence brings about a resolution to Ty Ty's obsessive search. After banishing Jim Leslie, Ty Ty looks off for a moment into the horizon while a bird's call twitters to life, signifying a new beginning. In the closing scenes, Ty Ty's change of heart is profound as he suddenly realizes that true contentment comes from the intangible strengths of human relationships.

Mann's hands-off approach to direction worked to great effect in *God's Little Acre*, and he extracted notable supporting performances from Jack Lord and Aldo Ray in their depictions of Southern manhood. As Ty Ty's eldest daughter, Helen Westcott etched a tortured portrait of unrequited love, while Tina Louise's first film role as the sultry Griselda was probably the best performance of her career. (In an interview with Frank Quinn in the *New York Times*, Ryan falsely predicted that Louise and costar Fay Spain were going to "come over like blockbusters with *God's Little Acre* and be established as stars.")

Rounding out the cast, Vic Morrow and Lance Fuller performed effectively, while Rex Ingram, Michael Landon, and Buddy Hackett completed the entourage of Southern types. In the central character of Ty Ty Walden, Ryan tied everything together with a grizzled, down-home depiction of the half-mad, God-fearing dirt farmer. He was proud enough of *God's Little Acre* to place it on his list of favorite films.

Reviews: "*God's Little Acre* is one of the few films I have seen in recent months that has *style* . . . a wholly delightful entertainment, so well-knit it is impossible to apportion the credit for its undoubted success to director, scriptwriter, artists . . .

or, for that matter, to the fine photography of Ernest Haller, or the imaginative music score of Elmer Bernstein . . . (a performance from Robert Ryan that is quite the best this over-typed Hollywood husky has given us), a man of lusty good humor, intense in his family loyalty and love of God." (P.G.B., *Films and Filming*, September 1958.)

"The denizens of *God's Little Acre* have been treated with dignity and intelligence in a folk comedy that is actually funny, realistic and rarely a lampoon. . . . Credit Robert Ryan with a superb performance as the farmer consumed by an exotic drive for gold and a devout wish to keep his family happy and at his side. As the graying, unshaven, middle-aged but still muscular patriarch, he makes a rough-hewn but memorable figure." (A.H. Weiler, *New York Times*, 8/14/58.)

"A very fine picture . . . adult, sensitive, intelligent . . . rousing, rollicking and ribald. . . . Scene after scene of striking power. . . . One of Mann's notable achievements. . . . Robert Ryan gives the performance of his career . . . as remarkable, perhaps, as Walter Huston's performance in *Treasure of the Sierra Madre*." (Powe, *Variety*, 5/14/58.)

". . .often ribald and frank in displaying the low and primitive qualities of the Walden family. It is handsomely photographed in black and white . . . ably directed by Mann . . . Robert Ryan is excellent as the father of the strange brood led by Jack Lord, Aldo Ray, and Tina Louise." (Philip T. Hartung, *Commonweal*, 6/13/58.)

"The picture has some striking merits. Chief among these is Ryan's performance as Ty Ty. Ryan makes him a vigorous and arresting patriarch. . . . The scene in which Ty Ty, struck down by one son, grovels, gnawing at the dirt, while another son hugs him, assuring him of love, is not only a kind of scene infrequently attempted in a Hollywood film, it is memorable. . . . Mann has directed the film with a keen eye for dramatic and pictorial composition, and with the aid of an expert cameraman, Ernest Haller, he has achieved some lovely shadings in black and white and some telling effects in depth." (Stanley Kauffmann, *New Republic*, 6/30/58.)

Lonelyhearts (5) (1958). United Artists, 102 min. *Director* Vincent J. Donehue. *Producer* Dore Schary. *Associate Producer* Walter Reilly. *Based on the book* Miss Lonelyhearts *by* Nathanael West, *and the play by* Howard Teichmann. *Screenplay* Dore Schary. *Art Director* Serge Krizman. *Set Decorator* Darrell Silvera. *Assistant Director* Clarence Eurist. *Wardrobe* Chuck Arrico, Angela Alexander. *Makeup* Abe Haberman, Frank Laure. *Music* Conrad Salinger. *Camera* John Alton. *Editor* Aaron Stell. *Cast* Montgomery Clift (Adam White), **Robert Ryan** (William Shrike), Myrna Loy (Florence Shrike), Dolores Hart (Justy Sargent), Maureen Stapleton (Fay Doyle), Frank Maxwell (Pat Doyle), Jackie Coogan (Gates), Mike Kellin (Goldsmith), Frank Overton (Mr. Sargent), Onslow Stevens (Adam's Father), John Gallaudet (Bartender).

The screen version of Nathanael West's novel, *Miss Lonelyhearts*, arrived reasonably faithful to the original except for the ending. When Dore Schary began to write the screenplay for *Lonelyhearts*, he thought West's tale of woe was unremittingly depressing. Moreover, he knew that movies with sad endings often had less success at the box office, so he decided to mix idealism and financial practicality. His final script had a neatly tied together ending from which everyone emerged with his or her problems magically resolved.

Although the agonized essence of West's book was left intact, some critics found Schary's ending too pat under the circumstances, while others were too emotionally shaken by its downbeat story to accept it. There were, however, a number of observers who appreciated Schary's creation of the film, despite its

moderate reception at the theaters. Thus, *Lonelyhearts* became another addition to the Ryan catalogue of critically acclaimed, commercially unsuccessful pictures.

Lonelyhearts examined a familiar theme in many Ryan films, that of the ignorance and decadence of man and of his ultimate corruptibility. Ryan depicted William Shrike, the anguished editor of the *Chronicle* newspaper, with the acerbic cynicism of a man betrayed too many times in life. Shrike has become the chronicler of the ills of mankind, which he sees and prints with sardonic relish on a daily basis. To his newly hired writer, Adam White (Montgomery Clift), Shrike asserts with conviction, "By tomorrow, our world diplomats may have so carefully managed our affairs, we may all be disappearing in atomic clouds."

As the sensitive, tormented writer of the "Miss Lonelyhearts" column in Shrike's newspaper, Montgomery Clift's Adam White presents an innocent image of unsullied concern, which heroically foils the story's cynical slant. On the one side stands the sarcastic, suspicious Shrike, on the other, the guileless, uncorrupted Adam, and their battlefield lies within the margins of the *Chronicle*'s "Miss Lonelyhearts" column, to which Shrike assigns Adam to initiate him to the "pitiful, dishonest people" who would resort to columns for the lovelorn.

Shrike deems the "Miss Lonelyhearts" column an unhallowed ground in which faceless people bare their anonymous, depraved souls to a pseudonymous byline, in the hope of salvation. He watches expectantly while Adam is slowly traumatized by his experience, and quickly begins to view him with the same suspicion he holds for the rest of the human race.

To his wife, Florence (Myrna Loy), Shrike announces, "Adam has been good because there's been no incentive to be bad. I'm intimate with the type." Part of the reason for Shrike's anger is that several years earlier, Florence committed adultery, and Shrike tortures her with guilt.

Perceiving that his wife is drawn to Adam's idealism, Shrike fires innuendos at her, and relentlessly badgers Adam. After enduring a torturous period writing to scores of pathetic souls, Adam asks to be taken off the "Miss Lonelyhearts" column. Shrike pounces on him with a vicious diatribe, and bristles intensely, "You, my knight exemplar, are a fraud. You talk of doing good, and at your first chance to ply your trade, you run like a scared surgeon at his first sight of an open abdomen. For a while, you were to me the true, heavenly picture of the nonexistent good samaritan. You'll have to continue samaritanizing or you're out of a job."

In Shrike's eyes, Adam has failed a crucial test, and when he retreats in embarrassment, Shrike proclaims to Florence, "He's a fake, a scribbling punk, trying to play the part of goody two-shoes. He'll steal my fillings when I lie dead on the street."

Shrike hopes that Adam will be corrupted and exposed as another hypocrite in a world of "fakes and frauds," and challenges him to "go out and meet one of your amateur authors of despair, deceit, duplicity, and debasement." When a lonely woman, Fay Doyle (Maureen Stapleton), writes to Miss Lonelyhearts about her loveless marriage, Adam agrees to see her, which results in an adulterous encounter.

Wracked with guilt over his impropriety, Adam gets drunk, assaults a coworker (Mike Kellin), and quits the Chronicle in despair. Shrike is initially triumphant about Adam's fall, and heralds to Florence, "Adam is not drunk, he is emancipated. The fortress is crumbled, the walls have been breached. Adultery, violence, and drunkenness have won the day."

Shortly thereafter, when Adam says his goodbyes at the newspaper, he is accosted by Fay Doyle's husband, Pat (Frank Maxwell), who has learned of her infidelity with Adam. As Doyle menaces Adam with a loaded gun, Adam

courageously faces him and confesses, while soothing the man's hurt with his genuineness. The picture ends as Adam reunites with his girlfriend, Justy (Dolores Hart), and Shrike has a change of heart from witnessing Adam's bravery. In the final frames, Shrike carries a bouquet of flowers to Florence to mend the emotional wounds he has inflicted.

Besides the characters of Ryan, Clift, and Myrna Loy, other members of the cast who encounter similar mental anguishes included Onslow Stevens, as Adam's incarcerated father, while Jackie Coogan and Mike Kellin were realistic as jaded reporters. In her first film, Maureen Stapleton delivered a harrowing depiction of the desperate wife, and Frank Maxwell was perfect as her confused husband.

The most dynamic character study in Lonelyhearts belonged to Ryan for his grim conveyance of Shrike's inner pain. Indeed, the picture possessed a film noir sensibility dealing with the themes of alienation and frustration, and Ryan performed his part with almost gleeful abandon. By now, such roles as the "wronged man who withdraws" had become his hallmark, and under the stage-trained directorship of Vincent J. Donehue, he struck a totally convincing pose as the tough, brutal editor of the Chronicle.

Of the critics who objected to Schary's pat ending, some felt that the characters had committed too many outrages against each other to be resolved so easily. In the New York Times, dated March 8, 1959, Bosley Crowther commented: "The pure and good and honest people who make beautiful films in Hollywood . . . persist in the fine and cheering notion that there is no scoundrel so evil and corrupt that a bright gleam of brave and noble action will not turn his cold heart to quivering mush. They are the vanguard of idealism, the invincible optimists."

Though Schary's undying penchant for idealism in the face of man's perversity lessened the pain inflicted by the original story, *Lonelyhearts* retained the brunt of the ennui West had infused in his book. Since Schary also produced the picture, it was set up with the same careful attention to detail which had marked his earlier work at RKO, and later, at MGM.

Cinematographer John Alton filmed *Lonelyhearts* using a process called "chiaroscuro" to give it a vintage look, and he created several effective interior scenes shot in modulated tones of grey and black. In particular, Alton's shooting of the scenes at Delehanty's, the "newshawk's pub" in which Shrike and Adam wage battle, projected the right amount of smoke-filled ambience.

Lonelyhearts attempted to examine a number of things about people and relationships, and it succeeded at most of them. It deserves high marks not only for its ambitious goals, but also for the skill and sincerity with which its message was conveyed.

Reviews: Bosley Crowther felt strongly enough about *Lonelyhearts* that he wrote about it on two occasions: "A clearly sincere endeavor to say something moving and profound about the danger of too-quick moral judgments and the virtue of loving thy fellow man is soberly made in Dore Schary's first independent film . . . Mr. Ryan is compelling throughout the better part of the film." (*New York Times*, 3/5/59.)

A few days later, Crowther wrote: "The authenticity of the ills of the characters are evidenced most impressively by Robert Ryan and Montgomery Clift . . . Mr. Ryan is superbly diabolic in a smirking, insinuating way." (*New York Times*, 3/8/59.)

Paul V. Beckley, of the *New York Herald-Tribune,* also devoted two columns to *Lonelyhearts:* "On the credit side of *Lonelyhearts* is a gallery of vivid characterizations. Robert Ryan is the editor who uses intellectual acumen as a meat axe on the softer heads around him . . . . It is a strong, serious effort to deal with a mordant and difficult story, and deserves

respect." (3/5/59)

"*Lonelyhearts* deserves respect. . . . Whatever reservations I have about the success of Schary's picture, I do feel that it is one of those films which ought to be seen by anyone seriously enough interested in movies to see and discuss them . . . Schary's movie is consistent, integrated, and certainly coherent. It is also relatively strong, vivid, and tense . . . Robert Ryan gives a tough, supple performance (despite some precosity in his cynicism) . . . Maureen Stapleton gives easily one of the best performances so far this year." (3/8/59.)

"The style of *Lonelyhearts* is both simple and surrealistic, and its story is a strange mixture of comedy and tragedy. It is an impressively grim picture with plenty of offbeat material." (Philip T. Hartung, *Commonweal,* 2/13/59.)

Day of the Outlaw (2) (1959). United Artists, 90 min. *Director* André De Toth. *Producer* Sidney Harmon. *Associate Producer* Leon Chooluck. *Screenplay* Philip Yordan. *Set Designer* Jack Polin. *Set Decorator* Lyle B. Reifsnider. *Music* Alexander Courage. *Makeup* Jack Dusick. *Wardrobe* Bob Martien, Elva H. Martien. *Sound* Ben Winkler. *Special Effects* Daniel Hays. *Camera* Russell Harlan. *Editor* Robert Lawrence. *Cast* **Robert Ryan** (Blaise Starrett), Burl Ives (Captain Bruhn), Tina Louise (Helen Crane), Alan Marshal (Hal Crane), Nehemiah Persoff (Dan), David Nelson (Gene), Venetia Stevenson (Ernine), Donald Elson (Vic), Helen Westcott (Vivian), Robert Cornthwaite (Tommy), Jack Lambert (Tex), Lance Fuller (Pace), Frank De Kova (Denver), Paul Wexler (Vause), Jack Woody (Shorty), William Schallert (Preston), Arthur Space (Clay), Michael McGreevey (Bobby), Betsy Jones Moreland (Mrs. Preston), Elisha Cook (Larry), George Ross (Clagett).

Day of the Outlaw was the one total misfire of the films on which Ryan collaborated with Sidney Harmon and Philip Yordan. Although director André De

Toth had made a number of above-average Westerns in the forties and fifties, his work on this one was as tedious as its Oregon location sequences were arduous. The film had a good cast in Burl Ives, Nehemiah Persoff, and several character actors, but the story lacked vitality and credibility.

In the Wyoming of 1880, Ryan's Blaise Starret is ostensibly feuding with Hal Crane (Alan Marshal) over barbed wire fences, but actually covets Crane's wife, Helen (Tina Louise). Just as the two men are about to have a gunfight, an ex–Army officer, Captain Bruhn (Ives), arrives in town with his gang, having just staged a payroll robbery.

Bruhn has been mortally wounded, but when he realizes his men are barely under his control, he agrees to leave the town with Starrett as a guide. Starrett leads the gang in the wrong direction, while along the way, they become greedy and kill each other one by one. In the end the whole gang is killed, including Bruhn, and Starrett returns to his town resolved to forget his desire for Helen.

Reviews: "Intended to provoke suspense, it succeeds only in demanding audience endurance.... The production has a top cast and many talented hands in the making of it.... De Toth's direction fails to create any definite characters and it does not establish any mood.... Ryan seems too intellectual for a characterization that has been given no background to support sensitivity." (*Variety*, 9/16/59.)

Odds Against Tomorrow (1959). United Artists, 95 min. *Producer-Director* Robert Wise. *Associate Producer* Phil Stein. *Based on the novel by* William P. McGivern. *Screenplay* John O. Killens, Nelson Gidding. *Art Director* Leo Kerz. *Set Decorator* Fred Ballmeyer. *Assistant Director* Charles Maguire. *Makeup* Robert Jiras. *Costumes* Anna Hill Johnstone. *Music and Music Conductor* John Lewis. *Sound* Edward Johnstone, Richard Voriseck. *Camera* Joseph Brun. *Editor* Dede Allen.

Cast Harry Belafonte (Johnny Ingram), **Robert Ryan** (Earle Slater), Shelley Winters (Lorry), Ed Begley (Dave Burke), Gloria Grahame (Helen), Will Kuluva (Bacco), Kim Hamilton (Ruth Ingram), Mae Barnes (Annie), Carmen De Lavallade (Kitty), Richard Bright (Coco), Lou Gallo (Moriarity), Fred J. Scollay (Cannoy), Lois Thorne (Eadie), Zohra Lampert (Girl in Bar), William Zuckert (Bartender), Mil Stewart (Elevator Operator), Paul Hoffman (Garry), Cicely Tyson (Fra), William Adams (Bank Guard), Allen Nourse (Police Chief of Melton).

As a latter-day *film noir*, *Odds Against Tomorrow* exploited most of the genre's elements in its structure, theme, and acting, to culminate in a vision of stark nihilism. Its story concerns a grim foray into the disjointed lives of a trio of losers uneasily joined on a bank robbery. Ryan, Harry Belafonte, and Ed Begley played the sorry men whose poorly conceived, ill-fated attempt to heist a payroll from a small-town bank in upstate New York ends in death for all three. Although the robbery is bungled by a series of mishaps, the thieves' ultimate undoing is an allegory on the theme of racial prejudice.

In this low-key, yet volatile, situation of intolerance among men, Ryan was the inevitable best choice as the dour, hard-bitten ex-convict, Earle Slater. He enlarged upon the type he had portrayed in *Crossfire*, and gave one of the best performances of his career. As the unfortunate recipient of Slater's depressed fury, Belafonte's Johnny Ingram had a simmering anger to complete the recipe for their cataclysmic demise.

The care that went into *Odds Against Tomorrow* was obvious. Independently backed by Belafonte's newly formed company, Harbel Productions, Belafonte had firm control over its conception, and hired the best in the business to create one of the cinema's most sophisticated explorations of race hatred. The brilliant eye of producer/director Robert Wise developed an ominous ambience by using the alienation inherent in the urban New York City setting. The city's windy, autumnal streets underscored the film's pervasive sense of bleakness, as Wise captured exactly not only the mood, but a visual sense of the melancholy to firmly ensconce *Odds Against Tomorrow* in the nether world of *noir* sensibility.

Moreover, Joseph Brun's camera work showed his instinctive knowledge of black and white film. Reminiscent of George Diskant's sharply delineated interior and exterior shooting in *On Dangerous Ground*, Brun added texture with beautifully modulated lighting. Filming over half of the picture within New York's crowded maze of apartment buildings, his fluid camera traveled up shadowy staircases, into creaky elevators and claustrophic flats, intensifying the characters' hemmed-in feelings. Several outdoor scenes, shot amid a hazy backdrop of the city's skyscrapers, offered an appropriate setting for the *noir* aspects of alienation and insignificance.

In addition to *Odds Against Tomorrow*'s outstanding physical execution, screenwriter John O. Killens's perceptive script clearly presented the polarizations man uses to perpetuate racism, without resorting to stereotypes. Although much attention was trained on Ryan's Slater as the primary source of the conflict, Johnny Ingram's biases completed the circle of discrimination, only less obviously so. Killens's realistic script depicted the origins of racism in subtle, insidious terms. (Killens, who is black, has the reality of experience to back him up.)

Ingram indicates his self-destructive streak by his gambling, while his feelings of inferiority are only inferred in brief disclosures. When he approaches his boss for a loan, a bodyguard asks him if he needs privacy; Johnny's response, "No, not for me," is deceptively self-effacing. Later, he complains of being "no good," and of having "bad luck." In one of the film's numerous biting exchanges of dialogue, his self-hatred shifts to others when he refers to his ex-wife's friends as "ofays,"

and then spits out cynically, "Why don't you wise up? It's their world and we're just living in it." Ingram sees himself as a helpless victim.

Slater's emotional problems are of a more disturbed nature. His racism is merely one facet in a sociopathic personality prone to impulsive acts and fits of depression. A fringe member of society, he is a product of the Depression and of Oklahoma's Dust Bowl, a loser who has spent his life running away. When he leaves his girlfriend, Lorry (Shelley Winters), to pull the bank job, he declares, "I've got somethin' now, and I'm gonna stick with it." His convoluted reasoning is both pathetic and ironic.

Part of Slater's loser syndrome stems from his temper. In a corner gin mill it surfaces when he beats up a soldier for calling him an "old man." Later, he confides his history of wandering to Lorry, "I been leavin' all my life," as well as his other prejudices, a "lousy Polack," and his antagonism toward authority figures, a "captain in the Army."

Yet despite his mean streak, Slater is presented in two romantic liaisons, one with his girlfriend and another with a neighbor from upstairs, Helen (Gloria Grahame). In one of the film's best scenes, Ryan gave one of his last portraits as a romantic screen figure, in a spare but beautifully conceived sequence involving Helen. When she asks Slater how he felt when he killed a man just before she seduces him, one is reminded of a similar scene in *On Dangerous Ground*. Accompanied by the seductive melody of John Lewis's superb jazz score, the scene was choreographed to cause audiences to cease any small talk. Ryan still had the ability to inspire sexual tension as well as dread.

Besides Ryan and Gloria Grahame, other *film noir* stalwarts such as Ed Begley, Will Kuluva, Lou Gallo, and Richard Bright (in one of the first films to portray homosexuals), contributed realistic depictions to fill out *Odds Against Tomorrow*'s grim ambience. In bit parts, Cicely Tyson,

Wayne Rogers, and Zohra Lampert did well, while singer Carmen De Lavallade and the Modern Jazz Quartet performed in a pungent scene in a Manhattan nightclub.

Robert Wise's direction was as relentlessly accurate as were his players' performances, and he came as close as possible to making a perfect movie. Film critics lauded the film, but its small budget and taboo topic lowered its possibility of wide recognition. But he and Ryan had a reputation for making pictures with a strong viewpoint, and they loved the film's social commentary enough to take a chance with it.

Reviews: "An absorbing, disquieting film.... On one level, *Odds Against Tomorrow* is a taut crime melodrama. On another, it is an allegory about racism, greed, and man's propensity for self-destruction.... Wise [has] produced and directed with an alert eye for sooty realism.... He has drawn fine performances from his players ... Ryan makes the flesh crawl as the fanatical bigot." (*Variety*, 10/7/59.)

"The tension builds well to a climax—thanks partly to director Robert Wise, partly to an able Negro scriptwriter named John O. Killens, but mostly to actor Robert Ryan, a menace who can look bullets, and smile sulphuric acid." (*Time*, 10/26/59.)

"A hard, nervous melodrama that has, for most of its length, an incisive, eager excitement.... Robert Ryan plays the hater, a man who never feels easy except in a rage.... Ryan and Begley are very forceful." (Paul V. Beckley, *New York Herald-Tribune*, 10/16/59.)

"A sharp, hard suspenseful melodrama.... Under the tight and strong direction of the realist, Robert Wise, the drama accumulates tensely, with fast, easy clarity, and the whole thing has an intensely sharp, true pictorial quality.... And from his excellent performances he got crisp and credible characters. Mr. Ryan is brilliant, cold and rasping, as a drifter from the South whose hatreds are ingrained and vicious, recalling the anti-Semitic killer he played in the melodramatic *Crossfire* a dozen years ago." (Bosley Crowther, *New York Times*, 10/16/59.)

"One is dazzled by the technical virtuosity with which the film is put over. The camera work of Joseph Brun is superb, there is no other word for it. The grey landscapes of wintry New York state, the smoky jazz club and the austere apartment houses as handled by Brun's camera are almost more expressive than the actors. ... An excellent performance from Robert Ryan. ... The cutting is a model of cinema craftsmanship, and the music score by the Modern Jazz Quartet's John Lewis is expert." (Derek Conrad, *Films and Filming*, 11/59.)

"Its theme, although done before, has vitality and interest. For all their grimness, the three title roles are excellently played, with Ryan as a bitter and tough criminal who thinks the world owes him a living. Obviously this is no pretty picture. Its determined realism deserves much respect, and so does its censure against bigotry and racial hatred. ... Belafonte, as the man who is the subject of Ryan's hatred, has a sense of dignity and a feeling of being driven beyond his strength. As a consequence, Ryan's skillfully portrayed hatred of him becomes all the more forceful." (Philip T. Hartung, *Commonweal*, 11/13/59.)

"The virtue of the picture—in addition to a blood stirring cast consisting of Ryan, Belafonte, Winters, Begley and Grahame, is the photography. The natural theatricality of the city and the river in upstate New York where the film was shot, under the cold light of racing cloud banks, has been brilliantly caught with no arch artiness.... It is a background of almost percussive tension." (Robert Hatch, *The Nation*, 11/28/59.)

Ice Palace (3) (1960). Warner Bros., C-143 min. *Director* Vincent Sherman. *Producer* Henry Blanke. *Based on the novel by* Edna Ferber. *Screenplay* Harry Kleiner. *Music* Max Steiner. *Orchestrator*

Murray Cutter. *Art Director* Malcolm Bert. *Set Decorator* George James Hopkins. *Assistant Directors* Russell Llewellyn, Gil Kissel. *Costumes* Howard Shoup. *Makeup* Gordon Bau. *Sound* Stanley Jones. *Camera* Joseph Biroc. *Editor* William Ziegler. *Cast* Richard Burton (Zeb Kennedy), **Robert Ryan** (Thor Storm), Carolyn Jones (Bridie Ballantyne), Martha Hyer (Dorothy Wendt), Ray Danton (Bay Husack), Diane McBain (Christine Storm), Karl Swenson (Scotty Ballantyne), Shirley Knight (Grace Kennedy), Barry Kelley (Einer Wendt), George Takei (Wang), Steve Harris (Steve at Age 16), William Yip (Chinese Maître d'), Stanford Jolley (Mr. Lawson).

Edna Ferber's sprawling tale of Alaska prior to its admission to statehood was a good idea for a movie, and with Ryan and Richard Burton starring, the finished product should have been better than it was. Warner Bros. put forth a reasonably firm effort in the production of *Ice Palace*, but when they cast several characters from the studio's bevy of young, nondescript stars, a measure of realism was lost. Although Warners spent a lot of money on the picture, its biggest problem had to do with its standard script, against which director Vincent Sherman could do little to improve it.

Ice Palace had enough romance and toughness to attract audiences, beautiful cinematography, and better than average acting from the stars, which included Carolyn Jones and Martha Hyer. Similar to Ferber's earlier novel about Texas tycoons in *Giant*, *Ice Palace*'s story followed two families through three generations of Alaskan heritage. One is led by Burton's power hungry Zeb Kennedy, the other by Ryan's righteous Thor Storm. The two become friends after Storm gives Kennedy a job and extends his hospitality to him, but when Kennedy steals Storm's girlfriend, Bridie (Jones), their connection turns to intense enmity.

Another conflict occurs when Kennedy's steamrolling business tactics threaten to ruin Alaska's fishing industry.

Storm, a fisherman by trade, undertakes to stop Kennedy, and the remainder of the story has to do with their 30-year battle that is increasingly concerned with their respective egos. While Kennedy's actions exploit Alaska's resources, Storm vows to stop him and they grow further apart.

Storm's future leads him into politics and a leading role in the promotion of Alaska for statehood. The resolution to the feud between Storm and Kennedy occurs when Kennedy leads a dangerous search mission for Storm, who is lost in the wilderness. Their friendship is rekindled when Kennedy has a change of heart and mends his ways. In the film's final scenes, Storm is shown giving speeches and campaigning for statehood, and the picture ends with Ryan's voiceover declaring pride in his new state, as the screen fades to a *National Geographic* type shot of Alaskan scenery.

The acting of Ryan, Burton, Carolyn Jones, and Martha Hyer labored to raise Ferber's story to a high level of soap opera, while supporting actors Jim Backus, Karl Swenson, Ray Danton, and Diane McBain kept the drama from going further, as if they were reenacting one of Warners' numerous television programs of the sixties. Nevertheless, Ryan's Thor Storm was one of his most positive portraits, and a total reversal of his recent Earle Slater. However, in *Ice Palace*, his romantic appeal was in its final stage of vitality, as reflected in his character's losing his woman (Bridie), because she was more attracted to a younger man (Kennedy).

Reviews: "An unusually strong human-conflict drama ... with director Vincent Sherman casting a knowing camera's eye on the scenic values of the territory involved, plus the added background ... rates it as an important production.... It can't miss being big." (*Variety*, 6/15/60.)

"This mingling of history and bittersweet romance, successful enough in book form, has proven irresistible to the movie companies.... *Ice Palace* will probably click along to the same silvery jingle as its predecessors.... Instead of Alaska in the foreground, there are Robert Ryan, Richard Burton, and Carolyn Jones — two men and a girl." (Arthur Knight, *Saturday Review*, 7/23/60.)

The Canadians (1) (1961). Twentieth Century–Fox, C-85 min. *Director* Burt Kennedy. *Producer* Herman E. Webber. *Screenplay* Burt Kennedy. *Wardrobe* Jim Dunlevy. *Sound* Arthur Bradburn. *Camera* Arthur Ibbetson. *Editor* Douglas Robertson. *Cast* **Robert Ryan** (Inspector Gannon), John Dehner (Frank Boone), Torin Thatcher (Sergeant McGregor), Teresa Stratas (The White Squaw), Burt Metcalfe (Constable Springer), John Sutton (Superintendent Walker), Jack Creley (Greer), Scott Peters (Ben), Richard Alden (Billy), Michael Pate (Chief Four Horns).

The Canadians rivaled *Escape to Burma* and *Alaska Seas* as one of Ryan's most forgettable pictures, and came during the hardest time of his career. Curiously, it also joined the list of films in which he was top-billed but which were box-office flops.

As Burt Kennedy's first job in the director's chair, *The Canadians* was a mediocre debut, made worse by a plodding screenplay which he also wrote. Strike two was in the casting of opera singer Teresa Stratas in one of the main roles, and the waste of talented actors, John Dehner and Torin Thatcher. In the lean plus column, the film featured beautiful scenery from the rolling plains of Saskatchewan and the Royal Canadian Mounted Police, which would have fit best into a travelogue for Canada.

The story of *The Canadians* followed a standard formula. A rancher (Dehner) and three gunmen travel north to Canada, searching for horses they believe stolen by Indians. After the men massacre an Indian village, Ryan's Inspector Gannon takes them into custody, but they escape, taking the White Squaw (Stratas) hostage. In the ensuing chase,

the woman gives her life saving Gannon, and the Indians arrive in time to drive the rancher and his men off a cliff. Gannon returns to headquarters, safe in the knowledge that he has upheld justice, and the film ends on a note of nationalistic Canadian pride.

Reviews: "Tedious.... The first British quota picture to be shot solely in Canada is a plodding, tepid drama.... The dull script is played out conscientiously but without much spirit.... Ryan, expressionless as his horse, gives a stolid performance." (*Variety*, 3/8/61.)

"Burt Kennedy's screenplay is uninventive, uneventful, and without even enough clichés to fill it out. ... Ryan, an actor who does have a sinewy manner, seems at times to be concealing with difficulty his awareness of just how slouchy drab is the material he is working with...." (Paul V. Beckley, *New York Herald-Tribune*, 6/1/61.)

King of Kings (5) (1961). MGM, C-165 min. *Director* Nicholas Ray. *Producer* Samuel Bronston. *Associate Producers* Noel Howard, Sumner Williams. *Screenplay* Philip Yordan. *Narration written by* Ray Bradbury. *Music* Miklos Rozsa. *Assistant Directors* Carlo Lastricate, Jose Maria Ochoa, Jose Lopez Rodero. *Choreography* Betty Utey. *Sets and Costumes* Georges Wakhevitch. *Set Decorator* Enrique Alarcon. *Sound* Franklin Milton, Basil Fenton Smith. *Second Unit Directors* Noel Howard, Sumner Williams. *Special Camera Effects* Lee Le Blanc. *Special Effects* Alex C. Weldon. *Camera* Franz Planer, Milton Krasner, Manuel Berenguer. *Editor* Harold Kress. *Cast* Jeffrey Hunter (Jesus Christ), Siobhan McKenna (Mary), **Robert Ryan** (John the Baptist), Hurd Hatfield (Pontius Pilate), Ron Randell (Lucius the Centurion), Viveca Lindfors (Claudia), Rita Gam (Herodias), Carmen Sevilla (Mary Magdalene), Brigid Bazlen (Salome), Harry Guardino (Barabbas), Orson Welles (Narrator), Rip Torn (Judas), Frank Thring (Herod Antipas), Guy Rolfe (Caiaphas), Maurice Marsac

(Nicodemus), Royal Dano (Peter), Edric Connor (Balthazar), George Coulouris (Camel Driver).

Ryan's role as John the Baptist in Nicholas Ray's reverent, orthodox account of the life of Christ was greeted with doubt by the public. Despite his own mixed emotions about taking a part far removed from his usual realm, he brought a divine poignancy to a character that had little potential for sustained dramatic impact because of its brevity. Although the running time of *King of Kings* was 165 minutes and Ryan appeared in a small segment, his importance in the story was pivotal to its outcome.

During the filming of *King of Kings*, quite a bit of press followed producer Samuel Bronston's lavish biography, and having been shot in Technicolor and 70 millimeter Super Technirama, the picture was visually stunning. Director Ray's studied "auteur" style, although out of place in the religious epic milieu, remained offbeat, emphasizing reverence and artistically conscious set designs to underline Philip Yordan's traditional screenplay.

One of the best aspects of *King of Kings* was in its unusual casting. Bronston chose 20th Century–Fox's young star, Jeffrey Hunter, to play Christ, because he saw in Hunter a face combining the "delicate sensitivity and virile masculine strength so commonly seen in the artistic representations of Christ." (*Films and Filming*, November 1960.)

In addition to Ryan and Hunter, the high quality cast included Siobhan McKenna, Frank Thring, Harry Guardino, Ron Randell, Rip Torn, and Hurd Hatfield. Since they all had previously been active on the stage, they meshed well with Ray's technique as an "actor's director."

Although Ryan's role was little more than a trenchant cameo, his involvement with the picture was symbolic of his dedication to films that had something to say over and above the mundane.

Reviews: Some critics reacted strongly to *King of Kings*. A review in *Time*, dated October 27, 1961, reflected confusion: "The corniest, phoniest, ickiest and most monstrously vulgar of all the big Bible stories Hollywood has told in the last decade."

Yet the same reviewer later went on to say: "Bronston's bust enjoys one solid virtue: a script precisely organized and competently prosed by playwright Philip (Anna Lucasta) Yordan, who has often quite sensitively reconciled the grandeurs of the King James version with the need for a fresh, contemporary tone.

"I am one of those who went to see *King of Kings* full of foreboding and who came away pleasantly surprised. . . . There are several noteworthy performances. . . . Robert Ryan, as John the Baptist, is better than I expected he would be in such a role, especially in the scene in which he baptizes the mature Christ, whom we see for the first time. In this important scene, Ray was inspired to have the camera record a shot of Hunter's blue eyes *reflecting* light. Nothing could more effectively suggest spirituality, and Ray correctly followed this shot with one of Ryan's eyes, pondering the nature of the Man who had come to be baptized." (Henry Hart, *Films in Review*, 11/61.)

"A major motion picture by any standard—as a production, as a script, for masterly management of scenes by its director, and as an entertainment. . . . It wisely substitutes characterizations for orgies. Nicholas Ray has brooded long and wisely upon the meaning of his meanings, has planted plenty of symbols along the path yet avoided the banalities of religious calendar art. . . . Off-type for him is Robert Ryan as John the Baptist, and he makes an attractive character of the holy man." (*Variety*, 10/11/61.)

The Longest Day (5) (1962). Twentieth Century–Fox, 180 min. *Directors* Andrew Marton, Ken Annakin, Bernhard Wicki. *Based on the book by* Cornelius Ryan. *Screenplay* Cornelius Ryan.

Additional Episodes Romain Gary, James Jones, David Pursall, Jack Seddon. *Music and Music Conductor* Maurice Jarre. *Thematic Music* Paul Anka. *Arranger* Mitch Miller. *Art Directors* Ted Haworth, Vincent Korda, Leon Barsacq. *Assistant Directors* Bernard Farrel, Louis Fitzele, Gerard Renateau, Henri Sokal. *Sound* Jo De Bretagne, Jacques Maumont, William Sivel. *Special Effects* Karl Baumgartner, Karl Helmer, Augie Lohman, Robert MacDonald, Alex Weldon. *Camera* Jean Bourgoin, Henri Persin, Walter Wottitz. *Helicopter Shots* Guy Tabary. *Editor* Samuel E. Beetley. *Cast* John Wayne (Colonel Vandervoort), Robert Mitchum (General Cota), Henry Fonda (General Roosevelt), **Robert Ryan** (General Gavin), Rod Steiger (Commander), Robert Wagner (U.S. Ranger), Richard Beymer (Schultz), Mel Ferrer (General Haines), Jeffrey Hunter (Sergeant Fuller), Paul Anka, Tommy Sands, Fabian (Rangers), Sal Mineo (Private Martini), Roddy McDowall (Private Morris), Stuart Whitman (Lieutenant Sheen), Eddie Albert (Colonel Newton), Edmond O'Brien (General Barton), Red Buttons (Private Steele), Tom Tryon (Lieutenant Wilson), Alexander Knox (General Bedell Smith), Ray Danton (Captain Frank), Henry Grace (General Eisenhower), Mark Damon (Private Harris), Steve Forrest (Captain Harding), John Crawford (Colonel Caffey), Ron Randell (Williams), Richard Burton, Donald Houston (Royal Air Force Pilots), Kenneth More (Captain Maud), Peter Lawford (Lord Lovat), Richard Todd (Major Howard), Leo Genn (General Parker), John Gregson (Padre), Sean Connery (Private Flanagan), Jack Hedley (Briefing Man), Michael Medwin (Private Watney), Norman Rossington (Private Clough), Irina Demich (Janine), Bourvil (Mayor), Jean-Louis Barrault (Father Roulland), Christian Marquand (Kieffer), Arletty (Mme. Barrault), Jean Servais (Admiral Jaujard), Curt Jurgens (General Blumentritt), Werner Hinz (Marshal Rommel), Paul Hartmann (Marshal Rundstedt), Peter Van Eyck (Colonel Ocker), Gert Frobe (Sergeant Kaffeeklatsch), Hans Christian Blech (Major Pluskat), Wolfgang Preiss (General Pensel), Heinz Reincke (Colonel Priller).

Ryan's appearance in *The Longest Day* was not a role of substance, yet the picture stranded no less than 30 other performers in cameo roles. The film represented his third cameo, after *The Boy with Green Hair* and *King of Kings*, in a list that grew substantially during the lean sixties.

The Longest Day was really a John Wayne–Robert Mitchum movie, wherein both stars upheld their reputations as he-men of the American cinema. Over and above the star attraction that the picture's producers amassed, *The Longest Day* was one of the first large scale epics to chronicle the Allied invasion of Europe on June 6, 1944.

Employing three directors to handle the dominant nationalities represented (America, Great Britain, Germany) was a wise decision by producer Darryl Zanuck, resulting in consistently arresting performances. Moreover, Cornelius Ryan's screenplay, adapted from his book of the same title, breathed with the immediacy of the period.

The film's only flaw, perhaps, was in its blatant use of major actors in bit parts. Besides Ryan's inconsequential role as a sympathetic general, Henry Fonda, Rod Steiger, Eddie Albert, Richard Burton, Richard Todd, Leo Genn, and many others performed well in brief roles.

Reviews: "In spite of its spectacular battle scenes, enormous scope, and frequent change of scene, *The Longest Day* has enormous clarity. Credit should go to Cornelius Ryan who wrote the screenplay from his own book. The officers come through best, such as Robert Ryan as Brigadier General James Gavin, and John Wayne as Lieutenant Colonel Ben Vandervoort." (Philip T. Hartung, *Commonweal*, 10/26/62.)

Billy Budd (5) (1962). Allied Artists, 123 min. *Director* Peter Ustinov. *Executive Producer* A. Ronald Lubin. *Producer* Peter

Ustinov. *Based on the novel* Billy Budd, Foretopman *by* Herman Melville, *and the play by* Louis O. Coxe, Robert H. Chapman. *Screenplay* Peter Ustinov, Robert Rossen, DeWitt Bodeen. *Music and Music Conductor* Anthony Hopkins. *Production Designer* Don Ashton. *Art Director* Peter Murton. *Costumes* Anthony Mendelson. *Makeup* Bob Lawrence. *Assistant Director* Michael Birkett. *Sound* Charles Crafford, Charles Poulton, Len Shilton. *Camera* Robert Krasker. *Editor* Jack Harris. *Cast* **Robert Ryan** (John Claggart), Peter Ustinov (Captain Vere), Melvyn Douglas (The Dansker), Terence Stamp (Billy Budd), Ronald Lewis (Jenkins), David McCallum (Lieutenant Wyatt), John Neville (Lieutenant Ratcliffe), Paul Rogers (Lieutenant Seymour), Lee Montague (Squeak), Thomas Heathcote (Payne), Ray McAnally (O'Daniel), Robert Brown (Talbot), John Meillon (Kincaid), Cyril Luckham (Hallam), Niall MacGinnis (Captain Graveling).

After three films in which his talents were ill-used, Ryan got top billing, as the demonic Master-at-arms John Claggart, in the powerful adaptation of Herman Melville's allegorical novel, *Billy Budd, Foretopman.* His performance was the key to the film's success, as the Claggart role had pitfalls in interpretation, and might easily have lapsed into caricature. But Ryan avoided crude exaggeration under Peter Ustinov's studied direction, and his Claggart epitomized the cold fervor of absolute evil that Melville saw as an inevitable corollary to the good in man.

Ustinov cowrote, with DeWitt Bodeen and Robert Rossen (who was uncredited in the billing), a realistic script that adhered to the flavor of the times. Melville wrote *Billy Budd, Foretopman* as a statement to Great Britain about its tyrannical naval system, to baptize people to the inhumane treatment of sailors on board Her Majesty's ships.

In fact, the service had become a breeding ground where the dregs of society mixed uncomfortably with the elite in an antithetical, antagonistic relationship. Naval justice was harsh and unbending, as men were routinely flogged, keelhauled, or hanged. (It is alleged that shortly after Melville's novel was published, the British Admiralty brought sweeping changes to its brutal system.)

The good versus evil conflict between Ryan's malevolent Claggart and the angelic Billy Budd (Terence Stamp) is mediated by Ustinov's Captain Vere, who represents the force for rationality and order in an irrational world. Yet although Vere, as the symbol of justice and the law, is the final arbiter of Budd's and Claggart's battle of wills, his decision to hang Budd when he kills Claggart has the hollow ring of hypocrisy. Ustinov's script carefully pointed out the ambiguities of law versus the ambivalence of justice, where good often goes unserved.

Billy Budd is a film of dichotomies. Claggart sees himself as a victim of a predatory world where he bitterly asserts, "Only the strongest teeth survive." Budd, on the other hand, has led an innocent existence in which his warmth has charmed the coldest hearts, until he meets Claggart's steeled barriers. When Budd is conscripted for duty on board Vere's man-o'-war, his luck changes for the worse, while Claggart's envy turns into a vendetta. In Budd's naiveté, he sees Claggart's comments, "Oh, Master Budd, you *do* make friends easily," and his grimace-like smile, as signs of friendship rather than as a malignant warning.

Ryan's spectral recreation of Claggart had a moving intensity, since he made the demon master-at-arms into a pathetic figure despite his evil. His hatred of men is explained in a scene in which Captain Vere demands, "Why are you so bent to such a sorry task?" to which Claggart solemnly replies, "I am what I am, and what the world has made me."

When Billy's ingenuousness nearly breaks down Claggart's wall of solitude, the latter becomes paranoid and sends him away, snarling, "You would charm *me* too," then, "Get away! *Get away!*"

From then on, fate consummates

with death as Budd and Claggart, the epitomes of right and wrong, perish due to human weakness. In a climactic scene, Claggart accuses Budd of mutiny and sedition, to which Budd strikes him with a fatal blow. Before dying, Claggart smiles ominously at Budd, knowing that he will die for the act.

In the ensuing court-martial, Billy is found guilty of murder and is hanged from the yardarm at dawn, to the shame of Vere and his fellow officers. Bound by an arbitrary code of justice, they are also its victims. At film's end, as Billy's corpse swings in the ocean breeze, the ship is suddenly fired upon by a French man-o'-war, and the last shot is of Captain Vere's arm jutting out lifelessly from under a splintered, fallen mast. The battle lends an ambivalent conclusion to the film, whose outcome is left to the viewer's discretion.

Peter Ustinov did a meticulous job of recreating the harsh life aboard ship in the 18th Century British Navy, where floggings, unfit food, and ill treatment were the standard lot for ordinary seamen. Amid such hardships, though, the sea is ever-present as a mysterious yet beautiful power, to help calm men's souls as they live and die.

Ustinov filmed *Billy Budd* off the coast of England and Spain on an authentic British frigate, capturing the realism of the times, while Robert Krasker's sharp black and white cinematography, done in Cinemascope, caught the breathtaking feel of the open seas, with vast, expansive shots of far horizons and sails rippling in the wind. Ustinov decided on black and white instead of color because he thought, "Color beautifies everything."

The cast, including Melvyn Douglas, Paul Rogers, John Neville, and David McCallum, worked well together under Ustinov's deft direction, and gave further clarity to the concise screenplay. As deprived able seamen, Ronald Lewis, Lee Montague, Thomas Heathcote, and John Meillon provided solid support, while Terence Stamp posed an angelic opposite to Ryan's tormented Master Claggart.

Ryan's interpretation of Claggart again succeeded in injecting pathos into a negative character. Many critics asserted that Ryan was the focal point of *Billy Budd*, and that it was one of his most complex roles. On the other hand, his vivid portrayal did little to offset his image of evil in people's minds. Nevertheless, *Billy Budd* was a remarkable piece of lasting value and artistic achievement.

Reviews: "Ustinov peopled his picture with British actors he knew were solidly reliable, like Paul Rogers and John Neville, and added two veteran Hollywood actors, Robert Ryan and Melvyn Douglas. Ryan . . . always a fine actor, had long wanted to play the part of Claggart. . . . His performance in *Billy Budd*, as an incarnation of evil, was one of the major contributions to the film's effectiveness." (*Ustinov in Focus*, Tony Thomas, A. Zwemmer, *London*, 1971.)

"Splendid film. . . . In a beautiful black-and-white production, the physical setting of the drama is flawlessly achieved. . . . Billy Budd's tormentor, as played by Robert Ryan, is a creature of cold, sadistic fervor. He is a Melville symbol of the cruel and completely unalterable evil that endlessly runs through the world, blind and without apparent reason, like a tornado or forest fire. . . . Mr. Ryan puts forth a taut and chilling picture as the demon master-at-arms." (Bosley Crowther, *New York Times*, 10/31/62.)

"A beautiful, terrifying, heartbreaking film. . . . The transformation [to the screen] is the more admirable for the fact that *Billy Budd* is essentially a morality play . . . Robert Ryan is the terrible Mr. Claggart who presides so zealously at floggings . . . once, after counting out ten lashes while a sailor is whipped, his mouth frames a silent "eleven." Then, standing alone at the rail, he continues to strike his own flank with his rattan crop, privately counting out lash after lash in seething frustration." (*Time*, 11/9/62.)

"Ryan is outstanding, whether smirking stiffly while a soldier is whipped at his orders, or recognizing suddenly how narrowly he has escaped succumbing to Budd's innocence. It is a penetrating realization of one of the most vivid and agile-minded villains on film." (Paul V. Beckley, *New York Herald-Tribune*, 10/31/62.)

"It is likely that *Billy Budd* will turn out to be the best and most important picture of the year . . . Robert Ryan is excellent in the role of Claggart, catching the almost inexplicable force of evil as he enjoys the floggings he oversees, disdains Billy's innocence, and looks with suspicion and envy on the young man's beauty and joie de vivre." (Philip T. Hartung, *Commonweal*, 11/16/62.)

". . . the real acting weight of the film comes from Robert Ryan as Claggart. His scenes, without reservation, have full command, and he brings the Master-at-Arms chillingly to life as a sadistic monster, as an astute killer of his own and other people's dreams.

In particular, there are three scenes which reveal the dark at the bottom of Claggart's psyche as surely as though they had been taken by flashlight: a magnificent moment when he stands broodingly alone on the side of the ship, his swagger stick beating out the leftover strokes of a flogging he had argued more heavily punished; a telling exchange between he and Vere in which he answers the former's probing with a curt "I am what I am, and what the world has made me"; and best of all, a dialogue with Billy in the prow of the ship late at night which takes on the aspects of a duel as both men reveal the extent of their opposing personalities." (John Cutts, *Films and Filming*, October 1962.)

The Battle of the Bulge (2) (1965). Warner Bros., C-187 min. *Director* Ken Annakin. *Producers* Milton Sperling, Philip Yordan. *Screenplay* Philip Yordan, Milton Sperling, John Nelson. *Music* Benjamin Frankel. *Song* Benjamin Frankel, Kurl Wiehle. *Art Director* Eugene Lourie.

Assistant Directors Jose Lopez Rodero, Martin Sacristan, Luis Garcia. *Technical Advisors* General Meinred von Lauchert, Colonel Sherman Jolle, Major Edward King. *Sound* David Hildyard, Gordon McCallum. *Camera* Jack Hildyard. *Editor* Derek Parsons. *Cast* Henry Fonda (Lieutenant Colonel Kiley), Robert Shaw (Colonel Hessler), **Robert Ryan** (General Grey), Dana Andrews (Colonel Pritchard), George Montgomery (Sergeant Duquesne), Ty Hardin (Schumacher), Pier Angeli (Louise), Barbara Werle (Elena), Charles Bronson (Wolenski), Werner Peters (General Kohler), Hans Christian Blech (Conrad), James MacArthur (Lieutenant Weaver), Telly Savalas (Guffy).

Ryan's first film appearance in three years was in one of the first large scale war epics of the sixties, and if nothing more gratifying could be said of the picture, at least Ryan was well paid for it. *The Battle of the Bulge* was his fourth film for producer Sidney Harmon, but from a creative viewpoint, it failed to ignite any serious critical attention.

Although *The Battle of the Bulge* had better than average box office success, its initial good fortune was principally due to its impressive cast, headed by Ryan, Henry Fonda, Robert Shaw, and Dana Andrews, and because it was filmed in Cinerama. The visual spectacle of soldiers engaged in close fighting amid the onslaught of German panzers provided sufficient visceral excitement to drown out Ken Annakin's lackadaisical direction.

Despite a strong screenplay, which was cowritten by Philip Yordan, Milton Sperling, and John Nelson, the cast could do little to elevate *The Battle of the Bulge* above the average. Included among the supporting cast could be found several American actors who had sought greener pastures in Europe, led by George Montgomery, Charles Bronson, Telly Savalas, and James MacArthur.

Robert Shaw's portrayal of an obsessed German panzer officer was the best written part in the cast, while fifties star

Dana Andrews occupied a subordinate position similar to Ryan's. Since 24 minutes were deleted from *The Battle of the Bulge* shortly after its release, perhaps it originally had more on its mind than blood and guts. Ryan's part as General Grey may have suffered the most in the editing room, and seemed to have been cut in scenes in which he must make crucial battlefield decisions, and in a few important scenes with Fonda. Thus, the narrative loses impact when it jumps from individual interactions to battle sequences in which its multitudes of soldiers remain faceless and nameless.

The Battle of the Bulge emerged with no significant creative imprint, and was neither a "Ryan" nor a "Fonda" movie, despite their efforts to make it so.

Reviews: "...what the intention of the film was, is never very clear. As a study in war, it is on the level of children playing with toy tanks and soldiers on the living room carpet. ... The screenplay gives hints of more serious intentions, and occasionally embarks on interesting discussions which are abruptly curtailed in the cause of providing more visual stimulation. ... In the hands of Frankenheimer or Wicki, the same subject would probably have been treated in more harsh and compelling terms. As it is, it remains a nostalgic return to the old style Hollywood glossy war epic, summed up rather neatly when Robert Ryan, as a general requesting supplies over the phone says, "Well, not later Fred, we're counting on you." (Robin Bean, *Films and Filming*, 2/66.)

The Crooked Road (1) (1965). Seven Arts, 90 min. *Director* Don Chaffey. *Executive Producer* Jack O. Lamont. *Producer* David Henley. *Based on the novel by* Morris L. West. *Screenplay* J. Garrison. *Music* Bojan Adamic. *Cast* **Robert Ryan** (Richard Ashley), Stewart Granger (Duke of Orgagna), Nadia Gray (Cosima), Marius Goring (Harlequin), George Coulouris (Carlo).

The Crooked Road was an embarrass-ment for everyone concerned with its making, and it more closely resembled a home movie than professional work. Primitively shot in Yugoslavia, the story bounced around haphazardly, resulting in a disjointed tale of overblown dialogue and confusing cabal.

In the title role as a crusading journalist, Richard Ashley, Ryan seemed to fare the best of the cast, although his past romance with Nadia Gray is only hinted. When they meet again in the present, their interaction is limited to a few sheepish looks, which must have left them as cold as audiences felt.

Costarring with Ryan as the supposedly malevolent Duke of a fictitious eastern European country, curiously named Orgagna, Stewart Granger played his role like a foppish spoiled brat. Although there is little evidence of the Duke's nefarious deeds, newspaperman Ashley embarks on a mission to expose him, as if he were after a Nazi war criminal.

While uncovering the Duke's dirty linen, Ashley brushes heads with two or three inept lackeys sent to kill him. These encounters only lead Ashley closer to a final showdown with his quarry. Naturally, Ashley succeeds in his one-man coup, the Duke is shot to death in a patently phony climax, and Orgagna is rescued from his medieval monarchy.

The Crooked Road's title was an appropriate metaphor to describe the picture, since, in addition to Don Chaffey's pallid direction and a contrived script, its editing seemed to have been done on a backwoods trail. Inevitably, the location shooting created minimal visual interest.

When Ryan carefully reviewed the script before accepting the Ashley part, he found that it had the prerequisites he wanted badly. He liked the heroism, the romance, and the foreign intrigue in exotic locales. *The Crooked Road* appeared very briefly to generally unfavorable reviews, and was released in England two years later, shortened by six minutes. It ranks in the top five of Ryan's worst films.

Reviews: "A hoary tale of a mythical dictator of a mythical Balkan domain threatened with exposure by a typically crusading newsman. Ryan is trapped in the role of the reporter.... It's a wonder they could all play it with a straight face—especially Ryan." (Bob Salmaggi, *New York Herald-Tribune,* 2/4/65.)

The Dirty Game (1) (1966). American International, 91 min. *Directors* Terence Young, Christian-Jacque, Carlo Lizzani. *Executive Producer* Richard Hellman. *Associate Producer* Eugene Tucherer. *Screenplay* Jo Eisinger. *Music* Robert Mellin. *Art Directors* Robert Gabriti, H. Weidman. *Sound* G. Mardiguian. *Camera* Pierre Petit, Richard Angst, Enrico Menczer. *Editors* Borys Leurn, Alan Osbiston. *Cast* Henry Fonda (Kourlov), **Robert Ryan** (General Bruce), Vittorio Gassman (Perego), Annie Girardot (Nanette), Bourvil (Laland), Robert Hossein (Dupont), Peter Van Eyck (Berlin C.M.), Maria Grazia Buccela (Natalia).

Ryan may have put bread on the table with *The Dirty Game,* but far from reviving his name, it nearly fell into permanent interment. Each of the film's three directors fashioned his own vignette of foreign intrigue; however, none of the stories were of lasting interest. One of the three, Terence Young, had made three James Bond thrillers (*Dr. No, From Russia with Love,* and *Thunderball*), while Christian-Jacque and Carlo Lizzani had distinguished themselves in European cinema. Nevertheless, the whole was less than the sum of its parts, since *The Dirty Game* bore no significant director's imprint.

As in *The Crooked Road, The Dirty Game* was shot overseas in West Germany, Africa, and Italy, featuring European screen notables Vittorio Gassman, Annie Girardot, Robert Hossein, and Peter Van Eyck. Joining Ryan in the European theater of acting was another American actor whose career had come up against mid-life crisis, Henry Fonda. *The Dirty Game* bore similarities to Ryan's growing list of pictures in which he popped in and out at strategic moments. In this installment he played an American Intelligence Chief, General Bruce, who is sent to Europe to oversee a prisoner exchange between the United States and Russia. While en route, he recalls three important cases he supervised.

Most critics noticed that the stories seemed disconnected and illogical, but that the film was serviceable fare within the James Bond sphere of high-tech gimmickry. American-International Pictures took over distribution of *The Dirty Game* and attempted to improve it in the cutting room. During the year after its release, it resurfaced in different cities with diminishing running times, ranging from 120 down to 87 minutes.

Ryan's General Bruce was another sketchily written part that left him obviously stranded. The *New York World Journal Tribune* commented, "Ryan keeps arriving late at the scene of each crime, lending a certain, undeniable sense of unity to the proceedings." His final line of dialogue, that "war is a hell of a way to make a living," had a ring of truth in light of his career, and probably was an opinion that he shared.

Reviews: "St. Vitus is the guilty patron saint of *The Dirty Game.* ... How it jumps around, from one vague encounter to another, from logic to illogic ... Ryan's presence at the opening and close of the picture is impossible to explain." (William Peper, *New York World Journal Tibune,* 9/22/66.)

"*The Dirty Game* has three directors doing acceptable if not unusual work. The pic cannily strives for action, suspense and comedy and is thus an item that should fit present interest in Cold War background pix..." (*Variety* [Paris], 7/21/66.)

The Professionals (5) (1966). Columbia, C-117 min. *Director* Richard Brooks. *Producer* Richard Brooks. *Based on the novel* A Mule for the Marquesa *by*

Frank O'Rourke. *Screenplay* Richard Brooks. *Art Director* Edward S. Haworth. *Set Decorator* Frank Tuttle. *Makeup* Robert Schiffer. *Wardrobe* Jack Martell. *Assistant Director* Tom Shaw. *Music and Music Conductor* Maurice Jarre. *Sound* Charles J. Rice, William Randall, Jr., Jack Haynes. *Special Effects* Willis Cook. *Camera* Conrad Hall. *Editor* Peter Zinner. *Cast* Burt Lancaster (Bill Dolworth), Lee Marvin (Rico Farden), **Robert Ryan** (Hans Ehrengard), Jack Palance (Jesus Raza), Claudia Cardinale (Maria Grant), Ralph Bellamy (J.W. Grant), Woody Strode (Jacob Sharpe), Joe De Santis (Ortega), Rafael Bertrand (Fierro), Jorge Martinez (Padilla), Maria Gomez (Chiquita), Jose Chavez, Carlos Romero (Revolutionaries), Vaughn Taylor (Banker), Robert Contreras, Don Carlos (Bandits), Eddie Little Sky (Prisoner).

The Professionals is a noteworthy film, and one of the best Westerns of the sixties. Director Richard Brooks, whose skilled hand has been put to good use in a number of films of high dramatic value, fashioned a fast-paced, laconic picture with an adult theme.

Loyalty and honor are the questions on trial in *The Professionals*, and Ryan, Lee Marvin, Burt Lancaster, and Woody Strode are the four men who deal with the subject in different ways. They are enlisted as soldiers-of-fortune by railroad magnate J.W. Grant (Ralph Bellamy), to rescue his kidnapped wife, Maria (Claudia Cardinale), from the Mexican bandit Jesus Raza (Jack Palance).

Set against a background of the divided factions waging the Mexican Revolution, Brooks's screenplay posed several intriguing moral questions. But although the ending fails to solve any of them, its tongue-in-cheek irony makes the film worth its often torturous journey. As Burt Lancaster's Dolworth discusses the rescue mission with his three comrades, he muses about its morality, "The only trouble is, who are the bad guys, and who are the good guys?"

The Professionals is also about changing values versus finding meaning in life. Of the four men, two (Marvin and Lancaster) are depicted as having previously fought side by side with Raza, for what is portrayed as a "noble" cause. But the picture questions their motives. Were they heroic or merely concerned with glory?

Ryan's Hans Ehrengard is the only member of the group who has no background in destruction, and thus becomes its conscience. Although called upon to shoot other men during the rescue attempt, he is depicted as a humane man, hired more for his ability as an expert horseman and animal handler than for his killing power. Ironically, it is his kindness that nearly foils their mission, when he saves several horses from being shot by Dolworth. Shortly after setting the riderless horses free, some of Raza's men find them and capture Dolworth.

The final paradox in *The Professionals* happens when Farden and Dolworth rescue Maria, only to find that she was not kidnapped, but fled home with Raza willingly. Moreover, she informs her rescuers that she and Raza are longtime lovers, and that her marriage to Grant was a family arrangement. But despite her news, they finish their mission, only to change their minds at the end of the film when they decide that Grant is the real kidnapper.

In the last scene, as Maria helps a wounded Raza into a wagon and rides off into the sunset, an infuriated Grant calls Farden a "bastard," to which Farden retorts, "That, sir, was an accident of birth, but you, sir, are a self-made man." *The Professionals* had plenty of gritty muscularity, but Ryan shared little of it. By this time he had achieved similar "star" recognition to that of his costars, Marvin and Lancaster, but his Ehrengard was the least developed of the three parts. The fate of Ehrengard epitomized the state to which Ryan was relegated in a number of pictures.

Reviews: "A sleek slam-bang adventure-suspense film ... you don't get this many old pros packed into one picture every day of the week ... every cliché has been set aglitter anew in sentence and scenery by actors of singular eptness... Robert Ryan is the humanitarian at heart..." (Judith Crist, *New York World Journal Tribune*, 11/3/66.)

"All outdoors and the lands adjacent thereto are barely enough to contain the abundance of hell-for-leather action and raw adventure that Richard Brooks has packed into *The Professionals*. Burt Lancaster and Lee Marvin are as tough as you'd expect them to be ... Robert Ryan and Woody Strode are laconic, and Claudia Cardinale is sultry and disheveled." (Bosley Crowther, *New York Times*, 11/3/66.)

The Busy Body (3) (1967). Paramount, C-101 min. *Producer-Director* William Castle. *Associate Producer* Dona Holloway. *Based on the novel by* Donald E. Westlake. *Screenplay* Ben Starr. *Music* Vic Mizzy. *Song* Edward Heyman, Johnny Green. *Art Directors* Hal Pereira, Roland Anderson, Al Roelofs. *Set Decorators* Robert Benton, Jack Mills. *Assistant Director* Andrew J. Durkus. *Makeup* Wally Westmore. *Sound* Harold Lewis, John Wilkin. *Special Camera Effects* Paul K. Lerpae. *Process Camera* Farciot Edouart. *Camera* Hal Stine. *Editor* Edwin H. Bryant. *Cast* Sid Caesar (George Norton), **Robert Ryan** (Charley Barker), Anne Baxter (Margo Foster), Kay Medford (Ma Norton), Jan Murray (Murray Foster), Richard Pryor (Whittaker), Arlene Golonka (Bobbi Brody), Charles McGraw (Fred Harwell), Ben Blue (Felix Rose), Dom De Luise (Kurt Brock), Bill Dana (Archie Brody), Godfrey Cambridge (Mike), Marty Ingels (Willie), George Jessel (Mr. Fessel), Audrie Magee (Mrs. Fessel), Mickey Deems (Cop), Choo Choo Collins (Woman), Paul Wexler (Mr. Merriwether).

Ryan's final picture for Paramount completed its ill-advised use of his talents versus the comedic banter of Sid Caesar, Jan Murray, Bill Dana, Godfrey Cambridge, Richard Pryor, Marty Ingels, and

others. *The Busy Body* fell into the hands of veteran producer/director William Castle, who had shown a flair for the light as well as the serious. The story belonged to the film's stars, and was a sufficient mixture of bodies turning up everywhere, gangsters chasing people, and empty coffins, to fit into the slapstick style of its mid–sixties comedians.

Sid Caesar plays an inept syndicate flunky, George Norton, who is accused of misplacing $1,000,000 which was hidden in the clothes of a murdered mob bill collector. The syndicate chief, Charley Barker (Ryan), sends his men after George to retrieve the loot, which in the meantime passes from place to place, and body to body.

During the money's journey, George's possessive mother (Kay Medford) and an ex-stripper, Margo (Anne Baxter), get involved in the action, and help uncover the culprit behind the missing money. At film's end, George learns that Barker set up the theft, and to cover his tracks, Barker tries to kill George on a city rooftop. In the nick of time, George's mother and girlfriend (Arlene Golonka) arrive and push Barker off the roof to his death.

Although Ryan was able to accommodate the rigors of *The Busy Body*, it was his first and only comedy.

Reviews: "A diverting suspense comedy spoof of modern crime syndicates, murder and grave-robbing... William Castle emphasizes comedy rather than gore amid good production values.... His direction has elicited some strong performances from Caesar, Medford, Baxter, Golonka, and Ryan..." (*Variety*, 2/1/67.)

"*The Busy Body* comes not to praise Sid Caesar but to bury him, and surrounding him in this tasteless Runyonesque rehash are such borscht belt holders as Murray, Dana, Jessel, and Mickey Deems..." (*Time*, 6/9/67.)

The Dirty Dozen (4) (1967). MGM, C-149 min. *Director* Robert Aldrich. *Producer* Kenneth Hyman. *Associate Producer*

Raymond Anzarut. *Based on the novel by* E.M. Nathanson. *Screenplay* Nunnally Johnson, Lukas Heller. *Music* Frank De Vol. *Songs* Frank De Vol, Mack David, Sibylle Siegfried. *Title Design* Walter Blake. *Art Director* W.E. Hutchinson. *Assistant Director* Bert Batt. *Sound* Franklin Milton, Claude Hitchcock. *Special Effects* Cliff Richardson. *Camera* Edward Scaife. *Editor* Michael Luciano. *Cast* Lee Marvin (Major Reisman), Ernest Borgnine (General Worden), Charles Bronson (Wadislaw), Jim Brown (Jefferson), John Cassavetes (Franko), Richard Jaeckel (Sergeant Bowren), George Kennedy (Armbruster), Trini Lopez (Jiminez), Ralph Meeker (Kinder), **Robert Ryan** (Colonel Breed), Telly Savalas (Maggot), Donald Sutherland (Pinkley), Clint Walker (Posey), Robert Webber (General Denton), Tom Busby (Vladek), Ben Carruthers (Gilpin).

The dearth of good roles was continuing to plague Ryan, and he was again cast in a "cameo" appearance in Robert Aldrich's violent, controversial war film, *The Dirty Dozen*. But MGM was more interested in his marquee value than anything else, and employed several other actors of similar stature in minor roles, including Ernest Borgnine, Robert Webber, Ralph Meeker, and George Kennedy.

For its time, *The Dirty Dozen* achieved a high level of technical efficiency in its climactic battle sequence however, a disturbing message remains at the film's core. *The Dirty Dozen*'s initial premise, that the Army would assign military prisoners to conduct an assassination raid against the Germans, was an indictment of the military's sacrosanct reputation. The film exploits extermination since the Dirty Dozen's mission leads them to the wholesale slaughter of civilians in the film's ending conflagration.

When the Dozen parachutes behind enemy lines to the chalet where high-ranking German officers relax, a warning siren gives them away, and the Germans and a number of civilians flee to a basement where they lock themselves in. Lee Marvin's Reisman coolly orders two of his men to pour gasoline down the basement's air vents, and they dump in a score or more of hand grenades. In the tremendous explosion the helpless people are shown being engulfed in flames, while Reisman and his remaining team make a triumphant getaway.

Aldrich had previously examined the ambiguities of war to better effect in *Attack*, and *Ten Seconds to Hell*, but he conceived *The Dirty Dozen* as an action/adventure film, rather than as serious food for thought. One of the film's major distinctions was its graphic depiction of violence, which would be considered tame by today's standards. The picture begins with Reisman witnessing an execution by hanging and committing mayhem on John Cassavetes' loud-mouthed Franko, then proceeds to increasing destruction and havoc.

Ryan's martinet Colonel Breed was one of his least important cameos, as his on-screen time lasted barely ten minutes, and his dialogue consisted of about ten lines. However, the role may have been abbreviated during the editing stage, since the origin of the antagonism between Reisman and Breed is implied but not explained. The character wasn't even a flattering one, since Breed is depicted as a classic example of officer ineptitude.

Reviews: "An astonishingly wanton war film . . . a raw and preposterous glorification of a group of criminal soldiers who are trained to kill and then go about it with hot, sadistic zeal." (Bosley Crowther, *New York Times*, 6/16/67.)

"An exciting, well-mounted and grimly realistic World War II drama." (*Variety*, 6/21/67.)

Hour of the Gun (3) (1967). United Artists, C-100 min. *Producer-Director* John Sturges. *Based on the novel* Tombstone's Epitaph *by* Douglas D.Martin. *Screenplay* Edward Anhalt. *Music* Jerry Goldsmith. *Art Director* Alfred C. Ybarra. *Set Decorator* Victor Gangelin. *Wardrobe* Gordon

Dawson. *Makeup* Charles Blackman. *Assistant Directors* Thomas Schmidt, Robert Jones. *Sound* Jesus Gonzalez Gancy. *Special Effects* Sass Bedig. *Camera* Lucien Ballard. *Editor* Ferris Webster. *Cast* James Garner (Wyatt Earp), Jason Robards (Doc Holliday), **Robert Ryan** (Ike Clanton), Albert Salmi (Octavius Roy), Charles Aidman (Horace Sullivan), Steve Ihnat (Andy Warshaw), Michael Tolan (Pete Spence), Frank Converse (Virgil Earp), Austin Willis (Anson Safford), Richard Bull (Fitch), Larry Gates (Clum), Karl Swenson (Goodfellow), Bill Fletcher (Jimmy Ryan), Robert Phillips (Frank Stillwell), Jon Voight (Bill Brocius), William Schallert (Herman Spicer), Lonnie Chapman (Turkey Creek Johnson), Monte Markham (McMasters), William Windom (Jack Vermillion), Edward Anhalt (Doctor), Walter Gregg (Billy Clanton), David Perna (Frank McLowery), Jim Sheppard (Tom McLowery), Jorge Russek (Latigo).

Hour of the Gun had an original running time of 101 minutes, but when United Artists pared the final version down to 90 minutes, some of Ryan's dour staging of gunman and cattle rustler Ike Clanton was wasted. One needed to depend on his brief appearances to establish credibility for his notoriety, and as completed, the film belonged to James Garner as Wyatt Earp, and to Jason Robards as Doc Holliday.

Director John Sturges made *Hour of the Gun* with his customary proficient sobriety beginning with a funeral scene, but the film continued at that pace until the final, anti-climactic face-off between Earp and Clanton in the courtyard of a hacienda. In his second film about the infamous gun battle at the O.K. Corral, Sturges conducted a psychological study of the relationship between Earp and Holliday, depicting Holliday as having a conscience over Earp.

After Clanton kills Virgil Earp and wounds Morgan Earp, Wyatt goes on a murderous vendetta, methodically gunning down Clanton's men. Holliday observes his friend's behavior with growing disgust, and finally confronts him. Other than the moral dilemma posed by Earp's vigilante-style justice, *Hour of the Gun*'s promise of excitement compared weakly with the earlier *Gunfight at the O.K. Corral*, which Sturges had directed in 1957. (*Gunfight at the O.K. Corral* featured Burt Lancaster as Earp, and Kirk Douglas as Doc Holliday. John Ireland played Clanton.)

Sturges hired a top cast, but these only partially helped the picture's turgid development. Among the ubiquitous group of townspeople in *Hour of the Gun*, Albert Salmi, Charles Aidman, Larry Gates, William Schallert, Karl Swenson, and Monte Markham, provided solid support. Clanton's henchmen were headed by surly Western stalwarts, Steve Ihnat, Michael Tolan, Robert Phillips, Jorge Russek, and Jon Voight, in his first film.

As in other films in which Ryan's role was minimal yet integral to the story, he exuded enough tension to easily carry off his abbreviated linchpin. At that point in his career, he could waltz through any part he was given, and since he was getting more involved with the theater, he chose film assignments that wouldn't interrupt his stage work.

Reviews: "*Hour of the Gun* is a totally conventional Western drama ... the man Wyatt Earp is after is Robert Ryan, who puts his customary contemptuous expression to better use than he puts his gun, which he doesn't unlimber until the damage to him is done.... The wonder is that John Sturges, a top director, has made such an obvious, slow film with his cast." (*New York Times*, 11/2/67.)

"Genuine zip and interest in the first half eventually dissipates into a talky, telescoped resolution, perhaps from final editing ... Ryan is a perfect heavy." (*Variety*, 10/4/67.)

Custer of the West (5) (1968). Cinerama, C-120 min. *Director* Robert Siodmak. *Producers* Philip Yordan, Louis

Dolivet. *Producer-Director of Civil War sequence* Irving Lerner. *Screenplay* Bernard Gordon, Julian Haleny. *Music and Music Conductor* Bernardo Segall. *Songs* Bernardo Segall, Will Holt, Robert Shaw. *Art Directors* Jean-Pierre D'Eaubonne, Eugene Lourie, Julio Molina. *Set Decorators* Antonio Mateos. *Makeup* Julian Ruiz. *Assistant Director* Jose Maria Ochoa. *Sound* Kurt Herrnfeld, Alban Streeter. *Camera* Cecilio Paniagua. *Editor* Maurice Rootes. *Cast* Robert Shaw (George Custer), Mary Ure (Elizabeth Custer), Jeffrey Hunter (Lieutenant Benteen), Ty Hardin (Major Reno), Charles Stalnaker (Lieutenant Howells), Robert Hall (Sergeant Buckley), Lawrence Tierney (General Sheridan), Kieron Moore (Chief Dull Knife), Marc Lawrence (Goldminer), **Robert Ryan** (Sergeant Mulligan).

Ryan had been pushing hard to regain his screen recognition, but his role as a gold hungry Army deserter in Robert Siodmak's well-told version of George Armstrong Custer's last days was generally overlooked. Although his character, the alcoholic, romantic Sergeant Mulligan, was only a ten-minute "cameo," it served as the film's conscience and provided the impetus for Custer's glorious destiny.

Custer of the West was filmed in Cinerama and had an original running time of two hours and twenty-five minutes. Despite the opinions of several critics that this *Custer* was the best of the lot about the enigmatic general, the film's epic length was a deficit at the box office. After its initial London engagement and several United States previews, *Custer of the West* was cut to two hours and released in a less expensive format, Super Technirama (70 mm).

In the starring role as Custer, Robert Shaw portrayed him as a taciturn, rigid martinet whose egocentrism caused his downfall. A number of Custer films have over the years suffered the fate of depicting him as merely a flamboyant, fairhaired dandy, but Siodmak's serious direction and Shaw's spartan interpretation suggested a driven, soulful glory seeker. On July 26, 1968, *Time* magazine noted, "This *Custer* comes much closer to the complex nature of its antihero than any earlier treatment." (Coincidentally, Siodmak became established in the *film noir* genre with *The Killers* (1946), *Cry of the City* (1948), *Criss Cross* (1949), *The File on Thelma Jordan* (1950). In 1953, he left the United States and returned to Europe.)

Producer Philip Yordan cast *Custer of the West* with a number of Hollywood veterans whose careers, like Ryan's, had traveled similar courses. Lawrence Tierney, as General Philip Sheridan, had appeared with Ryan in *Best of the Badmen* 16 years earlier, and this was one of his last roles. Character actor Marc Lawrence had played supporting parts in several tense dramas in the fifties, but had ended up in Europe in the sixties, while Jeffrey Hunter, who had come on strong as a 20th Century–Fox hopeful, had now joined the others overseas.

Ryan injected his performance as Mulligan with a resonance which several critics applauded. In two brief but intense scenes, one in the stockade, the other in the company quadrangle, Ryan portrayed agony and despair to perfection. In the perceptive screenplay, Mulligan's act of desertion and subsequent execution served to indict Custer's ruthlessness and to precipitate the Little Big Horn massacre. When Custer rejects Mulligan's plea for clemency, it is a galvanizing act which spurs him to fight his last pompous battle.

Reviews: "...the Cinerama effects ... and the spectacle remain, and they are briskly displayed under Robert Siodmak's direction ... the Bernard Gordon-Julian Halevy script is oddly topical as well as literate, and made more so by Robert Shaw's complex portrait of Custer, Mary Ure's subtlety as his wife, and Lawrence Tierney's interesting Sheridan.... The winning point is performance, and for a lagniappe, there's a slightly more than cameo-sized bit by Robert Ryan that shows in miniature, as Shaw does throughout, just how the pros perform." (Judith Crist, *New York*, 9/15/68.)

"The heart-in-mouth thrills of Cinerama lensing are meshed with the legend of Custer's last stand in this Spanish-shot Western.... The result is capable, audience-involving adventure on the visual level ... Robert Ryan guest-stars with a forceful cameo as a deserting, gold-hungry soldier." (*Variety*, 11/15/68.)

A Minute to Pray, a Second to Die (3) (1968). Cinerama, C-97 min. *Director* Franco Giraldi. *Executive Producer* Selig J. Seligman. *Producer* Alfredo Antonini. *Story* Albert Band, Ugo Liberatore. *Screenplay* Liberatore, Louis Garfinkle. *Art Director* Massimo Capriccioli. *Set Decorator* Guido Josia. *Costumes* Luciana Fortini. *Makeup* Michele Trimarchi. *Assistant Director* Franco Cirno. *Music* Carlo Rustichelli. *Sound* Fernando Prescetelli. *Camera* Alace Parolin. *Editor* Alberto Gillitti. *Cast* Alex Cord (Clay McCord), Arthur Kennedy (Roy Colby), **Robert Ryan** (Governor Lem Carter), Nicoletta Machiavelli (Laurinda), Mario Brega (Kraut).

As a prototypical entry in the spate of Italian Westerns directed by Sergio Leone and starring Clint Eastwood, *A Minute to Pray, a Second to Die* may have set the tone for what followed. However, the addition of Ryan, Arthur Kennedy, and Alex Cord offered enough gritty American masculinity to offset the swarthy sameness of the rest of the cast, whose faces were forgotten as soon as they left the screen.

The story of *A Minute to Pray, a Second to Die* has psychological undertones concerning Clay McCord's (Cord) mysterious malady, which at the film's outset appears to be psychosomatic in origin. Whenever he is faced down in a gunfight, McCord is stricken with a paralytic palsy. Complicating matters, a murderous band of bounty hunters is chasing him while he attempts to gain amnesty from New

Mexico Governor Lem Carter (Ryan). During his journey for forgiveness, McCord runs afoul of crooked, sadistic Sheriff Roy Colby (Kennedy), who doesn't believe in amnesty.

While McCord sets about making things right, he is portrayed as less evil than is implied from the number of men he kills. When he comes under the accepting gaze of the beautiful Laurinda (Nicoletta Machiavelli), whatever contrariness he possesses is vanquished for the sake of love.

After Colby arrests McCord, intent on seeing him hang, he escapes, but the bounty hunters follow him to a shack and attempt to burn him out. Colby tries to save him and is killed, but Carter arrives in time, and in the ensuing gunfight, the bounty hunters are killed.

Later, a doctor discovers that McCord's attacks are caused by a bullet lodged against his spine in an earlier gunfight. The bullet is removed, ending his paralysis, Carter grants him unconditional amnesty, and McCord rides off into the sunset. (Dubbed English version, 97 minutes. In the original uncut version, which lasted 103 minutes, McCord is killed by two bounty hunters who are unaware he has been given amnesty. In the distributor's pressbook, though, McCord tears up his amnesty papers after killing the bounty hunters and realizing he can never give up his life of crime.)

The work of Ryan, Kennedy, and Cord aside, the most impressive aspects of *A Minute to Pray, a Second to Die* concerned its location setting in the Italian Alps, and in its Technicolor Cinerama process. In terms of advancing Ryan's career, the film was the first in several years in which he had a significant part, albeit after accepting third-billing beneath Cord and Kennedy. Also, the part was a totally sympathetic one, depicting him as a benevolent patriarchal type.

There is irony in the casting of Ryan and Kennedy in *A Minute to Pray, a Second to Die*, because their careers resembled each other. Both actors settled for comfortable positions as second leads with occasional top-billing, and often shared similar character types in their movies, being cast frequently as sympathetic heavies with a sadistic streak, or as forgiving paternal presences. But Kennedy's malevolence was never quite as intense as was Ryan's, thus Ryan always held onto the number one position as the person to inspire absolute dread.

Reviews: "In the hard, driving tradition of *A Fistful of Dollars*, this Selmur Pictures presentation rates higher than the average in the category by virtue of sinewy action and a good name cast headed by Alex Cord, Arthur Kennedy and Robert Ryan. Occasionally the story falls into stereotype, but its overall effect is that of strong Western entertainment." (Mandel Herbstman, *Trade Review.*)

"Kennedy's role is largely reactive, while Robert Ryan has far more opportunity to demonstrate his professional skills." (*Variety,* 5/1/68.)

"What makes this mess bearable is the presence of two actors from Hollywood: Robert Ryan and Arthur Kennedy as a two-fisted governor and a leathery town marshal." (Howard Thompson, *New York Times,* 5/23/68.)

Anzio (1968). Columbia, C-117 min. *Director* Edward Dmytryk. *Producer* Dino De Laurentiis. *Based on the book* Anzio *by* Wynford Vaughan-Thomas. *Adaptors* Frank De Felitta, Giuseppe Mangione. *English Screenplay* Harry A. Craig. *Music* Riz Ortolani. *Song* Riz Ortolani, Jerome Pomus. *Art Director* Luigi Scaccianoce. *Set Decorators* Francesco Bronz, Emilio D'Andria. *Costumes* Ugo Pericoli. *Makeup* Amato Garbini. *Assistant Directors* Giorgio Gentili, Gianni Cozzo. *Sound* Aldo De Martini. *Special Effects* Walfrido Traversari. *Camera* Giuseppe Rotunno. *Editors* Alberto Gallitti, Peter Taylor. *Cast* Robert Mitchum (Dick Ennis), Peter Falk (Rabinoff), Earl Holliman (Stimler), Arthur Kennedy (General Lesly), **Robert Ryan** (General Carson), Mark Damon

(Richardson), Reni Santoni (Movie), Joseph Walsh (Doyle), Thomas Hunter (Andy), Giancarlo Giannini (Cellini), Anthony Steel (General Marsh), Patrick Magee (General Starkey), Arthur Franz (General Howard), Elsa Albani (Emilia), Wayde Preston (Colonel Hendricks), Wolfgang Preiss (Marshal Kesselring).

An all-star cast and one of Hollywood's greatest directors labored on *Anzio,* but a glance at the opening credits which listed Ryan as "special guest star," warned viewers that his role was a *cameo.* This premonition was validated when Ryan appeared very briefly at the film's beginning, as General Carson, and was not seen again until the end of the picture, when he is seen riding through recently liberated Anzio, waving triumphantly to the throngs of people.

Of the gallery of unimpressive war pictures that came out of the sixties, *Anzio* failed more than the others because of its mediocre production values. Having been filmed in Rome, it was primitive compared to American cinema, such as in its routine cinematography, tinny musical score, clumsy editing, and dubbed soundtrack. Director Edward Dmytryk might be allowed a momentary lapse in an otherwise highly distinguished career, and one must also forgive Ryan for accepting a throwaway part in order to keep his name alive on the screen.

Reviews: "*Anzio* is a very ordinary war movie with an epic title.... Having chosen as his subject the January, 1944, Allied Landings at Anzio, Dino De Laurentiis has surmounted most of the logistical problems that might be involved in such a venture by simply ignoring them ... in the cast are Arthur Kennedy and Robert Ryan, whose careers now seem to consist solely of playing the 'special guest star' in a series of schlocky European films." (Vincent Canby, *New York Times,* 7/25/68.)

"*Anzio* suffers from flat writing, stock performances, uninspired direction, and dull pacing ... it is ironic how many contemporary films now concentrate on instances of stupidity, which become so clear in hindsight. In the case of this film, two U.S. generals, Arthur Kennedy and Robert Ryan, play a cautious and a headline hungry type, respectively. Technical credits occasionally give a hype to the picture, but in general this war epic just flaps around." (*Variety*, 6/19/68.)

The Wild Bunch (5) (1969). Warner Bros.-Seven Arts, C-142 min. *Director* Sam Peckinpah. *Producer* Phil Feldman. *Associate Producer* Roy N. Sickner. *Story* Walon Green, Sam Peckinpah. *Second Unit Director* Buzz Henry. *Assistant Director* Cliff Coleman, Fred Gammon. *Music* Jerry Fielding. *Music Supervisor* Sonny Burke. *Art Director* Edward Carrere. *Wardrobe* Gordon Dawson. *Makeup* Al Greenway. *Sound* Robert J. Miller. *Special Effects* Bud Hulburd. *Camera* Lucien Ballard. *Editor* Louis Lombardi. *Cast* William Holden (Pike Bishop), Ernest Borgnine (Dutch Engstrom), **Robert Ryan** (Deke Thornton), Edmond O'Brien (Freddy Sykes), Warren Oates (Lyle Gorch), Jaime Sanchez (Angel), Ben Johnson (Tector Gorch), Emilio Fernandez (Mapache), Strother Martin (Coffer), L.Q. Jones (T.C.), Albert Dekker (Harrigan), Bo Hopkins (Crazy Lee), Dub Taylor (Mayor Wainscoat), Jorge Russek (Zamorra), Alfonso Arau (Merrera), Chano (Don Jose), Sonia Amelio (Teresa), Aurora Clavel (Aurora), Elsa Cardenas (Elsa), Fernando Wagner (German Army Officer), Paul Harper, Rayford Barnes (Men in Pike's Gang).

Ryan's role as an aging, semi-honorable bounty hunter in Sam Peckinpah's highly controversial, classic elegy to the dying West was an appropriate return to center stage. After appearing in a bunch of low budget, low quality films, most of which were made in Spain or Italy, Ryan's work for Peckinpah brought him back in the company of craftsmen.

The Wild Bunch was possibly Peckinpah's most important picture, coming at the end of a three-and-a-half-year hiatus from Hollywood. His eccentric,

argumentative personality had gotten him into trouble when his last film, *Major Dundee*, was considerably shortened, despite his vehement protests. He had gone into a self-imposed exile, but when producer Phil Feldman offered him *The Wild Bunch*, he licked his wounds and went at it with a vengeance. The result was a beautiful, shocking, tragic monument to the Western genre and the revival of a dying art form.

Despite its primitive title, *The Wild Bunch* was a major technical achievement, particularly in its use of slow motion photography that seemed to choreograph the violence. Lucien Ballard's remarkable cinematography and Louis Lombardo's precise editing worked together perfectly to create an intensely exciting visual sense of being there. But inevitable misconceptions cropped up regarding Peckinpah's message, because the script that he cowrote with Walon Green contained macho attitudes that clouded over the film's merits.

Moreover, some critics found *The Wild Bunch*'s violence excessive and a sign of Peckinpah's self-indulgence and preoccupation with gore for its shock value. Initial previews of *The Wild Bunch* in Hollywood and Kansas City ran 190 minutes, and some audiences came away horrified by its intense, explicit violence. It underwent three more deletions before its final release length of 145 minutes, but Peckinpah was satisfied with the results, having supervised the editing. He realized that the film's blood-letting had achieved new heights, and had expected that certain scenes would have to go. One cut eliminated several disembowelings occurring in the initial gun battle; however two others were flashbacks involving Ryan and Holden.

The critics who found fault with Peckinpah's excising had good reason for concern, as the relationship between Ryan's Deke Thornton and William Holden's Pike Bishop lacked sufficient development. A few observers commented ironically about Ryan's first important role in years being chopped up. Nevertheless, he had the power to overcome it, perhaps because he had grown accustomed to stretching more out of less.

Taken on face value for its resonance, quality of acting, music, and sheer spectacle, most of the alleged Western classics pale in comparison with *The Wild Bunch*. In his book, *The Great Movies*, William Bayer ranked it with *The Searchers, Shane*, and *Red River*, commenting: "It is a picture that dares to be excessive. Peckinpah courts condemnation and risks disaster by putting so personal and unorthodox a conception on the screen. Because he is successful, a case can be made that *The Wild Bunch* is not only great within the Western genre, but may be among the greatest films of the sixties."

The Wild Bunch is a film about loyalty, and within that context, Ryan's Deke Thornton served as its conscience, although in reality he is little better than Pike Bishop and his gang. Peckinpah described his characters as "violent, moronic criminals" (Paul Schrader, *Cinema*, Vol. 3, No. 5); even the law, as represented by Albert Dekker's ruthless Harrigan, is perverted. Thus, Thornton and Edmond O'Brien's uncouth Freddie Sykes emerge at the end in quasi-heroic fashion.

When Peckinpah cast *The Wild Bunch*, he brought together a score or more of actors whose faces had etched a familiar map in the Western genre. At that point, Ryan had starred in 15 Westerns and numerous television Westerns, a few of which remain today as superior examples of the genre. His Deke Thornton joined the ranks of portrayals whose stature was increased by the mere fact that Ryan was an established icon of the genre.

One of the best lines of dialogue belonged to Ryan, and his delivery of it carried more than a touch of ironic reality. As Thornton sits atop his horse, wearily gazing at the human refuse he has been forced to consort with, he states bitterly,

"We're after men, and I wish to God I was with them."

Reviews: "[*The Wild Bunch*] is very beautiful and the first truly interesting, American-made Western in years ... Ryan, Ernest Borgnine, and Edmond O'Brien add a ... resonance to the film.... It's a fascinating movie..." (Vincent Canby, *New York Times*, 6/26/69.)

"*The Wild Bunch* is Peckinpah's most complex inquiry into the metamorphosis of man into myth. Not incidentally, it is also a raucous, violent, powerful feat of American filmmaking.... [More] characteristic [of the film] are the sweeping visual panorama of the whole film (stunningly photographed by Lucien Ballard) and the extraordinarily forceful acting from a troupe of Hollywood professionals.... As the reluctant head of the band of bounty hunters, Robert Ryan gives the screen performance of his career." (*Time*, 6/69.)

"Those who go [to see the movie] will see a brilliantly made, thought-provoking movie.... It seems inappropriate to talk of *The Wild Bunch* as a beautiful film. But, in fact, it is beautifully made and full of spectacular visual images. Lucien Ballard's cinematography is often breathtaking... Holden [gives] an excellent performance, better than he has given in years and Robert Ryan is also excellent..." (Charles Champlin, *Los Angeles Times*, 6/15/69.)

"As a native-born Westerner, Peckinpah seems instinctively to affirm the power of the physical to express and transform the spiritual.... It is good to see William Holden and Robert Ryan, those tortured presences of the '50s, in roles with some moral tension." (Andrew Sarris, *Village Voice*, 7/31/69.)

"Peckinpah's forceful direction is a definite asset... Ryan is dramatically efficient as Holden's hunter.... Technically, the feature is of high quality, particularly color photography of Lucien Ballard, music by Jerry Fielding... Louis Lombardo's editing in second half is commendable." (*Variety*, 6/16/69.)

Captain Nemo and the Underwater City (2) (1970). MGM, C-106 min. *Director* James Hill. *Executive Producer* Steven Pallos. *Producer* Bertram Ostrer. *Based on the story by* Jules Verne. *Screenplay* Pip Baker, Jane Baker, R. Wright Campbell. *Art Director* Bill Andrews. *Costumes* Olga Lehmann. *Assistant Director* Ted Lewis. *Music* Walter Scott. *Sound* A.W. Watkins. *Camera* Alan Hume. *Underwater Camera* Egil S. Woxholt. *Editor* Bill Lewthwaite. *Cast* **Robert Ryan** (Captain Nemo), Chuck Connors (Senator Fraser), Nanette Newman (Helena), John Turner (Joab), Luciana Paluzzi (Mala), Bill Fraser (Barnaby), Kenneth Connor (Swallow), Allan Cuthbertson (Lomax), Christopher Hartstone (Philip), Vincent Harding (Mate/Navigator), Ralph Nosseck (Engineer).

Ryan's appearance in *Captain Nemo* was two steps backward after his big success the previous year in *The Wild Bunch*. The picture had a degree of elegance in its international cast, but compared to the 1955 Jules Verne fantasy, starring Kirk Douglas and James Mason, *Captain Nemo* was best suited for Saturday matinee fare.

The most exciting aspects of the film were its colorful photography and lavish but artificial set designs. The costumes, varying from garish to traditional, seemed odd under the circumstances. Ryan's garb was especially unusual, and resembled a train conductor's uniform. Others in the cast who seemed equally uncomfortable with the material included Chuck Connors, Nanette Newman, and Luciana Paluzzi.

Ryan did a valiant job with his part, infusing it with a world-weary cynicism which seemed appropriate, considering his own situation. His character's disillusionment with the society from which he was fleeing was a fitting metaphor for Ryan's real-life outlook.

Reviews: "Robert Ryan conveys just the right amount of channelled megalomania as the dictator captain ... the decor is suitably splendid and gaudy... Despite its determinedly lightweight nature, more so because it suffers from a lack of literary antecedents, it is still very entertaining, and just the right thing for a jaded child at Christmas." (*Films and Filming.*)

Lawman (5) (1971). United Artists, C-99 min. *Director* Michael Winner. *Producer* Michael Winner. *Screenplay* Gerald Wilson. *Assistant Directors* Michael Dryhurst, Malcolm Stamp, Jaime Contreras. *Art Director* Herbert Westbrook. *Set Decorator* Ray Moyer. *Music and Music Conductor* Jerry Fielding. *Makeup* Richard Mills. *Wardrobe* Ron Beck. *Sound* Terence Rawlings, Manuel Topete Blake, Hugh Strian. *Special Effects* Leon Ortega. *Camera* Bob Paynter. *Editor* Freddie Wilson. *Cast* Burt Lancaster (Jered Maddox), **Robert Ryan** (Cotton Ryan), Lee J. Cobb (Vince Bronson), Sheree North (Laura), Joseph Wiseman (Lucas), Robert Duvall (Vernon Adams), Albert Salmi (Harve Stenbaugh), J.D. Cannon (Hurd Price), John McGiver (Mayor), Richard Jordan (Crowe Wheelwright), John Beck (Jason Bronson), Ralph Waite (Dekker), William Watson (Choctaw Lee), Charles Tyner (Minister), John Hillerman (Totts), Robert Emhardt (Hersham), Richard Bull (Dusaine), Hugh McDermott (Moss), Lou Frizzell (Cobden), Walter Brooke (Harris), Bill Bramley (Marc Corman).

After the sheepish *Captain Nemo and the Underwater City*, Ryan returned to prominence in another impressive Western, which approached the stature of *The Wild Bunch*. The parallel between his role in *Lawman* and his real-life dilemma was striking, even to the character's name, Cotton Ryan. Ryan's proximity to his character contributed to a highly restrained performance which exuded an air of finality.

Although an Englishman, Michael Winner, directed *Lawman*, he demonstrated an instinctive flair for the Western, despite being much maligned by American critics. Unfortunately, the notoriety that has followed several Winner directed pictures starring Charles Bronson has overshadowed his more serious work.

Lawman approaches its subject in a literate manner rarely seen in Westerns, and was a psychological Western whose theme focussed on moral rectitude and self-destructive pride. (*Lawman* compares well with other underrated adult Westerns, including Anthony Mann's *Man of the West* (1958), Edward Dmytryk's *Warlock* (1959), David Miller's *Lonely Are the Brave* (1962), and Vincent McEveety's *Firecreek* (1968).) Gerald Wilson's realistic screenplay neatly included a large cast around the central struggle between Burt Lancaster's Marshal Jared Maddox and Lee J. Cobb's Vince Bronson. The ironic story follows Maddox, who is a rigid law enforcer whose inflexibility transcends justice, making him a victim of his principles.

The unbending character of Maddox shares company with many in the cast, who suffer from the same mental obstinacy that is an unpleasant side-effect of manhood. Besides Maddox, the others whose prideful souls are their undoing include Bronson's hot-headed foreman (Albert Salmi), a cowardly rancher (J.D. Cannon), and Bronson's son (John Beck).

Lawman begins with Bronson's drunken cowboys shooting up Maddox's town after a long cattle drive, and an innocent bystander being killed. Maddox rides to the town of Sabbath intending to bring the killers back for trial, but he runs into immediate opposition. At first, Bronson attempts to buy Maddox off, but when Stenbaugh goads Maddox into a showdown and is killed, Bronson's prudence turns to recklessness.

Maddox tracks down Bronson's cowhands, but a former lover (Sheree North) begs him to let the men go. When Maddox refuses to release a prisoner (Robert Duvall), she appears to have failed. While bringing his man to jail, Maddox has a change of heart and decides to give up his chase, but it is too late. Bronson

arrives in town with his son and a gunman (William Watson), and in the ensuing gunfight, Maddox kills Bronson's son and the gunman.

Distraught over his son's death, Bronson commits suicide, and Maddox shoots a fleeing man in the back, having been driven past the pale of the law. *Lawman* ends on a mordant note, with Maddox riding out of town amid the carnage of four dead men, while Ryan stands by as mute testimony to the safety of his non-committal actions.

Lawman gained added realism from the performances of its superior supporting cast. In particular, Joseph Wiseman, Robert Duvall, Richard Jordan, J.D. Cannon, Sheree North, and Ralph Waite gave portrayals of depth, while smaller roles were accurately delivered by John McGiver, Robert Emhardt, Walter Brooke, and John Hillerman.

Ryan functioned as *Lawman's* conscience and chief observer, cynically watching men walk down paths he has passed countless times before. Having seen life from both sides of the coin, he is bitter about the hypocrisy of mankind. Early on in *Lawman*, Ryan informs Maddox, "If you're a lawman, you're a disease. The people need you but they hate you."

Ryan's outlook is a product of his having been a casualty himself, and when Maddox recalls Ryan's reputation as a courageous keeper of the peace, Ryan tells him that what remains is "a bunch of yesterdays." Having reached the end of the line, Ryan describes his downfall to Maddox as "a long way down from the high country, with stops all the way down," and that "in Abilene I ran, in Acadia City I hid in a cellar, in Monmouth the Loring brothers made me eat dirt."

A few critics called Ryan's part a casting coup, because on the surface, the role seemed incongruous with his tough-guy image. But underneath, it conformed to a type he had set often, indeed, by then it warranted being called a "Ryan" type.

Reviews: "Robert Ryan is tremendous in the role of a broken-down hero who has become a bought-and-paid-for small town marshal." (Norma McClain Stoop, *After Dark,* 9/71.)

"The inflexibility of pride and self-determined authority is the main theme of this extraordinarily perceptive Western... Gerald Wilson's screenplay must rate as one of the best ever written for a Western, it has much to say but says it concisely ... Robert Ryan is exceptionally good as the sold-old marshal, who was once great but settled for an easy life of doing what he is told, a once great gunfighter who could never retain his old glory and never tries because he knows he never could." (Robin Bean, *Films and Filming,* 4/71.)

"The film's major surprise is its fine cast. Here Winner has outdone himself, beginning with the casting of Ryan as the weak, weary marshal." (Kathleen Carroll, *New York Daily News,* 8/5/71.)

"Some cutting dialogue and boiling psychological tension are the most winning things about *Lawman,* a potent but curiously exasperating Western with those three hardies Robert Ryan, Burt Lancaster and Lee J. Cobb." (Howard Thompson, *New York Times,* 8/5/71.)

"Working in a more conventional mode, Robert Ryan, Burt Lancaster, and Lee J. Cobb project magnitudes of star power in *Lawman.*" (*Playboy,* 11/71.)

The Love Machine (1) (1971). Columbia, C-108 min. *Director* Jack Haley, Jr. *Executive Producer* Irving Mansfield. *Producer* M.J. Frankovich. *Based on the novel by* Jacqueline Susann. *Screenplay* Samuel Taylor. *Music and Music Arranger* Artie Butler. *Songs* Brian Well, Ruth Batchelor, Artie Butler, Mark Lindsay. *Production Designer* Lyle R. Wheeler. *Set Decorator* George Hopkins. *Titles* Maury Nemoy. *Dialogue Coach* Kathleen Freeman. *Costumes* Moss Mabry. *Makeup* Hank Edds. *Assistant Director* Philip P. Parslow. *Sound* Les Fresholtz, Arthur Piantodosi. *Camera Effects* Butler-Glouner. *Camera* Charles

B. Lang. *Second Unit Camera* Frederick L. Guarino. *Editor* David Blewitt. *Cast* John Philip Law (Robin Stone), Dyan Cannon (Judith Austin), **Robert Ryan** (Gregory Austin), Jackie Cooper (Danton Miller), David Hemmings (Jerry Nelson), Jodi Wexler (Amanda), William Roerick (Cliff Dorne), Maureen Arthur (Ethel Evans), Shecky Greene (Christie Lane), Clinton Greyn (Alfie Knight), Sharon Farrell (Maggie Stewart), Alexandra Hay (Tina St. Claire), Greg Mullavey (Bob Summers), Edith Atwater (Mary), Gene Baylos (Eddie Flynn), Gayle Hunnicut (Girl at Party), Jerry Dunphy, Michael Jackson, Ted Meyers (Newscasters).

There was something curiously moribund about *The Love Machine,* over and above its being Ryan's first picture after his bout with cancer. Since the film was based on author Jacqueline Susann's novel of the same name, the imprint of her own terminal cancer condition may have filtered through into its plot. Most of the cast, including Ryan, limped through their parts, reenacting a succession of Hollywood high jinks which emerged as a series of banal clichés.

The Love Machine's biggest failing had to do with its initial premise. The story focused on a television newscaster with an unusual persona: on the surface, he is an intellectual chronicler of pressing social concerns; in private, he leads a lurid lifestyle of sexual conquests and perversions, and other forms of physical and emotional abuse. However, John Philip Law's vapid demeanor as the main character fails to depict him other than as an empty soul wracked with narcissistic loneliness.

In addition to script and acting deficiencies, Jack Haley, Jr.'s spotty direction left the cast to their own devices, and Ryan, Dyan Cannon, Jackie Cooper, and David Hemmings emerged the worse for wear. As the big-time television executive Gregory Austin, Ryan seemed to lack strength at times, especially in his scenes with Cannon, but in other sequences, he returned to form as a power-wielding manipulator of men. Symbolically, the role related to his own circumstances: in *The Love Machine*, his character has a heart attack but recuperates.

Reviews: "*The Love Machine* has enough dumb lines to qualify as a veritable anthology of unintentional humor, but it hasn't the energy or the wit or, finally, the commitment to its own absurdities to provide the exhilarating sense of life that is the real appeal of the good-bad movie. A lot of good people are wasted. Actors like Robert Ryan seem more and more like a precious natural resource, and to say that Ryan escapes this movie with his soul intact (as he does), is to say too little." (Roger Greenspun, *New York Times*, 8/15/71.)

"There's something to be said for the film version of *The Love Machine*. It's as superficial as the best selling novel. Among the people who revolve around John Philip Law, only Robert Ryan and Dyan Cannon are credible in their roles." (Barbara Wilson, *Philadelphia Inquirer*, 8/12/71.)

And Hope to Die (5) (1972). Twentieth Century–Fox, C-99 min. *Director* René Clément. *Producer* Serge Silberman. *Based on the novel* Black Friday *by* David Goodis. *Screenplay* Sebastian Japrisot. *Music* Francis Lai. *Camera* Edmond Richard. *Editor* Roger Dwyre. *Cast* **Robert Ryan** (Charley), Jean-Louis Trintignant (Tony), Aldo Ray (Mattone), Tisa Farrow (Pepper), Lea Massari (Sugar), Jean Gaven (Rizzio), Nadine Nabokov (Majorette), André Lawrence (Gypsy), Daniel Breton (Paul).

There is a certain cruel irony in the title *And Hope to Die*, since the picture came on the heels of Ryan's cancer diagnosis. His role in the film was a fascinating combination of several Ryan images, and gave him more with which to work than he had seen since the late fifties.

Again, he was the leader of a gang of societal misfits who were likeable in a sense, despite being murderers and thieves. His Charley Ellis had a humorous sagacity that reeked of fatalism, and which bore similarities to his Sandy Dawson in *House of Bamboo*. In both films he had delusions of omnipotence, declaring to a friend in *House of Bamboo*, "I was right, like always," while in *And Hope to Die*, one of his henchmen says with certainty, "Charley is always right."

French director René Clément trained his talents on the sublime and the visual, infusing surrealism into *And Hope to Die*'s gangster plotline. Beginning with a flashback of children playing in the streets of Montreal and an airplane crashing into a crowd of people, the film cuts to Jean-Louis Trintignant, fleeing from gypsies and ending up at Charley's island hideout. The flashbacks establish the film's *déjà vu* tone, and help to explain the connections between the characters.

And Hope to Die is about dreams and fantasies, past and present, and how the innocence of youth succumbs to the tragedy of experience. Youth is depicted as an ever-present state in the characters, and an introductory phrase from Lewis Carroll's *Alice in Wonderland*, "We are but older children, dear, who fret to find our bedroom near," suggests that the characters are still playing games. In adulthood, though, the games are deadly.

The picture never directly states that Charley and his gang have a past history, but inferences to a special bonding appear throughout the story. Charley carries the same penknife and bag of marbles as does one of the children in the flashback, and a Cheshire cat signboard at his house has a meaning that only he and his captive, Froggy (Trintignant), seem to know. Charley's girlfriend, Sugar (Lea Massari), cooks gourmet meals for the gang, while they sip coffee and chat amiably about a caper that includes kidnapping and murder.

With its haunting imagery and ethereal sound track, *And Hope to Die* had the style to compete with other films of its type. Yet its several references to psychic phenomena and the supernatural limited its appeal for average moviegoers. Moreover, when 20th Century– Fox edited the film from 140 minutes down to 99, a number of questions as to its metaphysics remained unanswered.

Clément had earned a reputation as a skilled visual craftsman beginning in the late forties, and had directed two successful French *films noirs*, *Purple Noon* (1959) and *Rider on the Rain* (1970). In *And Hope to Die*, his genius was again validated.

Ryan's last two pictures dealt with the theme of death, thus his depiction of a dying gangster going out in a wild outnumbered shoot-out with the police was an intriguing statement. One wonders how much determination Ryan needed to detach himself from his own ominous pathology in order to communicate Charley Ellis's inner pain.

Reviews: "Noted French filmmaker René Clément has brought off a crafty caper pic. . . . For once, French logic is eschewed and in its place is a gangster film that evokes nostalgia for the earlier lack of complications and crime-does-not-pay attitudes without any forced social or moral aspects. But it also adds another dimension by comparing it to children's games and giving it a sort of poetic envelope. . . . The violence is sharply done, not for its own sake, but as the childlike consequences of this deadly game. Robert Ryan has stature and authority as the aging chief who accepts death, with Trintignant mixing innocence and shrewdness as the fugitive with the solid will for survival. . . . The adroit script, excellent production dress of producer Serge Silberman, fine utilization of the rugged Canadian countryside and Montreal bustle, a catchy musical score by Francis Lai and topflight lensing by Edmond Richard all help give this a solid gloss which should insure this film good commensurate business around the world." (*Variety*, 9/19/72.)

"*And Hope to Die* is bound to be enshrined as an instant minor classic gangster movie, both for its exquisitely offbeat dialogue and convoluted plot . . . and the cast. Tough, old Robert Ryan, wounded and growling to his girlfriend, "You've never said no to me before." (Kevin Saviola, *Women's Wear Daily*, 11/30/72.)

"*And Hope to Die* is a provocative thriller which never goes soft or dull. . . . The continual remembrance of childhood is director René Clément's way of linking past and present in the game of life, and a bloody, cheerless game it is when the adults get to play it. . . . Ryan and the characters he matches wits with are vivid, sometimes amusing, even engaging, in spite of their trigger-happy fingers. . . . Clément sets the scene creatively, and peoples it with originals. Nor does the cast let him down, particularly Ryan, Trintignant, and Lea Massari as Ryan's not-quite-loyal mistress." (Frances Herridge, *New York Post*, 11/30/72.)

Lolly Madonna XXX (2) (1972). MGM, C-105 min. *Director* Richard C. Sarafian. *Producer* Rodney Carr-Smith. *Based on the novel by* Sue Grafton. *Screenplay* Rodney Carr-Smith. *Art Director* Herman Blumenthal. *Set Decorator* Jim Payne. *Music* Fred Myrow. *Song* Kim Carnes, David Ellingson. *Assistant Directors* Mike Moder, Terry Carr. *Sound* Charles W. Wilborn, Hal Watkins. *Special Camera Effects* Tim Smyth. *Camera* Philip Lathrop. *Editor* Tom Rolf. *Cast* Rod Steiger (Laban Feather), **Robert Ryan** (Pap Gutshall), Scott Wilson (Thrush Feather), Jeff Bridges (Zack Feather), Season Hubley (Roonie Gill), Katherine Squire (Chickie Feather), Timothy Scott (Skylar Feather), Ed Lauter (Hawk Feather), Randy Quaid (Finch Feather), Tresa Hughes (Elspeth Gutshall), Paul Koslo (Villum Gutshall), Kiel Martin (Ludie Gutshall), Gary Busey (Seb Gutshall), Joan Goodfellow (Sister Gutshall).

Lolly Madonna XXX was made at the lowest ebb of Ryan's life, and had a downcast tone which mirrored his depression. The film had a few things in its favor, in its lead casting of Ryan and Rod Steiger, and in its direction by Richard Sarafian. Also, the picture featured a cast of then little known actors, who have since gone on to major careers, such as Jeff Bridges, Gary Busey, Randy Quaid, Kiel Martin, and Ed Lauter.

Filmed near Knoxville, Tennessee, *Lolly Madonna XXX* deals with two backwoods families, the Gutshalls led by Ryan and the Feathers led by Steiger, who are feuding over the rights to a disputed meadow. The title refers to the signature on a letter which becomes the catalyst for a bloody confrontation between the two families. Along the way, various indignities and crimes are performed or intimated, such as kidnapping, insanity, rape, transvestism, incest, murder, and other abuses.

On one level, *Lolly Madonna XXX* might be seen as an allegory on war, in which a dispute turns friend into foe, and war results. At the end of the picture nothing is settled, which may be its point.

Ryan's performance as a thoughtful patriarch driven to violence lacked the energy of his Charley Ellis in *And Hope to Die*, and strongly reflected the elegiac feeling of his last films. For much of *Lolly Madonna XXX*, his part called for him to remain in a stationary position while importuning his sons to "think things over." It is only during the film's last few minutes that he returns to familiar form as an avenging angel when he takes action against the Feathers.

Reviews: "This is a brutal, violent, but superbly made film about the senselessness of hatreds, and how they can escalate into tragedy. . . . Ryan is an actor who has aged gracefully. He is still able to play a leading role with force. . . . Here he looks far older, and is more subdued. But at the climax we see the Robert Ryan of old, able to take charge and fight." (Jeffrey Lyons, *Rock*, 4/23/73.)

"If *Lolly Madonna XXX* wasn't so staggeringly unbelievable, I'd swear it was supposed to be a comedy. But it's played seriously, so the bloodshed and carnage and nasty sex are even more baffling. . . . It's an awful waste of talent to see Robert Ryan, Jeff Bridges, and Scott Wilson mixed up in this mess." (Rex Reed, *New York Daily News*, 2/23/73.)

Executive Action (5) (1973). National General, C-91 min. *Director* David Miller. *Producer* Edward Lewis. *Associate Producers* Dan Bessie, Gary Horowitz. *Story* Donald Freed, Mark Lane. *Screenplay* Dalton Trumbo. *Music* Randy Edelman. *Titles* Bill Brown. *Art Director* Kirk Axtell. *Technical Consultant* Steve Jaffe. *Research* Robert Polin, Kevin Van Fleet, David Lifton, Lillian Castellano, Penn Jones, Jr., Carol Rosenstein, Eda Hallinan, Barbara Elman. *Graphics* Ben Nay. *Sound* Bruce Bisenz, Kirk Francis, Jock Putnam. *Camera* Robert Steadman. *Editors* George Frenville, Irving Lerner. *Documentary Editor* Ivan Dryer. *Cast* Burt Lancaster (Farrington), **Robert Ryan** (Foster), Will Geer (Ferguson), Gilbert Green (Paulitz), John Anderson (Halliday), Paul Carr (Chris), Colby Chester (Tim), Ed Lauter (Operation Chief), Richard Bull, Lee Delano (Gunmen, Team A), Walter Brooke (Smythe), Sidney Clute (Depository Clerk), Lloyd Gough (McCadden), Richard Hurst (Used Car Salesman), Joaquin Martinez (Art Mendoza), William Watson (Leader, Team B), John Brascia, Dick Miller, Hunter Von Leer (Riflemen, Team B), Ed Kemmer (Reporter).

It is not surprising that Ryan accepted the role of Foster, a wealthy ultra right-wing conspirator, in *Executive Action*, since its script was written from left-wing thought processes. Based on events surrounding the assassination of John F. Kennedy, producer Edward Lewis got the idea to make the movie in the aftermath of Watergate, and pushed ahead with it despite advice to the contrary.

Lewis's decision to make *Executive Action* was influenced by actor Donald

Sutherland, who had approached him with material about the Kennedy assassination. The film was a social statement rather than a money-maker, and Lewis had difficulty finding a distributor for it. When National General Pictures finally picked it up, its national engagements were drastically limited. In a number of cities, *Executive Action* arrived and departed from theaters after only two weeks.

Some observers believed that *Executive Action* was hysterical liberal propaganda. In New York City, an NBC affiliate censored out a television commercial for the film, and announced, "...the violence portrayed is excessive and done in such detail as to be instructional and to invite imitation." (*New York Times*, November 8, 1973.)

Although the film's violent scenes were minor, consisting mainly of the assassins taking target practice at a dummy of Kennedy, the actual newsreel footage of the assassination and the gunning down of Lee Harvey Oswald produced a shocking effect transcending the imaginary.

The picture was probably the most controversial of Ryan's career, as its story attacked the core of the American right, exploring the premise that a small group of wealthy industrialists had Kennedy killed. Heading the conspirators, Ryan's Foster and Will Geer's Ferguson hire ex–CIA agent Farrington (Burt Lancaster) to execute their plan. The operation includes twin assassins firing at Kennedy from different vantage points, a Lee Harvey Oswald look-alike, and the paid involvement of Jack Ruby.

Executive Action's main interest was its political message. Trumbo's dry script consisted mostly of low-key discussions reflecting a leftist viewpoint about sinister powers running our country. (Trumbo stated in an interview: "After reading Josiah Thompson's marvelous study of the ballistics ... I was convinced that at least two men must have committed the Kennedy murder.... I have since discovered that even Lyndon Johnson thought J.F.K.'s death was the result of a conspiracy. He told that to Walter Cronkite ... in an interview conducted shortly before he died. But L.B.J. had the right to approve what was shown, and had that part cut out." (*Playboy*.) Thus, the picture presented little real challenge to those involved with its making. Director David Miller had done several notable suspense films (*Midnight Lace, Sudden Fear, Lonely Are the Brave*), and was able to build considerable tension out of a fact-based story whose conclusion viewers knew beforehand.

Although the dialogue never required the characters to raise their voices above a conversational tone, it had tremendous face-value impact because the cast was composed mainly of liberal thinkers. In addition, since Trumbo and Will Geer had been victims of reactionary venom years earlier, their connection with *Executive Action* was poetic justice.

Despite having a limited theatrical distribution, *Executive Action* did well at the box office, gaining recognition for its daring exploration. One critic of the picture accused Ryan of being a radical mouthpiece for producer Lewis. Although his dialogue contained one inflammatory line in which he coolly outlines a plot to create chaos among "Blacks, Puerto Ricans, and poverty-level Whites," it signified a supremacist attitude contradicting America's posture of racial and economic tolerance.

Since *Executive Action* was released shortly after Ryan's death, his fatalistic portrayal of Foster followed the trend of his last few pictures. Within the storyline, he again played an apocalyptic witness to events in which he was a participant.

Two scenes clearly depict his role: in the first, as Foster gives the go-ahead signal to the assassins, he bows his head and solemnly says to Lancaster's Farrington: "Ah, well ... it'll soon be over ... then there'll be nothing we can call our own but death ... that small model of the barren earth which serves as paste and cover to our bones ... by God's sake, let us sit upon the ground and tell sad stories of the death of kings."

The second powerful vignette occurs at film's end, when Foster receives an ominous phone call at his headquarters. After a brief conversation, he walks to the billiard table where his co-conspirators are nervously waiting, and announces that Farrington has just died of a heart attack. The closing frames show Ryan smiling grimly as he takes aim with his cue stick and strikes a ball sharply, as if to underscore his earlier prophetic words.

Reviews: "*Executive Action* offers a tactful, low-key blend of fact and invention.... The result is a cool, skillful, occasionally confusing argument for conspiracy... Lancaster and Ryan appear as pensive, practical semiacademics, rationally planning an act as bloody as a small foreign invasion.... Ryan is wonderfully benign and wry, wisely underplaying where others might have gone all out for evil." (Nora Sayre, *New York Times*, 11/8/73.)

"...This is a film which ... has a serious and controversial point of view... The millionaire schemers are played by such figures as Will Geer and the late Robert Ryan, whose performance here makes one regret more than ever the disappearance of an actor who never won the recognition he deserved." (Dilys Powell, untitled British review, 1/27/74.)

"...the hypothesis that Lee Harvey Oswald was merely a carefully chosen fall-guy and that the actual assassins were experts hired in a right-wing plot makes for chilling, unnerving, mostly compelling drama ... the acting is expertly understated. Will Geer and Robert Ryan play moneyed men who loathe Kennedy's policies and fear a Jack-Bobby-Ted dynasty." (*Cue*, 11/12/73.)

The Outfit (4) (1973). MGM, C-102 min. *Director* John Flynn. *Producer* Carter

De Haven. *Based on the novel by* Richard Stark. *Screenplay* John Flynn. *Music* Jerry Fielding. *Art Director* Tambi Larsen. *Set Decorator* James I. Berkey. *Assistant Director* William McGarry. *Sound* Richard Raguse, Jall Watkins. *Camera* Bruce Surtees. *Editor* Ralph E. Winters. *Cast* Robert Duvall (Macklin), Karen Black (Bett Harlow), Joe Don Baker (Cody), **Robert Ryan** (Mailer), Timothy Carey (Menner), Richard Jaeckel (Chemey), Sheree North (Buck's Wife), Felice Orlandi (Frank Stern), Marie Windsor (Madge Coyle), Jane Greer (Alma), Henry Jones (Doctor), Joanna Cassidy (Rita), Tom Reese (Man), Elisha Cook (Carl), Bill McKinney (Buck), Anita O'Day (Herself), Archie Moore (Packard), Tony Young (Accountant), Roland LaStarza (Hit Man), Roy Roberts (Bob Caswell), Edward Ness (Ed Macklin), Tony Anderson (Parking Attendant), Emile Meyer (Amos), Roy Jenson (Al), Philip Kenneally (Bartender), Army Archerd (Butler), Tony Trabert (Himself), Jeannine Riley (Prostitute), Charles Knapp (Motel Owner).

The Outfit was a throwback to the heyday of the *film noir* era, and had the right formula to revive an interest in the genre. Again, Ryan was cast as a gangland boss, but after having played major parts in his last several pictures, he slipped back into *cameo* status in *The Outfit*. Significantly, though, his role had a symbolic parallel not only to his life but to his reputation as the epitome of the *noir* male—lonely, cynical, and doomed. His last *film noir, Odds Against Tomorrow*, had been one of the final entries in the genre, thus his reprise in *The Outfit* gained added importance.

The Outfit centers on two men, Earl Macklin (Robert Duvall) and Cody (Joe Don Baker), who go against the syndicate (the outfit), and emerge ahead of the game. When the syndicate, headed by Ryan's Mailer, sends hit men after Earl and Ed Macklin for robbing a syndicate bank, Ed is killed and Earl takes on the syndicate to retrieve the bank loot. Aided by Cody, Macklin travels up the syndicate ladder toward Mailer. Since criminal activity is presented as the norm in *The Outfit*, its final confrontation, in which Macklin kills Mailer, is depicted as just retribution.

Thematically, *The Outfit* conformed to *film noir* in several respects. Being entirely concerned with the underworld, alienation and distrust are contagious emotions among the characters, from the top man, Mailer, down to his underlings and their molls. Mailer lives in a fortresslike mansion and is depicted as an edgy loner, drawn to but trapped by his illicit lifestyle. He travels surrounded by bodyguards, and his beautiful, neglected wife, Rita (Joanna Cassidy), who complains to him, "How long are we going to stay cooped up in his mausoleum?" The women in *The Outfit* are as immoral as are the men. Macklin's girlfriend, Bett (Karen Black), sets him up to be killed but loses her own life instead.

Producer Carter DeHaven put together a classic B-movie with style, casting the picture with a formidable gallery of heavies from the forties and fifties. Most notably, Elisha Cook, Jr., Timothy Carey, Marie Windsor, and Emile Meyer supported the film's inclusion in *noir* iconography, while their performances transcended the bit parts they were given. Director John Flynn had been an assistant director for Robert Wise on several films, thus *The Outfit*'s brisk action sequences had a flashy precision that compensated for its traditional screenplay.

Some critical reactions to *The Outfit* were negative, and had mostly to do with its scripting. One reviewer called it an "engagingly trashy mob melodrama helped by a solid supporting cast." Its faults aside, *The Outfit* registered a cut above other gangster films, and within the *film noir* cycle, its appearance after over a decade of absence indicated its value and durability as an art form.

Ryan had squeezed in *The Outfit* shortly before his death, and as in his last several pictures, the theme of death was integral to his character. Conforming to the moribund trend, Mailer loses his life in a dramatic shoot-out with Macklin at film's end, while eliciting a degree of sympathy when he dies, begging for his life. The showdown between him and Macklin carried fatalism to its natural conclusion.

Reviews: "Director/screenwriter John Flynn has obviously drawn on the rich traditions of the American criminal demimonde on film ... the late Robert Ryan as the Outfit boss taps his old reserves of projecting corrosive cynicism... Flynn does not abuse his actors, and the personality cameos are more than just spear carriers ... a good case can be made that Duvall, Black, Baker, and Ryan are at their peak impressiveness in recent years at this type of genre acting." (Tom Allen, *Village Voice*, 11/16/74.)

"One of the advantages of fashioning yarns concerning violent antihero types who take on guys with even darker ways is that the lesser of two evils has the freedom to successfully pull off murder and mayhem without being subjected to the just-retribution tradition of some crime-genre pix.... Black and Ryan both turn in solid efforts." (*Variety*, 10/24/73.)

The Outfit is a plain shoot-em-up equipped with some mighty good actors and better than tolerable girls.... All you can say about the picture is that it's well done, action-packed, has good mortality rates, and lets the good guys, if any, survive." (Archer Winsten, *New York Post*, 4/25/74.)

Duvall and Baker ... carry off John Flynn's ... fiction in high and flashy style, courtesy of Flynn's fast-paced, forthright direction.... Ryan's syndicate head is a piece of cake, but, as was his wont throughout his career, he gives dimension and complexity to the smallest ... of scenes." (Judith Crist, *New York*, 4/29/74.)

The Iceman Cometh (5) (1973). American Film Theatre, C-239 min.

Director John Frankenheimer. *Producer* Ely Landau. *Based on the play by* Eugene O'Neill. *Text edited by* Thomas Quinn Curtiss. *Camera* Ralph Woolsey. *Editor* Harold Kress. *Cast* Lee Marvin (Hickey), Fredric March (Harry Hope), **Robert Ryan** (Larry Slade), Jeff Bridges (Parritt), Martyn Green (The Captain), George Voskovec (The General), Moses Gunn (Joe Mott), Tom Pedi (Rocky Pioggi), Evans Evans (Cora), Bradford Dillman (Willie Oban), Sorrell Booke (Hugo Kalmar), John McLiam (Jimmy Tomorrow), Nancy Juno Dawson (Pearl).

The Iceman Cometh was the crowning achievement of Ryan's career, and a poignant message from the depths of his soul. It is a moot point to consider the extent to which Ryan was aware of the self-doubts he communicated in his cynical, whiskey-soaked portrait of Larry Slade. There seems to be little question that the personal crises he had struggled with throughout his life and of late led directly to the existential dilemma he embraced in Eugene O'Neill's dark journey into man's psyche.

Two obstacles facing director John Frankenheimer during filming concerned its four-hour length and its taking place in one setting. Relying on simplicity in the staging and on realistic set designs, he placed his players close enough together that several interactions could be seen at once. The modest budget under which he operated worked in his favor, almost as if the cast compensated for it by uniformly superb acting.

Except for a few alterations in dialogue, *The Iceman Cometh*'s screenplay remained faithful to the play, exuding all of O'Neill's bilious sarcasm and intellectual wit. Through the mouths of a dozen or so alcoholic lost souls, he explored man's need for illusion. Behind a hazy cloud of rot-gut booze and stagnant air, his characters drift in and out of a stupor, trading apprehensions about their 'pipedreams' and visits from the 'iceman,' O'Neill's metaphors for self-delusion and death

O'Neill probably would have reveled in Ryan's performance, and on the personal circumstances surrounding his acceptance of the Larry Slade part. In the spectacle of human misery on display at Harry Hope's dingy, down-and-out Last Chance Saloon, Ryan's Slade held court over questions of existence, proclaiming his freedom from 'pipedreams' and the 'iceman.'

The references connecting Ryan's persona with that of Larry were numerous and pungent in meaning. A beginning description of Larry as a "philosopher anarchist who knows all the answers" resembled an ethical standard with which Ryan had flirted in his past radical associations. Referring to existential abstractions about which he had become preoccupied, Ryan's Slade declares to his cronies, "The hell with the truth. The history of the world proves that truth has no bearing on anything. It's the lie of the pipedream that gives life to the whole misbegotten mad lot of us, drunk or sober."

To the bartender, Rocky, Larry denies dwelling on any illusions, and confesses, "Mine are dead and buried behind me. What's before me is the fact that death is a fine, long sleep and I'm damn tired, and it can't come too soon for me." In two of Ryan's most intimate exchanges, he spat out his words with a vehemence of self-awareness: "All I know is that I am sick of living; I'm through. I'm drowned and contented on the bottom of a bottle. Honor or dishonor, faith or treachery, they're nothing to me but opposites of the same stupidity that is the kingdom ruler of life, and in the end they'll both rot into dust in the same grave. All things are meaningless to me because they grin at me from the one skull of death."

Then: "You think when I say that I am finished with life, and tired of watching the stupid greed of the human circus, and I welcome closing my eyes in the long sleep of death, you think that's a coward's lie? So I'm afraid to live am I, and even more afraid to die, so I sit here with my pride drowned on the bottom of a bottle, keeping drunk so I won't see myself shaking in my britches with fright, or hear myself, whining and praying beloved Christ, let me live a little longer, at any price, if only for a few days or a few hours even, have mercy almighty God, and let me still clutch greedily at my yellow heart, this sweet treasure, this jewel beyond price, this dirty stinking bit of withered old flesh that is my beautiful little life."

As the final frames of *The Iceman Cometh* pass before us, the denizens of Harry Hope retreat once more into excess while Larry stands vigil on reality. Delivering his last lines of dialogue, he savors his words with the same masochistic pleasure as he would from a cheap shot of bourbon: "I'll never be a success in the grandstand or anywhere else. Life is too much for me. I'll be a weak fool looking at two sides of everything until the day I die, and may that day come soon. I'm the only real convert to death that Hickey made here, and from the bottom of my coward's heart, I mean that now."

Amid the din of his compatriots' drunken spectacle, and Sorrell Booke's cackling, "the days grow hot for Babylon," the camera zooms in on Ryan's face, pinched with resignation.

Heading the cast with Ryan were Fredric March, whose Harry Hope was a study in aged pathos (March had also been diagnosed as suffering from cancer. *Iceman* was his last film), and Lee Marvin, whose Hickey sounded the braggadocio of a true drummer. As it had been usually presented, the Hickey character was believed by some observers to have represented O'Neill. In Frankenheimer's production and in Ryan's interpretation, though, Larry Slade came through more clearly as the embodiment of O'Neill's besodden intellect.

In 1973, the prestigious National Society of Film Critics bestowed a posthumous special award on Ryan, calling his performance, "a consummate demonstration of acting skill at the end of a long, distinguished career." His competition for the Society's best actor award was stiff, against Marlon Brando—*Last Tango in Paris*, Al Pacino—*Serpico*, Robert De Niro—*Mean Streets*, Jack Lemmon—*Save the Tiger*, and others.

The Society's members who nominated Ryan included Charles Champlin (*Los Angeles Times*), Jack Cocks and Richard Schickel (*Time*), David Denby (*Harper's*), Roger Ebert (*The Chicago Sun-Times*), Pauline Kael (*The New Yorker*), and Paul D. Zimmerman (*Newsweek*). In Zimmerman's critique of *The Iceman Cometh*, he praised Ryan's performance as "exceptional in deep focus and sustained intensity," but he nevertheless placed second to Brando in *Last Tango in Paris*.

Although *The Iceman Cometh* was the best of the American Film Theater series of eight plays transferred to film, it now lays in ominous status. Its original producer, the Ely Landau organization, released the film in a limited theatrical engagement in the '70s. Shortly thereafter, however, Landau declared bankruptcy and the rights to ownership of the film have been in litigation ever since. As had been the case with Frankenheimer's *The Manchurian Candidate*, *The Iceman Cometh*'s availability for public or private viewing is at the mercy of the courts. Some movie buffs may have been lucky enough to have procured the film when it was available on video cassette a few years ago.

Reviews: "*The Iceman Cometh* is a success indeed. It is not merely a worthy production of a great play. It also possesses moments—most notably in the performance of Robert Ryan—of its own greatness. It is a film of extraordinary beauty and power.... The weight of the play falls on Robert Ryan, whose portrayal of Larry Slade is magnificent. Slade, the rummy poet anarchist, the man who likes to pretend he watches life with cynical dispassion from the grandstand, who claims to invite and welcome death, is a role full of traps. It is hard to separate Slade's sodden grandiloquence from O'Neill's own penchant for overstudding his dialogue. Ryan does it by animating and underscoring every line, each inflection with a vast, crumbling dignity, a lacerating honesty.... The movie most securely belongs to Robert Ryan, and it is an eloquent memorial to his talent. Ryan, who died of cancer in July, was ailing while he was making *Iceman*. In the circumstances, it would be easy to sentimentalize his performance. But such a measure would diminish its greatness. With the kind of power and intensity that is seldom risked, much less realized, it has its own pride and stature." (Jay Cocks, "An Eloquent Memorial," *Time*, 11/12/73.)

"The late Robert Ryan is amazing. He has enlarged the role of Larry, too frequently played as a glib, whining cynic, and invested him with something close to heroism. The doomed detached anarchist is less a copout in this interpretation than one fearful of exercising a huge power to affect other lives. His strength and dignity have almost created a new Larry." (*Variety*, 11/22/73.)

"*The Iceman Cometh* is played by a near-perfect cast including that great screen actor Robert Ryan, in his last role, the very personification of disillusioned integrity as the washed-up anarchist Larry Slade." (Philip French, *London Observer*, 9/7/80.)

"It is Robert Ryan, his face a wreck of smashed dreams, who provides the tragic dimension that makes this *Iceman* a moving, unforgettable experience. Ryan played this part in the shadow of his own death. He died this year, leaving behind a lifetime of roles too small for his talent and this great performance as epitaph." (Paul D. Zimmerman, *Newsweek*, 11/12/73.)

"There's a moving glimpse of the late Robert Ryan as the exhausted ironist who waits for death: the stern pity he levels on others is tempered with an occasional youthful smile." (Nora Sayre, *New York Times*, 10/30/73.)

"There are some fine performances from Robert Ryan, in the shadow of death both in and out of character, as Larry Slade, and from Fredric March as Harry Hope." (Molly Haskell, *Village Voice*, 11/8/73.)

"Look at the remarkable crevasses in the face of Larry Slade (the late Robert Ryan). Don't be shy. Come in close. Poke into his tired eyes." (Vincent Canby, *New York Times*, 11/11/73.)

The Inheritance (not rated) (1964) 58 min. *Producer/Director* Harold Mayer. *Associate Producer* Lynne Rhodes Mayer. *Writer* Millard Lampell. *Camera* Edmund B. Gerard, Jesse Paley, Leonard Stark. *Film Editor* Lawrence Silk. *Music Composer and Conductor* George Kleinsinger. *Song Pass It On by* George Kleinsinger, Millard Lampell. *Songs performed by* Pete Seeger, Judy Collins, Tom Paxton, Page Gaynes, Barry Kornfeld, Carla Rutolo, John R. Winn, Millard Lampell. *Sound* Al Gramaglia. *Narrator* **Robert Ryan.** *In cooperation with* Amalgamated Clothing Workers of America, AFL-CIO, CLC.

"Freedom doesn't come like a bird on the wing,
Doesn't come down like the summer rain
Freedom, Freedom is a hard won thing,
And every generation has to win it again."

This is the theme song and the theme of Harold Mayer's documentary. *The Inheritance* opens with the flood of immigrants that poured through Ellis Island in the early 1900s and explores a landscape largely unknown to the present generation. Using classic still photographs of the period, rare silent film and newsreel footage, as well as original shooting, the film unveils the dim sweatshops of the Lower East Side, coal mines and textile mills filled with children, the battlefields of World War I and the anxious years of the Depression.

In this setting we see the immigrants

struggle to become part of their new country, and labor's brutal battle to organize into a united movement during the 1930s. The actual footage of the Memorial Day Massacre at Republic Steel lends the power of authenticity to these scenes. The film moves through World War II and the Civil Rights movement of the 1960s as every generation fights again to preserve and extend its freedoms.

The Inheritance won awards at the Mannheim (Italy), Popoli (Italy), Melbourne (Australia), Edinburgh (Scotland) and Montreal (Canada), International Film Festivals, and is still relevant to the American scene. The *London Financial Times* said of the film: "It must become one of the films of our time. Anyone who fails to be moved by it is spiritually dead."

*   *   *

Stage Performances

Too Many Husbands (1939), by W. Somerset Maugham, Belasco Theatre, Los Angeles.

A Kiss for Cinderella (1940), by J.M. Barrie, with Luise Rainer. Ryan also appeared in various plays during summer stock in Dennis, Massachusetts; Maplewood, New Jersey; Arden, Delaware; Roslyn, Long Island.

Clash by Night (1941), by Clifford Odets, directed by Lee Strasberg. As Joe Doyle, with Tallulah Bankhead, Joseph Schildkraut, Lee J. Cobb, Schubert Theatre, Philadelphia, Pennsylvania, Belasco Theatre, New York.

Coriolanus (1954), by Shakespeare, produced and staged by John Houseman. As Coriolanus, with John Emery, Mildred Natwick, John Randolph, Will Geer, Alan Napier, Lori March, Jack Klugman, Jerry Stiller, Gene Saks, Michael Tolan, Jack Bittner, and others, Phoenix Theatre, New York.

Tiger at the Gates (1957), by Giraudoux, directed by Harold J. Kennedy, with John Ireland, Mary Astor, Marilyn Erskine, Ray Danton, and others, Sombrero Theatre, Phoenix, Arizona, Ivar Theatre, Los Angeles.

Founded the Theatre Group at UCLA, with John Houseman and Sidney Harmon (1959).

Murder in the Cathedral (1959), by T.S. Eliot, directed by John Houseman. As Beckett, with Richard Hale, Robert Gist, Theodore Marcuse, John Hoyt, Alan Napier, Joseph Ruskin, Robert Casper, Stephen Joyce, Pippa Scott, Doris Lloyd, Betty Harford, and others, Schoenberg Hall, UCLA.

Antony and Cleopatra (1960), by Shakespeare, staged by Jack Landau. As Antony, with Katharine Hepburn, Douglas Watson, John Harkins, Donald Davis, Patrick Hines, Earle Hyman, Anne Fielding, John Ragin, Morris Carnovsky, Will Geer, Clifton James, Sada Thompson, and others, American Shakespeare Festival, Stratford, Connecticut.

Mr. President (1962), by Howard Lindsay and Russel Crouse, music and lyrics by Irving Berlin, staged by Joshua Logan. As President Stephen Decatur Henderson, with Nanette Fabray, Anita Gillette, Jerrry Strickler, Jack Washburn, Charlotte Fairchild, Jack Haskell, Stanley Grover, Wisa D'Orso, John Cecil Holm, St. James Theatre, New York.

271

Othello (1967), by Shakespeare, as Othello, Nottingham Playhouse, Nottingham, England.

Long Day's Journey into Night (1967), by Eugene O'Neill, as James Tyrone, Sr., Nottingham Playhouse, Nottingham, England.

Founded the Plumstead Playhouse Repertory Company, with Henry Fonda and Martha Scott (1968).

Our Town (1968), by Thornton Wilder, directed by Leo Brady. As Editor Webb, with Henry Fonda, Estelle Parsons, John McGiver, Jo Van Fleet, John Beal, Anthony George, Mark Bramhall, Thomas Coley, and others, Mineola Theatre, Mineola, Long Island.

The Front Page (1968), by Ben Hecht and Charles MacArthur, directed by Leo Brady. Same cast as *Our Town*.

The Time of Your Life (1968), by William Saroyan. As the philosophic barfly, Millpond Theatre, Roslyn, Long Island.

The Front Page (1969), directed by Harold J. Kennedy. As Walter Burns, with Peggy Cass, Bert Convy, Doro Merande, Conrad Janis, John McGiver, Val Avery, James Flavin, Charles White, Harold J. Kennedy, Julia Meade (replaced by Helen Hayes), and others, Ethel Barrymore Theatre, New York.

Long Day's Journey into Night (1971), by Eugene O'Neill, staged by Arvin Brown. As James Tyrone, Sr., with Geraldine Fitzgerald, Stacy Keach, James Naughton, Promenade Theatre, New York.

Television
Performances, 1955–1973

Screen Directors' Playhouse. Episode: "Lincoln's Doctor's Bag." 12/14/55, NBC, 30 min. *Based on a story by* Christopher Morley. *Directed by* H.C. Potter. Lincoln: **Ryan;** Dr. Stone: Charles Bickford; Edwin Stanton: Willis Bouchey; Simon: Johnny Lee; Petitioner: Dennis King, Jr.

President Abraham Lincoln has recently become discouraged and saddened by the continuing war between the states. His physician attempts to cheer him up with the gift of a young puppy.

Zane Grey Theatre. Episode: "You Only Run Once." 10/5/56, CBS, 30 min. Matt: **Ryan;** Martha: Cloris Leachman; Hale: John Hoyt; Kroll: Howard Petrie.

A cattle rancher unknowingly hires two ranch hands who are wanted criminals. A vigilante mob discovers they are working for him, and accuses him of being an accessory to murder. He is subsequently marched off to be hanged.

Turn of Fate. Episode: "Silhouette of a Killer." 9/30/57, NBC, 30 min. Man: **Ryan;** Ellen: Cloris Leachman; Maria: Anna Navarro; Pop: Irving Bacon; Nate: Forrest Lewis; Sheriff: Robert Brubaker.

A weekly series of half-hour dramas with a rotating cast of stars, including David Niven, Charles Boyer, Jane Powell, and Jack Lemmon.

A man awakens on a lonely desert road to find he is the sole survivor of an auto crash. He sees that the wrecked car is a sheriff's patrol car, and that he is handcuffed, but he has no recollection of who he is. He staggers to a nearby ranch house and startles the girl who is alone there. She believes he is an escaped killer, and the drama ensues with some good suspense before coming to a satisfactory conclusion for the man.

Alcoa Theatre. Episode: "On Edge." 11/18/57, NBC, 30 min. Trilbridge: **Ryan;** Martha: Gail Kobe; Captain Posen: Edward Binns; Lieutenant Brackett: Fredd Wayne.

Although William Trilbridge is now a highly respected professor of philosophy at a California college, he had a dark past as a confidence man. His past now threatens to be detrimental to his new life, as the police discover his whereabouts.

Goodyear Theatre. Episode: "The Crowd Pleaser." 12/9/57, NBC, 30 min. Berry: **Ryan;** Bill Johnson: Stuart Whitman; Mary Whitman: Jean Willes; Mick Terrill: John Beradino; Vandy Vance: Stacy Harris.

Frank Berry was once a promising fighter, until he was decisively and badly beaten five years previously. He is now a boxing manager working with an impulsive young fighter, and is training him for an important bout. But the young man is impatient for better fights and bigger money, and his recklessness gets him into serious difficulty.

Alcoa Theatre. Episode: "The Face of Truth." 12/30/57, NBC, 30 min. Ripetti: **Ryan;** Mrs. Ripetti: Catherine McLeod; Father Boniface: John Marley; Bartender: Paul Burns.

After serving a long prison sentence, Mike Ripetti returns home. His wife hopes that he will settle down and make a decent home for her and their son, but Ripetti is concerned only with killing the man responsible for his conviction.

Alcoa Theatre. Episode: "Hidden Witness." 1/27/58, NBC, 30 min. Detective Jeff Banner: **Ryan;** Ann Palmer: Barbara Eiler; Joe Frazier: Lawrence Dobkin; Eddie: Michael Pate; Walter: Ned Wever.

Goodyear Theatre. Episode: "White Flag." 2/17/58, NBC, 30 min. Ryan was cast as the surgeon. No other members of the cast were listed.

A well-known heart specialist faces a difficult decision when he learns that a gang has successfully substituted its ailing leaders for another patient. It seems that the gang leader needs an extremely delicate operation to save his life, and the physician is the only one qualified to perform the surgery.

Goodyear Theatre. Episode: "The Seventh Letter." 3/17/58, NBC, 30 min. Lieutenant Joe Carter: **Ryan;** Louise Ryan: Virginia Gregg; Bobby: Eugene Martin.

A police lieutenant is assigned to an unusual case, the investigation of the murder of a mailman. Although on the surface the case appears routine, the detective begins to suspect that someone tried to retrieve a letter from the mailman, and when he refused to give it up he was killed.

Goodyear Theatre. Episode: "The Giant Step." 4/28/58, NBC, 30 min. Gunner's Mate Smith: **Ryan;** Captain Stemon: Harold J. Stone; Joe: Norman Alden; Nick: John Cliff.

During World War II two men are put ashore on the Japanese held island of Okinawa. Their mission is to capture alive a deadly snake, from which is extracted an ingredient for a valuable vaccine.

Alcoa Theatre. Episode: "The Perfectionist." 5/19/58, NBC, 30 min. Morton: **Ryan;** Mrs. Morton: Frances Rafferty.

For the past 15 years Ken Morton has worked as a teller in a small-town bank, and has finally devised what he considers to be a foolproof way of robbing the bank.

Playhouse 90. Episode: "The Great Gatsby." 6/26/58, CBS, 90 min. *Teleplay by* David Shaw. *Directed by* Franklin Schaffner. Jay Gatsby: **Ryan;** Daisy: Jeanne Crain; Nick Carraway: Rod Taylor; Myrtle Wilson: Virginia Grey; Jordan Baker: Patricia Barry; Dr. Edwards: Barry Sullivan; Ann Brewster: Kim Hunter; Robert Brewster: Alex Nicol; Morino: Hurd Hatfield; Captain Wilkins: Sebastian Cabot.

Zane Grey Theatre. Episode: "To Sit in Judgment." 11/13/58, CBS, 30 min. Parney: **Ryan;** John Washbrook: Harry Dean Stanton.

Sheriff Parney hangs a local badman found guilty of murder. The dead man's sons are just as bad as their father, and vow to kill Parney in revenge.

Zane Grey Theatre. Episode: "Trial by Fear." 6/11/59, CBS, 30 min. Oakley: **Ryan;** Tod Owen: David Janssen; Tuphill: Harold J. Stone; Sheriff Galt: Edward Platt; Baker: Raymond Bailey.

A gunslinger, Cob Oakley, is placed on trial for murder. One juror is certain that the man is innocent, although the rest of the jury believes him guilty. But before the jury can reach its verdict, the gunman escapes.

Zane Grey Theatre. Episode: "Interrogation." 10/1/59, CBS, 30 min. Kraig: **Ryan;** Corporal Durbin: Harry Townes; Interrogator: Alexander Scourby; Cota: Don Diamond; Gonzales: Rodolpho Hoyos; Palaza: Robert Contreras.

During the Mexican-American War of 1847, Captain Kraig has a well-earned reputation for bravery. He and Corporal Durbin are taken prisoner by the enemy and face torture and interrogation. Durbin begins to crack under the pressure, and Kraig pleads with him not to submit to the enemy.

Buick Electra TV Playhouse. Special "The Snows of Kilimanjaro." 3/25/60, CBS, 90 min. *Based on the novel by* Ernest Hemingway. *Teleplay by* A.E. Hotchner. *Directed by* John Frankenheimer. Walters: **Ryan;** Helen: Ann Todd; Marjorie: Janice Rule; Rhoda: Jean Hagen; Mrs. Leslie: Mary Astor; Editor: James Gregory; Molo: Brock Peters.

Harry Walters feels death closing in on him. Injured on a hunting trip, he is attended by his wife, as he languishes deliriously on an African plain, in the shadows of the snow-capped Mount Kilimanjaro. His mind is filled with bitter memories of the life he lived—his career as a writer, his adventures all over the world, and most vividly of all, the women he has known.

Wagon Train. Episode: "The John Bernard Story." 11/21/62, ABC, 60 min. Bernard: **Ryan;** Metsina: Perry Lopez; Larry Gill: Beau Bridges; Ben Gill: Cliff Osmond; Mrs. Budgen: Doris Kemper; Mr. Budgen: William Fawcett; Dr. Porter: Herbert Lytton.

Indians kidnap Mrs. Budgen from the wagon train, and in her place they leave a seriously ill Indian youth named Metsina. The Indians promise to return Mrs. Budgen if John Bernard can save the youth.

Kraft Suspense Theatre. Episode: "Are There Any More Out There Like You?" 11/7/63, NBC, 60 min. *Based on George Cuono's prize-winning novelette,* "The Brave and the Cool." *Script by* Luther Davis. *Directed by* Elliott Silverstein. Bollington: **Ryan;** Edna Bollington: Phyllis Avery; Janet: Katharine Ross; Paul Durbin: Adam Roarke; Althea Winton: Sharon Farrell; Willis Maudry: Peter Helm; Mr. McMurty: Jay Novello.

The telephone rings at the Bollington residence, shattering the quiet of a Christmas season evening at home. Tom Bollington learns that his daughter Janet and three college friends have been picked up by the police—they were out joyriding in their car when they killed a pedestrian. And to make matters worse, the youths are now acting evasive, and won't reveal who was driving the car. In fact, they are treating the tragic accident as just another holiday lark.

Breaking Point. Episode: "Better Than a Dead Lion." 1/20/64, ABC, 60 min. *Written by* Mort Fine *and* Shimon Wincelberg. Thompson: Paul Richards; Raymer: Eduard Franz; Lloyd Osment: **Ryan;** Eunice Osment: Bettye Ackerman; Walter Gosse: John Larkin.

Eunice Osment asks Thompson to help her husband, a famous author-adventurer who has become notably accident-prone of late, and she fears he is about to have a mental breakdown.

Eleventh Hour. Episode: "Who Chopped Down the Cherry Tree?" 1/29/64, NBC, 60 min. *Script by* Dick Nelson. Franklin "Hoppy" Hopp: **Ryan;** Myra Hopp: Peggy Ann Garner; Calvin Hopp: Richard Anderson; Ettinger: James Edwards; Jamison: Robert Brubaker.

Colorful "Hoppy" Hopp always sways the voters with his effusive, hayseed theatrics; and he also plays along with his younger brother's political machine—until the machine plans the biggest graft bag in state history.

Wagon Train. Episode: "The Bob Stuart Story." 9/20/64, ABC, 60 min. Cooper: Robert Fuller; Hale: John McIntire; Wooster: Frank McGrath; Stuart: **Ryan;** Janice Stuart: Vera Miles; Keith Lance: Tommy Sands; Felix Colton: Andrew Prine; Thomas Lance: William Smith.

Ex-lawman Bob Stuart gets into a fight on his wedding night, with an old enemy, Cooper Smith.

Bob Hope Chrysler Theatre. Episode: "Guilty or Not Guilty." 3/9/66, NBC, 60 min. *Script by* Roland Kibbee *and* Evan Hunter. Filmed in New York City as a pilot for a projected series about a New York City assistant district attorney. Dixon: **Ryan;** Collier: Leslie Nielson; Ralph Belmonte: Richard Beymer; Mrs. Collier: Diana Hyland; Frank Reeser: Robert Duvall; Ben Stafford: Leif Ericson; Catherine Rogers: Pippa Scott.

Prompted by the increasing crime rate, and the release of a suspected criminal, Gregg Collier organizes a citizens' committee to patrol the area. Assistant D.A. Andrew Dixon is hard pressed to catch the recently released criminal in a lie so that he can be arrested, and complicating the difficulty is Collier's rabble-rousing.

The Front Page. Special. 1/31/70, syndicated, 90 min. *Written by* Ben Hecht *and* Charles MacArthur. *Directed by* Harold J. Kennedy. Burns: **Ryan;** Hildy: George Grizzard; Mollie Molloy: Estelle Parsons; Mayor: John McGiver; Mrs. Grant: Vivian Vance; Bensinger: Harold J. Kennedy.

The brash and gutsy newspaper world of Prohibition Chicago comes alive as Ryan and George Grizzard star in this television version.

The action is fast-paced, and the language is spicy in the play that Tennessee Williams said "uncorseted the American Theatre with its earthiness and two-fisted vitality." Appearing with Ryan are fellow members of the Plumstead Playhouse, which was founded by Ryan, Henry Fonda, and Martha Scott, for the purpose of reviving the great American Classics. Helen Hayes, whose late husband Charles MacArthur, coauthored the play, introduces *The Front Page.*

A battle of wits unfolds between arrogant managing editor Walter Burns and his ace reporter, Hildy Johnson. Burns's efforts to keep Hildy from quitting are played out in a busy Chicago press room while rival newspapers try to scoop them on a pending execution and an upcoming mayoral election.

The Man Without a Country. Special. 4/24/73, ABC, 90 min. *Directed by* Delbert Mann. Nolan: Cliff Robertson; Vaughan: **Ryan;** Ingram: Beau Bridges; Danforth: Peter Strauss; Morgan: Walter Abel; Burro: John Cullum; Secretary of the Navy: Sheppard Strudwick.

In 1863, the young army officer, Philip Nolan, is accused of treason. At his trial, despite the efforts of his defense to clear him of charges, he spoils his chance for freedom after crying out in court, "Damn the U.S.!" His words become a harsh reality as he is banished to a lifetime at sea.

Narrations, Appearances
and Recordings

Narrations

Writings on the Sand, documentary about the history of the Nile River, PBS.

World War I, weekly documentary, 9/22/64–9/5/65, CBS, 30 min.

The Inheritance, motion picture depicting the influx of workers into America since 1900, set against a backdrop of the growth of unions. Produced by Harold Mayer for the Amalgamated Clothing Workers of America, 60 min.

The City of Ships, documentary on the history of the Port of New York, 12/18/64, NBC, 60 min.

A reenactment of Abraham Lincoln's second inaugural address, as Lincoln, on the east steps of the Capitol Building, 3/4/65.

The Poetry of Wallace Stevens, 2/28/68, NET (Channel 13, New York), 60 min.

Who Speaks for Man? documentary providing critical appraisal of the United Nations, NET (Channel 13, New York), 11/12/69, 60 min.

The Last of the Westerners, 2/4/70, ABC, 30 min.

The Poetry of Walt Whitman, 8/30/70, NET (Channel 13, New York), 30 min.

Appearances

A Tribute to Woody Guthrie, Carnegie Hall, New York, 1/68.

Broadway for Peace, Lincoln Center, 1/68.

Alexander Cohen's **The Scene** (New York based talk show), Channel 9, 2/11/68.

Celebration for the Reopening of the Ford's Theatre, with Henry Fonda and Fredric March, CBS, 1/68.

Recordings

The Gift of the Maji, and **The Last Leaf,** by O'Henry.

The Front Page, by Ben Hecht and Charles MacArthur, as Walter Burns, directed by Harold J. Kennedy.

Long Day's Journey into Night, by Eugene O'Neill, as James Tyrone, directed by Arvin Brown.

The Iceman Cometh, by Eugene O'Neill, as Larry Slade, directed by John Frankenheimer.

Mr. President, lyrics by Irving Berlin, as Stephen Decatur Henderson, directed by Joshua Logan.

Ryan Films
on Videocassette

Bombardier — 1943
The Sky's the Limit — 1943
Behind the Rising Sun — 1943
Crossfire — 1947
Berlin Express — 1948
The Boy with Green Hair — 1948
Return of the Badmen — 1948
Caught — 1949
The Set-up — 1949
Flying Leathernecks — 1951
The Racket — 1951
Clash by Night — 1952
Beware, My Lovely — 1952
The Naked Spur — 1953
Bad Day at Black Rock — 1954
Escape to Burma — 1955
The Tall Men — 1955

Back from Eternity — 1956
Men in War — 1957
God's Little Acre — 1958
Lonelyhearts — 1958
Ice Palace — 1960
King of Kings — 1961
The Longest Day — 1962
Billy Budd — 1962
The Battle of the Bulge — 1965
The Professionals — 1966
The Dirty Dozen — 1967
Anzio — 1968
The Wild Bunch — 1969
The Love Machine — 1970
And Hope to Die — 1972
Executive Action — 1973
The Iceman Cometh — 1973

Appendix A: Film Noir in the United States

The phenomenon of *film noir* in the United States originated as a result of the social upheaval caused by World War II, and from the rise of American gangsterism that preceded the war. Born from a strange conglomeration of social statement, studio economy-mindedness, and technological advancements in filmmaking, the *film noir* became a medium for expressing the turmoil of people's emotions. Although as an art form it has been difficult to identify the *film noir* cycle in terms of an exact life span, its thematic structure emerged and gathered momentum during the forties and early fifties. The war had weighed heavily on the hearts of Americans, thus the *film noir* evolved as an appropriate cathartic. Feelings of frustration and futility, combined against a backdrop of violence and sexuality, were fully exploited by Hollywood.

Viewed sociologically, returning American soldiers, disoriented from the cataclysm the war had forced upon them, were perhaps the hardest hit in their readjustment, and were susceptible to the lure of corrupt organizations. Within the criminal element indigenous to America, more global issues, such as the fear of Communism and the threat of nuclear weapons as a method of extortion, were sometimes tied to more basic *film noir* themes.

Several character motifs are central to *film noir*, such as the themes of alienation, obsession, and isolation, often presented within a paranoid framework. A typical *film noir* derives much of its meaning from existential and Freudian thought, as its characters are usually assailed by emotional turmoil and a constant struggle with random, painful events of life.

Film noir also presents the perverse in man, expressed as either sexual or violent aberrations from the social norm. Its people act out their conflicts in settings symbolizing negative moods, such as depression, repression, or suppression, and which are suggested by grimy waterfront hotels, corrupt big-city syndicates, or crowded, neon-lit honky-tonks. Frequently, the *film noir* protagonist only finds the solution to his dilemma through death.

Some of the best proponents of the *film noir* genre were European expatriates who had come to America in the late thirties, such as Fritz Lang, Max

Ophuls, Fred Zinnemann, and Jean Renoir. Their work strongly contributed to the concept of expressionism in *film noir*, and involved the interaction of key themes with unconventional visual styles. The higher echelon of American filmmakers instrumental to the *film noir* movement in the States included Robert Wise, Edward Dmytryk, Samuel Fuller, Anthony Mann, Nicholas Ray, and Robert Aldrich.

The *film noir* artist used the camera as a key stylistic device. The term "low-key" lighting, meaning "high contrast," was frequently used to create specific attitudes, such as harshness or desolation. Highly filtered camera work produced softer, more pleasant visual images.

Other camera techniques unique to *film noir* involved the extensive use of shadows, oddly angled shots, the shimmering effects caused by light and darkness falling on wet surfaces, and wide-angle lenses for perspective distortion. Innovations of the forties, such as high-speed lenses, more sensitive films, and an increased portability of camera equipment, helped to make *film noir* adaptable to location shooting.

Much of the popularity of *film noir* was bound in economic terms, and dependent on the changing values of our culture. Thus, it was doomed to a short life span. Its gradual decline resulted from the relative tranquility of the fifties, and by the end of the decade it had virtually disappeared.

Since then, attempts have been made to resurrect it, most notably in Don Siegel's *Dirty Harry* (1971), Robert Culp's *Hickey and Boggs* (1972), and John Flynn's *The Outfit* (1974).

More recently, Lawrence Kasdan's *Body Heat* (1982), Hal Ashby's *The Postman Always Rings Twice* (1981), and Joel Coen's *Blood Simple* (1985), have demonstrated the genre's viability and longevity in the contemporary market.

Ryan as a Noir Figure

Robert Ryan is a lasting icon of the *film noir* genre, and possibly its most important actor. Most of his portraits, while depicting people aloof to the norms of society, exemplified the genre's most salient traits. He was drawn to psychological dramas in which his acute portrayals ran a dizzying gamut of emotional instability and inner pain, ranging from quietly controlled to actively hostile. In the textbooks, his behaviors are listed as character disorders; in his *films noirs*, he becomes the tragic, existential psychopath.

Most of his characters were obsessed, paranoid, pathetic, sadistic, in short, integral to the core of *film noir*. His contributions were unique because he nearly always emerged evoking pathos, despite being either a thief, a murderer, or a psychotic. Several emotional themes ran through his roles, frequently of loneliness, depression, or frustration. Often he was a down-at-the heels protagonist, having been the victim of an unhappy childhood or a debilitating physical injury, cast to the mercy of fate and mankind.

A number of writers have noticed Ryan's skill as the *noir hero*. In one of the best books on the genre, *Film Noir: An Encyclopedic Reference to the American Style,* writer Julie Kirgo lauded his performance in Fritz Lang's passionate *Clash by Night,* and aptly encapsulated his work throughout the genre:

> As in many *noir* films, Robert Ryan delivers *Clash by Night*'s most anguished performance. As the model of the alienated man, pain constantly flickers beneath the sardonic mask of his face, although he holds his mouth tightly in check, and his powerful body in a useless rigidity. Ryan etches a complex portrayal of an unhappy personality whose miseries are expressed in acts of cruelty, but who is accepted with some degree of audience understanding.

Robert Ryan's Films Noirs

The Woman on the Beach: Director: Jean Renoir (1947)
Crossfire: Director: Edward Dmytryk (1947)
Berlin Express: Director: Jacques Tourneur (1948)
Act of Violence: Director: Fred Zinnemann (1948)
Caught: Director: Max Ophuls (1949)
The Set-up: Director: Robert Wise (1949)
The Woman on Pier 13 aka I Married a Communist: Director: Robert Stevenson (1949)
The Racket: Director: John Cromwell (1951)
On Dangerous Ground: Director: Nicholas Ray (1951)
Clash by Night: Director: Fritz Lang (1952)
Beware, My Lovely: Director: Harry Horner (1952)
House of Bamboo: Director: Samuel Fuller (1955)
Odds Against Tomorrow: Director: Robert Wise (1959)
The Outfit: Director: John Flynn (1973)

Appendix B:
The Oakwood School Today

Since its humble beginnings in Robert and Jessica Ryan's backyard in 1951, Oakwood now encompasses kindergarten through twelfth grade, and is rated as one of the best schools in the country. To further its programs and to extend itself to the less advantaged, the Robert and Jessica Ryan Memorial was founded in 1974. Its concept provided services for children with learning disabilities, advocated creative teacher training, and disseminated a humanistic social studies curriculum.

The social studies program was subsidized by a $10,000 grant from a founding parent in memory of Jessica Ryan, and was detailed in scope. It explored, through reenactment of arts, customs, and mythology, the cultures of both East and West from which our own has stemmed.

As a benefit for the Ryan memorial, on November 3, 1974, Sean O'Casey's *Juno and the Paycock* was presented at the Mark Taper Forum. Starring in the play were Jack Lemmon, Walter Matthau, and Maureen Stapleton, under George Seaton's direction. Before the play, John Houseman delivered a moving tribute to the Ryans, followed by a poignant film retrospective of Ryan's career, which was created by Lamont Johnson. Interspersed with vignettes from Ryan's best films, Johnson included interviews with Fritz Lang, Katharine Hepburn, John Sturges, and others. Joanne Woodward and Paul Newman narrated the retrospective, which concluded with Ryan's harrowing final speech from *The Iceman Cometh*.

Chapter Notes

Chapter 1.
1. Jeanne Stein, *Films in Review*, January, 1968.
2. *Ibid.*
3. Joseph Wershba, *New York Post*, March 7, 1963.
4. *Ibid.*
5. *New York Herald-Tribune.*
6. *Films in Review*, January, 1968.
7. *Films in Review*, January, 1968.
8. From a letter Ryan wrote to the Max Reinhardt Archives at SUNY (State University of New York at Binghamton).

Chapter 2.
1. Edward Dmytryk, *It's a Hell of a Life, but Not a Bad Living.*

Chapter 3.
1. *Films in Review*, January, 1968.
2. Alden Whitman, the *New York Times*, July 12, 1973.

Chapter 4.
1. Daniel J. Leab, *Journal of Contemporary History* (SAGE, London, Beverly Hills and New Delhi), 1984.
2. Charles Bitsch, *Cahiers du Cinéma*, August, 1958.
3. Thierry Génin, *L'Avant Scène*, August, 1970.

Chapter 5.
1. Dore Schary, *Heyday, An Autobiography.*
2. *Films and Filming*, March, 1971.

Chapter 6.
1. Patricia Bosworth, the *New York Times*, June 1, 1969.
2. Harold J. Kennedy, *No Pickle, No Performance.*
3. *Films and Filming*, January, 1968.
4. *Films and Filming*, March, 1971.

5. *Coronet*, Spring, 1963.
6. John Cutts, *Films and Filming*, July, 1961.

Chapter 7.
1. Glenn Loney, *Cue*, July 11, 1970.
2. From a prepared speech Spottswood presented at an Oakwood School function.
3. Pauline Kael, *5001 Nights at the Movies*.

Chapter 8.
1. Rui Nogueira and Nicoletta Zalaffi, *Cinema* (Paris), April, 1970.
2. William Otterburn-Hall, *Louisville Courier-Journal and Times*, June 7, 1970.
3. *Cinema* (Paris), April, 1970.
4. *Films and Filming*, March, 1971.
5. *Current Biography*, 1963.
6. Philip French, *Westerns*.
7. *Films and Filming*, March, 1971.

Chapter 9.
1. *No Pickle, No Performance*.
2. *Films and Filming*, March, 1971.
3. SANE Archives.
4. Joe Nivens, *San Bernardino Sun-Telegram*, October 4, 1959.
5. The *New York Times*, October 20, 1959.
6. *Saturday Review*, June 11, 1960.
7. Joe Hyams, *New York Herald-Tribune*, September 29, 1959.
8. SANE Archives.
9. *New York Sunday News*, August 27, 1967.
10. Jeremy Heymsfeld, *New York World-Telegram and Sun*, April 14, 1966.
11. *New York Sunday News*, August 27, 1967.

Chapter 10.
1. John Houseman, *Final Dress*.
2. *Philadelphia Bulletin*, May 23, 1969.
3. *Cue*, July 11, 1970.
4. Lee Silver, *New York Daily News*, July 28, 1960.
5. *Cue*, July 11, 1970.
6. Rick DuBrow, *New York Mirror*, December 9, 1961.
7. *Ibid.*
8. *Films and Filming*, November, 1960.
9. *New York Mirror*, December 9, 1961.
10. *Saturday Review*, October 28, 1961.
11. *New Republic*, November 10, 1962.
12. *New York Post*, March 7, 1963.

Chapter 11.
1. *Films and Filming*, January, 1968.
2. Wanda Hale, *New York Daily News*, March 14, 1966.

3. Promotional advertisement, courtesy Harold Mayer Productions.
4. George Horne, the *New York Times*, December 18, 1964.
5. *Louisville Courier-Journal and Times*, June 7, 1970.

Chapter 12.
1. *Films and Filming*, March, 1971.
2. Roberta Branden Gratz, *New York Post*, January 27, 1968.
3. The *New York Times*, June 1, 1969.
4. The *New York Times*, October 24, 1965.
5. *Philadelphia Bulletin*, May 23, 1969.
6. *Cue*, July 11, 1970.
7. Alvin Shuster, the *New York Times*, October 18, 1967.
8. Paul Schrader, *Cinema*, Volume 3, Number 5.

Chapter 13.
1. *No Pickle, No Performance*.
2. Louis Calta, the *New York Times*, July 23, 1969.
3. *No Pickle, No Performance*.
4. The *New York Times*, August 5, 1971.
5. *Playboy*, November, 1971.

Chapter 14.
1. Mary Murphy, *Los Angeles Times*, September 5, 1972.
2. George Gent, the *New York Times*, April 5, 1971.

Chapter 15.
1. *Los Angeles Times*, September 5, 1972.
2. *Ibid*.
3. Jeffrey Lyons, *Rock*, April 23, 1973.

Bibliography

In addition to the bibliography as an information source, important data were collected from film periodicals, newspapers, and trade magazines and also from material contained in film study courses and retrospectives.

Some material from the archives lacked dates, in which case no date is listed. Moreover, a chronological reference list would be confusing and unwieldy, thus no attempt has been made to recount every source date. Where possible, dates are listed in the text.

Newspapers: *Brooklyn Daily Eagle, Chicago Daily News, Chicago Sun-Times, Chicago Tribune, Hartford Courant, London Observer, Los Angeles Reader, Los Angeles Times, Louisville Courier-Journal and Times, Milwaukee Journal, New York Daily Mirror, New York Daily News, New York Herald-Tribune, New York Journal-American, New York Post, New York Times, New York World-Telegram, Passaic Herald News, Philadelphia Bulletin, Philadelphia Inquirer, San Diego Reader, Village Voice, Wall Street Journal.*

Film Periodicals: *American Film, Film Comment, Films and Filming, Films in Review, Photoplay, Sight and Sound, Take One, Theatre Arts.*

Trade Reviews: *Cue, Filmgoers' Daily, Hollywood Reporter, Motion Picture Herald, Showmen's Trade Review, Variety.*

Periodicals: *After Dark, Christian Science Monitor, Commonweal, Nation, New Republic, Newsweek, New York, New Yorker, Playboy, Real Paper, Rock, Rolling Stone, Saturday Review, Time.*

Cinema Revivals and University Retrospectives: *Film Notes,* Museum of Modern Art, Eileen Bowser, 1969, 1979; *Program Notes,* University of Texas, Department of Radio, Television, and Film, Austin, Texas, 1974, 1979, 1981, 1983, 1984; International Arts Society, University of Arizona, 1968; Toronto Film Society, 1974.

Allen, Steve. *Mark It and Strike It.* New York: Holt, Rinehart, and Winston, 1960.
Armour, Robert A. *Fritz Lang.* Boston: Twayne, 1977.
Basinger, Jeanine. *Anthony Mann.* Boston: Twayne, 1979.
Bayer, William. *The Great Movies.* New York: Ridge Press, 1973.
Bogdanovich, Peter. *Fritz Lang in America.* London: Studio Vista Limited, 1967.
Brooks, Tim and Earle Marsh. *The Complete Directory to Prime Time Network T.V. Shows—1946 to Present.* New York: Ballantine, 1979.

Cook, Bruce. *Dalton Trumbo*. New York: Charles Scribner and Sons, 1977.

Crist, Judith. *The Private Eye, the Cowboy, and the Very Naked Girl*. New York: Holt, Rinehart, and Winston, 1967.

Dmytryk, Edward. *It's a Hell of a Life, but Not a Bad Living*. New York: New York Times Books, 1978.

Dunne, Philip. *Take Two, A Life in Movies and Politics*. New York: McGraw-Hill, 1980.

Eames, John Douglas. *The MGM Story*. New York: Crown, 1975.

French, Philip. *Westerns*. New York: Oxford University Press, 1977.

Garnham, Nicholas. *Samuel Fuller*. New York: Viking Press, 1971.

Gow, Gordon. *Hollywood in the Fifties*. New York: A.S. Barnes, 1971.

Hardy, Phil. *Samuel Fuller*. New York: Praeger Press, 1970.

Higham, Charles, and Joel Greenberg. *Hollywood in the Forties*. New York: Paperback Library, 1970.

Hirsch, Foster. *The Dark Side of the Screen: Film Noir*. New York: Da Capo Press, 1981.

Houseman, John. *Violence, 1947: Three Specimens. Hollywood Quarterly*. Berkeley and Los Angeles: University of California Press, 1948.

_____. *Front and Center*. New York: Simon and Schuster, 1979.

_____. *Final Dress*. New York: Simon and Schuster, 1983.

Jensen, Paul M. *The Cinema of Fritz Lang*. New York: A.S. Barnes, 1969.

Jewell, Richard B., and Vernon Harbin. *The RKO Story*. New York: Arlington House, 1982.

Kael, Pauline. *I Lost It at the Movies*. Boston: Little, Brown, 1965.

_____. *Reeling*. Boston: Little, Brown, 1976.

_____. *Kiss, Kiss, Bang, Bang*. Boston: Little, Brown, 1978.

_____. *5001 Nights at the Movies*. Boston: Little, Brown, 1982.

Katz, Ephraim. *The Film Encyclopedia*. New York: Perigee, 1979.

Kennedy, Harold, J. *No Pickle, No Performance*. Garden City, New York: Doubleday, 1978.

Kitses, Jim. *Horizons West*. London: Thames and Hudson, 1969.

Kreidl, John Francis. *Nicholas Ray*. Boston: Twayne, 1977.

Mellen, Joan. *Big Bad Wolves—Masculinity in the American Film*. New York: Pantheon, 1977.

Morgenstern, Joseph, and Stefan Kanfer, editors. *An Anthology by the National Society of Film Critics, 1973–74*. New York: Simon and Schuster, 1969.

O'Brien, Pat. *The Wind at My Back*. Garden City, New York: Doubleday, 1964.

Ott, Frederick W. *The Films of Fritz Lang*. Secaucus, New Jersey: Citadel, 1979.

Parish, James Robert. *Actors' Television Credits*. Metuchen, New Jersey: Scarecrow Press, 1973.

_____. *The Tough Guys*. Carlstadt, New Jersey: Rainbow Books, 1977.

Sayre, Nora. *Running Times: Films of the Cold War*. New York: Dial Press, 1982.

Schary, Dore. *Heyday, An Autogiobraphy*. Boston: Little, Brown, 1979.

Shipman, David. *A Story of Cinema*, Volume One. New York: St. Martin's Press, 1982.

Silver, Alain, and Elizabeth Ward, editors. *Film Noir: An Encyclopedic Reference to the American Style*. Woodstock, New York: Overlook Press, 1979.

Silver, Charles. *The Western Film*. New York: Pyramid, 1976.

Skolsky, Sidney. *Don't Get Me Wrong, I Love Hollywood*. New York: Putnam and Sons, 1975.

Thomas, Tony. *Ustinov in Focus*. London: A. Zwemmer, 1971.

Ustinov, Peter. *Dear Me*. Boston: Little, Brown, 1977.

Walsh, Raoul. *Each Man in His Time*. New York: Farrar, Straus, and Giroux, 1974.

Index

Numbers in **boldface** indicate photographs.

A

Abel, Walter 276
About Mrs. Leslie 59,
74–**75**, 98, 220–221
Ackerman, Bettye 275
Acosta, Rodolpho 214,
227–228
Act of Violence **31**, 32,
193–196, 281
Adamic, Bojan 247
Adams, Julia 214–215
Adams, William 237
Adler, Buddy 82, 224
Adler, Robert 218, 226
After Dark 260
Agar, John 42, 200–201
Ahn, Philip 182
Aidman, Charles 252
Akins, Claude 86
Alarcon, Enrique 241
Alaska Seas 74, 81, 115,
219–220, 241
Alaves, Jose Lopez 226
Albani, Elsa 255
Albert, Eddie 117, 152,
180–181, 243
Alcoa Theatre (tv) 92, 273–
274
Alden, Norman 274
Alden, Richard **114**, 241
Aldrich, Robert 138,
250–251, 280
Alexander, Angela 234
Alice in Wonderland (story)
261
All Kneeling (novel) 203–204
Allen, Dede 237
Allen, Gene 228
Allen, Steve 106–108
Allen, Tom 266

Alloway, Lawrence 217
Alpert, Hollis 231
Alton, John 223, 234, 236
Altwies, James 193, 198, 200
Amalgamated Clothing
Workers of America 269
Amelio, Sonia 256
American Civil Liberties
Union 63, 109, 130, 132
American Friends' Service
Committee 31, 63, 108
American Shakespeare
Festival 113–115
Ames, Leon 184
Ames, Stephen 195
Amy, George J. 211
And Hope to Die 163, 261–
263, 278
Anderson, Herbert **10**, 198
Anderson, John 263
Anderson, Richard 276
Anderson, Robert 185
Anderson, Roland 180, 250
Anderson, Tony 265
Andes, Keith 211, 228–229
Andrews, Bill 258
Andrews, Dana 135, 246–
247
Andrews, Robert Hardy
200–202, 205
Angeli, Pier 246
Angold, Edit 202
Angst, Richard 248
Anhalt, Edward 251, 252
Anka, Paul 243
Anna Christie (play) 169
Anna Lucasta (play) 242
Annakin, Ken 242, 246
*An Anthology by the Na-
tional Society of Film
Critics* 154

Antonini, Alfredo 254
Antony and Cleopatra (play)
113–115, 141, 174, 271
Antrim, Harry 194
Anzarut, Raymond 251
Anzio 139, 255–256, 278
Arau, Alfonso 256
Archer, John 205
Archerd, Army 265
*Are There Any More Out
There Like You?* (tv) 275
Arlen, Harold 181
Arletty 243
Armstrong, Robert 193
Arness, James 214–215, 221
Arnold, Gary 153
Arnt, Charles 183, 195
Arrico, Chuck 234
Arthur, Maureen 260
Artists Help All Blacks 132
Ashby, Hal 280
Astaire, Fred 16, 181–182
Aston, Don 244
Astor, Mary 32, 92, 194,
271, 275
At Your Service (play) 9
Athanas, Verne 227
Atkinson, Brooks 14, 79
Atwater, Edith 260
Auer, John H. 17, 182
Avant Scène 37, 39, 53, 71
Averback, Hy 65
Avery, Phyllis 275
Avery, Val 152, 272
Axtell, Kirk 263

B

Babcock, Fay 223
Bacall, Lauren 149

Bacher, William A. 226
Back from Eternity 91, **93**, 228–229
Bacon, Irving 273
Bad Day at Black Rock 59, 74–**76**, 81, 83, 85, 98, 115, 221–223, 278
Bagdasarian, Ross 219
Bailey, Raymond 274
Bakaleinikoff, Constantin 180, 182, 183, 184, 185, 187, 189, 191, 193, 198, 200, 202, 203, 205, 206, 208, 211, 213
Baker, Jack 211
Baker, Jane 258
Baker, Joe Don 265–266
Baker, Pip 258
Baker, Roy 85, 218–219
Baldwin, Walter 193, 207
Balkan, Adele 195
Ball, Lucille 128
Ball, Suzann 215
Ballard, Lucien 191–192, 218, 227–228, 252, 256
Ballmeyer, Fred 237
Bancroft, George 180
Band, Albert 254
The Band 144
Bankhead, Tallulah 13–14, 271
Banks, Peter 116
Barbour, Dave 202
Barker, Lex 189, 193
Barnes, Clive 79, 151, 153–154, 161
Barnes, George 195
Barnes, Howard 186, 197
Barnes, Mae 237
Barnes, Rayford 146, 256
Barnett, Vince 208
Barr, Richard 152
Barrault, Jean-Louis 243
Barrie, J.M. 271
Barry, Gene 219, 228–229
Barry, Patricia 274
Barrymore, John 137
Barsacq, Leon 243
Barstow, James S. 193, 206
Barzman, Ben 195
Basinger, Jeanine 94
Batchelor, Ruth 260
Batt, Bert 251
The Battle of the Bulge 66, 135, 246–247, 278
Bau, Gordon 191, 193, 195,

198, 240
Bauchens, Anne 180
Baumgartner, Karl 243
Bavier, Frances 214
Baxter, Alan 198–199
Baxter, Anne 139, 250
Bayer, William 257
Baylor, Hal 198
Baylos, Gene 260
Bazlen, Brigid 241
Beal, John 65, 149, 272
Bean, Robin 247, 260
Beary, Bud 184
Beaton, Betsy 195
Beaumont, Hugh 65, 108, 180
Beaumont, Kathryn 65, 108, 180
Beck, John 258–259
Beck, Ron 258
Beckley, Paul V. 111, 214, 236, 239, 241, 246
Beddoe, Don 207
The Bedford Incident 106
Bedig, Sass 252
Beery, Wallace 4
Beetley, Samuel E. 193, 243
Begley, Ed **104**, 208–209, 237–239
Behind the Rising Sun 16–17, **18**, 278
Bel Geddes, Barbara **34**–35, 196
Belafonte, Harry 108, 145, 237–239
Belfor, Barbara 107
Bell, James 183, 206, 220
Bellamy, Ralph 130, 179, 249
Benchley, Robert 181
Benedict, Brooks 179
Benjamin, Richard 152, 189
Bennett, Joan **22,** 24, 187–189
Bentley, Elizabeth 201
Benton, Robert 250
Beradino, John 273
Berenguer, Manuel 241
Bergen, Frances 221
Berger, Ralph 186, 192, 195, 208
Berkey, James I. 265
Berlin Express **29,** 31, 59, 191–192, 278, 281
Berlin, Irving 124–125, 271, 277
Bernaduccio, Daniel 228
Bernstein, Elmer 229–231

Berry, John 29, 63
Bert, Malcolm 240
Bertrand, Rafael 249
Bessie, Dan 263
Best of the Badmen 56, 205–206, 253
Best, Willie 179
The Best Years of Our Lives 15
Better Than a Dead Lion (tv) 275
Betz, Carl 218–219
Beware, My Lovely 63–64, 69–**70**, 213–214, 281
Beymer, Richard 243, 276
Bezzerides, A.I. 50–51, 208
Biberman, Abner 179, 180, 182
Bice, Robert 184, 214
Bickford, Charles 24, 187–189, 273
Big Bad Wolves – Masculinity in the American Film (book) 40
The Big Combo 27
Billy Budd, Foretopman (novel) 244
Billy Budd xii, **119**–121, 243–246, 278
Binns, Edward 273
Birkett, Michael 244
Biroc, Joseph 240
Bisenz, Bruce 263
Bissell, Whit 227–228
Bittner, Jack 271
Black, Karen 265–266
Black Friday (novel) 261
Black Sunday 165
Blackman, Charles 252
Blake, Amanda 220
Blake, Manuel Topete 258
Blake, Walter 251
Blanke, Henry 239
Blech, Hans Christian 243, 246
Blewitt, David 260
Block, Libbie 196
Blood Simple 280
Bloom, Harold Jack 216–217
Bloom, William 218
Blue, Ben 250
Blue, Monte 180
Blue Denim 107
Blumenthal, Herman 262
Bob Hope Chrysler Theatre (tv) 138, 276
The Bob Stuart Story (tv) 276

Bodeen, DeWitt 244
Body and Soul 198
Body Heat 280
Boehm, Sydney 226
Boemler, George 221
Boetticher, Budd 70, 214–216
Bogart, Humphrey 72
Bogeaus, Benedict 223–224
Bois, Curt 35, 196
Bombardier 15–**16**–17, 278
Bond, Ward 57, 208–210
Bondi, Beulah 228–229
Booke, Sorrell 267
Boone, Richard 96
Booth, Shirley 74–**75**, 98, 220–221
Borgnine, Ernest 76, 139, **146**, 154, 222, 251, 256–257
Born to Be Bad 46, **47**, 59, 203–205
Borzage, Lew 223
Bosworth, Patricia xiii, 99–100
Bouchey, Willis 273
Bourgoin, Jean 243
Bouvil 243
Bow Tamely to Me (story) 223
Bowser, Eileen 200
The Boy with Green Hair 32–**33**, 195–196, 243, 278
Boyer, Charles 92, 273
Boyer, Lyle 186, 187
Boyle, Charles, P. 214, 215
Boyle, Edward 8–9
Boyle, Edward G. 196
Bradburn, Arthur 241
Bradbury, Ray 107, 241
Brady, Leo 149–150, 272
Brady, Ruth 196
Bramhall, Mark 272
Bramley, Bill 258
Brando, Marlon 32, 74, 268
Brandt, Janet 231
Brandt, Louis 231
Brascia, John 263
The Brave and the Cool (novella) 275
Bray, Robert 189, 193
Breaking Point (tv) 130, 275
Brecht, Bertolt 87, 102
Brega, Mario 254
Brennan, Walter 56, **76**, 205–206, 222–223, 227–228
Breslin, Howard 222
Breton, Daniel 261
The Brick Foxhole (novel)

22, 25, 189
Bridges, Beau 172, 275, 276
Bridges, Jeff 164, 166–168, 262–263, 267
Brigandi, Phil 198, 200
Bright, Richard 237–238
Brissac, Virginia 179, 184, 220
Broadway for Peace Show 144–145, 277
Brodie, Don 227
Brodie, Steve **28**, 186, 187, 189–190, 193
Bronson, Charles 246, 251
Bronston, Samuel 115, 241–242
Bronz, Francesco 255
Brooke, Walter **10**, 184, 258–259, 263
Brooklyn Daily Eagle (newspaper) 184
Brooks, Richard 22, 25, 189, 248–250
Brown, Arvin xiv, 40–41, 59, 87, 90, 156–157, 159–162, 164, 168, 277
Brown, Bill 263
Brown, Harrison 106
Brown, Helen 198
Brown, Jim 251
Brown, Joyce 176
Brown, Malcolm 216, 222
Brown, Robert 244
Brown, Vanessa 97
Brown, Wally 183
Brubaker, Robert 273, 276
Brun, Joseph 237–239
Bryant, Edwin H. 250
Buccela, Maria Grazia 248
Buetel, Jack 205
Buick Electra TV Playhouse (tv) 111, 275
Bulburd, Bud 256
Bull, Richard 252, 258, 263
Burke, Sonny 256
Burnett, W.R. 207
Burns, Paul E. 200, 227, 274
Burr, Raymond 214–215
Burton, Richard 111, 117, 240–241, 243
Burton, Robert 218
Busby, Tom 254
Busey, Gary 164, 262–263
The Busy Body 139, 250
Butler, Artie 260
Butler, Gerald 49, 208

Butler, John 198
Butler-Glouner 260
Buttons, Red 243

C

Cabeen, Ross 65
Cabeen, Wendy 65
Cabot, Bruce 56, 205
Cabot, Sebastian 274
Cadwalader, Jessica 9, 10
Caesar, Sid 139, 250
Cagney, James 4
Cagney, Jeanne 179
Cahiers du Cinéma 53, 156
The Caine Mutiny 30
Caldwell, Erskine 231
Cambridge, Godfrey 250
Cameron, Elisabeth 109, 195
Cameron, Ian 109, 195
Campbell, R. Wright 258
The Canadians **114**–115, 241
Canby, Vincent 255, 257, 259, 269
Cannon, Dyan 260–261
Cannon, J.D. 155, 258–259
Capriccioli, Massimo 254
Captain Nemo and the Underwater City 152, 258
Cardenas, Elsa 256
Cardinale, Claudia **137**, 249–250
Carey, Gary 35, 208
Carey, Harry, Jr. **81**, 223–225
Carey, Leslie I. 214
Carey, Olive 208
Carey, Timothy 172, 219, 265–266
Carlos, Don 249
Carlson, Richard 179
Carmody, John 172
Carnes, Kim 262
Carney, Alan 183
Carnovsky, Morris 271
Carpenter, Claude 180, 181, 182
Carr, Paul 263
Carr, Terry 262
Carradine, John 183
Carrere, Edward 256
Carroll, Kathleen 260
Carroll, Lewis 261
Carroll, Madeline 180
Carr-Smith, Rodney 262
Carruthers, Ben 251

Carson, Jack 179
Carson, Johnny 143
Carter, Harry 218
Carter, Janis 42, **45**,
 200–201, 206
Casey, James 187
Casper, Robert 271
Cass, Peggy 152, 272
Cassavetes, John 251
Cassidy, Joanna 265–266
Castegnaro, Mario 196
Castellano, Lillian 263
Castle, William 139, 250
Cathcart, Daniel B. 221
Catlett, Walter 195
*Cattle Annie and Little
 Britches* 48
Caught 33–**34**, 35–37, 53,
 56, 196–198, 278, 281
Cavanaugh, Florence S. 184
Cavens, Al 211
*Celebration for the Reopening
 of the Ford's Theatre* (guest
 appearance) 277
Chaffey, Don 247
Challee, William **54**
Chamberlin, Howland 207
Chambers, Wheaton 202
Champion 38, 198
Champlin, Charles 172,
 257, 268
Chandler, Raymond 50
Chaney, Lon, Jr. 180
Chano 256
Chaplin, Charlie 4, 133
Chapman, Hugh 187
Chapman, Lonnie 252
Chapman, Robert H. 244
Charlton, Peter 107
Chase, Frank 214
Chavez, Jose 249
Chekhov, Anton 4
Cheshire, Harry 200
Chester, Colby 263
Chicago Sun-Times 268
Chierichetti, David vii
Chooluck, Leon 229, 236
Christian, Mady 184
Christian Science Monitor
 219, 226
Christian-Jacque 248
Cinema 147, 257
Cirno, Franco 254
Citizen Kane 15, 42
City Beneath the Sea 70,
 215–216
The City of Ships (narra-

tion) 132, 277
Clark, Carroll 181, 184, 202,
 205, 211
Clark, Fred 228–229
Clark, James B. 224
Clark, Ken 227
Clark, Mary Ellen vii
Clarke, David 195, 198
Clarke, Mae 214
Clash By Night 13–14, 59,
 67–69, 80, 210–212, 271,
 278, 281
Clatworthy, Robert 214
Clavel, Aurora 256
Clément, René 163,
 261–262
Cliff, John 205, 274
Clift, Montgomery 99–101,
 234–236
Clute, Sidney 263
Cobb, Lee J. 13, 155, **157**,
 258–260, 271
Coch, Edward, Jr. 214
Cockrell, Francis 218
Cocks, Jay 269
Codee, Ann 202
Coe, Peter 219, 223
Coen, Joel 280
Coffin, Tris 228
Coghlan, Frank, Jr. 179
Cohen, Albert J. 214, 215
Cohen, Alexander 277
Cohn, Art 37, 198–199, 201
Colbert, Claudette 12, 43,
 47, 202–203
Coleman, Cliff 256
Coleman, C.C., Jr. 219
Coleman, Robert 151
Coley, Thomas 272
The College Widow 4, 179
Collier, William, Jr. 179
Collinge, Patricia 184, 185
Collins, Choo Choo 250
Collins, G. Pat 200, 208
Collins, Judy 130, 144, 269
Collins, Ray 207
Collins, Russell 222, 231
Comanche Station 214
Combat (novel) 229
Come Back, Little Sheba 74,
 220
Comer, Sam 220
Committee for Friendly
 World Broadcasting 108
Committee for the First
 Amendment 107, 127
Commonweal 182, 189, 191,

195, 207, 214, 216, 218,
 219, 223, 229, 233, 236,
 239, 243, 246
Conlin, Jimmy 208
Connery, Sean 243
Connor, Edric 242
Connor, Kenneth 258
Connors, Chuck 258
Conrad, Charles 218
Conrad, Derek 239
Conrad, William xiv, 207
Considine, Tim 221
Conte, Richard 27
Contreras, Jaime 258
Contreras, Robert 249, 275
Converse, Frank 252
Convy, Bert 152, 272
Coogan, Jackie 227,
 234–235
Cook, Alton 212
Cook, Eddie 101, 111
Cook, Elisha 172, 236,
 265–266
Cook, Willis 249
Cooke, Alistair 141
Cooper, Gary 12, 19, 86, 180
Cooper, George **28**,
 189–190
Cooper, Jackie 260
Coote, Robert 191–192
Cope, John 180
Corby, Ellen 220
Corcoran, William 186
Cord, Alex **143**, 254–255
Coriolanus (play) 78–79, 110,
 113, 115, 141, 174, 271
Cormack, Bartlett 207
Cornthwaite, Robert 236
Coronet 22, 53
Corrigan, Lloyd 179
Cosby, Bill 132
Costello, Delores 179
Coulouris, George 242, 247
The Count of Monte Cristo
 (novel) 107
Courage, Alexander 236
Cousins, Norman xiv, 106
Cowl, Jane 202
Cox, Aileen Babs 202
Coxe, Louis O. 244
Cozzo, Gianni 255
The Crack Within the Ring
 (novel) 22
Crafford, Charles 244
Craig, Alec 179
Craig, Harry A. 255
Crain, Jeanne 99, 274

Crawford, Broderick 180
Crawford, Joan 90
Crawford, John 243
Creber, Lewis 218
Crehan, Joseph 180
Creley, Jack **114**, 241
Crenna, Richard 138
Criss Cross 253
Crist, Judith 138, 249–250,
253–254, 266
Cromwell, John 42, 60,
202, 207, 281
Crone, George 183
Cronjager, Edward 205
Cronkite, Walter 264
The Crooked Road 135–136,
247–248
Crosby, Bing 127
Crosby, John 99
Crossfire 25–**26**, 27–**28**, 42,
50, 53, 59, 75, 83, 189–
191, 196, 207, 278, 281
Crouse, Russel 271
The Crowd Pleaser (tv) 92,
273
Crowther, Bosley 190–191,
195, 198, 203, 210, 226,
227, 231, 235–236, 239,
245, 250, 251
Cry of the City 253
Cue 64, 78–79, 115, 197, 221,
265
Cullum, John 276
Cully, Russell A. 186, 187,
189, 191, 193
Culp, Robert 132, 280
Cuono, George 275
Curran, Joe 6–7
Curtis, Tony 99
Curtiss, Edward 215
Curtiss, Thomas Quinn
267
Custer of the West 142–143,
252–254
Cuthbertson, Allan 258
Cutter, Murray 240
Cutts, John 75–76, 190,
221, 246

D

D'Agostino, Albert S. 180,
181, 182, 183, 184, 185, 186,
187, 189, 191, 193, 195, 198,
200, 202, 203, 205, 206,
207, 208, 211, 213

Dale, Michael 215
Damn the Defiant 120
The Damned 32, 196
Damon, Mark 243, 255
Dana, Bill 139, 250
d'Andriz, Emilio 255
Dano, Royal 116, 242
Danton, Ray 92, 240, 243,
271
Darby, Ken 226
Darien, Frank 187
Darrell, Steven 226
Darrin, Sonia 196
Darwell, Jane 184
Davenport, Harry 183
David, Mack 251
Davidson, Adele 107
Davidson, Gordon 111
Davies, Richard 181
Davis, Donald 271
Davis, Frank 187
Davis, Luther 275
Davis, Sammy, Jr. 67
Dawn, Jack 194
Dawson, Gordon 251–252,
256
Dawson, Nancy Juno 267
Day, Laraine 42, 200–201
Day of the Outlaw 66,
102–103, 236–237
Dayton Productions 92
Deacon, Richard 227–228
Dear Brutus (play) 8
D'Eaubonne, Jean-Pierre
253
De Bretagne, Jo 243
Dee, Frances 14
Deems, Mickey 250
The Defenders (tv) 138
De Felitta, Frank 255
De Grasse, Robert 184
De Haven, Carter 265–266
Dehner, John 86, **114**, 241
Dekker, Albert 146, 148,
154, 256–257
De Kova, Frank 236
Delano, Lee 263
De Laurentiis, Dino 115, 255
De Lavallade, Carmen 145,
237, 239
Delmar, Vina 220
De Luise, Dom 250
De Martini, Aldo 255
Demich, Irina 243
DeMille, Cecil B. 29, 116,
180
Denby, David 268

De Niro, Robert 268
Denning, Richard 11–12,
179, 180
Denny, Reginald 223
De Packh, Maurice 227
Depinet, Ned 200
De Santis, Joe 249
The Detective Story 68, 92,
94
De Toth, André 103, 236–
237
De Vol, Frank 251
De Witt, Louis 231
Dexter, Brad 224–225
De Yong, Joe 179, 180
Diamond, Don 275
*Dick Powell's Zane Grey The-
atre* (tv) 91–92, 273, 275
Dillman, Bradford 166, 267
Dinelli, Mel 64, 213
Dinken, Bernard vii
Dinovitch, Abe 198, 202
The Dirty Dozen 138–139,
250–251, 278
The Dirty Game **137**, 248
Dirty Harry 280
Diskant, George E. 50, 64,
207, 208–210, 213, 238
Dmytryk, Edward 12, 16,
28, 30, 63, 179, 182, 184,
185, 189–191, 255, 259,
280, 281
Dobkin, Lawrence 274
Dobson, James 206
Doctor Faustus (play) 141
Dr. No 248
Doctor Strangelove 106
Dolivet, Louis 253
Domergue, Faith 34–35
*Don't Get Me Wrong, I Love
Hollywood* (book) 76
Donavan, Hobart 223
Donehue, Vincent J. 101,
234–235
Doniger, Walter 219
Doran, D.A. 65
Doran, Marion 65
Dorfman, William 191, 200
D'Orso, Wisa 271
Doucette, John 224–225
Douglas, Don 182
Douglas, Kirk 28, 32, 38,
98, 252, 258
Douglas, Melvyn 57, 120,
128, 244–245
Douglas, Paul 68–69,
211–212

Doyle, Frank 195
Dreier, Hans 180
Drew, Ellen 180
Dryhurst, Michael 258
Dubov, Paul 198
Duclow, Geraldine vii
Dudley, Doris 202
Duff, Warren 184, 185
Dumke, Ralph 219
Duncan, William 179, 180
Dunlevy, Jim 241
Dunne, Finlay Peter 107
Dunne, Philip xiv, 107–108,
    118, 138, 165, 171
Dunnock, Mildred 159
Dunphy, Jerry 260
Dupuis, Art 207
Durant, Ariel 141
Durant, Will 141
Durgin, Cyrus 124
Durkus, Andrew J. 250
Duryea, Dan 86
Dusick, Jack 236
Duvall, Robert 155, 258–
    259, 265–266, 276
Dwan, Allan 81, 233–234
Dwyer, Marlo 189, 200
Dwyre, Roger 261
Dylan, Bob 124, 144

E

Eagle in a Cage (tv) 131
Ebert, Roger 268
Ebo, Elaine vii
Ebsen, Buddy 65
Edds, Hank 260
Edelman, Randy 263
Edouart, Farciot 180, 220,
    250
Education for Peace (book) 79
Edwards, Bruce 180, 184
Edwards, Heidi 65
Edwards, James 198, 230,
    276
Eight Steps to Peace 95
Eiler, Barbara 274
Eiseman, Alvord 222
Eisenhower, Dwight D. 108
Eisinger, Jo 248
Eisler, Hanns 187
Ekberg, Anita 91, 93, 228–
    229
El Cid 94
The Eleventh Hour (tv) 130,
    275

Eliot, T.S. 62, 110, 271
Eller, Carl 172
Ellingson, David 262
Elliot, Biff 224
Elman, Barbara 263
Elson, Donald 236
Emerson, Emmett 228
Emery, John 271
Emhardt, Robert 155,
    258–259
Enright, Ray 23, 32, 184,
    186, 192
Epstein, Mel 219
Ericson, John 76, 222–223
Ericson, Leif 276
Erskine, Marilyn 92, 271
Escape to Burma 80, 81, 115,
    223–224, 241, 278
Eurist, Clarence 234
Evans, Evans 267
Evans, Gene 191
The Execution of Private
    Slovik 48
Executive Action 98, 173–
    174, 175, 263–265, 278

F

Fabian 243
Fabray, Nanette 10, 123,
    271
The Face of Truth (tv) 92,
    274
Fadiman, William 49
Failsafe 106
Fairbanks, Douglas, Sr. 4,
    73, 133
Fairchild, Charlotte 271
Falk, Peter 152, 255
Farber, Manny 186, 191,
    200, 210, 212, 218
Farrar, David 223
Farrel, Bernard 243
Farrell, Sharon 260, 275
Farrow, John 228–229
Farrow, Tisa 261
Fawcett, William 219, 275
Fegte, Ernst 179
Feldman, Phil 146, 256
Fellows, Robert 180, 184,
    185
Fenton, Frank 181
Ferber, Edna 111, 239–240
Ferguson, Frank 196, 208
Fernandez, Abel 219
Fernandez, Emilio 146, 256

Ferrer, Mel 43, 202, 203–
    204, 243
Fessler, Bailey 180
Fetherston-Haugh, R.C. 180
Fielding, Anne 271
Fielding, Jerry 256, 258, 265
Fields, Al 184
52 Pick-up 165
The File on Thelma Jordan
    253
Film Comment 51
Film Noir 24–25, 26, 28, 60,
    64, 91, 103, 189–191, 196,
    197, 198, 208–210, 211, 213,
    216, 224–225, 235, 237–
    238, 253, 262, 265–266,
    279–281
Film Noir: An Encyclopedic
    Reference to the American
    Style (book) 64, 200, 210,
    214, 281
Film Noir: The Dark Side of
    the Screen (book) 27, 60
Filmgoers' Daily 188
Films and Filming 75, 116,
    190, 221, 228, 233, 239,
    246, 247, 258, 260
Films in Review 219, 242
Final Dress (book) 110
Fine, Mort 275
Firecreek 259
Fisher, Clay 226
A Fistful of Dollars 255
Fitzele, Louis 243
Fitzgerald, F. Scott 113
Fitzgerald, Geraldine 160,
    162, 272
Fix, Paul 179
Flannery, William 179
Flavin, James 152, 179, 272
Fleming, Rhonda 218
Fletcher, Bill 252
Flippen, Jay C. 206
Flowers, Bess 200, 203
Flying Leathernecks 56–57,
    58, 206–207, 278
Flynn, John 265–266, 280,
    281
Fonda, Henry 86, 97, 117,
    131, 135–136, 145, 149–151,
    243, 246–248, 272, 276,
    277
Fong, Benson 182
Fontaine, Joan 46, 47,
    203–204
Forbes, Louis 223
Forbes, Mary 184

Ford, John 4, 98, 155, 179
Ford, Wallace 198
Forrest, Steve 243
Forrest, William 207
Forte, Joseph 202
Fortini, Luciana 254
Foster, Lewis R. 179
Foster, Preston 180
Foulger, Byron 179, 205
Fowler, Hugh S. 227
Fowley, Douglas 214
Foy, Eddie, Jr. 180
Fragos, George 211
Farmer, Virginia 203
Francis, Anne 222
Francis, Kirk 263
Frankel, Benjamin 246
Frankenheimer, Evans xiv,
  166–167, 176, 267, 268
Frankenheimer, John xiv,
  95, 111–113, 165–168, 170,
  175, 267, 275, 277
Frankovich, M.J. 260
Franz, Arthur 255
Franz, Eduard 130, 275
Fraser, Bill 258
Frawley, William 179
Freberg, Stan 107
Freed, Donald 173–174, 263
Freeman, Joel 222
Freeman, Kathleen 260
The French Connection II 165
French, Philip 86, 269
Frenville, George 263
Fresco, Dave 198
Fresholtz, Les 260
Frings, Ketti 220
Fritz Lang in America
  (book) 69
Frizzell, Lou 258
Frobe, Gert 243
From Here to Eternity 194
From Russia with Love 248
Front and Center (book) 49,
  78
The Front Page 149–155, 158,
  272, 276
The Front Page (recording)
  277
Fry, Christopher 92
Frye, Gilbert 211
Fuchs, Jay 153
Fuller, Lance 231–232, 236
Fuller, Leland 227
Fuller, Robert 276
Fuller, Samuel xiv, 38–39,
  82–83, 207, 224–226,

  280–281
Fulton, John P. 220
Funke, Lewis 114–115

G

Gable, Clark 31, 73, 84,
  205, 226–227
Gabriti, Robert 248
Gage, Erford 14, 183
Gaines, Richard 184
Gallaudet, John 179, 234
Gallitti, Alberto 255
Gallo, Lou 237–238
Gam, Rita 241
Gamet, Kenneth 206
Gammon, Fred 256
Gancy, Jesus Gonzalez 252
Gangelin, Victor 251
Gangway for Tomorrow 17,
  183
Garbini, Amato 255
Garcia, Juan 226
Garcia, Luis 246
Gardiner, Charles H. 187
Garfinkel, Louis 254
Garfunkel, Art 124
Garland, Judy 128
Garland, Tommy 215
Garmes, Lee 196
Garner, James 139, 252
Garner, Peggy Ann 276
Garrison, J. 247
Garson, Greer 74, 221
Gary, Romain 243
Gasparre, Dick 211
Gassman, Vittorio 248
Gates, Larry 252
Gates, Nancy 182
Gateson, Marjorie 181
Gausman, Russell A. 214
Gaven, Jean 261
Gaynes, Page 269
Gebert, Gordon 206
Geer, Will 144, 174, 263–
  265, 271
Geesken, Terry vii
Génin, Thierry 39, 53, 71
Genn, Leo 243
Gennaro, Peter 67, 124
Gentili, Giorgio 255
Gentleman's Agreement 190
Gentry, Race 230
George, Anthony 150, 272
George, George W. 200–201
Gerard, Edmund B. 269

Gershenson, Joseph 214
Gershwin, Ira 128
Gerstad, Harry 189
Ghost Breakers 179
Giannini, Giancarlo 255
Giant 111
The Giant Step (tv) 274
Gibbons, Cedric 193, 216,
  221, 222
Gidding, Nelson 237
The Gift of the Maji
  (recording) 277
Giglio, Sandro 224
Gilbert, Billy 179
Gilchrist, Connie 194
Gillette, Anita 125, 271
Gilliatt, Penelope 154
Gillitti, Alberto 254
Ging, Jack 130
Ginsberg, Alan 124, 144
Giraldi, Franco 254
Girardot, Annie 248
Giraudoux, André 92, 271
Gist, Robert 271
Givot, George 182
Glass, Everett 205, 218
Gleason, Jackie 97
Glover, Edmund 185
God's Little Acre 66, 94,
  96–97, 231–234, 278
Goddard, Paulette 179, 180
Gold Medal Studios 103
Golden Gloves 11, 12
Golden Horizons (novel) 186
Goldoni 9
Goldsmith, Jerry 251
Goldstone, Richard 37, 198
Golitzen, Alexander 215
Golonka, Arlene 250
Gombell, Minna 193
Gomberg, Maxine 107
Gomberg, Sy 107
Gomez, Maria 249
Gomez, Thomas 44,
  200–201
Goodfellow, Joan 262
Goodis, David 261
Goodwin, Harold 180
Goodyear Theatre (tv) 92,
  273, 274
Gorcey, Bernard 198
Gordon, Bernard 253
Goring, Marius 247
Gottlieb, Sanford 106
Gough, Lloyd 263
Gow, Gordon 85
Gozie, Bernie 216

Grace, Henry W. 193, 243
Graff, Wilton 196
Grafton, Sue 262
Graham, Fred 200
Grahame, Gloria 189–190,
    237–239
Grainger, Edmund 206–207
Gramaglia, Al 269
Granet, Bert 191
Granger, Stewart 247
Grant, Cary 32, 40, 46, 57,
    73, 88, 205
Grant, James Edward 201,
    206
Grant, Kirby 180
Grapewin, Charles 180
Grau, Gil 187, 195
Gray, Nadia 247
Gray, Peter 224
Grayson, Charles 200–202
The Great Gatsby (novel)
    99, 274
The Great Movies (book) 257
Green, Gilbert 263
Green, Johnny 250
Green, Martyn 267
Green, Walon 256
Green, William 198
Greenberg, Joel 27, 198
Greene, Howard W. 180
Greene, Shecky 260
Greenleaf, Raymond 214
Greenspun, Roger 261
Greenway, Al 256
Greer, Jane 172, 265
Gregg, Virginia 274
Gregg, Walter 252
Gregory, James 275
Gregson, John 243
Grey, Virginia 274
Greyn, Clifton 260
Griffin, G.F. 180
Griffith, D.W. 133
Griffith, Edward H. 181
Grizzard, George 155, 276
Gross, Jack 186–188, 192,
    200
Gross, Roland 181, 184, 187,
    198, 200, 208
Grover, Stanley 271
Grubb, Jack 191
Guardino, Harry 116,
    241–242
Guarino, Frederick L. 260
Guernsey, Otis L. 182, 191,
    192, 196, 201, 203, 215
Guilfoyle, Paul 200–201

Guilty or Not Guilty (tv)
    138, 276
Guinness, Alec 120
Gunfight at the O.K. Corral
    252
Gunga Din 15
Gunn, Moses 166, 267
Guthrie, Arlo 144
Guthrie, Woody 144
Gwenn, Edmund 27
The Gypsy Moths 165

H

Haas, Charles 65
Haas, Emily 65
Haberman, Abe 234
Hackett, Albert xiv, 124,
    158, 165, 171, 173, 176
Hackett, Buddy 231, 233
Hagen, Jean 275
Haines, William Wister 207
The Hairy Ape (play) 169
Hale, Barbara 32, 195
Hale, Richard 110, 271
Halevy, Julian 253
Haley, Jack, Jr. 260
Hall, Conrad 249
Hall, John vii
Hall, Robert 253
Haller, Ernest 229–230,
    231–234
Hallinan, Eda 263
Hallmark Hall of Fame (tv)
    131
Hallward, Joy 203
Hamilton, Kim 104, 237
Hamilton, Neil 179, 180,
    181
Hammerstein II, Oscar 128
Hampden, Walter 180
A Handful of Heaven (story)
    181
Hanscom, Marion vii
Harbin, Vernon 204
Hardin, Ty 246, 253
Harding, Vincent 258
Harding, William vii
Harford, Betty 271
Harkins, John 271
Harlan, Russell 236
Harline, Leigh 184, 195,
    200, 224
Harmon, John 214
Harmon, Sidney xiv, 65–66,
    71–72, 94, 97, 100–101,

110–111, 135, 229, 231–232,
    236, 246, 271
Harper, Paul 256
Harper's 268
Harrigan, William 58, 206
Harris, Jack 244
Harris, Richard 120
Harris, Stacy 273
Harris, Steve 240
Harrison, Doane 179
Hart, Dolores 100, 234–235
Hart, Henry 242
Hartman, Paul 243
Harstone, Christopher 258
Hartung, Philip 182, 189,
    190, 207, 214, 216, 218,
    219, 223, 228, 229, 233,
    236, 239, 243, 246
Harvey, Harry 186, 187, 189
Harvey, Jack 215
Harvey, Lew 184, 193
Harvey, Michael 191, 193
Haskell, Jack 271
Haskell, Molly 269
Hatch, Robert 200, 210,
    214, 223, 239
Hatfield, Hurd 241–242,
    274
Hathaway, Henry 228
Hattie, Hilo 215
Hatton, Raymond 179
Havens, Richie 144
Hawks, William B. 226
Haworth, Edward S. 249
Haworth, Ted 243
Hay, Alexandra 260
Hayakawa, Sessue 224–225
Haydn, Richard 221
Hayes, Alfred 69, 211–212
Hayes, George Gabby 21,
    186, 193
Hayes, Helen 145, 154–155
Hayes, Lee 144
Haynes, Jack 249
Hays, Daniel 236
Hayward, Jim 219
Hayward, Leland 124
Hayworth, Rita 90
Head, Edith 220
Heathcote, Thomas 244–
    245
The Heavies (book) 109, 195
Hecht, Ben 149, 154–155,
    272, 276, 277
Hecht, Harold 98
Hedley, Jack 243
Hedrick, Earl 220

Heflin, Van **31**–32, 194–195
Hehr, Addison 224
The Heiress 213
Helen of Troy 53
Heller, Lukas 251
Hellman, Richard 248
Helm, Peter 275
Helmer, Karl 243
Helton, Percy 198–199, 202, 220
Hemingway, Ernest 87, 111–113, 275
Hemmings, David 260
Hempstead, David 17, 181, 184
Henley, David 247
Henry, Buzz 256
Henry, William 179
Hepburn, Katharine xiv, **112**, 113, 115, 122, 271, 282
Her Twelve Men 74, 221
Herbstman, Mandel 255
Herman, Al 180, 182, 183, 189, 191, 213
Herridge, Frances 262
Herrmann, Bernard 208–209
Herrnfeld, Kurt 253
Herzbrun, Bernard 214
Heston, Charlton 128
Heydt, Louis Jean 184
Heyman, Edward 250
Hickey and Boggs 280
Hickman, Darryl 198
Hickman, Dwayne 195
Hicks, Russell 179
Hidden Witness (tv) 274
High Noon 194
Higham, Charles 27, 198
Hildyard, David 246
Hill, James 258
Hillerman, John 258–259
Hinds, Samuel S. 195
Hines, Patrick 271
Hinz, Werner 243
Hirsch, Foster 27, 60
Hitchcock, Alfred 46
Hitchcock, Claude 251
Hobson, Laura A. 221
Hodgins, Earle 193
Hoffman, Herman 222
Hoffman, Paul 237
Hoffmann, Walter xiv
Hogan, James 179, 180
Hogan, Michael 187
Holden, William 128, **146**, 154, 256–257

Hollander, Frederick 191, 196
Holliman, Earl 219, 255
Holloway, Dona 250
Hollywood in the Fifties 85
Hollywood in the Forties 39, 198
Hollywood Quarterly 24–25, 188
Hollywood Reporter 51
Holm, John Cecil 271
Holmes, Taylor 194, 213
Holt, Nat 186, 192
Holt, Will 253
Homes, Geoffrey 219
Hoover, J. Edgar 179
Hope, Bob 179
Hopkins, Anthony 244
Hopkins, Bo 256
Hopkins, George James 240, 260
Hopper, Hedda 29, 179
Hopper, Jerry 219
Horizons West 70–71, 214–216
Horner, Harry 64, 213–214, 281
Horowitz, Gary 263
Hossein, Robert 248
Hotchner, A.E. 275
Hough, Stanley 226
Hour of the Gun 98, 139–**140**, 251–252
House, Billy 186, 187
House Committee on Un-American Activities 28, 31, 57, 97, 128, 184–185, 196
House, Lionel 202
House of Bamboo 59, **81**–83, 224–226, 261, 281
Houseman, John xi, xiv, 4, 25, 39–40, 49–51, 74, 78–79, 87, 102, 110, 131, 145, 174, 208–210, 221, 271
Houston, Donald 243
Houston, Norman 186
How Green Was My Valley 107
How Red Was My Valley: Hollywood, the Cold War Film (article) 202
Howard, John 180
Howard, Kathleen 203
Howard, Noel 241
Howard, Trevor 120
Hoyos, Rodolpho 275
Hoyt, John 110, 271–273

Hubbard, John 214
Hubley, Season 262
Hudson, Rock 214–215
Hughes, Howard 13, 33–35, 37, 42–43, 56–57, 60, 69, 94, 198, 200, 204, 207
Hughes, Tresa 262
Hull, Henry 218–219
Hume, Alan 258
Hunnicut, Gayle 260
Hunt, J. Roy 186, 187, 189, 193
Hunt, Marsha 82
Hunt, Norman 108
Hunter, Evan 276
Hunter, Jeffrey 85, 116, 227–228, 241–242, 243, 253
Hunter, Kim 99, 184–185, 274
Hunter, Thomas 255
Hurst, Richard 263
Hussey, Ruth 19, 184–186
Huston, Virginia 207
Hutchinson, Max 196
Hutchinson, W.E. 251
Hutton, Robert 207
Hyams, Joe 86
Hyer, Martha 187, 240
Hyland, Diana 276
Hyman, Earle 271
Hyman, Kenneth 250
Hymer, Warren 183

I

I Lost It at the Movies (book) 120
I Married a Communist (The Woman on Pier 13) 13, 42–**43, 44**–45, 56, 60, 200–202, 205, 281
Ibbetson, Arthur 241
Ice Palace 111, 239–241
The Iceman Cometh (recording) 277
The Iceman Cometh xiii, 39, 165–**168, 169**, 266–269, 278, 282
Idiot's Delight (play) 149
Ihnat, Steve 252
Indrisano, John 36–37, 198
Inferno 71, **73**, 85, 218–219
Ingels, Marty 250
Ingram, Rex 231
The Inheritance (narration) 128–131, 269–270, 277

Interpretations of Life (book) 141
Interrogation (tv) 275
Ireland, John 92, 252, 271
The Iron Major 17–18, 184
Irving, Richard 208–209
It's a Hell of a Life, but Not a Bad Living (book) 12
Ives, Burl 128, 236–237

J

J.B. (play) 149
Jacks, Robert L. 227
Jackson, Anne 149
Jackson, Michael 260
Jackson, Warren 193
Jaeckel, Richard 139, 172, 251, 265
Jaffa, Henri 180
Jaffe, Steve 263
Jagger, Dean 222–223
James, Clifton 271
Jane Eyre 42
Janis, Conrad 152, 272
Janssen, David 274
Janssen, Eilene 220
Japrisot, Sebastian 261
Jarre, Maurice 206, 243, 249
Jarrico, Paul 28
Jeffreys, Anne 186, 193
Jennings, Al 221
Jennings, Gordon 180
Jennings, Talbot 223
Jenson, Roy 265
Jessel, George 250
Jewell, Richard B. 204
Jiras, Robert 237
The John Bernard Story (tv) 275
John Birch Society 117–118
Johnson, Ben 146, 256
Johnson, Lamont xiv, 48–49, 57, 62, 65–67, 82, 84, 102, 105, 110–111, 161, 169, 282
Johnson, Lyndon 145, 173, 264
Johnson, Nunnaly 251
Johnson, Toni 65
Johnstone, Anna Hill 237
Johnstone, Edward 237
Jolle, Colonel Sherman 246
Jolley, Stanford 227, 240
Jones, Carolyn 240–241
Jones, Henry 265

Jones, Isaac 220
Jones, James 243
Jones, James Earl 124
Jones, L.Q. 95, 146, 230, 256
Jones, Penn, Jr. 263
Jones, Robert 252
Jones, Stanley 240
Jordan, Richard 258–259
Josia, Guido 254
Journal of Contemporary History 202
Joy, Leatrice 179
Joy, William 184
Joyce, James 87, 113
Joyce, Stephen 271
Juno and the Paycock (play) 282
Jurgens, Curt 243

K

Kael, Pauline 34–35, 80, 120, 170, 197, 223, 268
Kalmus, Natalie 180, 195
Kandel, Aben 184
Kanter, Hal 220
Kaper, Bronislau 194, 216–217, 221
Kaplan, Abbott 100–102
Karlan, Richard 207
Kasdan, Lawrence 280
Kass, Robert 219
Kauffmann, Stanley 101, 117, 234
Kaufman, Millard 222
Kazan, Elia 131
Keach, Stacy 162, 272
Keating, John 79
Keating, Larry 218–219
Keats, John 35
Keene, Tom 26, 189, 191, 193
Keith, Brian 219–220
Keith, Robert 230
Keller, Walter E. 185, 187, 200
Kelley, Barry 206, 240
Kelley, DeForrest 81, 224–225
Kelley, Walter 230
Kellin, Mike 101
Kellum, Terry 181, 182, 183, 193
Kelly, Gene 149
Kelly, Paul 179, 189–190, 202

Kemmer, Ed 263
Kemper, Charles 52, 54, 208–209
Kemper, Doris 275
Kenneally, Phil 172, 265
Kennedy, Adam 230
Kennedy, Arthur 86, 254–256
Kennedy, Burt 241
Kennedy, George 139, 251
Kennedy, Harold J. xiv, 68, 90, 92–93, 150–155, 158, 163, 271–272, 276, 277
Kennedy, John F. 108, 125, 129, 173–174, 263–265
Kennedy, Robert 145
Kent, Ted J. 214
Kerr, Donald 198
Kerr, Walter 161
Kerz, Leo 237
Kibbee, Roland 276
Kilian, Victor 184
Killens, John O. 237–239
The Killers 253
Killy, Edward 180, 184, 185, 198
Kimlin, Newell 222
King and Country 32, 196
King, Brett 206, 207
King, Henry 228
King, Dennis, Jr. 273
King, Major Edward 246
King, Martin Luther 145
King of Kings 115–116, 241–243, 278
Kingsley, Sidney 68
Kipling, Richard 219
Kirgo, Julie 281
Kirk, Mark Lee 226
Kirk, Phyllis 228–229
Kirkpatrick, Jess 198
Kish, Joe 214
A Kiss for Cinderella (play) 12–13, 271
Kiss, Kiss, Bang, Bang 197, 223
Kissel, Gil 240
Kitses, Jim 71
Kitty Foyle 184
Kleiner, Harry 224–225, 239
Kleinsinger, George 269
Klugman, Jack 271
Knapp, Charles 265
Knight, Arthur 116, 240–241
Knight, Shirley 240

Knox, Alexander 117, 243
Knudtson, Frederick 203
Knute Rockne — All American
  17
Kobe, Gail 273
Koerner, Charles 29
Kolb, Clarence 181
Korda, Vincent 243
Kornfeld, Barry 269
Kortner, Fritz 191
Korvin, Charles **29**, 191–192
Korwin, Norman 69
Koslo, Paul 262
Kraft Suspense Theatre (tv)
  275
Kram, Arthur 220
Krasker, Robert 244–245
Krasna, Norman 69, 211
Krasner, Milton 37, 198–
  199, 241
Kreidl, James 51
Kreig, Frank 211
Kress, Harold 241, 267
Krizman, Serge 234
Kroeger, Berry 194
Krumgold, Sigmond 179
Kuller, Morine 65
Kuller, Sid 65
Kuluva, Will 237

L

La Blanche, Ernest E. 184
Ladel, Norman 125
Lai, Francis 261–262
Lambert, Jack 236
Lamont, Jack O. 247
Lampell, Millard xiv, 89–
  90, 98, 105, 109, 122, 127–
  129, 131–133, 136, 142, 144,
  158, 164, 176, 269
Lampert, Zohra 237, 239
Lancaster, Burt 28, 32, 63,
  74, 98, 128, 138, 155, 157,
  173–174, 175, 249–250,
  252, 258–260, 263–265
Landau, Ely 267
Landon, Harold 180
Landon, Michael **96**, 231
Lane, Charles 180
Lane, James 195
Lane, Mark 173–174, 263
Lang, Charles B. 260
Lang, Fritz 68–69, 211, 279,
  281, 282
Langella, Frank 159

Lardine, Bob 109
Lardner, Ring, Jr. 29, 63,
  124
Larkin, John 275
Larsen, Tambi 265
Lasky, Jesse, Jr. 180
The Last American Hero 48
The Last Leaf (recording)
  277
The Last of the Westerners
  (narration) 277
Last Tango in Paris 268
LaStarza, Roland 265
Lastricate, Carlo 241
Laszlo, Aladar 182
Laszlo, Ernest 220
Lathrop, Philip 262
Latimer, Jonathan 228
Laure, Frank 234
Laurents, Arthur 196
Lauter, Ed 164, 262–263
Lauter, Harry 207
Lavery, Emmet 181
Law, John Philip 260–261
Lawford, Peter 181, 243
Lawman 155–**157**, 258–260
Lawrence, André 261
Lawrence, Barbara 221
Lawrence, Bob 244
Lawrence, Marc 253
Lawrence, Robert 236
Leab, Daniel J. 202
Leachman, Cloris 273
Lease, Rex 228
Le Blanc, Lee 241
Lee, Johnny 273
Lee, Peggy 67
Lee, Ruth 208
Lehmann, Olga 258
Leicester, James 223
Leigh, Janet xiv, 32, 71–**72**,
  194, 216–218
LeMay, Alan 180
Lemmon, Jack 92, 268, 273
Leonard, Archie 198
Leonard, Jack R. 202
Leonard, Robert Z. 221
Leonard, William Torbert vii
Lerner, Irving 253, 263
Lerpae, Paul K. 250
Leslie, Joan 181, 203–204
Leslie, Nan 187–188
Leurn, Borys 248
Leutzinger, Ted R. xiv
Levene, Sam **28**, 189–190
Levinson, Nate 189, 191
Levitt, Alfred Lewis 195

Lew, Shirley 182
Lewin, Esther 107
Lewis, Blake 200
Lewis, Edward 98, 165, 173,
  263–264
Lewis, Forrest 273
Lewis, Gene 186
Lewis, Harold 250
Lewis, John 237–239
Lewis, Ronald 244–245
Lewis, Ted 258
Lewthwaite, Bill 258
Liberatore, Ugo 254
Life 116
Lifton, David 263
Lincoln's Doctor's Bag (tv) 273
Lindfors, Viveca 241
Lindgren, Harry M. 180
Lindsay, Howard 122, 271
Lindsay, Mark 260
Lipman, William R. 179, 180
Lipton, David 65
Lipton, Sylvia 65
Little Sky, Eddie 249
Lizzani, Carlo 248
Llewellyn, Russell 240
Lloyd, Doris 271
Loeffler, Louis 226
Logan, Joshua 122, 271, 277
Lohman, Augie 243
Lolly Madonna XXX 164–
  165, 262–263
Lombardo, Louis 256
London Financial Times 269
London, Jack vii
London Observer 269
Lonely Are the Brave 259
Lonelyhearts **100**, 100–101,
  109, 234–236, 278
Long Day's Journey into Night
  59, 139–142, 159–162, 272
*Long Day's Journey into
  Night* (recording) 277
The Longest Day 116,
  117–118, 242–243, 278
Lontoc, Leon 215
Loo, Richard 182
Lopez, Perry 275
Lopez, Trini 251
Lord, Jack 97, 231–233
Lorentz, Pare 14–15
Los Angeles Reader 37
Los Angeles Times 172, 257,
  268
Losey, Joseph 32, 63, 195
Louise, Tina **102**, 231–233,
  236–237

Lourie, Eugene 246, 253
The Love Machine 159, 260–261
Love, Montagu 180
Low, Jack 227
Low, Warren 220
Lowe, David 151
Loy, Myrna **100**, 128, 234–236
Lubin, A. Ronald 243
Luciano, Michael 196, 251
Luckham, Cyril 244
Lukas, Paul 179, 191–192
Lundigan, William 218
Lupino, Ida 50–51, **70**, 208, 210, 213–214
Lyon, Richard 195
Lyons, Jeffrey 165, 263
Lytton, Herbert 275

M

Mabry, Moss 260
McAnally, Ray 244
Macalastry, Mary 4
MacArthur, Charles 149, 154–155, 272, 276, 277
MacArthur, James 246
McBain, Diane 240
Macbeth (play) 78
McCallum, David 244–245
McCallum, Gordon 246
McCambridge, Mercedes 107
McCarthy, Eugene 145
McCarthy, Joseph 49, 57, 97, 109
McCoy, Horace 179, 180
McDermott, Hugh 258
McDonald, Francis 180
MacDonald, Joe 224
MacDonald, Kenneth 189, 193
MacDonald, Robert 243
McDowall, Roddy 117, 243
McEveety, Vincent 259
McGarry, William 265
MacGinnis, Niall 244
McGiver, John 149, 151–152, 155, 258–259, 272, 276
McGivern, William P. 237
MacGowan, Kenneth 102
McGrath, Frank 276
McGraw, Charles 139, 191, 250
McGreevey, Michael 236
MacKenzie, Joyce 207

McKinney, Bill 265
McLaglen, Victor 179
MacLane, Barton 180–181, 185, 205
MacLean, Fred 222
McLeod, Catherine 274
McLiam, John 166, 267
MacMurray, Fred 12
Mad with Much Heart (novel) 50, 208
Mademoiselle 22
Maeterlinck (play) 9
Magee, Audrie 250
Magee, Patrick 255
The Magnificent Ambersons 15
Maguire, Charles 237
Majewski, Virginia 208–209
Major Barbara (play) 82
Major Dundee 256
Maltin, Leonard 39, 60, 98, 101, 156, 224
Mamakos, Peter 214, 216
Man of the West 259
The Man Who Asked Why (novel) 22
The Man Without a Country (tv) 172, 276
The Manchurian Candidate 165, 268
Mangione, Giuseppe 255
Mankiewicz, Herman 42, 201
Mann Anthony 70–71, 94, 97, 158, 216, 218, 229–231, 259, 280
Mann, Daniel 74, 220
Mann, Delbert 102, 172, 276
Mansfield, Irving 260
Mantley, John 202
Mara, Adele 228
March, Fredric 128, 145, 165–169, 267, 269, 277
March, Joseph Moncure 38, 198
March Lori 271
Marcuse, Theodore 271
Marden, Adrienne 218
Mardiguian, G. 248
Margo 182, 183
Marine Raiders 15, 19–**20**, 23, 94, 185–186, 189
Marker, Harry 202
Markham, Monte 252
Markle, Fletcher 107
Marley, John 274
Marlowe, Scott 230

Marquand, Christian 243
Marquette, Desmond 205
Marsac, Maurice 241
Marshal, Alan 236–237
Marshall, E.G. 138
Marshall, George 179
Marshek, Artie 219
Martell, Jack 249
Martien, Bob 236
Martien, Eva H. 236
Martin, Chito 180
Martin, Dean 67
Martin, Douglas D. 251
Martin, Eugene 274
Martin, Kiel 166, 262–263
Martin, Philip, Jr. 184, 185
Martin, Richard 184, 185
Martin, Strother 146, 256
Martinez, Joaquin 263
Martinez, Jorge 249
Marton, Andrew 242
Marvin, Lee 75–**76**, 107, 138, 165–168, 222–223, 249, 250, 251, 267
Marx, Groucho 128
Mason, James 196–197, 258
Massari, Lea 261–262
Massey, Raymond 97
Mateos, Antonio 253
Mathers, Lester 200
Mathews, George 215–216, 227–228
Matthau, Walter 282
Maugham, W. Somerset 10, 87, 271
Maumont, Jacques 243
Max, Edwin 198
Maxwell, Frank 234–235
Mayer, Harold xiv, 128–129, 269
Mayer, Louis B. 63
Mayer, Lynne xiv, 128–129, 269
Mayo, Archie 4, 179
Mayo, Virginia 85, **88,** 227
Mazurki, Mike 16, **18,** 182
Meade, Julia 154, 272
Meadows, Jayne 107–108
Meadows, Roy 184
Mean Streets 268
Medford, Harry 191
Medford, Kay 250
Medwin, Michael 243
Meeker, Ralph 71–**72**, 139, 216–218, 251
Meillon, John 244–245
Meisel, Myron 37

Mellen, Joan 40
Mellin, Robert 248
Mellor, William 216–217,
  219, 222–223, 228–229
Melville, Herman 120, 244–
  245
Men in War 66, 94–**95**,
  229–231, 278
The Men 32
Menczer, Enrico 248
Mendelson, Anthony 244
Menjou, Adolphe 29
Merande, Doro 152, 272
Mercer, Johnny 181
Meredith, Charles 195, 228
Meredith, Madge 186
Metcalfe, Burt 241
Metty, Russell 181, 182, 184
Meyer, Emile 172, 226, 265
Meyer, Richard C. 229, 231
Meyers, Ted 260
Middleton, Robert 227
Midnight Lace 264
A Midsummer's Night Dream
  (play) 9
Miles, Vera 276
Milland, Ray 12
Millar, Marjie 220
Miller, David 173, 175, 259,
  263–264
Miller, Dick 263
Miller, Harley 185
Miller, Michael 230
Miller, Mitch 243
Miller, Robert J. 256
Miller, Sidney 179
Millican, James 179
Mills, Jack 211, 250
Mills, Richard 258
Milner, Victor 180
Milton, Franklin 241, 251
Minciotti, Silvio 211
Mineo, Sal 243
Mintz, Jeffrey vii
A Minute to Pray, A Second
  to Die 139, 142–**143**, 254–
  255
Miracle on 34th Street 27
Mishkin, Leo 17–18
Miss Lonelyhearts (book)
  234
Mister Dooley 107
Mr. Klein 32
Mr. President 122, **123**, 124–
  126, 139, 271, 277
Mrs. Miniver 74
Mitchell, Cameron 224–

225, 226
Mitchell, Millard 71–**72,**
  216–218
Mitchum, Robert 28, 31,
  60, 63, 117, 131, 157, 189–
  190, 207, 208, 212, 243,
  255
Mizzy, Vic 250
Moder, Mike 262
Modern Jazz Quartet 239
Molieri, Lillian 214
Molina, Julio 253
Monroe, Marilyn 69, 211
Monroe, Tom 214
Montague, Lee **119**, 244–
  245
Montell, Lisa 223
Montgomery, George 246
Montgomery, Robert 29
Montoya, Alex 223, 228
Moore, Archie 172, 265
Moore, Cleo 208–209
Moore, Kieron 253
Moorhouse, Bert 202
More, Kenneth 243
Moreland, Betsy Jones 236
Moreno, Rita 118
Morgan, Henry Harry 220
Morgan, James 221
Morganstern, Joseph 153
Morley, Christopher 273
Morris, George 51
Morris, Johnny 179
Morrison, Barbara 216
Morrow, Vic **96**–97,
  230–231, 234
Mosconi, Willie 133
Mother Courage (play) 102
Movies on TV 216
Moyer, Ray 258
Mozsa, Miklos 241
Muirhead, Janice vii
A Mule for the Marquesa
  (novel) 248
Mullavey, Greg 260
Murder in the Cathedral
  (play) 110, 271
Murphy, Tom 159
Murray, Don 108
Murray, Jan 139, 250
Murton, Peter 244
Musuraca, Nicholas 180,
  183, 185, 200, 203, 211
Mutiny on the Bounty 120
My Life and My Films
  (book) 188
Myrow, Fred 262

N

Nabokov, Nadine 261
Naish, J. Carrol 68, 179,
  182, 211–212
The Naked City 48
The Naked Spur 70–71, **72**,
  216–218, 278
Name, Age, and Occupation
  14–15
Napier, Alan 110, 271
Nathan, George Jean 170
Nathanson, E.M. 251
Nation 186, 191, 200, 210,
  212, 218, 223, 239
National Committee for a
  Sane Nuclear Policy
  (SANE) 99, 106–109, 132
National Society of Film
  Critics 268
Natteford, Jack 192
Natwick, Mildred 271
Naughton, James 162, 272
Navarro, Anna 273
Nay, Ben 263
Neal, Tom 182
Nelson, David 236
Nelson, Dick 276
Nelson, John 246
Nemoy, Maury 260
Nervig, Conrad A. 194
Ness, Edward 265
Neville, John 121, 139, 244–
  245
New Republic 26, 101, 117,
  200, 210, 234
New York 253–254, 266
New York Daily Mirror 183
New York Daily News 260,
  263
New York Herald Tribune
  24, 79, 99, 111, 186, 191, 192,
  193, 196, 197, 201, 203, 206,
  214, 215, 223, 226, 231,
  236, 239, 241, 246, 248
New York Morning Telegram
  17–18
New York Post 262, 266
New York Sunday News 109
New York Times 14, 79, 99,
  114, 125, 130, 132, 141, 151,
  153, 154, 156, 161, 172, 186,
  188, 191, 192, 193, 195, 198,
  201, 203, 205, 206, 210,
  212, 215, 218, 219, 220,
  226, 227, 228, 231, 233,
  235–236, 239, 245, 250,

251, 252, 255, 257, 260, 261, 264, 265, 269
New York World Journal Tribune 248, 249–250
New York World Telegram and Sun 125, 212
New Yorker 150, 268
Newill, James 180
Newman, Lionel 227
Newman, Nanette 258
Newman, Paul 102, 282
Newsweek 153, 170, 268
Newton, Marianna 107
Nicholson, Emrich 215
Nicol, Alex 220, 274
Nielson, Leslie 276
Nightmare Alley 27
Niven, David 92, 273
Nixon, Richard 145
No Pickle, No Performance (book) 90
None So Blind 187–188
Norin, Gus 196
Norman, Maidie 220
Normand, Robert 230
Norris, Jay 187, 189
North, Edmund 227
North, Sheree 155, 258–259, 265
Northwest Mounted Police 12, 179–180
Nosseck, Ralph 258
Nottingham Playhouse 139
Nourse, Allen 237
Novello, Jay 275
Nugent, Frank 226

O

Oakwood School 65–67, 71, 79, 82, 93–94, 99, 102, 282
Oates, Warren 146, 256
Obeler, Arch 182
Ober, Philip **47**, 202–203, 220
Oberon, Merle **29**, 31, 191–192
O'Brien, Edmond 117, 138, 146, 243, 256–257
O'Brien, Pat 15–17, **18**, 19, 32, 136, 180, 181, 184–185, 195–196
O'Casey, Sean 282
Ochoa, Jose Maria 241, 253
O'Connell, Arthur 227–228
O'Connor, John 172

O'Day, Anita 265
Odds Against Tomorrow 59, 103, **104**–105, 237–239, 265, 281
Odets, Clifford 13, 29, 211, 271
Odetta 144–145
Odlum, Floyd 37
Of Human Bondage 42
O'Hanlon, James 202
O'Hara, Shirley 26
O'Henry 277
Okey, Jack 198, 203, 207
Oliver, Edith 150
Olivier, Laurence 46
O'Morrison, Kenny 198
On Dangerous Ground 48–**52**, **53**–54, 56–57, 60, 64, 69, 208–210, 281
On Edge (tv) 92, 273
On the Beach 106
One Man's America (book) 141
One on One 48
O'Neal, Charles 192
O'Neill, Eugene 62, 107, 139–141, 159, 165, 167, 170, 267–268, 272, 277
Ophuls, Max 33–35, 56, 99, 196–197, 279, 281
Oremback, Al 213
Orlandi, Felice 265
O'Rourke, Frank 248–249
Orry-Kelly 191
Ortega, Leon 258
Ortolani, Riz 255
Osbiston, Alan 248
Osborne, Bud 193
Osmond, Cliff 275
Ostrer, Bertram 258
O'Sullivan, Maureen 171, 173, 175–176
Othello 78, 141–142, 272
Our Town 149–150, 272
The Outfit 172, 265–266, 280, 281
Overman, Lynn 180
Overton, Frank 234

P

Pacino, Al 268
Padelford, Morgan 195
Page, Gale 220
Paige, Robert 179
Paiva, Nestor 208–209
Palance, Jack 138, 249

Paley, Jesse 269
Pallos, Steven 258
Paniagua, Cecilio 253
Paris, Jerry 220
Parolin, Alace 254
Parrish, Anne 203–204
Parrish, Robert 196
Parslow, Philip P. 260
Parsons, Derek 246
Parsons, Estelle 149, 155, 272, 276
Parsons, Harriet 211
Pass It On 269
Pate, Michael 241, 274
Patterson, Elizabeth 181
Pawley, Charles 187
Paxton, John 25, 189–190
Paxton, Tom 269
Payne, Jim 262
Paynter, Bob 258
Peace or Atomic War (book) 106
Peck, Ann 228
Peck, Gregory 128
Peckinpah, Sam 145–147, 153, 256–257
Pedi, Tom 267
Peper, William 248
Pepper, Barbara 218
Pereira, Hal 220, 250
The Perfectionist (tv) 274
Pericoli, Ugo 255
Perkins, Kenneth 223
Perkins, Osgood 153
Perna, David 252
Perry, Harry 191
Persin, Henri 243
Persoff, Nehemiah 230, 236
Persons in Hiding (novel) 179
Peter Gunn (tv) 48
Peters, Brock 275
Peters, Hans 193
Peters, Ralph 207
Peters, Scott 241
Peters, Werner 246
Petit, Pierre 248
Petracca, Joseph 227
Petrie, Howard 207, 273
Philadelphia Bulletin 124
Philadelphia Inquirer 261
Phillips, Robert 252
Phillips, W.H. 200
Phipps, William 189
Photoplay 22, 26, 184, 187, 200, 208, 221, 224, 227, 228
Pianthodosi, Arthur 260
Pickett, Clarence 106

Pihodna, Joa 205
Pine, Philip 198, 230–231
Pine, William H. 179
Pinky 107
Pirandello (play) 9
Planer, Franz 241
Platt, Edward 227–228, 274
Playboy 156, 260
Playhouse 90 (tv) 98, 274
Plumstead Playhouse 149–151
The Poetry of Wallace Stevens (narration) 277
The Poetry of Walt Whitman (narration) 277
Poitier, Sidney 132
Polglase, Van Nest 223
Polin, Jack 236
Polin, Robert 263
Polk, Rudolph 196
Pollack, Dee 213
Poore, Dan 214
Poplin, John S., Jr. 231
Porfirio, Robert 64, 210, 214
Port Royal, the Ghost City Beneath the Sea (book) 215
Porter, Don 152, 207
Portman, Clem 187, 189, 191, 195, 198, 200
The Postman Always Rings Twice 280
Potter, H.C. 85, 273
Poulton, Charles 244
Powell, Dilys 265
Powell, Jane 92, 273
Power, Tyrone 27, 97
Powers, Mala 215–216
Powers, Tom 214
Preiss, Wolfgang 243, 255
Prentiss, Paula 152
Prescetelli, Fernando 254
Prest, Pat 206, 208
Preston, Robert 56, 180, 205–206
Preston, Wayde 255
Previn, André 194, 222–223
Price, Vincent 97
Price, Will 187
Prine, Andrew 276
Pringle, George A. 180
Pritchard, Herbert 214
The Private Eye, the Cowboy, and the Very Naked Girl (book) 138
The Professionals **137**–139, 248–250, 278
The Proud Ones 85, **88,** 227–228

Provost, Jon 228–229
Prud'Homme, Cameron 228–229
Pryor, Richard 250
Puglia, Frank 184
Puig, Eva 180
Purple Noon 262
Pursall, David 243
Putnam, Jock 263

Q

Quaid, Randy 262–263
Quarry, Robert 224
Quayle, Anthony 120, 139
Queen of the Mob 12, 179
Quinn, Anthony 70, 102, 179, 180, 215–216
Quinn, Frank 183, 233
Quinn, Howard 202

R

Rabin, Jack 231
The Racket 59–60, **61,** 207–208, 278, 281
Rackin, Martin 180, 185
Rafferty, Frances 274
Ragin, John 271
Raguse, Richard 265
Rainer, Luise 12, 271
Raitt, John 118
Randall, William, Jr. 249
Randell, Ron 241–242, 243
Randolph, John 271
Rathvon, N.P. 190
Rawlings, Terence 258
Ray, Aldo 94–**95,** 97, 229–231, 231–233, 261
Ray, Anthony 230
Ray, Lois 227
Ray, Nicholas 42–43, 49–51, 53, 56–57, 60, 115, 201–202, 203–204, 206, 207–210, 241–242, 280, 281
Raymonds, Jack 198
Read, Herbert 79
Reagan, Ronald 143
Rebecca 46
Red River 257
Reed, Rex 263
Reed, Robert 138
Reed, Walter 180, 181, 193, 214–215
Reeling (book) 170

Reese, Tom 265
Reeves, Richard 207
Reifsnider, Lyle B. 231, 236
Reilly, Walter 234
Reincke, Heinz 243
Reinhardt, Max 9, **10,** 64, 153, 171–172
Reinhardt, Wolfgang 196
Reisberg, Harry E. 215
Reiss, Stuart A. 224
Renateau, Gerard 243
Renie 193
Renoir, Jean **22**–23, 29, 183, 187–189, 280, 281
Return of the Badmen **30,** 32, 56, 186, 192–193, 205, 278
Reynolds, Adeline 182
Rice, Charles J. 249
Richard, Edmond 261–262
Richards, Lloyd 183
Richards, Paul 130, 275
Richards, Robert L. 193
Richardson, Cliff 251
Rider on the Rain 262
Riley, Jeannine 265
Rios, Lalo 215
Risdon, Elisabeth **47,** 202
Riste, Tom 214
The RKO Story (book) 204
Roarke, Adam 275
Robards, Jason, Jr. 139, 152, 176, 252
Robards, Jason, Sr. 186, 193
Rober, Richard 200
Roberts, Roy 172, 265
Roberts, Steve 208
Roberts, William 221
Robertson, Cliff 172, 276
Robertson, Douglas 241
Robinson, Edward G. 40, 77
Robson, Mark 198
Robson, May 180
Rock (magazine) 263
Rodero, Jose Lopez 241, 246
Roelofs, Al 250
Roerick, William 260
Rogell, Sid 49–50, 200, 202
Rogers, Ginger 17, 19, 181, 184
Rogers, Grayson 186, 193
Rogers, Lela 185
Rogers, Paul 121, 139, 244–245
Rogow, Lee 221

Rolf, Tom 262
Rolfe, Guy 241
Rolfe, Sam 216
Romero, Carlos 249
Romero, Ramon 215
Romus, Jerome 255
Roope, Fay 219, 227
Roosevelt, Franklin 14
Root, Lynn 181
Rootes, Maurice 253
Rosenstein, Carol 263
Ross, Anthony **52**, 208–209
Ross, Arthur 107
Ross, George 236
Ross, Katharine 275
Rossen, Robert 198, 244
Rossington, Norman 243
Rosson, Arthur 179
Rotunno, Giuseppe 255
Royal Canadian Mounted Police 12, 180
Ruiz, Julian 253
Rule, Janice 275
Runaway Train 54
Running Time: Films of the Cold War (book) 27
Ruskin, Joseph 271
Russek, Jorge 252, 256
Russell, Jane 84–86, 226–227
Russell, William D. 205–206
Rustichelli, Carlo 254
Rutenberg, Joseph 221
Rutolo, Carla 269
Ryan, Cheyney xiv, 17, 33, 64, 68, 82, 85, 87, 113, 118–119, 127, 133, 139, 143–144, 164, 175–176
Ryan, Cornelius 242–243
Ryan, Dick 202, 203
Ryan, Irene 187
Ryan, Jessica xiv, **10**, 22–23, 33, 61, 63–68, 71, 87–90, 105, 113, 117–119, 122, 129, 130, 132, 142, 144, 157, 159–160, 162, 166, 171, 286
Ryan, Lisa xiv, 67, 87–89, 105, 113, 118–119, 124, 129, 133, 139, 142, 152, 175–176
Ryan, Mabel 3–4, 7–8, 126
Ryan, Timothy (father) 3–4, **5**, 7
Ryan, Timothy (son) xiv, 23, 64, 68, 81, 84, 87, 98, 113, 118–119, 127, 133, 136,

139, 143–145, 164, 175–176
Ryan, Vickie 113
Ryen, Richard 183

S

Sacristan, Martin 246
Saint, Eva Marie 102
Saks, Gene 271
Sale, Virginia 186
Salinger, Conrad 234
Salmaggi, Bob 248
Salmi, Albert 155, 252, 258–259
Sam Benedict (tv) 138
Sanchez, Jaime 146, 256
Sande, Walter 187, 207, 222
Sanders, Hugh 206
Sands, Tommy 243, 276
SANE (National Committee for a Sane Nuclear Policy) 99, 106–109, 132
Sanford, Erskine 200
Santoni, Reni 255
Sarafian, Richard 164–165, 262–263
Saroyan, William 149, 151, 272
Sarris, Andrew 257
Saturday Review 106, 116, 221, 231, 240–241
Savalas, Telly 246, 251
Save the Tiger 268
Saviola, Kevin 262
Sawtell, Paul 186, 193
Sayre, Nora 27, 265, 269
Scaccianoce, Luigi 255
Scaife, Edward 251
The Scene (guest appearance) 143, 277
Schaefer, Natalie 196
Schaffner, Franklin 99, 274
Schallert, William 236, 252
Schappert, Elizabeth xiv, 79
Schary, Dore 25, 28–29, 37, 57, 99, 102, 109, 176, 189–190, 191–192, 195–196, 198, 222–223, 234–236
Schaumer, Ed 227
Schenk, Nick 222
Scheuer, Steven H. 216
Schiffer, Robert 249
Schildkraut, Joseph 13–14, 68, 271

Schilling, Gus **52**, 208–209
Schlom, Herbert 205
Schmidt, Arthur 179, 180
Schmidt, Thomas 252
Scholl, Jack 180
Scholl, Jerome 180
Schrader, Paul 146–137, 257
Schulman, Leo Morton 196
Schunzel, Reinhold 191
Schuster, Harold 185
Schweitzer, Albert 106
Scollay, Fred J. 237
Scott, Adrian 25, 28, 30, 63, 189
Scott, Lizabeth 207
Scott, Martha 149–151, 155, 272, 276
Scott, Pippa 110, 271, 276
Scott, Randolph 21, 186, 193
Scott, Timothy 262
Scott, Walter 258
Scott, Walter M. 224
Scott, Zachary 203–204
Scourby, Alexander 275
Screen Directors' Playhouse 85, 273
The Searchers 257
Seaton, George 282
Seay, George 179
Seconds 165
The Secret Fury **43**, 202–203
Seddon, Jack 243
Seeger, Pete 130, 144, 269
Segal, George 152
Segall, Bernardo 253
Seiderman, Maurice 231
Seligman, Selig J. 254
Sen Yung, Victor 230
Serling, Rod 107
Serpico 268
Servais, Jean 243
The Set-up **36**–41, 50, 53, 82, 105, 115, 198–200, 230, 278, 281
Seven Men from Now 214
The Seventh Letter (tv) 92, 274
Sevilla, Carmen 241
Shakespeare, William 78, 113–115, 141, 174, 271, 272
Shane 257
Shane, Maxwell 179
Shannon, Harry 193, 226
Shannon, Richard 219
Sharp, Henry 179

Shaw, David 99, 274
Shaw, George Bernard 4, 82
Shaw, Robert 135, 246, 253–254
Shaw, Tom 249
Shearer, Douglas 194
Shenandoah (play) 173
Sheppard, Jim 252
Sherman, Vincent 239–240
Shilton, Len 244
Shimada, Teru 224
Shipman, David 74, 121
Shirley, Anne 180
Shoup, Howard 240
Showmens' Trade Review 198, 210
Sickner, Roy N. 256
Siegel, Don 280
Siegfried, Sibylle 251
Sight and Sound 221
Silberman, Serge 261–262
Silhouette of a Killer (tv) 92, 273
Silk, Lawrence 269
Silver, Charles vii
Silver, David 224
Silvera, Darrell 180, 181, 182, 183, 184, 185, 187, 188, 191, 193, 195, 198, 200, 213, 234
Silverstein, Elliott 275
Simon, Paul 124
Simpson, Robert 218
Simpson, Russell 226
Siodmak, Curt 191
Siodmak, Robert 252–253
Sister Beatrice (play) 9
Sivel, William 243
Six Characters in Search of an Author (play) 9
Skirball, Jack 202
Skolsky, Sidney 76
The Sky's the Limit 16–17, 278
Slack, Freddie 181
Slaff, George xiv
Slattery's People (tv) 138
Slavin, George F. 200–202
Smith, Art 196
Smith, Basil Fenton 241
Smith, Solomon 33, 118–119, 122
Smith, Williana 33, 118–119, 122
Smith, William 276
Smyth, Tim 262

The Snows of Kilimanjaro (tv) 111, 275
Snyder, William E. 206
Soderlund, Jean vii
Sokal, Henri 243
Sokoloff, Vladimir 9, 67, 71, 75
Solomon, Jack 231
Sommer, Edith 203
Southern California Committee for Refugees 108
Space, Arthur 236
Spain, Fay 231, 233
Sparks, Robert 203
Sparkuhl, Theodor 179
Spawn of the North 74, 219
Speak, Jean L. 187, 186, 193
Spelling, Aaron 219
Sperling, Milton 102, 246
Spock, Benjamin 124
Spottswood, Marie 79
Springer, John xiv, 89
Squire, Katherine 262
Stack, Robert 81, 224–225
Stalmaster, Lynn 206
Stalnaker, Charles 253
Stamp, Malcolm 258
Stamp, Terence 244–245
Stang, Arnold 152
Stanley and Livingstone 107
Stanley, Kim 160
Stanton, Harry Dean 274
Stanwyck, Barbara 68–69, 80, 211–212, 223–224
Stapleton, Maureen xiv, 100, 234–236, 282
Stark, Leonard 269
Stark, Richard 265
Starr, Ben 250
Steadman, Robert 263
Steele, Anthony 255
Steiger, Rod 91, **93**, 107, 117, 228–229, 243, 262–263
Stein, Phil 237
Steinbeck, John 13
Steiner, Max 239
Stell, Aaron 234
Stepanek, Karel 215
Sterling, Jan 219–220
Stevens, George 111
Stevens, Inger 107
Stevens, Leith 213
Stevens, Louis 214
Stevens, Onslow 234–235
Stevens, Wallace 277
Stevens, William 183, 191, 195

Stevenson, Adlai 72–73
Stevenson, Robert 42, 200–201, 281
Stevenson, Venetia 236
Stewart, James 71–**72**, 86, 216–218
Stewart, James G. 180, 182, 183
Stewart, Margie 180
Stewart, Mil 237
Stiletti, Mario 211
Stiller, Jerry 271
Stine, Hal 250
Stine, Harold 191
Stockwell, Dean **33**, 195–196
Stokes, Vera 208
Stollery, David 221
Stone, George E. 180
Stone, Harold J. 274
Stone, Milburn 207
Stoney, Jack 200
Stoop, Norma McClain 260
A Story of Cinema (book) 74, 121
Stout, Archie 180
Strasberg, Lee 13, 102, 271
Stratas, Teresa 241
Strauss, Peter 172, 276
Streeter, Alban 253
Strian, Hugh 258
Strickler, Jerry 271
Strode, Woody 138, 215, 249–250
Strong Boy 4, 179
Strong, Leonard 180, 182
Strudwick, Sheppard 172, 276
Stuart, Marvin 194
Students for a Democratic Society 144
Sturges, John 65, 98, 139, 221–223, 251–252, 282
Sturges, Preston 34
Sturtevant, John 186, 187, 189
Stutz, Sophia 231
Sudden Fear 264
Sullavan, Margaret 128
Sullivan, Barry 99, 221, 274
Sullivan, Gardner C. 180
Sullivan, James W. 206
Sunset Boulevard 27
Surtees, Bruce 265
Surtees, Robert 194
Susann, Jacqueline 159, 260

Suspicion 46
Sutherland, Donald 251,
　263–264
Sutters, Jack vii
Sutton, John 241
Swanson, Gloria 4, 27
Swenson, Karl 240, 252
Sylos, Frank 196, 229

T

Tabary, Guy 243
*Take Two, A Life in Movies
　and Politics* (book) 118
Takei, George 240
Talbot, Nita **52**, 208–209
The Tall Men 84, **86**, 226–
　227, 278
The Tall T 214
Talman, William **61**, 200,
　207
Tamiroff, Akim 180
Taubman, Howard 125, 141
Taylor, Don 206
Taylor, Dub 146, 256
Taylor, Joan 208
Taylor, Peter 255
Taylor, Rod 99, 274
Taylor, Samuel 260
Taylor, Vaughn 249
Teal, Ray 220
Teichmann, Howard 234
Television Movies: 1985–1986
　39, 60, 71, 98, 101
Ten North Frederick 107
Tender Comrade 17, 19,
　184–185
Terrell, Ken 227
Terry, William 183
Texas Rangers Ride Again 12,
　180
Thatcher, Torin 241
Thaxter, Phyllis 194
Theatre Arts 214, 216
They Live by Night 49
Thomas, Dylan 62, 102
Thomas, Norman 106
Thomas, Tony 245
Thomas, William C. 179
Thompson, Howard 156,
　193, 206, 215, 219, 255,
　260
Thompson, Josiah 264
Thompson, Rex 221
Thompson, Sada 271
Thomson, James S. 185

Thorne, Lois 237
Thring, Frank 241–242
Thunderball 248
Tierney, Lawrence 205, 253
Tiger at the Gates (play)
　92–94, 271
Time 182, 188, 190, 193, 201,
　217, 223, 226, 239, 242,
　245, 250, 253, 257, 268
The Time of Your Life (play)
　149, 151, 272
Tirpak, John vii
To Sit in Judgment (tv) 92,
　274
Tobias, George 198–199
Todd, Ann 275
Todd, Richard 243
Todd, Sherman 181, 184,
　191, 206, 207
Tolan, Michael 252, 271
Tombstone's Epitaph (novel)
　251
Too Many Husbands (play)
　10, 271
Toomey, Regis 180, 195
Toporow, Roman 191–192
Torn, Rip 116, 241–242
Totter, Audrey 198–199
A Touch of Evil 27
Tourneur, Jacques 191–192,
　281
Tover, Leo 187, 202, 226
Towland, Adela 202
Townes, Harry 275
Trabert, Tony 172, 265
Tracy, Spencer 4, 40, 57,
　76, 222–223
Trail Street **21**, 23, 186–187
The Train 165
Travers, Henry 180
Traversari, Walfrido 255
Travilla 226, 227
Tremayne, Les 207
Trevor, Claire 56, 205–206
Trail by Fear (tv) 92, 274
Tribby, John E. 189
A Tribute to Woody Guthrie
　(guest appearance) 277
Triesault, Ivan 221
Trimarchi, Michele 254
Trintignant, Jean-Louis 163,
　261–262
Trumbo, Dalton 29–30, 63,
　173–174, 184–185, 263–264
Tryon, Tom 243
Tsiang, H.T. 182
Tucherer, Eugene 248

Turetsky, Phil 107
Turn of Fate (tv) 273
Turner, John 258
Turner, Paulette 214
Tuttle, Frank 249
TV Movies 224
Twist, John 180, 205
Tyler, Tom 180, 193, 205
Tynan, Kenneth 130
Tyner, Charles 258
Tyson, Cicely 237–238

U

UCLA Film Archives 37
Udall, Stewart 145
Ulysses 87
Under Milkwood (play) 102
United World Federalists 31,
　95, 106, 130
Unnatural Causes 48
Ure, Mary 253
Ustinov in Focus (book) 245
Ustinov, Peter 119, 243–245
Utey, Betty 241

V

van Bark, Virginie xiv
Vance, Vivian 202, 276
Van Eyck, Peter 243, 248
Van Fleet, Jo 272
Van Fleet, Kevin 263
Van Praag, Van 229
van Schmus, Albert 196
Variety 24, 56, 57, 111, 192,
　195, 197, 208, 214, 215,
　220, 223, 229, 233, 239,
　240, 241, 242, 248, 250,
　251, 252, 254, 255, 255–
　256, 257, 262, 266, 269
Vaughan-Thomas, Wynford
　255
Vendetta 34
Vermilyea, Harold 203
Verne, Jules 152, 258
Vernon, Glenn 187
Vickers, Martha 185
Village Voice 257, 266, 269
*Violence, 1947: Three
　Specimens* 25
*Violent America: The
　Movies–1946 to 1964*
　(book) 217
Visart, Natalie 179

The Visitor (play) 6, 8
The Voice of Man 108
Voight, Jon 54, 252
von Lauchert, General
 Meinred 246
Von Leer, Hunter 263
Von Zerneck, Peter 191
Voriseck, Richard 237
Voskovec, George 166, 267
Votrian, Peter 221
Vuolo, Tito 207
Vye, Murvyn 223

W

Wade, Russell 180, 184, 185
Waetherwax, Paul 213
Wagner, Fernando 256
Wagner, Max 207
Wagner, Robert 117, 243
Wagon Train 91, 119, 130,
 275–276
Waite, Ralph 155, 258–259
Wakeling, Gwen 223
Wakhevitch, Georges 241
Wald, Jerry 69, 211
Waldis, Otto 191
Walker, Clint 251
Walker, Vernon L. 180,
 184, 185
Wallace, Charles E. 194
Wallace, Richard 180
Wallenberg: A Hero's Story 48
Walling, Paula 187
Wallis, Hal. B. 98, 220
Wallsten, Cynthia 122, 158
Wallsten, Robert xiv, 13,
 21, 72, 73, 82, 88–89, 122,
 124, 126–127, 158, 171
Walsh, Joseph 255
Walsh, Raoul 84, 226
Walters, Barbara 127
Warburton, John 216
Ward, Amelita 181, 183
Ward, Luci 192
Warlock 259
Warner, Jack 135
Warren, Eda 228
Warren, Phil 186
Warrick, Robert 223
Warrick, Ruth 184
Washburn, Jack 271
Washington Post 153, 172
Watkins, A.W. 258
Watkins, Hal 262
Watkins, Jall 265

Watkins, Pierre 179
Watson, Douglas 271
Watson, William 258–259,
 263
Watt, Nate 223
Watts, Richard, Jr. 153
Waxman, Franz 228–229
The Wayfarers 9
Wayne, Fredd 273
Wayne, John 29, 56, **58**,
 62, 77, 86, 118, 158,
 206–207, 243
Weaver, Dennis 214–215
Webb, Robert D. 227–228
Webb, Roy 180, 182, 183,
 184, 185, 189, 211
Webber, Herman E. 241
Webber, Robert 139, 251
Webster, Ferris 262
Weidman, H. 248
Weiler, A. 188, 192, 212,
 218, 233
Weinstein, Henry 165
Weiss, Nathan Norman 24,
 188
Welch, Robert 118
Weldon, Alex C. 241, 243
Well, Brian 260
Welles, Orson 27, 241
Wellman, Harold 211
Werle, Barbara 246
West, Morris L. 247
West, Nathanael 99, 101,
 234, 236
Westbrook, Herbert 258
Westcott, Helen 231, 233,
 236
Westmore, Wally 180, 250
Wever, Ned 274
Wexler, Jodi 260
Wexler, Paul 236, 250
Wheeler, Lyle R. 218, 224,
 226, 227, 260
Which Way the Wind?
 (narration) 108
The Whistle in the Dark
 (play) 159
White, Charles 151–152, 272
White, Dan 214, 218
White, Dean 193
White Flag (tv) 274
White, George 216
White, Jacqueline 189, 193
White, Jesse 228–229
White, Sammy 220
Whitehead, O.Z. 213
Whiting, Barbara 213

Whitman, Stuart 243, 273
Whitman, Walt 174, 277
Whitmore, James 82, 107
*Who Chopped Down the
 Cherry Tree?* (tv) 275
Who Speaks for Man?
 (narration) 277
Wicki, Bernhard 242
Widmark, Richard 57, 212
Wiehle, Kurl 246
Wilborn, Charles W. 262
Wilcox, Jim 118
The Wild Bunch xiii, 145–
 146, **147**–148, 152–156,
 256–258, 278
Wild Calendar (novel) 196
Wild, Harry 187
Wilde, Cornel 128
Wilder, Billy 53
Wilder, Thornton 107, 149,
 272
Wilke, Robert J. 86, 205
Wilkin, John 250
Willes, Jean 273
Williams, Adam 206
Williams, Sumner 208, 210,
 241
Willis, Austin 252
Willis, Edwin B. 193, 222
Willoughby, Barrett 219
Wilmas, James 213
Wilson, Barbara 261
Wilson, Freddie 258
Wilson, Gerald 156, 258–
 260
Wilson, Louise 196
Wilson, Mitchell 187–188
Wilson, Scott 164, 262–263
Wincelberg, Shimon 275
Winchester '73 94
Windom, William 252
Windsor, Marie 172,
 265–266
Winkler, Ben 236
Winn, John R. 269
Winner, Michael 155–156,
 258–260
Winsten, Archer 266
Winters, Ralph E. 265
Winters, Shelley 237–239
Wise, Robert xiv, 37,
 53–54, 62, 103, 105, 109,
 180, 184, 198, 237–239,
 266, 280, 281
Wiseman, Joseph 155,
 258–259
Wolcott, Earl 195

Wolf, William 153
Wolfe, Ian 184, 208, 220, 221
The Woman on Pier 13, (I Married a Communist) 13, 42–**43, 44**–45, 56, 60, 200–202, 205, 281
The Woman on the Beach 22, 23–24, 52, 183, 187–189, 196, 281
Women's Wear Daily 262
Wong, Iris 182
Woods, Harry 186, 187, 205
Woodward, Charles 152
Woodward, Joanne 102, 282
Woody, Jack 236
Woolsey, Ralph 267
World War I (tv narration) 131, 277
Worth, Constance 198
Wottitz, Walter 243
Woulfe, Michael 200, 211
Woxholt, Egil S. 258

Wright, Will 194, 226
Wright, William H. 193, 216
Writings on the Sand (narration) 277
Wyatt, Jane 107
Wynn, Keenan 107

Y

Yamaguchi, Shirley 224–225
Ybarra, Alfred C. 251
Yip, William 182, 240
Yordan, Philip xiv, 30, 40, 46, 65–66, 75, 76, 77, 86, 94–95, 97, 103, 116, 134–135, 142, 158, 229, 231, 236, 241–242, 246, 253
You Only Run Once (tv) 273
Young, Carleton 205, 206
Young, Collier 193, 213
Young, James R. 182
Young, Robert 189–190

Young, Terence 248
Young, Tony 265
Young, Victor 180, 220, 226
The Young Lions 30
Youngstein, Max 107
Yurka, Blanche 179

Z

Zane Grey Theatre 91–92, 273, 275
Zanuck, Darryl 82, 243
Ziegler, William 240
Zilzer, Wolfgang 182
Zimmerman, Paul D. 170, 268
Zinnemann, Fred xiv, 32, 193–195, 280, 281
Zinner, Peter 249
Zinsser, William K. 223, 226, 231
Zitter, Ruth vii
Zuckert, William 237